# Security and Everyday Life

# Routledge Advances in Criminology

# Security and Everyday Life

## Edited by Vida Bajc and Willem de Lint

Routledge
Taylor & Francis Group
New York   London

First published 2011
by Routledge
711 Third Avenue, New York, NY 10017

Simultaneously published in the UK
by Routledge
2 Park Square, Milton Park, Abingdon, Oxon OX14 4RN

*Routledge is an imprint of the Taylor & Francis Group, an informa business*

© 2011 Taylor & Francis

Typeset in Sabon by IBT Global.

*Library of Congress Cataloging-in-Publication Data*

Security and everyday life / edited by Vida Bajc and Willem de Lint.
    p. cm. — (Routledge advances in criminology ; 10)
  Includes bibliographical references and index.
  1. Internal security—Social aspects.   2. Security, International—Social aspects.
3. Public safety.  I. Bajc, Vida.   II. De Lint, Willem, 1959–
  HV6419.S43 2011
  363.2—dc22
  2010031811

ISBN13: 978-0-415-99768-3 (hbk)
ISBN13: 978-0-203-83252-3 (ebk)

# Contents

## PART I
## Public Spaces and Collective Activities

## PART II
## Struggle and Resistance

## PART III
## Law, Citizenship, and the State

## PART IV
## Global Agendas, Local Transformations

# Figures and Tables

# Acknowledgments

No book is ever done without a long list of people who, in one way or another, contribute to its completion. We are especially grateful to Don Handelman. We also thank Elijah Anderson, Peter Andreas, Prosper Bernard, Charles Bosk, Jean-Paul Brodeur, Arthur Cockfield, Diana Crane, Jose Miguel Cruz, Benoît Dupont, Gil Eyal, Gary Alan Fine, Myra Floyd, Hugh Gusterson, Lisa Hajjar, Jonathan Hiskey, Alastair Iain Johnston, Elihu Katz, Jeroen de Kloet, Giselinde Kuipers, Dani Lainer-Vos, Bettina Lange, David Lipset, David Lyon, Douglass Messey, Kathleen Moore, Costas Nakassis, Aihwa Ong, Faye Pike, Robert Pike, James Ron, Carolanne Saunders, Carroll Seron, Benjamin Sims, Elisabeth Sköns, Regina Smardon, Philip Smith, David Snow, David White, and Elia Zureik. We are also grateful to Routledge Series Editors, Benjamin Holtzman and Max Novick; the Surveillance Studies Centre at Queen's University, Kingston, Canada; the Writing Center at Methodist University; and the Queen's University Library for their support and assistance.

*Vida Bajc*

This collaborative project on security has engaged a cacophony of opinion and sometimes even discordant voices offering contrasting observations on the nature of the field. That is as it should be. I thank the contributors for their forbearance, especially Reem Bahdi for your indefatigable spirit of justice, and Sirpa Virta for the constancy of your wise counsel. Thanks also to Pat O'Malley and Mark Neocleous for inspiration, and to Jean-Paul Brodeur posthumously, whose passing is a great loss for Canadian policing and security studies. Thanks to my students, Christian Pasiak, Shannon Speed, Ryan Cotter, Ryan Gostlow, and Adam Pocrnic, for the high level of engagements over the years. I owe a deep debt of gratitude to Perry Pittao for her superb professionalism and for helping me over some troubled seas and, of course, to Vaughen, for not abandoning ship in the face of the tallest storm clouds we have ever encountered.

*Willem de Lint*

# Introduction

## Security Meta-Framing: A Cultural Logic of an Ordering Practice

*Vida Bajc*

## INTRODUCTION

This volume is a contribution to our understanding of the dynamics associated with seeing in all sorts of everyday social situations and cultural phenomena a potential threat to security. The range of such phenomena and activities is wide and diverse. Drug use and street crime, expressions of religious, cultural, or political identity, migration across state territories or state borders, collective public gatherings from sports games to state-sponsored public events—even being in public buildings such as courthouses, schools, hospitals, airports, or city halls—have all become intimately intertwined with the fear that they may be associated with intentions to undermine what is seen as security in everyday living. Popular expressions such as "we need more security here," "security will be very tight during the event," "there is a lot of security around that area," or "there is a lot more security here now than there used to be in the past" attest to this development. Such expressions connote public interpretations of the dynamics associated with what I call security meta-framing (Bajc 2010), an ordering principle of social life that holds security as its central value. Public understanding of security meta-framing captures a number of elements associated with these dynamics, among them an apparatus of institutions and their operatives, surveillance practices and technologies, and a particular kind of social order and perception of safety.

Bureaucratic institutions and their various satellites, including private enterprise, comprise an apparatus of organizations and professionals that claim expertise in the matters of public orderliness. The apparatus arbitrates on what is acceptable public conduct and what types of individual or group behavior count as abnormal and thereby potentially threatening to security. Their operatives are credentialed professionals who see themselves as expertly trained in ways that the general public is not. Historian Andrew Bacevich (2007: xii) writes about the U.S. state apparatus, for example, that "viewing the average citizen as uninformed, fickle, and provincial, members of this elite imagine themselves to be sophisticated, sagacious, and coolly analytical." Their authority rests on their assertion that they serve in the name of the state as well as in the interest of the public. Their decision as to which situations and phenomena constitute a threat to security is legitimized by their claim to expert knowledge not only about what is safe and what is dangerous but also which actions should constitute a response to their classification of threats. This security apparatus is an outgrowth of what Foucault (2007) calls "governmentality," a particular rationale of governing that appears in Western Europe in relation to the idea of the state, variously called modern state, sovereign state, national state, or nation-state (see Tilly 1990). This rationale articulated notions of sovereign power over a delineated territory and human activity within its boundaries and of appropriate public conduct that was to benefit the prosperity of the state as well as the well-being of its population. According to Sassen (2008), the state became possible through the articulation of the idea of secular authority as exclusive over a particular territory, with clearly delineated boundaries, through the institutionalization of a system of constitutional forms of rights. These notions helped set the stage for the rise of a global system of apparatuses of governance, based on particular expertise, technologies, legal norms, and management techniques.

The know-how of the security apparatus relies to a large extent on technologies, techniques, and procedures of bureaucratic surveillance. By bureaucratic surveillance, I mean processes of methodical accumulation of information, classification of this information into exclusive categories, and articulation of expert knowledge to respond to this information (Bajc 2007a). Some of the more familiar manifestations of these processes of surveillance for the purposes of security that we encounter in everyday life-situations are security checkpoints, requests for biometrics, closed-circuit television cameras, monitoring of digital transactions, or mass-mediated requests in public spaces to "report suspicious behavior." Through the processes of surveillance and its technological developments, the apparatus is able to track human behavior in real time, as it is happening. The routine tracking of human behavior in real time enables the apparatus not only to evaluate at any moment whether this behavior follows the understanding of appropriate public conduct and the vision of orderliness as conceived by the apparatus, but also to react swiftly to any stimuli that may come from the data. In practice, such response to the data depends as much on an extensive and reliable network of informants as on the availability of computer software for data processing and analysis and relies heavily on profiling of human behavior. These visions of social situations and phenomena in which there may be human activity that could potentially undermine security are supported by statistical probability estimates that help envision potential threats, consider human activities beforehand, and foresee how they may likely play out (Desrosières 1998). Statistical modeling, computer games, and other inventions of information-processing technologies and techniques facilitate anticipations and predictions of situations and phenomena classified as potentially threatening to security. The processes of bureaucratic

surveillance are an outgrowth of a particular kind of a system of classification through which the world is divided into exclusionary categories.
As anthropologist Don Handelman (2004: 19–38) describes, rather than
organizing the world according to how things are connected and how
they work together, this type of classification seeks to identify in every
occurrence specific characteristics, and then divide the world according
to these attributes into exclusive categories so that each phenomenon and
activity can be positioned into a single category. It is this kind of thinking, based on bureaucratic surveillance, exclusionary classification, and
probability statistics, that enables the security apparatus to raid a home
of an undocumented migrant worker or deny a person the right to board
an airplane. This thinking is related to the same rationality that underlies the mechanisms of governance mentioned earlier.

The activity of the security apparatus and its means of bureaucratic
surveillance also reflect deeply seated, common-sense cultural assumptions about social order and disorder. They help generate a specific perception of social reality and a particular understanding of how the world
works. They connote a domain of experience in which the public has the
feeling of being protected from or—alternatively—of being exposed to,
potentially harmful irregularities in public life. Therefore, it also reflects
a certain set of understandings of what is an acceptable orderliness in
interpersonal public conduct and, at the same time, communicates fear
of forces of disruption. Although there are multiple understandings of
just what this reality of security might or should entail, there is in this
multiplicity, as Beck (1992) has suggested, nevertheless a common expectation on the part of the public that something must be done to control
forces of chaos. This public expectation, as much as the activities of the
security apparatus practiced to respond to these expectations, entail a
belief in the potentials of technology to control uncertainty and prevent
disruption. There seems to be an assumption that the security apparatus
and its surveillance technologies and practices can, in fact, shield the
public from the forces of potential disorder and that everything possible
will be done to achieve this goal. This belief also entails a fear of the
possibility of a certain kind of technology to be in the hands of an enemy
who can create mass destruction of life and property.

The security apparatus, its means of surveillance, and particular cultural understandings of order and disorder in public life provide a cultural
and institutional environment within which notions of threats to security
can be normalized and particular responses to threats expected. They provide conditions of possibility within which the classification of a security
problem is able to emerge as a powerful organizing principle, articulating
a particular way of ordering everyday life. An ordering principle of social
life is an organizational logic of sociality that has the capacity to subsume
other rationales for ordering human relations and has the potential to subordinate other social activities to its own order. In this way, such a principle
defines the parameters and the conditions of how life should be lived and

articulates a particular way of organizing sociality. I call this ordering principle *security meta-frame*. Its logic is cultural in that it makes sense within a particular kind of cosmological understanding of the world, which, in this case, has decidedly Western European origins. The tendency to see a threat to security in ever larger domains of private and public life suggests that security meta-framing has two general qualities. It is expansive in that its potential is to spread. It is also totalizing in that it is able to subsume within its domain other ordering principles of social life. As Waever (1995) emphasizes, a classification of a particular issue as a threat to security implies a sense of urgency that can be seen as a crisis of survival of the social unit as a whole to the point that all other social issues and concerns may become irrelevant unless this particular threat is stopped. The activity of classifying social situations and cultural phenomena as a threat to security therefore has a tendency to subsume within its taxonomy other principles of social organization. In a given historical and socio-cultural context, security meta-frame has the potential to be elevated to the top of the collective priorities and, in this way, become the dominant ordering principle in a collectivity.

My conception of security meta-framing, an analytical tool with which I try to capture the dynamics associated with the growing dominance of security as an organizing principle of everyday life, is derived from the communication theory of Gregory Bateson. In his most well-known works, *Steps to an Ecology of Mind* and *Mind and Nature,* Bateson argues that human communication has the capacity to convey messages with multiple meanings simultaneously and at multiple levels of abstraction.[1] Therefore, Bateson reasons, this would create confusion unless some of that communication also contained information about how to interpret the rest of what is conveyed. For this to be intelligible, the interlocutors need a way of discerning which part of the communication conveyed is the basic message and which part carries instructions on how to interpret the basic message. Bateson expresses this idea of communication about communication with a prefix "meta" and articulates this relationship through a theory of framing. He proposes to think of a meta-communicative message as a frame in such a way that whichever information defines the given frame also provides the receiver with instructions about how to understand the messages which relate to that frame. To articulate this relationship between a frame as a meta-message and some basic communication to which it is directed, Bateson draws on the theory of logical types by Whitehead and Russell (1910), conceived—among other matters—to find a mathematical solution that would eliminate the emergence and formation of a logical paradox. A logical paradox is created by a situation in which a particular statement is simultaneously self-negating; for example, simultaneously true and false. In a logical system, such as mathematics that is held together through self-consistency based on set theory, such a paradox is impermissible because it undermines the system's premises. The proposed solution is to arrange statements into a hierarchy of sets such that a set of phenomena is positioned at a lower level and a set about this set of phenomena is positioned at a higher level. In this way, self-consistency is achieved when one refers to phenomena only when they are at the same level; that is, of the same type.

Bateson often refers to types as *classes*. For Bateson (2000a), this hierarchy makes possible for communication at the level of class to be clearly differentiated from its contents. Following the theory of logical types, a class of phenomena must be specifically distinguished from its contents—that is, its members—because the confuting of class and member is a prime cause of the formation of logical paradox. This implies that confusion in communication is avoided when the interlocutors understand a class; that is, a frame as a meta-message which instructs how to interpret the member of that class, that is, the message to which the frame is directed. In this formulation, sets of phenomena are classified into exclusionary categories and arranged hierarchically, such as the Russian matryoshka doll, so that the message of the frame is always of a higher order and value and is, therefore, always meta-communicative to all other basic messages it subsumes. When this hierarchy is not recognized, individuals receiving the messages are faced with a paradoxical situation in which they must choose between clearly delineated sets of messages that do not overlap, are at the same level of abstraction, and are contradictory to each other. Bateson (2000b) names such inability to discriminate between basic messages and meta-messages a double bind. A double bind is a paradoxical situation in which individuals are in a position where they are aware that it is vital that they make the right choice, and yet whichever option they choose will negatively affect all others. This paradoxical position resembles a situation where messages are at the same level, meaning that they are imbued with the same values or ethos—yet they are contradictory to one another. One way out of the double bind opens up when new information is introduced in such a way that it is recognized by the receiver as meta-communicative to all other messages already received; that is, as a new understanding that can re-establish, yet can also change, a hierarchy of messages.

Bateson (1958), of course, understands very well that mathematical logic of clearly delineated hierarchies of classes is a poor approximation of the complexities of human communication. Indeed, exclusionary framing based on logical typing is only one of the possible kinds of framing. Handelman (2006a), for example, formulates an alternative kind of framing based on the idea of the Möebius surface, a ring which turns inward and outward at the same time so that the inside and the outside are inherently intertwined and the boundary between them is blurred and cannot be clearly delineated. Handelman (2004, 2006b), however, knows full well that there are specific contexts in which the dynamics of communicative interaction do resonate closely with exclusionary framing, particularly in situations involving the bureaucratic system of the modern state and its form of exclusionary classification, an example of which are the dynamics associated with securitization as discussed in this volume. When the classification of security is included among the messages communicated, the public is typically presented with a situation in which the choice of security is valued more highly than the choice of other values that organize social life in a modern state—such as democracy, the right to privacy, the right to legal council, or human rights—in such a way that security appears as an obvious choice in relation to which the loss of some aspects of other values is seen as a reasonable and worthwhile sacrifice for what the value of security promises to deliver. When the value of security is elevated above other principles of social organization in a modern state, it becomes a meta-frame in relation to which other social activity becomes referenced and in accordance to which all other social life becomes organized.

What I call security meta-framing is more than what the common-sense understanding of the term "frame" or "framing" may suggest. The words "frame" and "framing" have a wide popular appeal and are used frequently in common parlance as in the sense of "giving a story a particular spin" or "making you see something in a particular way." In this sense, Simmel (1994: 17) writes that a picture frame, a molding which surrounds a painting, serves to "solve the problem in the visual sphere of mediating between the work of art and its milieu, separating and connecting." Similarly, framing is frequently used in various fields of social research as an analytical concept; however, its usage tends to be mechanical and typological, missing the very important epistemological aspect of this form of interpersonal communication and activity. Goffman (1986: 8–11) popularized the concept of framing in terms of a "frame of reference," as "a framework that could be appealed to for the answer" to the question "What is it that's going on here?" as a "strip . . . cut from the stream of ongoing activity . . . a raw batch of occurrences that one wants to draw attention to as a starting point for analysis," and a "slogan to refer to the examination in these terms of the organization of experience."

For Bateson, framing is an integral component of human communication because interpersonal communication involves exchanging messages at multiple levels of abstraction, where some messages carry instructions on how to interpret other messages being communicated. Framing organizes, interprets, and directs the basic part of the communication exchange. The security meta-frame, in the sense of 'framing' used by Bateson, is profoundly consequential in its social effects. When security is elevated to the level of the dominant ordering principle of social life, the security meta-frame becomes a condition of possibility within which are articulated not only thought but also practice. This condition of possibility is grounded in what I call elsewhere *a governmentality of potentialities* (Bajc 2007a), a rationale of governing that uses information gathering through surveillance technologies and techniques, statistical probabilities, computer modeling, profiling, and secrecy as means to envision or discover threats to security and then pre-empt such envisioned threats from materializing; that is, to deliver security by seeking to control the future. Security meta-framing is an outcome of this ordering practice.

## GOVERNMENTALITY OF POTENTIALITIES

The prominence of security discourses in contemporary public as well as private life speaks to the fact that security is a very powerful cultural construct. The emergence of security as a dominant ordering principle of daily living is related to a particular cultural logic of ordering of social life that developed in Europe around the idea of the formation of a territorially defined sovereign state and the rationale with which such a state is to be governed. The state emerges in relation to, and then supersedes, previous forms of organizational hierarchies—namely, the Church, the empire, and the feudal arrangements of authority—by establishing a new apparatus of authority that is grounded in sovereign rights over a specific territory, membership in the collectivity on this territory, and protection of territorial and membership boundaries. This authority comes to be articulated and formalized through a system of codified laws and regulations that legitimate the workings of the apparatus. The new rationality of governing, what Foucault (2007) terms "governmentality," relies on information gathering and data analysis through which the state comes to know the lives of the people in its territory, turn the collectivity of people with various feudal kinship ties into a state's population, and perfect probability estimates to be able to predict, plan, anticipate, or pre-empt transformations of social life and otherwise control potentialities of the population's behavior.

This form of the state is not some kind of a natural outgrowth from the previous hierarchies of order. Nor is it a kind of spontaneous transformation through a string of historical events. As Sassen (2008: 80) writes, the shift toward a sovereign, territorially bound state did entail reorientation of certain medieval practices, yet before the state could come to existence, it "needed to be imagined and personified." Similarly, Foucault (2007) argues that much intellectual energy has been invested into developing the idea of the state, its manifestations, and its transformations. An understanding of the conditions necessary for the state to exist and the state's existence to be sustained develops through ongoing reflexive thought and calculated practice. According to Foucault, the reasoning of the state and the ways in which it can be brought to existence as an alternative to the Church, the Empire, or some version of indigenous feudal kinship relations requires thinking of the state in its own terms. This means reflecting on its functioning in such a way that there develops a body of knowledge, reasoning, apparatuses, and mechanisms to establish and then support its existence and transformations.

First, the formation of the state establishes a physical demarcation of a geographical area it claims as its own territory and, with it, a clear separation between people who belong to the state and those who do not. These binary distinctions raise concerns with boundary maintenance, preoccupation with border control, and efforts to regulate movement of people in and out of the state. To this end, there develop apparatuses that monopolize the authority over movements of people, invent procedures to identify each and every member of its collectivity, require from each individual in its territory proper documentation, and implement codified laws that determine who may or may not cross the border or the state territory and under what conditions (Torpey 1998).

Second, as the territorial boundaries impose control over movements of people, they encircle certain groups of people within a spatial enclosure. In the pre-state Europe, the people who found themselves within this enclosure felt they were part of various nomadic groups, families, kinship groups, migrant groups, itinerant traveling groups, and various urban and rural settlements. They had loyalties to various indigenous hierarchies, and their ways of life followed the patterns of their own various internal structures of relations. This raises the question of how to reorder the lives of the people within the territorial boundaries for the needs of the state; that is, how the productivity of every citizen can effectively contribute to the prosperity of the state. An efficient management of this process would minimize disorder and irregularities in the workings of the people and the economy in favor of rational and controlled planning of social life. Apparatuses and mechanisms are set up to first separate each individual from his or her kinship group and then turn such an individual into what Foucault calls a "governable subject." The totality of such individuals can now comprise what becomes thought of as a population, a collectivity whose different aspects of life can be subjected to governing, management, and planning by the apparatuses. It is this population that is eventually able to see itself as a nation, a people who belong to a particular state. Governing in an organized and standardized fashion is achieved through what Sassen (2008: 6) calls a "centripetal scaling" under the umbrella of the state. This centripetal scaling is a hierarchy in which the state seeks to subsume under its domain human activity within its territory through the institutionalization of sovereign authority by means of a system of formally codified rules and regulations in which formally written law of what is and is not allowed overrides the various versions of indigenous agreements and localized legal practices. Foucault (2008: 44) refers to this authority as "centripetal discipline," a mechanism which "isolates a space that it determines a segment," and within this isolated space "concentrates, focuses, and encloses."

Foucault (2008) suggests that this transformation of peoples into a governable population found affinity with already-existing dynamics that developed through Christianization of Europe. What he labels "the pastoral" encompasses a particular way of life of a group of people under the protective shield of its leadership. The pastor is responsible for the well-being of all the individual believers from the time they are born to the moment of their death, following them wherever they go so that they may be able to find the path to ultimate fulfillment. The believers, in turn, as individuals and as a group, learn to follow the pastor's leadership and put their souls in the hands of a good shepherd so that they may be able to reach the eternal life. Foucault suggests that this is a type of authority that administers the entire existence not only of a group as a whole but of each and every person as an individual and also as a member of a collectivity. To the leader, the pastoral power is a responsibility of having to protect the souls of each individual from harm and to shield one and all from misfortune. The pastoral form of authority over the souls of men, Foucault suggests, is the background for the development of governing of the population as a calculated practice of apparatuses and mechanisms so that the authority over the spiritual is transitioned into a newly forming authority over the political. In these terms, such a population comes to expect that action will be taken in the face of a threat to security by the security apparatus.

Third, the exclusive authority and rights over a territory and its population bring to existence a reciprocal principle in relation to territorial sovereignty of other states, effectively establishing a system of states, each situated along the other and each in competition with the other so that the security of a given state is also dependent on its relation to other states. Through this principle of the interstate system, each state is compelled to protect its own sovereign rights against the aspirations, interests, and needs of other states (Buzan, Waever, and de Wilde 1998). Following Foucault (2007), preservation and maintenance of the state within this system require a method of governing that can simultaneously foster the growth of the economy, the well-being of the population, and the strengthening of the apparatuses put in place to maintain various forms of authority and rights, as well as protection of the state from external intrusions on its sovereignty.

Waever (1995) notes that by the height of the Cold War period, the practices and reasoning of the apparatuses with authority over security had developed into a domain of relations with its own patterns of communication, mutual activity, state and private institutions of public order and state defense, research institutions, sets of issues and agendas, rules of conduct, and professionals who claimed legitimate authorities in leading its activities. These elite professionals and entrepreneurs are firmly entrenched in their positions of power and deeply immersed in their own ways of reasoning and practice. Although there are variations in different historical moments and sociocultural contexts, Waever emphasizes that the defense of state sovereignty nevertheless always remains the central issue because, as these elites see it, if the sovereignty of a given state were to be undermined, the state would be defeated and would, in Waever's (1995: 52) words, "find itself laid bare to imposition of the conqueror's will." In such a case, all other concerns in the society would become irrelevant because the state would no longer be in a position to resolve them. These elites reason that the security of the state should, therefore, always be the highest priority, with all other issues subordinated to this end, and a threat to state security must be addressed immediately with all the necessary means. In the case of the United States, for example, Bacevich (2007) shows that professionals entrusted with the matters of state security have come to comprise a small group of professionals who form a closed circle of members keeping each other in power and reinforcing each others' views, legitimacy, and relevance with minimal regard to the democratic process of deliberation and decision making. Since World War II, Bacevich maintains, this security elite has come to believe that the survival of the American state is always at risk. Nelson (2007) documents how this rationale helped create a powerful complex of private and state institutions, dominated by private corporations and supported by academic research institutions, which are concerned with the production of means to maintain security. These elite are convinced that to be able to provide any level of security requires endless struggle and sacrifice on the part of the citizenry, constant preparation and readiness for war, and vigilant uncovering of secret plots and intentions of enemies of the state and its population.

The security apparatus and its mechanisms of management and control have emerged into a powerfully efficient system, capable of mobilizing populations on a huge scale to respond to what they label a security threat. The development of nuclear weapons and means to deliver them worldwide made the fear of threat to a nation more plausible. Anthropologist Joseph Masco (2006) describes, for example, how the invention of the atomic bomb at the U.S. nuclear research and experimental complex in Nevada, and the subsequent experimentation of its destructive potential, nurtured an environment in which the scientists perceived their work to be a part of a state of emergency in a country that could be a victim of a nuclear attack at any moment. This mentality was disseminated to the general public through the mass media as a form of collective fear in which the destructive power of the bomb could be imagined by envisioning one's home and city devastated by a nuclear explosion. Through various public spectacles in the form of large-scale exercises of responses to and televised visions of nuclear attacks, Masco (2008) suggests, the public internalized perceptions and feelings of insecurity and the need to give these issues a priority above any other public concerns. These mobilization exercises are also aided by the global system of technologically advanced mechanisms of control that are able to track, direct, and block the movement of people and information worldwide. Through these technological visions, it becomes possible to imagine how surveillance technology can help solve the security problem at all levels of social organization and successfully push for the interpretation of every problem as a security problem once such technological imaginary is possible (Bogard 1996). Other major military powers, such as Israel, subjected their own population to similar experiences of internalization of fear. This subjection helped the Israeli security complex develop what Kimmerling (1985) calls "routine security tension," which supports the social and institutional mechanisms that shift easily between routine daily life and a total mobilization against a perceived threat, as the decisions by the security apparatus demand. These mechanisms are grounded in conditions of emergency that are already deeply embedded in the everyday life of the Israelis. In this way, every crisis becomes an elaboration of already deeply internalized perceptions and behaviors of emergency.

How such activities are envisioned and strategies are conceived to pre-empt them are shrouded in secrecy, as security elites seem to have a distrust of the democratic process. This includes the elites in states where the choice of political organization is democracy and the actions of the government are subject to accountability to its citizens. At least in the case of the United States, Chesney (2007) suggests, secrecy seems to have been a part of the workings of the security apparatus since the state's inception. The centrality of secrecy for the functioning of the state, however, becomes particularly pronounced during what Bacevich (2007) calls the Long War.[2] This refers to a reconfiguration of the mechanisms of security throughout the period that began in the last half of the previous century, beginning with World War II (1941–1945) as a truly global war, followed by the Cold War (1947–1989) as a standoff between two opposing global superpowers, a short post–Cold War intermission (1990–2001), and now the global War on Terror (post–September 11, 2001 [9/11]) as an amorphous, inconclusive, open-ended, and infinitely expansible pre-emptive violence to impose the vision of order by the security apparatus on a global scale.

The public is often reminded of the merits of secret operations of the apparatus. Chesney (2007: 1263–1266) states, for example, that this was also evoked after the Watergate crisis where President Richard Nixon used executive privilege to try to prevent a disclosure of transcripts of conversations by the White House that would implicate the president in the scandal. Shortly after the media revealed the surveillance scandal to the public, the U.S. attorney general delivered his address to the Association of the Bar of the City of New York on the topic of government secrecy. He reminded his listeners of how state secrecy helped end World War II, referring to the work of secret agents who were able to decode messages encrypted by the German machine, and argued that secrecy is needed by any state to acquire intelligence information to be able to efficiently perform its central function, which is providing security for its citizens. With the growing reliance on global market forces, deregulation, and privatization in the current global age, Sassen (2008: 168–184) demonstrates that secrecy has become a vehicle for restricting access to information by the public about the activities of the security apparatus, accumulation of executive powers and government authority, and erosion of privacy rights. We may say that the Long War, spanning from World War II through the Cold War into the War on Terror, has made secrecy an acceptable form of governing not only among the members of the state security apparatus but also among the citizenry.

For the purposes of planning, envisioning, or pre-empting human activity, these networks of apparatuses of security and their mechanisms depend on the ability to acquire information, classify and process that information, and then effectively analyze it. Governmentality of potentialities is intimately dependent on continuous and methodical acquisition, accumulation, and processing of information about each individual and the collectivity as a whole. Today, the ever-improving technologies and techniques of surveillance generate enormous amounts of data that are channeled from numerous sources into centralized databases, often run by private firms. These data are continuously compiled and stored indefinitely for the purposes of data mining today and in the future, which means using sophisticated computer software to look for clues that help the apparatus envision even more possibilities of future threatening behavior. As I discuss elsewhere (Bajc 2007, 2010), information processing, combined with probabilistic thinking, makes it possible to profile individuals and groups into those who are safe and those who are potentially dangerous, those who may threaten security, and others who may not. Surveillance data combined with probabilistic analysis and profiling, Desrosières (1998) suggests, enable explanations about current human behavior and provide ideas on how that behavior may change in the future. They guide choices in terms of dealing with uncertainty, and offer tools to summarize otherwise unimaginable human diversity. They enable creation of categories through which the social world can be known, managed, and transformed by establishing a relation between social activity and the future. When security becomes a dominant ordering principle, analysis of surveillance data becomes the means to imagine and envision threats to security and conceive of strategies through which such events can be pre-empted.

To understand the dynamics associated with this rationale of governing and the rise of the security meta-framing, it is crucial to grasp the type of classification that underlies these mechanisms; namely, exclusionary classification. Classifications are frameworks through which we learn about the world and make sense of the social and natural environments around us. As far as we know, we are not able to think outside any particular classification, but how we classify the world does vary cross-culturally (Durkheim and Mauss 1963). This implies that classifications are cultural constructions we use all the time but rarely reflect on. These classifications guide our actions and thought, but we do not customarily think about them. They are means that help us think and act on the world rather than concepts we think about. What makes the task of analyzing this particular cultural logic of ordering practice even more challenging is the fact that the classification which underlies the workings of the security apparatus and its meta-framing is so pervasive that we take it for granted. It underlies the workings of state bureaucracy, provides impetus to the development of science, spurs technological innovations, and is also the basis of the operation of the Western legal system. For these reasons, it may be best to illuminate the logic of understanding the world through exclusionary classification and its consequences by a way of comparison.

Through exclusionary classification, we know the world by the principle of discrimination (see Handelman 2004: 19–28). When we try to identify phenomena and social activities, we look for elements that are their distinct representations; we create a category for such elements and then locate them within these established categories. Within each of these major categories, we then divide these elements into subcategories, and within each subcategory, into sub-subcategories, and so on, forming a hierarchical grid in such a way that each category subsumes all the ones below. In this way, we are able to assign every living and nonliving thing a distinct property and every such property a specific taxonomy. When we discover a new property for which no classification exists, we can simply invent one. Such hierarchies of classifications are purposefully created by a variety of professionals, such as statisticians representing population trends, scientists outlining the taxonomy of a particular species, or agents of the security apparatus analyzing surveillance data. Through exclusionary classification we take the complexity and the interconnectedness of everything that surrounds us and try to break it down into ordered hierarchies of distinct classes. We seek a priori generalizations to fit the huge diversity of phenomena and activities into predefined hierarchies of taxonomies in which each class frames the ones below. Such linear thinking also underlies security meta-framing, which I discuss in the following text.

An alternative way of understanding the world is to look not for distinctions but rather for connections. Such a principle of classification was articulated by philosopher Ludwig Wittgenstein (1953). Classification, through what he terms "family resemblances," seeks to connect the world through likenesses and interrelationships. Through this classification, we do not look for elements in a phenomenon or activity that have the same thing in common, nor do we make up a category and then put them into this category. When we look for connections, we do not create taxonomies with clear distinctions and fixed boundaries, such as safe and unsafe, secure and dangerous. Rather, we take a characteristic of a phenomenon and match it with a similar characteristic in an unrelated activity. In this way, our classification results in a series of relationships that connect one thing to another in a chain-like string where the totality of such connections has no one thing in common and does not connect all things at the same time. Such lateral thinking creates a network of overlapping similarities. This type of classification is closer to those created through tradition and reflexive practice, and as archaeologists suggest, approximates the knowledge of the ancients who sought explanations through connections rather than distinctions (Frankfort 1978). Russian developmental psychologist Lev Vygotsky (1962) describes such lateral thinking in children who group together objects that seem, to adults, inherently unrelated because they are not grouped on the basis of essential characteristics, but rather on complexes of associations in which a block is added to the chair because of a similar color, and the block and the chair to a book because of a similar shape. Exclusionary classification in which taxonomies are formed by grouping together elements with the same essential characteristics, Vygotsky concluded, must be taught by adults to be learned by children. Schools are, therefore, the primary institution in which linear thinking is thought and lateral perceptions discouraged.

Exclusionary classification also supports modern bureaucracy, enables the governmentality of potentialities, and underlies the security meta-framing. What makes the work of these mechanisms and apparatuses possible, Handelman (2004) suggests, is the systemic nature of their dynamics. These dynamics, he argues, are most powerful when the systematic becomes systemic in the way it is able to operate various forces in relation to one another. Exclusionary classification operates in such a way that it enables the information to be divorced from the human beings to whom it pertains. Once the information is detached from the person, the processing of that information can take on inertia of its own. Without regard for the actual human beings, data about them can be compiled, classified into any kind of categories the professionals see fit, and reclassified for any purpose. Each classification opens up possibilities to imagine and envision future human activity. So, too, for each classification, specifications can be devised for how to act on those visions and imaginaries to prevent them from happening. The ever-perfected computer capabilities allow for ongoing accumulation of huge amounts of data, limitless storage of these data for the purposes of data mining, and analysis of these data with inventive software capabilities. In this way, the system is able to absorb and process any type and amount of information and then project future human behavior from that information without crisis. Because it is possible to extract identifiable information about any social phenomenon and classify that information into exclusionary categories at will, the system of governmentality of potentialities can be self-sustaining in that it is able to deal with ambiguity and need not encounter information blocks that would lead to its failure. Much of these dynamics occur away from the public eye, but when they do enter the public sphere they tend to take the form of security meta-framing. Like the bureaucratic system of the security mechanisms, security meta-frame is itself hierarchical, based on exclusionary classification and on discriminating between options rather than connections between them. The security meta-frame consists of a series of nested frames, which, as with the matryoshka doll, constitute a series of encompassing and encompassed levels of classification.

## SECURITY META-FRAMING

The citizenry is rarely given an opportunity to evaluate security measures. There seems to be scant public education about the intricacies of the mechanisms put in place to exert control over public spaces, and little public debate on information gathering and analysis used for profiling citizens and noncitizens alike. The security apparatus values executive power to make swift decisions and secrecy over open public discussion and congressional

debates, not the least, as Sassen (2008: 183–184) suggests, b
ter takes time and attracts public attention and in this way
the urges for immediate pre-emptive action. When particular
activities the apparatus deems a potential threat to security
the public domain, the information tends to be presented in
the messages conveyed are to be interpreted by the public as ......
or insecurity, where security becomes an obvious choice. The primary facili-
tator of this information to the public is the mass media. We are informed
through detailed accounts about the personal life of suspected perpetrators,
including their family background, education, work history, leisure habits,
friendship circles, neighborly relations, and religious practices. These are, we
are told, ordinary people, liked by their neighbors, coworkers, and family,
whose lives suddenly took the wrong turn. Meticulous descriptions are provided about how the security apparatus pieced together and reconstructed
that path wrongly taken: meetings with certain people, trips abroad to particular countries, shifts in political views, changes in religious practices, and
changes in personality. We have an opportunity to see maps and photographs
of their intended activities with all that could have transpired if it were not
prevented. We are actually provided with certain details about the prompt,
pre-emptive, and forceful counteractivity of the apparatus through which, we
are told, these intended activities were indeed prevented. We are also offered
an evaluation of which technologies and techniques utilized in this case need
to be perfected for the future. We are told that rules and regulations which
fall within the legislative domain of the security apparatus will be made more
stringent. At the same time, we are warned that this counteractivity could
have been even more effective if human rights legislation were more flexible,
more amenable to the swift pre-emptive activity of the apparatus. To give an
example, in the summer of 2010, we were receiving information about Faisal
Shahzad and explosive materials left in a car in Times Square, in the middle
of New York City. As these details were released, we were also informed
that the US attorney general was proposing a broad new exception to the
Miranda rights established in 1966, which require that suspects be told that
they have the right to remain silent and to consult a lawyer before their statements are used as evidence. At the same time we were told that the security
apparatus advised that the No-Fly list be checked much more frequently and
much more attention paid to "the warning signs."[3]

Such information communicates messages that are meant to be interpreted
by the public in meta-communicative terms; that is, as a logical choice between
two distinct realities organized according to exclusionary premises—either
security or insecurity. Security, characterized by order, safety, and well-being
of everyone involved, is possible if the population embraces the measures of
the security apparatus. The absence of security measures implies the alternative; namely, potential disorder, fear, uncertainty, and destruction. The two
realities, security and insecurity, are made to be juxtaposed in exclusionary
terms as either one or the other but never both, so that the context becomes

ιess and less relevance in assigning or determining meaning. Communi-ᴢated in this way, the security apparatus seeks public support in hopes that there would be little confusion on the behalf of the public over which reality is preferable. The purpose of providing this information in such a way seems to be for the public to identify security as meta-communicative to all other information received. With security seen as the highest of values and so the highest of levels, it determines meaning almost entirely in its own terms; that is, with the exclusion of context as a modifier of meaning. Through this, the meta-message of security becomes a frame that communicates how other messages received in relation to this frame are to be interpreted. The security meta-frame carries the message of order, which may be summarized thusly: to achieve safety and orderliness, it is necessary to control human interaction and human mobility through surveillance technologies and procedures, profiling, and pre-emptive action on behalf of the security apparatus. These measures may not always be convenient and may sometimes run against the democratic values, such as human rights and privacy, but they are the only way to achieve security. We will have security as long as the public does its best to comply with the measures implemented by the security apparatus.

Security meta-framing is grounded in exclusionary thinking and based on exclusionary classification that generates categories of human activity as either safe or dangerous, either enabling order or creating chaos. For this type of framing to communicate successfully, the interlocutors must be able to interpret the hierarchy of the information provided in such a way that the meta-message of security is habitually identified and the rest of the information understood in relation to the security meta-frame. In this manner, the thinking of the security apparatus is that the quest for security always overrides any concerns associated with the effects of surveillance and security measures. This is the kind of thinking the security apparatus seeks to impose on the public. This dynamic of security meta-framing and its shortcomings are perhaps best understood by legal scholars of privacy who are concerned about what they see as a trend of diminishing expectations of privacy on the part of the public (Cockfield 2007). They argue that with rapid expansion of surveillance technologies and techniques, coupled with data gathering, processing, and dissemination, the message of security has come to encompass that of privacy. This means that the message of security dictates how the message of privacy is to be received. In Bateson's terms, the message of privacy becomes subsumed within the hierarchy of classes of messages under the overarching umbrella of the message of security. According to Solove (2007), the message of security communicates that the state has the need to secure its own existence to be able to provide security for the population. The message of privacy communicates that the apparatus is collecting various kinds of information about people, including where we shop, where we travel, and whom we call, but if collecting such information helps the apparatus uncover people's bad intentions, it is a small price to pay in exchange for the protection of the state. The former is directed to the society as a whole while the latter is directed to each individual who is to see his or her own privacy interests in relation to the need for security by the state and the society as a whole. The public is able to identify security as the meta-message because the messages are communicated in such a way as to demand the hierarchical resolution of what is actually an ambiguous relationship. The complexities of each side are condensed to give the appearance of a binary opposition that can have only one correct outcome: privileging and therefore valuing security over privacy. This, however, means valuing all of the complexities and nuances of security over all those of privacy. The result is the totalization of the value of security over that of privacy. In this way, Solove (2007: 747) writes, privacy is made to appear like a trivial concern, "thus making the balance against security concerns a foreordained victory for security."

Security meta-framing works well when the information provided to the public is received in such a way that the hierarchy of messages is made as clear as possible so that ambiguity and confusion can be avoided. In Bateson's (1972b: 459) famous formulation, information "is a difference which makes a difference." This would mean that we are surrounded by infinite visual and auditory stimuli so that our sensory receptors cannot possibly register them all and must, therefore, filter them out. What does enter our mental processes from this limitless amount of stimuli are selected elements that make us aware that something has happened which is different in such a way that it actually made a difference in our lives. Such a change, Bateson suggests, becomes information. What we register as information, change, or difference depends on our personal experience, collective memory, and a particular sociohistorical context. In the post-9/11 world, information about security threats broadcast by the media makes a difference because it resonates with the images of destruction associated with the burning of the Twin Towers of the World Trade Center in New York and, as Masco (2008) would suggest, imaginaries of "what could have happened" associated with the use of technological potentials of weapons of mass destruction by the wrong people.

When the information provided no longer makes a difference, when it is no longer registered as the meta-message of security, it leads to confusion. In Bateson's terms, this is when the hierarchy of messages turns into a choice between two equal values, a binary choice between, for example, security or privacy—but not both. In terms of thinking by the security establishment, such a binary is evidence of failure on the part of the security apparatus, because it opens up a space for negotiation and mediation between the opposing binaries. When messages appear as binaries, confusion stems from the uncertainty about which one to choose. People find themselves unable to identify the hierarchy of messages and, through this, the meta-message that carries instructions about how to interpret other messages received. Such ambiguity renders problematic which messages communicate what and how the entirety of information is to be interpreted. Such confusion means inability to understand which messages communicate order and what is to be understood as insecurity. It seems to be this continuous, almost simultaneous, switching back and forth between order and insecurity, safety and chaos that generates ambiguity and creates uncertainty. This opens up a space for contestation, questioning, and deliberation on the part of the public. In conditions of binary opposition, both poles of the binary are on the same level of abstraction and so, of the same value. The theory of logical types obviates this by insisting on hierarchy between the poles, hierarchy that encompasses the poles within a higher meta-level or class. From the standpoint of security thinking, binaries or multiplicities on the same level of abstraction are rejected because this denies and negates the basis for control by security.

To make sense of these dynamics of switching between contradictory orders of messages where one denies the other, Bateson (1956) envisions this situation as a logical paradox of the self-referential variety. A logical paradox, Wilder and Collins (1994: 87) explain, "always arise[s] from a problem posed and found to be unsolvable within the frame of given axiomatic systems." Paying attention to paradox, they suggest, exposes a number of taken-for-granted assumptions about rationality in the Western philosophical traditions, as well as the Western conventional wisdom. In the Western tradition, ideas are evaluated on the basis of binary truth—they are either true or they are false, but they cannot be true and false at the same time. As a matter of comparison, Wilder and Collins point out that, in the Eastern thought, paradox does not represent a concern because paradoxical statements stand as a form of truth in themselves, an opportunity to grow and create, rather than an inconsistency to be corrected. In the practice of Zen Buddhism, what the Western view would call a paradox is used as a teaching device to reach the path to enlightenment. The Chinese and the Japanese languages seem to have no concept that approximates the notion of the paradox as it is known in the Western philosophy. Our understanding of paradox, Wilder and Collins write, is related to the Western privileging of human reason and utopian visions of order rather than the embracing of perplexity, indeterminacy, and ambiguity in human behavior. Paradoxes are, therefore, analytically very interesting because they help us understand culturally and contextually specific responses.

An often-mentioned example of paradox of the self-referential variety is the one posited by Epimenides: "All Cretans are liars." Epimenides was himself a Cretan, so with this statement he wanted to demonstrate an example of an illogical, nonsensical, contradictory message because if it is true that all Cretans are liars, than he must not be telling the truth. But if he is telling the truth, then he must be lying. Because the premise of this reasoning is the either/or logic (i.e., the statement is either true or false but cannot be both), to make sense of this communication one is running in circles. Bateson (1956) draws inspiration from these contradictory premises to envision the relationship between communication and meta-communication and relies on the theory of logical types to articulate this communicative relationship through the notion of framing. Philosophers and mathematicians Alfred North Whitehead and Bertrand Russell (1910) argue that the communication by Epimenides contains two different levels of abstraction: the class "the Cretans," denoting those who live on the island of Crete, and the actual people on the island. Their solution is to change the value of one category in relation to the other, thereby creating a hierarchy of value. Following their reasoning, a class—in this case, the Cretans—cannot be a member of the class of the phenomena it denotes, here being the actual people living on the island, because the class is of a higher logical type than the phenomena it denotes. In terms of meta-communication, the class encompasses, subsumes, and orders its members. The members do not order the class. Epimenides, a member of the class of Cretans, therefore, should not be caught in self-referential paradox, because the class, in this case, liars, should not be confuted with a member of that class, here, Epimenides the Cretan who may or may not be a liar.

When the juxtaposition of security and insecurity does not lead to security meta-framing—that is, when the meta-message of security is not recognized and so security is not identified as the value, higher than any other—a contradiction between the messages is exposed. This becomes obvious when juxtaposition of the choice between messages of security and insecurity becomes exposed as a paradox, illuminating an unbearable situation in which we think that we are in a position in which whatever we choose will result in an intolerable loss. If we choose to entrust our lives to the protection of the security apparatus and its surveillance technologies and procedures, our privacy, freedom of movement, and human rights are seriously undermined. But if we reject these measures to keep our freedoms, we expose ourselves to the mercy of people who may have destructive intentions. Matters of safety and well-being are vitally important to our lives, so rather than ignoring the paradox as unproblematic, the public feels compelled to respond. We must choose a meta-communicative message because it is crucial that we distinguish accurately what kinds of messages are being communicated and yet we are not able to distinguish between the logical types of the messages we receive because one set of messages denies the others. Bateson (2000b) calls this situation a double bind, a binding relationship from which it may be difficult to escape.

In some cases, Bateson (2000b) notes, a double bind can stimulate creativity and spontaneity and lead to novel solutions. Such is the case with learning in Zen Buddhism where the master may use double binds to encourage movement along the path toward enlightenment. Bateson (2000b: 208) describes an example where the master holds a stick over the student's head and says authoritatively: "If you say this stick is real, I will strike you with it. If you say the stick is not real, I will strike you with it. If you do not say anything, I will strike you with it." A student may react spontaneously, instinctively, or even reflexively by simply reaching up to the master's hand, getting hold of the stick, and just taking it away from the master. Such an outcome is possible under certain conditions. This student is unburdened by fear of authority and liberated from the limitation to think in binary terms. The master would not see this reaction as a ridicule of the master's authority or dismissal of an intention to communicate a set of important messages to the student. The master is actually trying to teach such emancipation, freedom, and spontaneity and would, therefore, see this as the student's step closer to enlightenment.

In meditation and often also in therapy (see Wilder and Collins 1994), double binds are intentionally created by authoritative figures to help individuals overcome such paradoxical situations. This, however, is not the case with double binds that result from the failure of security meta-framing. Because security meta-framing involves a bureaucratic system of a state apparatus and is predicated on binary classification, a way out of a double bind calls for a hierarchical solution. Such a solution means to identify among the messages communicated a meta-message that interprets all others. This means receiving additional information that will, in the eyes of the public, make a difference. According to Handelman (1992), such new information enables a change in values given to the contradictory messages. It generates a new understanding, which has the capacity to change the value assigned to the self-negating messages in such a way that it establishes a hierarchy between the messages. Once the messages are hierarchically organized in relation to one another, one set of messages is able to emerge as a message at a meta-level in relation to the others.

Security meta-framing in relation to privacy in the context of law offers another interesting possibility. As currently interpreted in legal terms, privacy is the right of an individual and defined through a common denominator which comprises sufficient and necessary elements that demarcate what privacy is and clearly separates privacy from other concerns (see Cockfield 2007). In this way, and coupled with the perception by the public that diminished privacy rights is a small price to pay for security, the information about the loss of privacy in relation to surveillance and other security measures is not likely to either be received by the public and the courts alike in meta-communicative terms or lead to a double bind. For this reason, Solove (2008) proposes to break away from exclusionary classification of privacy and to instead conceptualize privacy through a plurality of connections between different aspects of life so that a clear-cut decision between privacy and security would not be possible. By focusing on sufficient conditions, one is forced to include and exclude various aspects of life in which privacy is present, and in this way misses its various forms. Through Wittgenstein's family resemblance theory, Solove shows how it becomes possible to see that privacy has many dimensions, each related to different aspects of social and individual life in such a way that one affects the other and the overall quality of life of the whole community. In this way, it is possible to identify many specific aspects of privacy in different situations without the burden of adhering to a unifying common denominator. Privacy becomes a cluster of distinct things, situations, and dimensions of experience that are related through a chain of interconnections rather than one common denominator. Understood in such terms, the public would be able to see the multiple dimensions of privacy as intimately and inseparably related to the quality of life of the entire society in which no one dimension of privacy could be singled out as unnecessary in relation to the value of security.

When no spontaneous or instinctive reaction is achieved, no outside interference is introduced, and so no new information that makes a difference is acquired, Bateson envisions a situation that leads to systematic distortions and eventual self-destruction. A repeated and prolonged exposure to double binds, Bateson and others argue, leads to schizophrenia (Ruesch and Bateson 1951). In a schizophrenic situation, the ongoing contradiction becomes emotionally burdening, making people oscillate between love for security and hate of the loss of privacy, love for democracy but hate toward a particular classification of individuals. When the public cannot sort out the messages, people become overburdened and emotionally overloaded, and may react in extreme ways described as paranoia. Without the ability to find a solution, Bateson (2000b: 211–212) writes, the public becomes "like any self-correcting system which has lost its governor; it spirals into never-ending, but always systematic, distortions." One could argue that this means the abdication of democracy on the part of the citizenry.

## THE CHAPTERS

This volume is a cross-national and interdisciplinary mix of original and thought-provoking empirical and conceptual contributions of case studies from different parts of the world. The chapters are divided into four sections, which follow this introductory discussion, and conclude with summary remarks by Willem de Lint. In Part I, *Public Spaces and Collective Activities*, we begin with two contexts in which the dynamics of security meta-framing are extremely intensified and, therefore, very visible: airports and state-sponsored public events. These two cases allow us to study how the apparatus envisions the social reality of security, the process through which such social reality is constructed, and the maintenance of this reality through self-correcting behavior on the part of the public. In both cases, it is essential for the security apparatus to avoid any ambiguity in communication so that the meta-message of security can be identified immediately and without confusion by the people involved. In these securitized spaces, there is little tolerance for any social behavior that has the potential to generate uncertainty and indeterminacy. Mark Salter discusses one example of such behavior; namely, joking. The "no-joking" signs at the airports suggest that the security apparatus is aware of the potentials of humor. Humor opens up a possibility of questioning or exposing the arbitrariness of the social order at the airport envisioned and imposed by the security apparatus. Its prohibition tries to ensure that no social context is created in which people boarding an airplane would question the underlying assumption that the extreme control measures at the airport are for the good of the people and that the security experts know best how to protect them. The attempt to eliminate humor from this social space is an effort to avoid a double-bind, that is, an effort to avoid a situation where the security-insecurity paradox would be exposed because the meta-message of security would not be identified. Humor, Bateson (1953) argues, makes us laugh precisely because its symbolism leads us through a thought process that works by way of contradiction and ambiguity to be able to arrive at the punch line. When passing through the checkpoint, for example, passengers are expected to follow the rules: take off their shoes, put their belongings on the conveyer belt, and walk through the metal detector. If a sound is released by the machine, the passenger is ordered to step back, remove from his or her body what ever elements are thought to be triggering the sound, and then walk through the metal detector again. This is to be repeated for as long as the metal detector is releasing the sound. If, during such a moment, a joke is shared between the passengers and a security operative and the joke makes people laugh, a double bind may potentially be created. The operative is put in a position where he or she must effectively distinguish between a truthful intent and a harmless joke – but is unable to do so. On their part, the passengers, during the shared moments of laughter collectively ignore the operative's requests and - like the student of Zen Buddhism mentioned earlier – grab their luggage off the conveyer belt, put their shoes back on, and bypass the metal detector. The prohibition of humor seeks to eliminate such situations. In the social reality of security as designed by the security apparatus, there is little tolerance for alternative realities and little acceptance for other ways of being in the world. The airport is an example of a social space within which the security apparatus makes every effort to indefinitely maintain the reality of security.

How does social reality of security come to exist? Using the case of the visit of the late Pope John Paul II to Jerusalem, I demonstrate, step-by-step, the process through which such reality is constructed in the context of public events. Public events are collective activities that, for the duration of the event, are able to reorder social life according to their own script. Their temporary, often cyclical, nature allows us to observe the process of transformation of social life in a public space from everyday routine living, to a social reality of the event, and then back to the routine life. For these reasons, such events offer themselves as empirically rich and analytically fruitful phenomena for the study of the epistemology of security meta-framing in its actual affects on social life. Using detailed ethnographic data, I show that this process involves a total transformation of everyday life for the duration of the event. The purpose of this reordering of social life is to eliminate uncertainty from the living environment as best as possible and establish a social space of maximum control. The process begins when a public event is classified by the apparatus as an activity that can potentially be a threat to security. With this classification, the apparatus takes over the public space in which the event is to be staged, encircles the space with an impermeable boundary, separates insiders from outsiders and the safe from the dangerous, creates a sterilized zone of safety, and reorders the movement of people within the enclosure. All available resources are mobilized to this end, and the public is expected to adjust its routine daily life according to the rules of the apparatus. I make a provocative argument that, if we analytically separate the process of re-ordering performed by the security apparatus from the performance of the actual public event, we see that the process of security meta-framing of reality of safety has a ritual form. The implication is that through the form of ritual, the performance of surveillance in the name of security gains legitimacy and acceptance in the eyes of the public. What I call "security meta-ritual" effectively avoids the double bind by communicating to the public that it is in the interest of everyone involved that the public event unfolds without disturbance. Every successful performance of the security meta-ritual reinforces its meta-constitution in relation to whichever public event it seeks to protect and re-establishes the hierarchy of maximum control through security over the uncertainty of everyday life.

Part II, *Struggle and Resistance,* offers two examples in which the security meta-framing is effectively questioned with analytically very interesting outcomes. The first case details resistance of one person, while the second presents us with a group struggle. Interestingly, as the two chapters illustrate, the notion of security seems to be a powerful cultural construct, as in neither case does facing a security–insecurity paradox lead to negating the value of security all together. Nevertheless, it does seem to open up a space for alternative visions of social reality. Liora Sion presents a case of an Israeli-born Jewish woman by the name of Tali Fahima who fails to identify security as the meta-communicative message and begins to question the security meta-frame as it is lived in Israel/Palestine. At some point in Fahima's life, the information she has been receiving from the Israeli institutions on such issues as education, religion, the media, and the military, as well as various other constituents of the security apparatus, no longer seems self-evident, so she finds herself in a double bind. As Sion describes, Fahima is confused; she has always been told that Palestinians do not belong to the state of Israel but now she sees that Palestinians are actually human beings and that she, as an Israeli, is partly responsible for the path their lives have taken. Fahima's reaction to her discovery of this paradox is to seek more information from alternative sources. On her own and apart from any of the established channels, she commences Internet conversations with Arabs and Palestinians, invites Palestinians for a visit to her home, and initiates meetings with Palestinians in a refugee camp. Through this activity, she begins to blur the clear-cut boundaries between us and them, the good and the bad, the safe and the dangerous—classifications, established and enforced by the Israeli state security apparatus. As is the case with any such bureaucratic system, the working of the Israeli security apparatus is predicated on clearly defined classifications—for example, religious, secular, Palestinian, Israeli, Muslim, Jewish, Christian, peacenik, and terrorist—and the system is not capable of dealing with the ambiguities Fahima has created. Not surprisingly, the response of the apparatus has been to try to reorient Fahima, to force her back into the designated taxonomies; that is, taxonomies with which the security apparatus operates. Fahima is told that she must choose between any of the available categories: be a loyal Israeli or go and live with the Palestinians. She is pressured, harassed, interrogated, tried in court, imprisoned, publically humiliated by the apparatus and the mass media alike, and abandoned by the Israeli public. The goal is to force her to succumb to the security meta-frame from which she sought to escape. The case is ongoing, and Fahima is unpredictable. As of this writing, Fahima has been abandoned by the Israelis but accepted by the Palestinians. She recently converted to Islam and currently lives in a Palestinian town.

Kathleen Staudt presents a case of security meta-framing of the U.S.-Mexico border and the articulation of a collective resistance to its tendencies. The stretch of nearly 2000 miles is a culturally diverse, socially vibrant, and economically interdependent area, populated by people of Hispanic, European, and Native American descent, among others. With the classification of border migration as a security threat, the border area is beginning to resemble a military zone, where concrete wall, watch towers, barbed wire, night vision cameras, movement sensors, endless other surveillance technologies, and untold numbers of border control operatives work to achieve maximum control over migration through the area. The social consequences of this fortification of the border are an example of the power of security meta-framing to reorder social life. Its effects penetrate physically, socially, culturally, and emotionally through the closely knit and interdependent local communities. As Staudt details, the bureaucratic arm of the security apparatus reaches deep into this social fabric, severing families, relatives, coworkers, and friends through exclusionary classifications. Security meta-framing is forcing people in a position where they are asked to choose their loyalties between their kin or their state. Particularly the Hispanic population, however, is well aware of the security–insecurity paradox. Yet, in this poverty-stricken region, dominated by the minority of white Anglos, resistance has taken time to build momentum. Recently, Hispanics have been elected to public office, nongovernmental organizations established to provide legal council to immigrants, and documentaries filmed to record harassment by the U.S. Border Patrol agents. There have been lawsuits, school walkouts, and civil disobedience to block the construction of the border wall. Interestingly, as Staudt shows, this resistance is not articulated against the value of security. Rather, the questioning of the security meta-frame is leading in the direction of a struggle over how to define security as the meta-message. From the standpoint of the state apparatus, terrorism puts the survival of the nation at risk and must be counteracted by using military means. Those who resist this meta-message, on the other hand, are articulating their counteractivities as the struggle for human security. This entails a mix of values including human rights, individual freedom from state intrusion, respect for constitutional rights, and faith-based principles. Whereas the double bind opens up a space for a battle over who should determine what the classification of security should actually entail, Staudt suggests that the security meta-framing by the state apparatus nevertheless seems to hold firmly, winning over the local articulations of human security.

The power of the state and its security apparatus to have control over security meta-framing is grounded in the ability to classify and re-classify individual behavior at will. This power is enhanced through televised demonstrations of the state's ability to pre-empt visions of chaos and destruction, the practice of secrecy, and pressures to modify legal norms to accommodate the needs of the apparatus. In Part III, *Law, Citizenship, and the State*, contributors demonstrate how the push for security as the dominant value through what I described earlier as governmentality of potentialities have been undermining the very basis of democratic principles of the modern state, the rule of law and the relationship between the citizen and the state. As Willem de Lint discusses, mass-mediated demonstrations of successful pre-emptive activity by the apparatus are crucial for their legitimacy in the eyes of the public. The public expects action on the part of the apparatus, lest it be thought of as "weak on security." At the same time, particularly in a democratic state, the apparatus is expected to demonstrate to the public that it is taking action in the face of chaos and uncertainty. Each reinforces the other so that, as Masco (2008) would suggest, both resonate with the collective memories on the part of the public and the apparatus alike of the destructive potentials of technologies in the hands of the wrong people. In Bateson's terms, this opens up a space of tolerance on the part of the public not only for secrecy but also for normalization of the so-called "exceptional security measures" by the apparatus.

Reem Bahdi documents the case of a number of Arabs and Muslims who came to be secretly classified as terrorists by the security apparatus of Canada and treated in violation of the law. She details several examples: the Canadian state apparatus was directly implicated in handing its own citizens and residents into the hands of the apparatus of another state, its denizens were kept in solitary confinement in Canadian jails for months without legal council, and individuals were confined to their homes through house arrest during which their family members were forced to surveil and police them. When these cases entered the public sphere and the lawyers began preparing lawsuits against the state, the apparatus simply created a new classification that denied the right to sue the state and labeled those who sought to claim such rights unpatriotic and therefore a national security threat. Bahdi concludes that there may be variations in the way apparatuses of different states with democratic political organizations support the meta-message of security when extraordinary measures are employed in the case of terrorism suspects. Although the United States publically claims that extraordinary measures are necessary in exceptional times, such claims are rarely publically made by the Canadian state. Instead, the Canadian apparatus claims that individual rights should be balanced in relation to collective rights so that if individual rights threaten the collectivity, individual protections should give way to the well-being of the group.

In the case of Western law, writes King (1993), any social issue or event that requires determination by the court has to be decided in binary terms, legal or illegal. These categories are mutually exclusive so that social activity cannot be simultaneously interpreted as lawful or unlawful. To be considered a part of the scope of law—that is, to fall within the boundaries of the legal system—any social practice, no matter how complex, needs to be coded in these binary terms and must be formulated in such a way that it can be arbitrated as either in accordance with the law or against the law.

Gabe Mythen analyzes the case of counterterrorism legislation in the United Kingdom. The new legislation seeks to legalize the governmentality of potentialities; that is, the tendency of the apparatus to act pre-emptively rather than arbitrate over an act already committed. This legislation, Mythen shows, is based on imaginaries of some abnormal human activity in the future and on anticipation of worse-case scenarios. The public expects that the governing institutions will act. The state apparatus is pushing to bend the existing law and to undermine the existing regulation to be able to act swiftly, bypassing the checks and balances currently in place. Through this push for new legislation, certain fundamental grounds of Western law are undermined, including the right to remain silent under questioning, the right to be released when no charges have been pressed, and the maxim that an individual is innocent until proven guilty of an actual unlawful activity.

Chapters in Part IV (*Global Agendas, Local Transformations*) demonstrate how the totalizing nature of the security meta-frame, as it expands globally, is able to define the parameters and the conditions of how everyday life should be lived at very micro-levels in three different parts of the world: the European Union (EU), Latin America, and China. Sirpa Virta documents the ambition by the governing bodies of the EU to impose homogeneous, unionwide surveillance measures on the populations of the member states in light of the new classification of "homegrown terrorism." Included in this new taxonomy is a specification that this type of terrorism can appear in any of the states of the EU, that visible signs of such "growth" include "radical behavior" and "recruitment," and that the apparatus must act on these signs to pre-empt and prevent whatever human activity may transpire as a result of this. The signs that communicate to the apparatus what entails radical behavior are interpreted through what Foucault (2003) analyzed as the understanding by the apparatus of what constitutes abnormal individual thought and lifestyle. Clues include changes in social, religious, or political convictions; refusal to shake a woman's hand; or changes in appearance such as growing a beard or wearing a particular kind of clothing. This new classification, Virta suggests, is administered through a highly centralized and bureaucratized security apparatus that is dominated by the police, intelligence organizations, and secret service, institutions with limited language skills and cultural knowledge to interpret intentions of individuals in the culturally and socially highly diverse population of Europe. The security meta-frame, she suggests, nevertheless resonates locally due to people's growing sense of fear.

Cultural behavior, Jiang Fei and Huang Kuo argue, is also at the center of security concerns in China where the state is anxious that the younger generations may be embracing cultural ways of the West, thereby relinquishing the Maoist traditions of discipline and respect of authority. In its ambition to dominate the global economy, the Chinese state had no choice but to join the global capitalist economic circles. By opting to embrace capitalism, China was forced to open its doors to multinational corporations, including what Fei and Kuo call transnational media corporations. To create a new market for their goods among the Chinese, corporations such as Disney, Time Warner, and others have been eager to promote the culture of consumption and consumer spending as well as the Western values associated with individualism. The Chinese state fears that, what Baudrillard (1981) calls the "seduction of the symbols of capitalism," will lure the Chinese youth away from the value of the Chinese version of socialism and its Maoist traditions. The result has been a not-so-subtle power struggle over the hearts and the minds of the Chinese, which the Chinese state is trying to articulate through the security meta-frame. Fei and Kuo use the ancient Chinese teachings on the art of war (Lian Heng and He Zong) to demonstrate these dynamics between the anxious Chinese state and the ambitious foreign media corporations. In their provocative analogy of the similarities between ancient Chinese war strategies and the contemporary securitization of culture by the state, Fei and Kuo illustrate how this struggle influences the lives of the Chinese people.

Nelson Arteaga Botello documents a similar expansionist ambition of the security meta-framing of everyday living, this one by the United States over the entire region of the Americas. Through two foreign aid policies, the Merida Initiative and the Columbia Plan, the U.S. Congress seeks to implement a security and economic infrastructure over the entire region. This top-down imposition, Botello shows, has had particular effects on the ground. In the fast-growing Latin American urban centers, he suggests, social inequality, underemployment, and neighborhood crime loom large so that people are seeking protection. Rather than improving the grossly inadequate social services, however, it is the surveillance practices of the security apparatus that are being put in place instead. Military and police surveillance permeates down to neighborhood relations, reshaping the social fabric as well as the physical landscape of these communities along class and racial lines. The public space is being carved into zones and corridors of intensive protection for those with the means. Neighborhood watch groups, private guards, and sophisticated surveillance technologies protect the well-being of the privileged residents who are housed in walled-off gated neighborhoods, who work and shop in zoned-off commercial districts, and are able to move from zone to zone through carefully surveilled routes. The exterior of this grid is left to violence, malnutrition, crime, and fear of open spaces. The boundary is maintained not only by the apparatus but also by the privileged residents who are encouraged to work closely with the apparatus and report any of their observations of abnormal behavior. Here, in the absence of effective social services or strong kinship or communal ties, the globalizing tendency of the security meta-frame meets the communal needs for safety and economic well-being.

As Willem de Lint discusses in his concluding remarks, with the empirical evidence and its accompanying theoretical reflections, this volume is a contribution to what is emerging as a research agenda on the dynamics associated with treating a wide variety of social activities and phenomena in everyday life as a threat to security. Attention to these issues was first given by Barry Buzan, Ole Waever, and colleagues at the Peace Research Institute at the University of Copenhagen. Today, their scholarship is referred to as the Copenhagen School.[4] Their efforts have sparked a very diverse set of approaches and research initiatives, among others in France (e.g. Bigo 2002; Balzacq 2005) and in Canada (e.g. de Larrinaga and Salter 2010). The introduction of security meta-framing derived from the communications theory of Bateson offers this research agenda a framework to theorize in historical and cultural-comparative terms at micro and macro levels how the security imperative is shaping the conditions of possibility of how everyday life is articulated through practice as well as through thought.

## NOTES

1. For an overview of the extensive scholarship of Gregory Bateson and its contemporary significance, see biographies by Charlton (2008) and Lipset (1980).
2. The Long War is a central theme in the Cold War espionage novels of John Le Carré who was, in his early career, himself a former spy for MI5.
3. See "Holder backs a Miranda limit for terror suspects." Charlie Savage, *The New York Times*, May 10, 2010; and "Militant's path from Pakistan to Times Square." Andrea Elliott, *The New York Times*, June 23, 2010.
4. A review of this scholarship is beyond the scope of my argument here. For most recent work see Buzan and Waever (2009, 2007); Buzan and Hansen (2009); Stritzel (2007); and Williams (2003).

# Part I

# Public Spaces and Collective Activities

# 1 "No Joking!"

*Mark B. Salter*[1]

## AIRPORT SECURITY IS (NOT) A JOKE

The airport has become a complex and overdetermined site and sign of the new security that has come under increased academic scrutiny, which enables and constrains differential mobility by systems of surveillance and control; the management of vision, space, and time; and by harnessing affect or emotion (Lyon 2003; Adey 2008). Airports are also a sign of the politics of everyday life; they represent the dream of free, technologically enabled mobility and the vulnerability that this global network lays bare (Augé 1995; Gordon 2004; Iyer 2001). Fuller and Harley say "the airport is a complex machine, a series of interdependent and cross-reference systems, functions, jurisdictions and modalities. What the airport is, depends on where you are in it, and how and why you are travelling through it" (2005: 17). As a signal site of 'national' security, Feldman observes, "The ramping-up of security procedures at the airport produces a kind of condensation point for anxieties surrounding the balance between liberty and security in the political community as a whole" (2007: 334). Because of the complexity and vulnerability of the civil aviation system, airports have become hypersecuritized spaces, where policies, technologies, and methods of control that would be unimaginable elsewhere are commonly accepted. This chapter builds on previous critical analyses of airports and the subjectivities created by their modes of care and control (Adey 2004; Lyon 2006; Salter 2007).[2] Airports are the subject of sustained analysis in the study aviation business, transport and human geography, tourism studies, surveillance studies, anthropology, law and society, and political science (Salter 2008).

The design, structure, and architecture of the airport should also be a subject of serious analysis. A number of airport theorists, such as Adey, Lyon, and Lloyd (all, 2003) draw attention to the way that consumer and bureaucratic spaces are arranged to maximize "dwell-time" and way-finding. In addition to the overdesign of terminals facilitating continual movement, sorting, and self-navigation, there is an international semiotic system of airport signs that condition behavior. Foucault makes an argument about

Bentham's prison design (the Panopticon): the architecture itself of the prison that renders all prisoners as silhouettes to a (possibly staffed) guard tower "induce[d] in the inmate a state of conscious and permanent visibility that assures the automatic functioning of power. So to arrange things that the surveillance is permanent in its effects, even if it is discontinuous in its action; that the perfection of power should tend to render its actual exercise unnecessary" (1977: 201). Fuller extends this kind of semiotic-design critique through an analysis of the use of windows in modern airport terminals that "have the power to arrest a crowd around a commodity, corralling them in chic bars overlooking the runway as they wait for their call, but also guiding them where to go next. Such guidance is necessary, given the multiplicity of regulatory and commercial zones with the airport" (2008: 164). In addition to guiding passengers, airport staff, and bureaucrats, airports are pedagogical spaces, teaching their inhabitants about the politics of mobility. All of the signs, designs, and structures educate passengers on how to behave in a way that makes the security apparatus work more smoothly, and facilitates their travel. This architectural and semiotic power has a panoptic effect: passengers come to self-police their behavior. Aatola argues that actually "airports teach people the central rituals of acknowledgements that are needed to navigate in the Byzantine structures of the modern hierarchical world order" (2005: 261). He connects the quotidian aspects of the airport to the larger geopolitical context:

> The omnipresent system of signs, codes and instructions define the airport experience . . . checks, instructions, prohibitions and warnings from the monotonous 'Watch your step' and 'unattended bags will be destroyed' to threats of fines and imprisonment provide the context . . . however, its pedagogical function is to instruct and prescribe about the 'natural' and 'apolitical' character of the contemporary imperial order (264).

These monotonous signs are important, precisely because they are not understood as political. Fuller analyzes the importance of signage within the airports: "we obey the signs: whether we believe or not is in many ways irrelevant. Each time I am frisked at the airport, it is done ostensibly with my welfare in mind; if I don't consent to being protected, I can't get on the airplane" (2002: 137). This chapter interrogates this obedience without belief and this docile acceptance of a particular kind of protection.

To add to these connections between the affective and security within cultural logics of control at the airport, I examine the joke at the airport. Anxiety leads to joking. But, while anxiety is permitted and even required to make the security system function, joking is prohibited (Salter 2007). From an anthropological point of view, jokes "[poke] a hole through often-undiscussed but official versions of everyday reality, exposing their contradictions the arbitrary basis of their social power" (Paolucci and Richardson

2006: 334). Freud would say that we joke precisely about what we fear. A joke means "'Look! Here is the world, which seems so dangerous! It is nothing but a game for children—just worth making a jest about!'" (1961: 433). Jokes undermine the whole claim that security is serious and thus that the security measures are necessary, exceptional, and not up for political debate.[3] This chapter interrogates the securitization of everyday life through an analysis of the "no-joking" rule at airports. The no-joking rule plays (or at least attempts to) three roles: to deter verbal attempts at undermining the call to security at the airport; to interiorize the policing of exterior signs of obedience; and to deny a sense of community between the joker and the agent of the state. At its root, the prohibition of humor is precisely an attempt to reveal the ambiguity or ambivalence of the invocation of security. As such, whether jokes occur at the airport or about the airport, the underlying security appeal—airports and civil aviation security is serious and requires special, exceptional limitations on freedom for the purpose of security—is destabilized by jokes and humor. As in the Panopticon, it is not the overt use of power but the belief in the structure of power that induces the effect of self-policing. The destabilization of the security discourse comes in the telling of jokes about everyday life—even if different jokes, in different contexts, told by different actors to different audiences have different effects. The urgency of the no-joking message belies the underlying incredibility of the airport security claim. Although no-joking signs in airports are the most overt attempt, legal, regulatory, or policy that prohibits joking in other airport zones and the social prohibition against making particular jokes (such as about September 11, 2001 [9/11]) are equally part of the same political contestation of the limits of the possible, the sayable, the laughable in everyday life.

A new awareness or sensitivity to the no-joking rule is representative of the securitization of everyday life in which the content of our speech is self-policed to avoid any ambiguity. Self-policing by travelers is a crucial tactic of aviation security authorities, and I have argued elsewhere that the predisposition to confession plays an important role in this (Salter 2006: 180–183). Parks argues that the new American security screening procedures "terrorize interiority" (197), and the real focus of screening is the traveler's presentation of self because "no object is un-threatening in the war on global terror" (198). She offers as evidence of the importance of affect and obedience the new civil penalties that can be issued by the Transportation Security Administration (TSA) for "attitude" (188). It is also illustrated in the presentation of trusted traveler programs or the self-streaming of passengers (expert, casual, and family) at a number of airport screening points (Curry 2004; Thurlow and Jaworski 2006). Why the new emphasis on the no-joking rule? With the new investments in screening equipment (including new scanners, x-ray machines, and explosive detection units) and new procedures (such as self-streaming, risk analysis, and No-Fly lists), what extra security does the no-joking rule add?

A typical TSA sign reads: "Attention: Making any jokes or statements[4] during the screening process may be grounds for both criminal and civil penalties. All such matters will be taken seriously. We thank you for your restraint in this matter."[5] These signs are often present right before the pre-board screening checkpoints.[6] Some airports also have the no-joking signs as part of a media display on television screens broadcast to travelers waiting in line before they arrive at the checkpoint or in the public space of the terminal. This message is repeated in numerous TSA brochures, pamphlets, and Web sites: "Belligerence, inappropriate jokes and threats are not tolerated. Jokes and/or comments about threats to passengers or the aircraft will be taken seriously and can result in criminal or civil penalties for the passenger."[7] In some TSA literature, the bullet heading for this item is "Security is serious," in others simply "Think." The Canadian Air Transport Security Authority (CATSA) and Transport Canada have similar public messages: "Never joke or talk[8] about weapons or hijacking while going through screening. It's against the law and penalties could be severe, including fines or jail."[9]

An Australian press release regarding their no-joking rule further demonstrates the limits of the state. The deputy prime minister justifies the rule against jokes on the grounds of utility, customer service, and a call that security is 'serious.' "These sort of jokes distress passengers and staff. They are expensive to deal with and cause delays, because we have to take them seriously and carry out searches just in case they're not, in fact, jokes. If you are stupid enough to make joke threats about aviation security, you won't just miss your flight. You could end up with a $5,500 fine and a criminal record—and that's no joke."[10] Anderson is right to be wary of the unintentional joke.[11] CATSA relaxed the interpretation or application of the no-joking rule in 2007 (although not the aviation security regulations themselves, which are the responsibility of the federal Transport Canada). A memo set a discretionary boundary between "careless and inflammatory" speech, which was not to be prosecuted, and "false declarations" that are threats to civil aviation. Examples provided included: "I am going to set fire to the airplane with this blowtorch" (false declaration) versus "What do you think I look like, a terrorist?" (careless or inflammatory)."[12] The CATSA spokesperson said, "screening officers were not discerning the context in which the declaration or the statement was made. And they were a little bit too quick on the trigger."[13] Calling (unarmed) screening officials "quick on the trigger" in interpreting security threats seems ham-fisted but demonstrates how thin the line is between statements and jokes. It is precisely an unintentional joke, while a CATSA spokesperson speaks to the press about the importance of security, that indicates how close the joke relates the security claim. This "slip of the tongue" also demonstrates the impossibility of policing the unconscious.[14]

No-joking rules were in place at airports before 9/11, as were prosecutions of false threats, but there is now a new public sensitivity to security. In addition to a number of high-profile prosecutions for individuals joking about bombs or other weapons at screening points since 9/11, security consultants and private individuals routinely try to demonstrate the weaknesses in airport security.[15] These failures "reveal that imagining and staging security breeches has become a national preoccupation and an obsessive management ritual" (Parks 2007: 189). Although one might assume a cultural taboo regarding humor about 9/11 itself or airport security after the failed shoe-bombing or transatlantic plots, jokes circulated almost immediately (Brigham 2005; Kuipers 2005).[16] Ellis records jokes about the World Trade Center attacks being posted within 2 hours of their collapse (2002). The horrifying images of the event were quickly interpolated through a Photoshopped picture of a tourist, taken with an attacking airplane in the background, which when debunked as a spoof was then itself further parodied (Frank 2004: 650). The shoe bomber, the No-Fly list, and the new millimeter wave scanner were each quickly made fun of through editorial cartoons, late-night comedians, on the Internet, and through commercials.[17] Anthropologists and folklorists have identified disaster joke-cycles that often follow public tragedies (such as the Challenger disaster and earthquakes). Oring (1987) describes these jokes as related not to the disaster itself but rather the mediated representation of the disaster. Joking in this context goes through several stages as the trauma event becomes narrativized in the communal imagination (Ellis 2001). Humor seems a natural and human response to anxiety and to trauma, but there is also a special sensitivity to security; how are these balanced at the airport?

## BE SERIOUS

A joke is a disruption of meanings for humorous effect, or "a play upon form. It brings into relation disparate elements in such a way that one accepted pattern is challenged by the appearance of another which in some way was hidden in the first" (Douglas 1991: 296). In Fine's words, "they twist the normal order of the world" (2004: 224). Jokes are inherently dialogic and depend on a particular and receptive audience. As Oring describes, "Jokes depend upon a community of knowledge and interpretations. Jokes communicate only when audiences are able to simultaneously access similar yet unstated categories, orientations, and experiences" (1987: 278). Not only are jokes culturally dependent but require this shared "community of knowledge and interpretations" precisely because jokes involve a disruption of explicit and implicit assumptions, roles, or statements. Because of this play with common factors between joker and audience, jokes can also reinforce and create community (Fine and de Soucey 2005). In this anthropological sense, jokes are parts of particular group cultures that rely upon and play with implicit and explicit knowledge common to members.

Freud's analysis of the joke has been important to literary and cultural studies of humor. The Freudian description of laughter is essentially a kind of static shock of the unconscious: "a sum of psychical energy which has hitherto been used for cathexis is allowed free discharge" (1960: 200). The TSA sign that "appreciates restraint"—rather than obedience, compliance, or cooperation—clearly operates under this theory of humor. The emphasis on restraint illustrates the need to internalize security procedures (i.e., to repress the desire to joke to release the fear of the paternal 'no'). Freud explains that the linguistic form of the joke creates and then disperses psychic tension within the audience. "The words of the joke [the audience] hears necessarily being about in him the idea or train of thought to the construction of which great internal inhibitions were opposed in him too" (201). Thus, humor depends upon the play of meanings that reveal what has been repressed (the infantile, the childish, the sexual, the bodily, the forbidden, or the taboo). This is why so much of the joking around airport security involves nudity or racial stereotypes. The paranoia about flying naked and invasive personal screening plays on the taboo of the biological body and of cultural assumptions about the naked and the clothed. Freud identifies several different kinds of jokes: "obscene, aggressive (hostile), cynical (critical or blasphemous)" (1960: 161). Plainly the majority of jokes about the efficacy of airport screening can be understood as cynical or critical. It is interesting that the majority of editorial cartoons or jokes do not play on the gendered stereotypes more familiar to the 1960s of the air crew (Trudy Baker's *Coffee, Tea, or Me? The Uninhibited Memoirs of Two Airline Stewardesses* [1967] or the 'mile-high' club), but show no reticence playing on racial/ethnic stereotypes of young Arab men as terrorist. Examining television commercials that use the airport setting can demonstrate this shift in what is acceptable material for a public joke.

Jokes also revel in a surplus of meaning and a play between potential explanations. Oring argues that "humor depends on the perception of an *appropriate incongruity*" (2003: 1).[18] The key of interpreting jokes must be the multiplicity of meanings, and the play between explicit and implicit meanings. For example: Two psychoanalysts meet on the street, one says to the other, "Hello, how am I?" This plays on an inversion of the usual formalities of social interaction (which would be 'how are you?'), which itself refers to the inherent narcissism of the self, invoking the childish time when that narcissism was socially and psychologically acceptable. The joke also points to the particular analyst–analysand relationship peculiar to Freudian psychoanalysis. Freud also discusses the "sceptical [*sic*]" joke that works precisely in "attacking [ . . . ] not a person or an institution but the certainty of our knowledge itself" (161). Much absurdist humor works in this way. Examples include Woody Allen's joke "there is the fear that there is an afterlife but no one will know where it's being held" or Steven Wright's joke "what is the speed of dark?" I would argue that when cynical jokes about the efficacy of security measures are met with the skeptical jokes that question the possibility of providing absolute security, we see the most dangerous kind of joke. The satiric news site *The Onion* presents a clear example of this kind of joke regarding the U.S. Federal Aviation Administration (FAA): "FAA considering passenger ban."[19] Citing a fictional FAA spokesman, the story concludes:

> Improved explosive-detection systems, fortified cockpit doors, more plainclothes sky marshals aboard planes, and mandatory anti-hijacking training for flight crews—none of it could eliminate the possibility of another Sept. 11 with 100 percent certainty," Gemberling said. "This will." "We've tried every possible alternative, but nothing has worked," Gemberling continued. "For all our efforts, we keep coming back to the same central problem: humans."

The joke depends upon a common knowledge of the purpose of the airline system (to move human beings) and the managerial rhetoric of security screening efficiency. The background assumption that the object of security is the traveling public is confounded by the nature of threat. This is similar to jokes and editorial cartoons depicting naked passengers or treating passengers as luggage.[20] The joke also plays on the impossibility of providing "100 percent certainty." No system can be risk free or totally secure, even though that is the common goal. Thus, the joke becomes that only a particular stereotype (e.g., police officer, bureaucrat, regulator, counterterrorism czar) would think that eliminating humans would make the system secure. However, these skeptical jokes also point to a fundamental tension at the start of the state's desire and ability to 'know' and 'manage' its population.

## THE EPISTEMOLOGICAL TENSION OF THE LIBERAL STATE

It is the success of liberalism to convince its citizens to police themselves in the name of freedom. Foucault writes that at the beginning of the 19th century, for example, "everywhere you see this stimulation of the fear of danger, which is, as it were, the condition, the internal psychological and cultural correlative of liberalism. There is no liberalism without a culture of danger" (2008: 67). The birth of the modern state is characterized by the gathering and marshalling of data: a different view of governing, which is not about prohibition but rather about the management of populations and the guarantee of circulation. Foucault examines particular sites, such as the prison and the clinic, within which the collection and management of information becomes a form of control. Thus, Foucault discusses networks of power and knowledge, which understand power to be productive of particular authorities and expertises (2000a: 131). I have argued elsewhere that the airport is a similar institution (Salter 2007). The security function of the state at the airport poses a particular epistemological problem: if the chief concern of liberal government is 'not to govern too much,' how does the government govern threat, risk, and security 'just enough'? We can see how increased securitization at airports, and in particular the production of a particular kind of protection requires the restriction on the freedom to move, or as Bigo puts it, "the paradoxical liberty 'to go anywhere except where one wants to go'" (2007: 26).

Jokes and their prohibition are crucial to the functioning of the national security state, because the state seeks to be a producer, arbiter, and manager of knowledge. Jokes—particularly ones that question the possibility of knowledge—are dangerous because they provide a space for untruths, which is not necessarily connected to mendacity. The no-joking rule adheres most often to official sites of truth/power (e.g., the courtroom, the interrogation cell, the clinic).[21] Foucault is useful for examining functions of the no-joking rule. As with the oath, the allegiance, and the confession, the rule attempts to fix the core epistemological tension of the state. He makes the case that confession is crucial to contemporary subjectivity: "I think we should consider it a highly significant event in the relations between the subject and truth when truth-telling about oneself became a condition for salvation, a fundamental principle in the subject's relationship to himself, and a necessary element in the individual's membership of a community" (2001: 364). This confession, when performed in front of an agent of the state, becomes an examination, and carries with it all of the religious overtones of its history (2000b: 5). However, because the agents of the state cannot know what is in the hearts and minds of its citizens (obedient or deviant), all attempts to fix knowledge regarding the inner realm of the citizen simply display the possibility of resistance and revolution. This is one of the great tricks of the disciplinary state, as Foucault suggests, that the strongest chains are in the mind (1977: 102). This dynamic is exacerbated by the nature of the war on terrorism, as it has been by previous anticolonial struggles. How does the state distinguish between political and non-political violence?[22]

Within this larger biopolitical picture, tactical tools are mobilized to facilitate self-policing. One of these tactics is the embedding of a confessionary impulse—or rather the encouragement of a particular kind of examination that is readable by agents of the state—at multiple sites of control such as the airport. Foucault points to the invention of this kind of examination:

> How is it that in Western Christian culture the government of men demands, on the part of those who are led, not only acts of obedience and submission but also 'acts of truth,' which have the particular requirement not just that the subject tell the truth but that he tell the truth about himself, his faults, his desires, the state of his soul, and so on? How was a type of government of men formed in which one is required not simply to obey but to reveal what one is by stating it? (1997: 81).

For example, in the court of law, not only do lawyers and judges take an oath of loyalty to the interests of justice, but each individual witness swears on a holy book to tell "the whole truth and nothing but the truth." This explicit oath is an attempt to compel truthfulness when no compulsion can be made. The medical clinic also requires an exhaustive detailing of symptoms, which are denarrativized in traditional diagnosis, separated from the history or identity of the individual and treated as a 'case.' Other interfaces between state and citizen, such as the airport security-screening checkpoint, make use of this confessionary complex.

Joking is the opposite of confession. Confession is an absolute reckoning of the self that affirms the authority of the audience to collect that information and make a judgment about the character of the confessor. Joking undermines both the claim to knowledge and the authority to judge. "The joke then represents a rebellion against that authority, a liberation from its pressure" (Freud 1960: 149). This is part of the reason that poststructural (and postmodern) philosophers are so fond of laughter as a strategy of critique, precisely because it demonstrates the limits, the assumptions, and the slippages of authority. Foucault links the start of his *Archeology of Knowledge* to laughter: "this book first arose out of a passage in Borges, out of the laughter that shattered, as I read the first passage, all the familiar landmarks of my thought . . . breaking up all ordered surfaces and all of the planes with which we are accustomed to tame the wild profusion of existing things, and continuing long afterwards to disturb and threaten with collapse our age-old distinction between the Same and the Other" (1970: xv). Laughter is "something that exceeds the thinkable and opens the possibility of 'thinking otherwise' bursts in through comical, incongruous, or paradoxical half-openings in discourse . . . it is [Foucault's] philosophical signature on the irony of history" (de Certeau 1986: 194).

The no-joking rule at the airport demonstrates precisely the inability of the state to distinguish between truthful and untruthful statements in the examination. In the same way that swearing on a Bible demonstrates an anxiety about a witness's ability or intention to tell the truth, the no-joking rule demonstrates an anxiety about the lack of ability to take a joke, to tell what is a joke, to laugh and to still maintain security, and to distinguish between real threats and jokes. It tears at the construction of the image of state agents as experts in security. This is the tension: the more the state seeks knowledge and certainty, the more it demonstrates its inability to hold a monopoly on truth or identity. Ambiguity, on which jokes rely, fundamentally undermines the presentation of certainty that is crucial to security performances. The airport checkpoint (as with the border, the court, or the clinic) is a performative site: a sociopolitical space in which identities are performed for a particular state audience and then authorized or marginalized (Wonders 2006). Aatola argues that: "within the airport frame a different set of expectations and rules constitutes expressive behaviour than that by which normal life outside the frame proceeds" (2005: 264). Joking, by its nature as disruptive and polyvalent, plays with the expected relationship between joker and the agent of the state precisely because it questions the institution's ability to make knowledge claims about the joker. Joking undermines the claim of the agent to make discretionary judgments about real, serious threats and unreal, trivial humor.

## JOKES TOLD AT THE AIRPORT

The vast majority of jokes about post-9/11 airports involve the new screening requirements or procedures (counting those involving gels, liquids, shoe removal, and scanners). I will next examine the importance of the no-joking rule as demonstrated in its exceptions; that is, when it is possible to make jokes about airport security? Because jokes critical of security procedures are a relatively easy case to make, I will use two quick examples from former President George W. Bush and David Letterman's "Top Ten" List. A critical case will then be examined (joking on Southwestern Airlines during the safety announcement). The joking on Southwest creates a sense of community between the joker and the audience. Each of these breeches in the no-joking rule demonstrates a function of the joke that resists the securitization of everyday life: the gravity of the threat or the competency of the state to manage that threat; the community between passengers and security agents; and the social stigma of visible signs of obedience or resistance.

### One-Liners

President Bush joked in a foreign policy speech to a university audience "security is strong at the airports. I hope they stop taking shoes off the elderly. [Laughter.] I must confess, they haven't taken my shoes off in a while [Laughter]".[23] Security around the president is so tight that he is assumed to be benign; also, he is playing with new security rules that require the removing of footwear (a response to the nearly successful attempt by Richard Reid to blow up American Airlines flight 63 from Paris–Charles de Gaulle Airport to Miami International Airport on December 22, 2001). These practices of screening are based on an industry-wide belief: the default security regulation should apply to every traveling individual.[24] When there is random screening, it is assumed to be as (statistically) effective as targeted screening, because targeting or profiling is always imperfect.[25] Thus, the procedures are ridiculed because they inappropriately target a group we all assume to be obviously benign and do not target someone so obviously dangerous as President Bush. David Letterman's (2004) Top Ten List on "How to Improve the Department of Homeland Security" concluded: "Instruct airport screeners to hit everybody in the nuts," demonstrating both the general belief in the inefficacy of airport screening and the interjection of the bodily (the biological and the sexual) into the realm of the everyday.[26] This particular joke also reveals the gendered assumptions of the traveling 'public' as predominantly male and aggressive, while security screening is portrayed as an emasculating (indeed, castrating) process. These brief jokes are typical and unremarkable, displaying a causal and shallow critique of airport security procedures as ineffective in target and method.

## Southwest Airlines

Southwest is a large, low-cost airline that is one of the most admired companies in the United States with a high reputation for customer satisfaction (Freiberg and Freiberg 1996; Gittelle 2002).[27] Its corporate mission is defined as: "dedication to the highest quality of Customer Service delivered with a sense of warmth, friendliness, individual pride, and Company Spirit."[28] Within the organization, employees come first and are expected to translate that care and concern to the passenger.[29] Humor and 'fun' are a cornerstone part of this brand (Freiberg and Freiberg 1996: 205). This is reflected in corporate strategy: "I want flying to be a helluva lot of fun," said Southwest Chairman Herb Kelleher. "Life is too short and too hard and too serious not to be humorous about it" (64). Here in this major statement of business philosophy, Kelleher directly contradicts the TSA's statement that being 'serious' means no joking. In hiring, recruiters ask potential employees how they have used humor in their place of work (66). The Southwest brand is built on customer service, and joking is seen as a clear sign of a positive attitude toward customers.[30] There is also a foregrounding of the crew as individuals, rather than simply abstract safety or security professionals. The focus on flight attendants is also part of the Southwest corporate strategy, which prioritizes employees (and then expects employees to prioritize passengers) (Miles and Mangold 2005). This commitment to humor is further demonstrated by two recent print advertisements. The majority of American Airlines have recently begun charging for checked luggage in an effort to balance rising fuel prices. Southwest's response advertisement reads: "What have they been smoking? Apparently, your rolled-up $20s."[31] The advertisement contrasts the additional costs of other airlines (e.g., check-in, phone reservation, snack fees). Similarly, another print advertisement is designed as a coupon, which reads "Don't' #$*!% me over. (Southwest is the only airline that accepts this coupon.)"[32]

This sense of humor is also present throughout the flight. A safety/security briefing at the beginning of each flight is mandated by national aviation authority (e.g., FAA, Transport Canada, Civil Aviation Authority). This briefing includes the operation of the seatbelt and oxygen masks, the designation of emergency exits, and the plan for evacuation (and lifejackets in the unlikely event of a water landing). The FAA Advisory Circular sets the problem of obedience and risk:

An alert, knowledgeable person has a much better chance of surviving any life- or injury-threatening situation that could occur during passenger-carrying operations in civil aviation. Therefore, the Federal Aviation Administration (FAA) requires a passenger information system for U.S. air carriers and commercial operators that includes both oral briefings and briefing cards. Every airline passenger should be motivated to focus on the safety information in the passenger briefing; however, motivating people, even when their own personal safety is involved, is not easy. One way to increase passenger motivation is to make the safety information briefings and cards as interesting and attractive as possible.[33]

There is ample evidence in social psychology that a key to resilience in the face of crisis or disaster is informed and engaged individuals (Flynn 2007: 154–165). Thus, the safety announcements provide crucial information about how passengers might help in their own survival in the "unlikely" event. But it is difficult to motivate passengers to contemplate their own mortality, something that is demonstrated in the fear of flying. In addition, it is difficult to compel passengers to self-police in this way, the absurdity of which is demonstrated in a recent announcement "it is our policy that passengers remain seated during the flight." The safety announcements have become normalized, essentially regulatory hoops for the air crew with no surprises for the passengers. The Southwest safety/security announcements are complex; the passengers are all assumed to be such seasoned travelers that the safety announcement has become background noise that is mostly ignored.

On Southwest, the safety announcement is full of jokes (Freiberg and Freiberg 1996: 209–210). Southwest encourages individual flight attendants to include their own jokes, and this variation from the FAA script also helps keep passenger attention. I want to argue that these jokes perform some particular function, which is to create a sense of community among Southwest customers and between crew and customers. The joking on Southwest interrupts this normalcy. In addition to promoting the brand of Southwest as 'fun,' this play on the safety/security announcement helps identify and naturalize areas of anxiety. The humor requires and creates a common community between the joker/flight attendant and the passenger/audience. For example, "there may be fifty ways to leave your lover, but there are only six ways to leave this aircraft . . ." which builds upon knowledge of 1970s folk singer Paul Simon and the scenarios for potential evacuation of the aircraft (209). The announcement continues "the location of exits is clearly marked with signs overhead, and by red and white disco lights . . . made you look!" (209). With this joke, the authority of the flight attendant is displaced, because he or she has both made a joke and played a joke on the passenger to accomplish the security function. Similarly, flight attendants often joke about their treatment by passengers: "This is a no whining, no complaining, no smoking flight" or "If you are unhappy with our service, there are six emergency exits on this flight . . ." Both of these jokes equate the FAA regulations with good passenger–flight attendant relationships, increasingly important in a time of air-rage but also a demonstration of the corporate brand of putting employees first. The flight attendant and passengers both know that there is a regulatory requirement to review the safety features of the aircraft, but in doing so with jokes, Southwest creates a sense of common community. In essence, the common authority that the jokes are directed toward is the regulator (i.e., the FAA). Cultural theorist Gayatri Spivak makes a similar point when she is denied boarding by a gate agent: "Don't say, 'We can't accept you.' That sounds very bad from one human being to another; next time you should say: 'The regulations are against it'; then we are both victims" (1990: 65).

The next case provides an interesting look at common communities built by the objects of government policy. Each of these jokes or quotidian practices confronts the securitization of everyday life obliquely and demonstrates the potential for resisting even the most totalizing of practices. The inversion of the No-Fly list and the funny safety announcements demonstrate precisely the function of the no-joking rule: to self-police ambiguity and to embody the acceptance of new security measures. Southwest is successful—as a joker—because the audience understands the multiple frames of reference: security, customer service, and employee relations. This raises another question: given the power and predominance of the discourse of national security, how are these jokes tellable? Within the structure of the joke, the jokers are still obedient, docile subjects of the national security state. The flight attendant meets the requirements of the FAA regulations. The former president still flies (often with the elderly). The jokes carry potential for protest, but it is a sly, circuitous, and indirect form of criticism more often about the ability of the state to provide security, to know its citizens, or to create a common community.

## MANAGEMENT OF AFFECT

Considerations of the management of affect or emotion are more plentiful in cultural studies and anthropology than in security studies, but it is quickly becoming an important area of research. Adey in particular has analyzed how "the affective expressions of hope, fear, joy, sadness, and many others, as well as the constitutive mundane bodily motions that occupy the airport terminal, may not be as distanced from power and control as we might think. In fact, they are central to their perpetuation as certain triggers—designed-into the terminal space—are intended to excite bodily and emotional dispositions at an unconscious and pre-cognitive register" (2008: 439). This chapter takes a small slice of that emotional range to examine how the airport uses anxiety as a tool of social control. This insight also stems, for us, from Foucault and his analysis of the Panopticon, a prison composed of entirely visible cells with a hidden central guard tower. Foucault suggests that the Panopticon is the perfect architecture of incarceration because the configuration of space itself "induce[s] in the inmate a state of conscious and permanent visibility that assures the *automatic* functioning of power . . . the surveillance is permanent in its effects, even if it is discontinuous in its action" (1977: 201). However, rather than give primacy solely to the guard or the architect, the generation of affect, particularly the airport, is the result of a number of different government, market, and social forces without any necessary coordination. Haggerty and Ericson (2000) argue that the "assemblage" is a better model for understanding surveillance and control in complex environments. Different agents, ideas, symbols, institutions, and motivations all act on the mobile individuals at the airport, resulting in a management of affect that is greater than the intentions, capabilities, or even desires of any one part of the system (Salter 2008). Thus, police aim to deter and detect petty theft. Merchants aim to increase sales through an exploitation of 'dwell-time.' Counterterror agencies aim to harden the target of the airport while facilitating surveillance. Airlines aim to increase flow through the security checkpoints. Security screening personnel aim to moderate and normalize flows through checkpoints. Immigration officials aim to limit preliminary examinations to 1 min or less, while allowing for secondary examinations to fulfill a security mandate. Passengers just want to pass through the airport as quickly as possible with as little 'hassle' as possible. Refugees want to be safe. The essence of neoliberalism as an ideology of control is the emptying of public space of signs of community or solidarity, particularly since the atomistic consumer-citizen-subject is far easier to control and manipulate.

Isin argues that the conception of the neoliberal subject as rational and calculative hides the affective and emotional. As such, he argues, "the figure that also occupies a central role in our times is the neurotic citizen who governs itself through responses to anxiety and uncertainties" (2004: 223). A Freudian account of neurosis describes its birth from the repression of libinal instincts necessary for group and 'civilized' life. Repression is necessary for society, which creates neurotic behavior (substituting the repressed desire for another object). Our desire for absolute and total freedom, imagined as infantile or erotic, is translated into more socially acceptable desires for wealth, travel, and domesticity and an inevitable neurotic compulsion that those substitutes can never provide the sought-after satisfaction. This is a clear problem of the safety or security state. Individuals crave absolute and total security, such as they imagined when they were children and largely ignorant of a world outside of their relationship with their mother. Even at the moment of the recognition of the father figure, and the beginnings of the Oedipal complex, it is clear that absolute and total freedom is unobtainable. Substitutions begin and neuroses start. Citizens want that the safety or security state will provide absolute and total security, and know that it cannot. The quest for security is replete with substitutions, which the state is more than willing to provide. It cannot guarantee safety in the workplace and so invents worker's insurance (Ewald 1991). It cannot guarantee automobility and so invents traffic safety codes (Packer 2003). It cannot guarantee airport security screening and so it creates No-Fly lists (Salter 2008a). But, these incomplete solutions themselves generate the anxiety that recursively greases the cogs of the system. The failure of the insurance industry to predict 9/11 has led to the creation of new lines of catastrophe insurance. The failure of the government to prevent 9/11 has led to the creation of the Department of Homeland Security. Anxiety is not a failure of the national security state but its necessary impulse. Fear is the machine that drives the expansion of securitization. The continual shadow of failure justifies the expansion of the ambit of security measures.

## SECURITIZATION OF EVERYDAY LIFE

The no-joking rule plays a signal role in the securitization of everyday life at airports. It represents an increase in the anxiety of state agents because of this epistemological tension. The state defines its role as the knowledge and thus management of security but cannot determine the threat vector or the appropriate solutions. And so, the justification of an unknowable threat enables governance through insecurity and the application of policing tactics to previously public and private spheres of personal conduct (Bigo 2002). The global War on Terror has become intertwined with everyday practices: the administration seeks to "discipline domestic behavior by linking it to external danger . . ." (Campbell 2007: 129). Security is a contested domain of politics but also requires the assent of the securitized.[34] Mobility—particularly the international mobility—afforded by air travel is seen as crucial to the global organization of capital, politics, and social life. Furthermore, the risks associated with the openness of a networked society have been made plain over the history of civil aviation. Because the airport is understood to be a crucial and vulnerable node in the global mobility regime, extraordinary security measures can be assayed with little resistance, particularly because the airport's population is continually in transit. Thus, in the face of clear imperatives for aeromobility[35] and in the absence of a clear population that must consent to new security measures, we must include quotidian resistances to new incursions on personal conduct.

What this analysis has demonstrated is that we must examine both the context of securitization as well as the practices of everyday life that are implicated in and created by that securitization. President Bush urged Americans to 'go shopping' as an antidote to terror while simultaneously making those purchase patterns accessible for risk analysis; New Orleans infrastructure renewal was neglected in favor of antiterror spending; and a war in Iraq was financed by increased debt and deficit that led to high oil prices. The imposition of the no-joking rule at airports and the evidence from Southwest demonstrate that language—as a proxy for intentions, identity, and politics—is a serious site of daily contestation. By examining artifacts of everyday life, we are able to highlight the power and the limits of the securitization discourse.

I want to end with a joke from a colleague in the aviation security field. His grandmother asks him, as an expert, the chances of a bomb getting through security. He tells her one in a million. The grandmother says, well, she lives in a city of a million and is always running into people she knows on the street, so she is anxious about flying. Well, says the expert, a bomb exploding may not destroy the airplane. Well, asks the grandmother, what are the chances of two bombs getting through security? That's one in five million, says the expert. So, the grandmother takes a bomb with her every time she flies. This joke gets at the core of the securitization of everyday life and the epistemological tension of the state. First, we do not understand risk, and so we depend on experts to parse that risk and make sound judgments about what risk is politically, socially, and economically acceptable. But, second, we do not understand threat. The joke is funny, to the extent that it is, because the idea of a grandmother carrying a bomb on an airplane is ridiculous and what we fear, that we cannot face the radical uncertainty of not knowing. In the face of a lack of understanding of risk and threat, particularly within a liberal mood, we are not simply willing but eager to cede freedoms for the promise of security. However, there is a power in the joke itself. Every system of power and every attempt at securitization requires some degree of consent by the securitized. Joking demonstrates a capacity to play language in ways that fundamentally unsettle the claims to knowledge, security, and authority that justify the securitization of everyday life.

## NOTES

1. I would like to acknowledge the support of the Social Sciences and Humanities Research Council of Canada. Also, thanks to Benjamin Muller for his thoughtful and continuing conversations about everyday security and particularly for reading an earlier draft of this chapter. My thanks go to Kate McInturff and my child, probably office mates, colleagues, and probably also random strangers, for laughing at more than one joke about airport security.
2. In this chapter, I refer to the common experiences of security screening, rather than the differential screening of individuals and groups based on (risk) profiling. I also bracket the question of intention.
3. There is extensive literature in International Relations on the process of securitization (See Introduction and Balzacq 2005; Buzan, Waever, de Wilde 1998; Stritzel 2007; Williams 2003).
4. An alternate, more specific sign reads: "regarding bombs and/or threats."
5. The TSA reminds travelers "Threats made jokingly (even by a child) can delay the entire family and could result in fines." TSA. 2008. Traveling with

Children. http://www.tsa.gov/travelers/airtravel/children/index.shtm. (accessed 1 June 2008).

6. This chapter does not examine border or immigration security checkpoints, although a similar argument could be made about no-joking rules at those frontiers and ports-of-entry. Security checkpoints are defined as the site (most often a chokepoint in the terminal architecture) where passengers and their carry-on baggage are screened for prohibited items before proceeding to the 'sterile' area of the concourse. For an introduction see Jenkins (2002).

7. TSA. 2008. Summer Travel Tips. http://www.tsa.gov/assets/pdf/summer_tips.pdf. (accessed 1 June 2008).

8. Earlier comments refer to "making small talk."

9. CATSA. 2008. How to avoid spring break security delays at the airport. http://www.catsa-acsta.gc.ca/english/media/rel_comm/decollage_takeoff.shtml. (accessed 1 June 2008).

10. Media Release by the Hon John Anderson MP. New Aviation Security Laws. 10 March 2005. Last accessed on Decemner 28, 2009. Available at http://parlinfo.aph.gov.au/parlInfo/download/media/pressrel/9NFF6/upload_binary/9nff63.pdf;fileType%3Dapplication%2Fpdf.

11. Anderson, Jon. 2005. Security Jokes Could be Bad for your Wealth, Deputy Prime Minister, Minister for Transport and Regional Services. March 10. A37/2005.

12. Beeby, D. Air passengers get wiggle room on "bomb jokes." *Canadian Press*, July 10, 2007.

13. Beeby, D. Air passengers get wiggle room on "bomb jokes." *Canadian Press*, July 10, 2007.

14. This could be an example of a Freudian slip, when a speaker says one word but means your mother.

15. Journalists, experts, and lay citizens have all attempted this.

16. This chapter will avoid the existing literature on jokes in extreme conditions, such as totalitarian rule or the Holocaust (see examples: Davies 2007; Dundes and Hauschild 1983).

17. Wrigley's "Chewphoria" (http://www.youtube.com/watch?v=j4tXCs4KgmU); Bluefly "Always there when you have nothing to wear" (http://www.youtube.com/watch?v=Vbi6y3KnAUo ) and most prominently Underdak's underwear commerical (http://www.youtube.com/watch?v=tvL41iY7nd0)—which features a female security guard forcing an attractive man to strip to his underwear—another female security guard ends the commercial with the line 'One day, you're going to get caught.' (accessed 10 September 2008).

18. There is a debate among humor theorists as to whether jokes require a 'release' or simply recognition (Fine 2004).

19. Onion, The. 2002. FAA Considers Passenger Ban. *The Onion* 38 (38). October 16. Available at: http://www.theonion.com/content/node/27687. (accessed 16 October 2002).

20. An archive of editorial cartoons is available: http://www.cagle.com/news/AirportSecurity2/main.asp.

21. Thus, the jokes that depend on literal interpretations of 'truth telling' jokes, such as lawyer/witness testimony, doctor/patient, or insurance form jokes (e.g., Attorney: ALL your responses MUST be oral, OK? What school did you go to? Witness: "Oral." "Patient: Doctor, Doctor, I broke my arm in two places! Doctor: Stay out of them places," or "An invisible car came out of nowhere, struck my car and vanished")

22. The Canadian Anti-Terrorism Law (C-36) makes inspiration part of the criminal act: "the need for proof of religious or political motive . . ." (Roach 2003: 54).

23. Bush, George W. 2006. President Discusses Global War on Terror at Kansas State University. Office of the Press Secretary, Washington, D.C.

24. Pilots and air crew, who are subject to multiple checks as a part of their job (and then have access to the control of the airplane itself) argue that they should not be subject to the same screening as the unknown passenger, but this argument has not found a receptive audience in Canada, the United States, the United Kingdom, or Australia.

25. On the dominance of mathematical thinking in aviation security, see Salter (2008).

26. http://www.cbs.com/latenight/lateshow/top_ten/index/php/20041215.phtml. (accessed 15 December 2004).

27. Southwest Airlines, 2006. We Weren't Just Airborne Yesterday. http://southwest.com/about_swa/airborne.html. (accessed 10 September 2004).

28. Southwest Airlines. 2008. Our Mission. http://southwest.com/about_swa/mission.html. (accessed 10 September 2004).

29. It should be noted that the acceptable bounds of humor have certainly changed for Southwest. Its original advertisements relied on particularly sexist stereotypes of flight attendants (in 'hot pants') as part of its appeal. A print ad advertised a "Lovev Seat" surrounded by said flight attendants. See Southwest Airlines. 1972. "Remember What It Was Like Before Southwest Airlines? You Didn't Have Hostesses in Hotpants. Remember?" http://southwest.com/multimedia/hotpants.mpg. (accessed 10 September 2004).

30. Examples: 2006. Funny Stuff. *nuts about southwest* available at: http://www.blogsouthwest.com/2006/06/09/funny-stuff. (accessed 13 September 2004).

31. Southwest Airlines . 2008. What have they been smoking? http://www.swa-media.com/swamedia/pod_smoking.pdf. (accessed 13 September 2004).

32. Southwest Airlines. 2009. Coupon. http://www.swamedia.com/swamedia/pod_coupon.pdf. (accessed 15 January 2009).

33. FAA. 2003. *Advisory Circular. Passenger Safety Information Briefing and Briefing Cards* AC No: 121–24C. Department of Transportation, July 23.

34. For a contrasting view, Balzacq (2008) argues that securitization can take place without the consent of a popular audience.

35. A term in use by Peter Adey in his upcoming work.

# 2 Security Meta-framing of Collective Activity in Public Spaces
## Pope John Paul II in the Holy City

*Vida Bajc*[1]

## INTRODUCTION

Whether we watch them on television or participate in situ, large-scale public events are occasions that draw attention to the involvement of the state security apparatus in how such events are practiced. The visit of the late Pope John Paul II to Jerusalem in 2000 prompted the headline of *The Jerusalem Post* to read "The Biggest Security Blitz to Guard Pope Here." The Summer Olympic Games in 2004 in Greece were so infused with security that the *LA Times* dubbed them 'the Summer Security Games.' More than 7 miles of barricades, rooftop sharpshooters, scores of cameras, and body searches of each and every person who entered the grounds of the Capitol in Washington D.C. were used during the second inauguration of President George W. Bush in 2005. So forthcoming were the Turkish surveillance and security measures during the 2006 visit of the current Pope Benedict XVI that the *New York Times* was prompted to report on helicopters hovering over Ankara, police commandos in uniforms spread throughout the streets, and sharpshooters trigger-ready on the rooftops of the buildings overlooking the path of the Pope's entourage. I suggest that through these surveillance technologies and procedures, a security apparatus—an assemblage of different agencies, institutions, professionals, private enterprises, and technologies, mobilized for the purpose of providing security—frames how such public activity is practiced.

The security apparatus works under the assumption that uncertainty of the mundane social life and its potentialities of disorder are a threat to the practicing of public events. Such uncertainty is understood to be something dangerous and potentially violent. Included in this assumption is another premise; namely, that during public events, disorder cannot be tolerated. The apparatus therefore seeks to control unpredictability to be able to ensure that public events will take place as intended and without any disturbance. My analysis of the involvement of the security apparatus in the second inauguration of President Bush in Washington D.C. in 2005 suggests that for a security apparatus, control of uncertainty during public events means the ability of its operatives and technologies to create a safe enclosure by controlling movement of people, objects, and information to and within this social space (Bajc 2007b). This study also demonstrates that the process itself through which the apparatus brings about this social space of safety has a ritual form. What I call security meta-ritual is a process of control of space and time, through which the security apparatus transforms social reality so that public activity can unfold within the domain of this secured space and time.

This relationship between the ritual activity of the security apparatus and the practicing of the public event is hierarchical in that the public activity is subjected to the order created through the transformative activity of the security apparatus. This hierarchy can be expressed in terms of a meta-relationship. The prefix 'meta' signifies a higher level activity about a lower level phenomenon; that is, the security meta-ritual is a kind of ritual activity performed to shape the process of another ritual—namely, the public event. I suggest that through this hierarchical relationship, conditions are created for the security meta-ritual activity to frame the process of the public event it purports to protect. I base my argument on the nature of meta-framing, originally articulated by Bateson (2000 [1972]) in his essay "A Theory of Play and Fantasy." I use the case of the visit of the late Pope John Paul II to Jerusalem in March 2000 and the security meta-ritual performed by the Israeli security apparatus to demonstrate how security practices meta-framed the course of the Pope's visit.

## UNCERTAINTY AND THE META-FRAMING OF SAFETY

As anyone who recently attended public rituals of the kind discussed here has been able to observe, the geographical area within which people gather to participate in the event is sectioned off from the rest of the social environment and encircled by a physical barrier. The barrier, closely guarded by the security operatives, is impermeable except for the specific number of designated openings through which only those approved by the apparatus are able to enter. Within the enclosure, there are few if any signs of normal routine daily life; small stores and coffee shops are closed, there are no random cars or bicycles passing by or parked on the street, people do not stroll about along the pavement, and the traffic lights do not serve their usual purpose. It is only outside the enclosure and farther away from its barrier that social life resembles the routine daily life as it is lived in that area. We observe that within the enclosure, a new social reality is brought into existence with the purpose of providing an ordered and controlled social space for public ritual activities.

For this new security-sanctioned order of safety to emerge and exist as such for the duration of a public ritual, the people involved need to see and interpret this reality as being void of danger and safe for a public event. This means that participants see the order inside the enclosure as qualitatively different in relation to the uncertain and potentially dangerous reality that lies outside its boundary; that is, the boundary which maintains the enclosure is understood as clearly and effectively separating the two realities. This suggests that the boundary is the point of reference in relation to which the two realities are distinguished and kept apart. The chain of fences, metal barriers, metal detectors, concrete blocks, surveillance cameras, and security operatives physically separate the social activity inside the enclosure from whatever goes on outside of its domain. These various elements of the security apparatus communicate to the people within the enclosure that the reality of which they are a part is indeed safe. As participants' transition through metal detectors, surveillance cameras, identity confirmation, and body searches for explosives, they confirm the validity of this transformative process of the security meta-ritual. Should the people involved perceive this transition from the reality of uncertainty into the reality of safety as ambiguous or ineffective, and the boundary between uncertainty and certainty as permeable and porous, the clear distinction between disorder and order, uncertainty and safety, vulnerability and protection would be dissolved. I suggest that what enables this perception of the distinction between the uncertain world of the every day and the safety inside the bounded domain is meta-framing.

In thinking about this process, I follow the principles formulated by anthropologist Gregory Bateson (Bateson 2000a [1972]). Bateson studied the evolution of communication and the development of human language. During his observations of how young monkeys interact, Bateson noticed how, at some moment, the monkeys were sitting around idling, then, at the next, they began to play, and after a series of interactions they stopped playing and went back to idling. This play looked very much like combat yet monkeys understood that it was play. They would bite each other as if they were fighting yet those bites were not bites of combat but playful nips. The monkeys were using the behavior of combat to play, denoting that what would otherwise be understood as combat was in this instance understood as play.

Bateson concluded that monkeys were able to exchange messages with each other in ways that were meaningful to them at multiple levels of abstraction; that is, their exchange of information was meta-communicative. The signals they were exchanging with each other not only communicated a change from just sitting around in boredom to some different activity. That same exchange of information also conveyed that this new reality in which they were engaging was to be understood as play. What subsumed all other messages exchanged was the meta-message "This is Play." This meta-message, Bateson reasoned, was able to frame the new reality as play because the new reality was defined in relation to, and as distinct from, the reality which immediately preceded it, namely, the not-play. This distinction between what was before and what succeeded it was maintained through a clear-cut boundary between the two realities. This boundary became a point of reference for how the new activity was to be interpreted. The boundary that framed the new activity was the meta-message "This is

Play." Bateson emphasized that this formulation of framing applied to situations in which there is "an instance of signals standing for other events" and where "actions denote, but are different from, other actions" such as in ritual, play, threat, and deceit (Bateson 2000a [1972]).

For Bateson, this cultural capacity to envision and create a new reality is an epistemological problem: what is the process through which a particular reality comes to exist as such? This problem becomes focused on the framing of an emerging reality rather than the frame itself. It is centered on the process through which a frame and the reality it encloses come to exist rather than the nature and the working of that frame. In Bateson's terms, framing means meta-communication. Framing provides a direction and sets the parameters for a sequence of developments through which one social activity becomes separated from another. This hierarchical relationship between the two realities established through meta-communicative framing subordinates the new social world to the meta-message of its boundary. The boundary that comes to separate the new reality from its surrounding is a meta-message which frames, shapes, and articulates the social activity within its domain. It frames the social activity because it is a meta-message.

This particular epistemological position treats framing as a linear process; that is, the formation of conditions under which a particular kind of social activity emerges is a unidirectional process which begins with some basic reality and concludes with the newly emerging social world in such a way that the activity within the new reality is subordinated to the meta-message of its boundary. This formulation results in a deterministic relationship which renders the content within the enclosure dependent on the meta-message that its boundary has come to represent. This reasoning also gives primacy to cognitive communication over emotional and embodied experiences and leaves aside the perceptions of reality through the aesthetics of social space.

Sociologist Erving Goffman (1986 [1974]), who based much of his frame analysis on Bateson's case, tried to avoid this linearity by formulating his essay as a question of the organization of conditions that make a particular interpretation of an experience of reality possible. For Goffman, this meant abandoning Bateson's meta-logic, introducing variability into the relationship between a frame and the activity within the frame through the concept of keying and that of lamination, and refocusing frame theory to make it applicable to all social situations. Goffman's work redirected frame theory toward questions about different types of frames, how frames are put together, and how they are used. This has become the foundation for the study of framing in much of social sciences, particularly the research on reception of mass-mediated communication, human cognition in interpersonal communication, power and persuasion in politics, and formation and agility of social movements (see Benford and Snow 2000). Largely unexplored, however, remain the processes through which conditions are created so that a particular reality and the frame which sustains it are brought to existence.

A major effort in this direction is the work of anthropologist Don Handelman (2006a, b) through his analysis of ritual and play. Handelman makes it an important point of departure the emphasis on differences in how parameters are set for a new reality to emerge. These parameters, argues Handelman, are culturally specific. Different contexts yield different types of processes through which frames and the realities they enclose come to exist. This would suggest that different initial conditions generate different kinds of forms of social organization that then enable variable types of frames to emerge. Handelman refers to the Batesonian framing through hierarchical interdependency as a "lineal" type. This type of framing depends on establishing a clear distinction between the reality inside the frame and that which remains outside by imposing a clear-cut boundary between them. Elsewhere, Handelman (2004: 3–42) suggests that this exclusionary logic is characteristic of bureaucratic systems. Such cultural systems generate realities with impermeable and unambiguous boundaries that divide the world into exclusive categories. Each element in the social world must fit into an assigned category. Participation in one reality excludes a person from the possibility of being a part in another reality. In this sense, the pinnacle of creation through this logic is the security apparatus itself for which social life is divided into clear-cut categories of safe and dangerous, unpredictable and certain, pure and polluted, desirable and undesirable.

I suggest that exclusionary meta-framing can help us understand how the security apparatus separates public ritual activity from the uncertainty of the everyday life and frames the course of a public event by bringing to existence a reality of public safety. Following the logic of exclusionary meta-framing, for the reality of safety to be conceived there needs to be willingness on the part of those who initiate the framing to set apart from the reality of the everyday life. To desire differentiation means to envision the new order as qualitatively different in relation to that given reality. As envisioned by the security apparatus, the reality of safety is a kind of social world in which all possible uncertainties and indeterminacies should be eliminated. Nothing may be left to chance. All possible future scenarios are envisioned and preempted so that all human and nonhuman activity can be in its proper place, ordered according to the template of the apparatus, and controlled by the apparatus throughout the duration of the public event.

In the case of public ritual activity, this vision begins to emerge into what will become a new reality when an initiative is provided to separate the public event from the uncertainty of the daily life. This initiative comes from the security apparatus that designates a particular public event as vulnerable to disruption. Because disorder is threatening to the apparatus whose conception of the world is made of unambiguous categories, the apparatus declares that the public event must be protected from interference. This designation and the decision to protect the event are communicated to the public through the mass media. This mass-mediated information also communicates the initiative to separate the public activity from the routine everyday life. This allows for a cognitive shift by the public away from the daily life and its uncertainties and indeterminacies, and diverts public attention toward whatever is coming. Once the public perception is shifted, it does not take some random path. Rather, this shift is diverted in a particular direction by those who do the framing. This renders framing meta-communicative in that the direction of communication is from the apparatus via the mass media toward the public. Neither does the new reality begin to take a random form. What is to take shape is patterned after something already known and meaningful to the public. That is to say, the emerging reality is qualitatively different in relation to the reality from which it is differentiated but familiar in that it resonates with some aspects of the collective memory of those involved. This meta-communication sets the conditions and lays out the parameters that will enable the creation of the reality of safety: surveillance and sanctioning by the apparatus of all movement to and within what will become the reality of safety.

As Goffman (1986) emphasizes, framing is as much a matter of mind as it is of the organization of social activity but it is also a specific human experience of that activity in a particular place and time. Framing is cognitively conceived and communicated, but what enables framing to materialize is that it is practiced and experienced through a particular form of social organization and social ordering. The analysis of the second presidential inauguration of President Bush demonstrates that the kind of social ordering which enables setting in motion the process through which the reality of safety is brought to existence has a ritual form (Bajc 2007b). This security meta-ritual is a ritual of order the purpose of which is to effectively and efficiently perform the separation from uncertainty and the transformation of people and their sociocultural space so that a reality of safety can be made possible. This is a type of ritual whose practice is aimed neither to achieve social solidarity nor reaffirm social membership, as is the case with the Durkheimian kinds of ritual. This type of ritual is performed to facilitate change on the social world for the purpose of some social activity. The elements that comprise the process of this type of ritual, however, are common to other kinds of ritual practices. All possible resources are mobilized to achieve the ritual outcome. The people involved are all expected to follow the ritual script as it is meant to be performed. The transformation involves purification of a designated physical space and people within it. The meaning of the meta-constitution of the security ritual is in the belief that the security apparatus of the modern state and its technologies and techniques can be effectively utilized to prevent disorder and control uncertainty in all contexts and for all purposes.

Once the unpredictable world of uncertainty has been kept outside of the domain of the reality of safety and the new reality brought to existence through separation of insiders from outsiders and safe from unsafe, what enables the emerging social world to exist as different is a boundary that encloses the new activity and keeps it separated from everything else in that context. In line with Bateson's reasoning, to be able to keep the two social worlds effectively separated, the boundary must communicate to those implicated within the enclosure how they are to interpret the new activity. This boundary is therefore a meta-message that conveys to the people involved how they should orient themselves within the new reality. The boundary communicates to the people involved the Batesonian meta-message of "This is Order." This message means that the reality of safety is void of uncertainty, ordered according to the template of the apparatus, and therefore secure. It is meaningful to the people involved because they have gone through the transformative process of the security meta-ritual. They understand that beyond the boundary of the reality of safety lies the uncertain and potentially dangerous world. The meta-message conveys that conditions are now created for the public event to take place as intended. Within this controlled space, the public event will be able to unfold, step by step, day by day, following the structure of the public event but always in relation to the meta-message of the security apparatus: "This is Order."

In the following text, I discuss the process of the security meta-framing of the visit of the late Pope John Paul II to Jerusalem in March 2000. The ailing Pope had an extended stay in the area that lasted for 6 days, and he moved within the Israeli and the Palestinian communities, crossing national, religious, and political boundaries not customarily crossed. The Israeli security apparatus announced the process of separation from the uncertainty of daily life in Jerusalem through Operation Old Friend, a process which shifted attention away from the daily routine social life in the city and directed people's focus on practices through which the apparatus began to create the reality of safety. This security meta-ritual mobilized all security forces and their technologies. It achieved cooperation of the Israelis and the Palestinians, the secular and the religious, the local and the foreign pilgrims. The purification process created a 'sterile zone' of safety and kept those deemed unsafe outside its domain. Inside this reality and through its meta-message, communicated symbolically through the images of the Pope's body, the apparatus framed every step of the activities of the Pope's visit. I present two examples of the framing of the Pope's activities: the open-air mass on the Mount of Beatitudes and the Pope's unplanned return to the Church of the Holy Sepulchre for prayer on Calvary. The data are a part of my ongoing ethnographic field research in Jerusalem (see Bajc n.d.).

## THE NEWS OF THE POPE'S VISIT TO JERUSALEM IN 2000

Security meta-framing of public events is most visible when such events require extensive participation of the general public and when their activities occupy extensive public areas and disrupt the daily routine social life. In this regard, the coming of the Pope John Paul II to Jerusalem in March 2000 was an extraordinary event. It was not simply a visit of another dignitary whose whereabouts could be reduced to a handful of invited politicians and journalists and contained at the prime minister's residence in

Jerusalem. The visit required public participation unlike any other in that not only the local dignitaries and officials but also Christians locally and from around the world were expected to attend. It interchangeably involved the religious and the secular, the political and the nonpolitical, and multiple spaces populated by the Israelis and the Palestinians. The activities surrounding the visit stretched out across a large geographic area and lasted 6 days, from March 21 to March 26, which is far beyond a regular visit of a dignitary.

The Pope's arrival was announced with the 'shock' notice. There were rumors in the city that Pope John Paul II might be coming on a pilgrimage in 2000 to honor the Jubilee Year, a Roman Catholic tradition that encourages the followers to visit the biblical sites in the Holy Land and the holy sites in Rome (see Macioti 2002). Yet, no one knew for certain whether he was coming, and there was hardly any mention about it in the Israeli or the Palestinian media. Weeks before his scheduled arrival, it was suddenly announced that the Pope was coming to Jerusalem. Such 'short notice' tends to be typical, particularly for events that are planned, designed, and carried out in a way that allows them to be fully broadcast live on domestic and international television. These broadcasts interrupt the daily routine television programming and keep the audiences in front of their television screens so that the social process of viewing in people's homes creates a ritual connection to the event outside (Dayan and Katz 1992).

The Pope's journey had a profound symbolic significance for several issues: religious claims to Jerusalem by Christians, Jews, and Muslims in the context of the peace negotiations between the Israelis and the Palestinians; the reconciliation between Christian and Jewish theology; and the attempts by the Vatican to legitimate both the already established state of Israel and the continuous struggle for Palestinian statehood. The visit took place when the Israeli–Palestinian peace process was at its peak. The significance of these events began to be widely debated on Israeli and Palestinian streets and closely followed by their media.

In light of this context, the visit was designed to symbolically reconcile the complex dynamics of social relations between the three monotheistic religions represented in the city. This required crossing of spaces and intergroup boundaries usually not routinely transgressed in Jerusalem. It necessitated taking on several different roles not customarily a part of state visits. For John Paul II, this was the first visit to the Holy Land. As a pilgrim he requested a series of private visits and prayers at various sites scattered throughout the area. He was flown with his private entourage in a helicopter between places along the Jordanian border, the West Bank, and northern Israel. His visit was also a carefully orchestrated diplomatic attempt to set into motion an interfaith dialogue between the three monotheistic religions represented in Jerusalem and encourage the political dialogue between the two political entities. This, too, required movement between the Palestinian and the Jewish populated areas. The Pope met with the Ashkenazi and the Sephardi chief rabbis in the Jewish Quarter in the Old City. He visited the Israeli president at his residence in west Jerusalem as well as the late Palestinian Chairman Yasser Arafat at his residence in Bethlehem. He also held an inter-religious meeting between the heads of the three religions in the Palestinian-populated east Jerusalem.

The Pope also had to be a pope. He responded to invitations of a number of small Christian communities in Jerusalem to visit their respective churches. This meant movement through narrow, windy streets and alleys of the Old City of Jerusalem and moving through the Christian, Jewish, and Muslim neighborhoods, lines rarely crossed by political dignitaries. It also meant physical exposure and close proximity to members of these communities. The height of the visit was his open-air Mass for Youth at the Mount of Beatitudes in the northern part of Israel by the Sea of Galilee. During the tenure of John Paul II, such masses were known to attract a very large number of pilgrims from the Catholic countries around the world. This meant that there also had to be a way to allow at least some Christians from inside Israel, the West Bank, and Gaza to participate. It is the scope of this public event that made the process of the security meta-ritual and its framing of the Pope's visit unusually visible.

## SETTING PARAMETERS AND CONDITIONS FOR THE CREATION OF REALITY OF SAFETY: THE TRANSFORMATIVE PROCESS OF THE SECURITY META-RITUAL

The process of separation from uncertainty and the shift in public perception was distinctly marked with a name of its own: Operation Old Friend. The play on the words "old friend" is a reminder of the long-unresolved relationship between Christians and Jews and, more recently, between Israel and the Vatican. The notion of "operation" signifies agency, a large-scale process of treatment of the body, an individual body in medicine and a social body in the military. It is a treatment with a series of acts that remedy its injury and deformity with precision and efficacy. If "Old Friend" is a conundrum attributed to the play of historical forces beyond control, "operation" is a noun of confidence and exactness of the military and the surgical type of intervention.

The "shock" notice of Operation Old Friend was the starting point of the unfolding of the security procedures as ritual, framing the cognitive shift in a specific direction. It came with the announcement of "the biggest security operation ever for a visit to Israel."[2] The security operation was considered 'unprecedented.' As the prominence of the security apparatus in its role of exerting order under conditions of uncertainty has grown in the eyes of the public, such superlatives in the working of the apparatus are becoming increasingly common (see also Bajc 2007b). They endow the security practices in their goal of eliminating uncertainty with ritual power. The media continuously attributed 'the scale of the operation to the sensitive religious significance of the pontiff's visit.' Indeed, the 'unprecedented operation' was not related to a threat to the life of the Pope. The media continuously reassured its audiences that the protective measures were "not based on any intelligence information on a threat to the Pope."[3] To the security apparatus, uncertainty does not mean knowledge or prediction that disorder will actually occur. Rather, uncertainty means a possibility of disorder of the kind that can not be allowed or tolerated.

## Resonance with Collective Memory

This framing of the shift in perception made sense to the Israeli public, and it resonated with their collective memories. Benford and Snow (2000: 619) write that resonance refers to "why some framings seem to be effective or 'resonate' while others do not" (see also Snow and Corrigall-Brown 2005). In the case of security meta-ritual, framing resonates with people because it draws on their collective memory. Kimmerling (1985) reports that, at least until the visit of Anwar el-Sadat to Israel in 1977, the Israeli society perceived every instance of warfare in the series of wars with its neighbors as a threat to the whole society. A possible defeat in a war would be perceived as a total annihilation of the Israeli society. Israeli institutions, from the Israeli Defense Forces to the Jerusalem Holocaust Museum, remain committed to the vision of Israel as a 'nation-in-arms' that must be able to protect itself from any attempt of destruction (Handelman 2004: 105). The absence of threat and the loss of such collective memory would take away the meaning and therefore the existence and the practice of the security meta-ritual.

An accident few days before the Pope arrived enlivened the reality of the threat and the possibility that something could go wrong in the minds of many people in Jerusalem. The public was informed shortly before the visit that "a wind gust blew down the stage" at the Mount of Beatitudes "on which the Pope was to have stood to speak to some 100,000 people during his visit to Israel next week." The church officials were publicly blamed for the accident because they chose not to cancel their contract with a Palestinian company after the security apparatus took over the arrangements for the event. "The project administration at the prime minister's office, in charge of the preparations for the Pope's visit," the media reported, "claims that the church representatives are responsible for the collapse, because they chose the contractor who built it." The report concluded that "dozens of Israel Electric Corporation Workers were recruited to rebuild the stage, 30 meters long [and] 20 meters wide."[4] One of the officials from the Catholic Church actively involved in overseeing the planning and the performance of the Pope's visit lamented over this issue: "The Israelis were good hosts," he related, "but they lacked awareness." To perform a mass you need an altar, he explained, a table-like structure behind which the priest stands as he performs the mass and on which the various elements used in the administering of the mass are laid. "And they were building this huge altar that was going to be put on the stage" where all that was needed was a small table.[5]

These details were lost among the Israeli public. Rather, the accident resonated deeply among the people at home and on the street as well as in the media because it recalled a similar accident in another event from the past. A bridge collapsed under a visiting Australian sports team during the 1997 Maccabiah Games, also called the Jewish Olympics, causing several team members to drown and left others injured. The collapse of the stage at the Mount of Beatitudes reassured the meta-framing of the security apparatus and the parameters and conditions it set for the creation of the reality of safety; namely, total control over each and every step surrounding the Pope's visit through total control of mobility of people, objects, and information. The incident strengthened the validity of the process of the security meta-ritual and its constitutive elements: total mobilization of all possible resources, expected cooperation of all involved, and purification of places and people.

## Mobilization of All Resources

The transformative process of the security meta-ritual demanded total mobilization of all possible forces. First and foremost, this included the media itself. It is through the mass media that the apparatus communicates its framing intensions and initiates the shift in public perception. Through the system of 'pooling,' a pre-paid arrangement between the state that organizes an event and a few major media corporations, it was ensured that only a handful of journalists were able to accompany the Pope and follow him on his route. Such an arrangement details exactly who is to be present in situ, how the event performers are to enact their role, and where the cameras are to be positioned during the process. It also specifies where the members of the security apparatus and its technologies are to be positioned in relation to these arrangements. Some 3,000 other journalists, who were not permitted to be present in situ at the events, rotated between the press centers in Bethlehem and in Jerusalem. Journalists complained bitterly about the press center in Bethlehem for what they saw as lack of organization. They praised the press center in Jerusalem where the footage, which had been filmed by the 'pool' and broadcast live on five TV channels, was transmitted simultaneously onto five huge television screens at the convention center. In addition to simultaneous viewing of coverage from multiple television channels, the press center in Jerusalem provided the journalists with printed leaflets with up-to-date information regarding sites visited, numbers of people at any given site, names of people present, contact information of spokespersons, and a great variety of other information regarding history, society, politics, and culture in Jerusalem. No such services were provided at the press center in Bethlehem, which offered a modestly equipped room staffed by a few volunteers. The two press centers served as hubs from which the majority of the journalists who came to cover the Pope's visit were reporting to their own respective media houses. The journalists sat at desks with high-speed Internet connections and transmitted their stories. In this way, the media engaged the audiences in the security meta-ritual by communicating and detailing its transformative practices.

Other elements of the security apparatus and its network of agencies were immediately mobilized. This included specially trained individuals and their institutions such as "the entire police force," the Border Police, the General Security Service, the Israeli Defense Force, and the "various civil bodies."[6] It also included specific technologies and techniques for surveillance of the mobility of individuals and objects such as surveillance cameras "set up in Bethlehem and Nazareth and monitored in Jerusalem."[7] Throughout the Old City of Jerusalem, long before the Pope's visit, surveillance cameras had been placed visibly and conspicuously on the edge of the stone walls at every intersection and in the middle of every street. Each is facing its own direction, together covering a full spectral gaze of the entire space between the walls. The cameras continuously gaze at the daily movement of people and objects through the narrow streets and alleys of the Old City: merchants and their display of consumer goods, children hand-pulling carts full of merchandise, tourists, pilgrims carrying wooden crosses along Via Dolorosa, clergy on their way to service, housewives and their daily food shopping, and children running errands. The Pope would have nothing to fear. "From the very moment" he arrived, he was "under constant surveillance by the special VIP unit" of the General Security Service.[8] All agents of security, those placed outside of the national boundaries, those positioned within, and those placed on the edge of borders with neighboring countries, all worked together toward a common goal of creating the reality of safety, ordered according to the vision of the security apparatus.

A reality of safety as conceived by the apparatus is a social space that is void of all uncertainty. For that reality to come to exist as such, uncertainty must be left outside of its domain. Everything must be done for uncertainty to remain in the social world beyond its boundary. Any presence of indeterminacy within the reality of safety would be considered a failure of the performance of the security meta-ritual because it would undermine the meta-message of "This is Order." Therefore, while this process can stretch the limits of available social and natural resources, the security meta-ritual will nevertheless be performed according to the script because after the fact, the question always remains: could it not have been done more perfectly? Was it not possible to eliminate all uncertainty? One of the security meta-ritual performers publicly defended his decision to overextend the resources in the following terms: "The finance minister is blaming me for creating an unexpected deficit in the Israeli budget." He noted that the Israeli government spent $7 million to prepare the sites. "About 5000 people [were] deployed each day," he emphasized. Yet, despite the use of so many people, "God forbid, if something happens, people will say why not 10,000?"[9]

The shift in perception away from the everyday and toward the new reality was framed in the direction of 'the biggest security operation' and set the total surveillance and control of all mobility using all available means as the conditions that would unable the creation of the reality of safety. The statement "God forbid, if something happens, people will say why not 10,000" most lucidly captures the underlying logic built into the script of the security meta-ritual, the practicing of the form of social ordering through which the security apparatus transforms the everyday life to bring to existence the reality of safety during public events. The reality of safety is characterized by an assumption that uncertainty—that is, events that have not yet occurred—can be prevented from happening through pre-emptive actions made possible through total control of all social activity. Conventional risk assessment analysis in economics or in medicine, for example, is a process of the weighing of possible risks against the costs associated with future actions so that steps to be taken in the future are those that are most cost-effective. The security meta-ritual, in contrast, is expected to bring to existence absolute certainty. This is predicated on having absolute control over what can possibly happen in the future. The pre-emptive actions are not weighted against the cost-effective activity. They are driven by the urge for maximum control of the ritual space and the human movement within. Beck (1995) observes that this urge to eliminate uncertainty is grounded in the belief that the security apparatus and its technologies and scientific knowledge are capable of bringing the uncertain under control. When uncertainty, perceived as a form of threat, resonates with collective experiences of the past, the perceptions of the reality of safety are subordinated to the meta-framing of the apparatus and the conditions it set for achieving that reality. Therefore, every measure possible will be taken to ensure that the creation of the reality of safety is made possible and all available resources and all activity will be subordinated to this end.

## Cooperation of All Involved

To subordinate human activity to the security meta-framing means to get people to agree to adjust their behavior in accordance with the security imperative. For many people in Jerusalem, the security meta-ritual was disruptive to their day-to-day life. The streets leading through the center were blocked off closer to the area of the Old City and the public transportation was rerouted. While some Jerusalemites may have been indifferent or perhaps even not agreeable to the Pope visiting the city, they accepted that, once the Pope arrived, there was no other choice but ordering of people's movement to ensure the visit would not be interrupted. A city official lamented that some people in Jerusalem complained that using all available means toward the goal of the reality of safety inconvenienced their life by overly disturbing their daily routine. "This week some people are not happy that they can't move around the city," he lamented. Yet, he added, these disturbances would be accepted as necessary because people in Jerusalem understand the need for security and elimination of uncertainty. "It's important that the Pope will come and leave healthy," he emphasized. "We want to avoid any possibility that anyone would do something that would cause damage. You don't need to convince people about this. They know it is important that the visit goes smoothly."[10] The security apparatus assumes that the people in Jerusalem will cooperate and willingly adjust their activities in relation to the parameters set by the apparatus.

Rituals require cooperation. As Dayan and Katz (1992: 19) assert in their analysis of the organization and the working of the media events, "public approval is required for an event to succeed; official events cannot be imposed on the unwilling or unbelieving." Indeed, not only Jerusalemites cooperated. So did the "Palestinian counterparts," as the media called them, those who in times of real warfare are on the side of the enemy. The Palestinians did not simply cooperate. As the media reported, they participated as an "equal partner" from the "areas under their jurisdiction." At the time of the visit, the area beyond the so-called Green line of 1967 was divided into three areas of jurisdiction. The Israelis assigned are C to themselves. Area A was given to the Palestinian Authority. Area B had a status of shared control by the two. But even the local politics was subordinated to the security imperative. The Palestinians worked together with the Israelis "in preparing for the medical arrangements" such as "appoint[ing] a cardiologist of their own to accompany the Pope during the visit to Bethlehem and other areas under [the Palestinian] jurisdiction." With forces now joined, no less than "17,695 police officers [would] be responsible for securing the Pope—and the tens of thousands of pilgrims expected with him—throughout the country and the Palestinian Authority areas." In the same breath, the report continued that "the Pope [would] spend a full day in Bethlehem and a half-day in Nazareth,"[11] effectively blurring the boundaries between the Palestinians inside Israel who are Israeli citizens and therefore move freely, such as those living in Nazareth, and the Palestinians who live beyond the 1967 border and enjoy no such freedoms, such as those in Bethlehem.

Great efforts were also made to achieve full cooperation from the incoming pilgrims, who, at least at that time, were not accustomed to the security procedures that have long been a part of life for the people in Jerusalem. The Israeli border crossing procedures were known to be long and tedious. Many visitors felt them insulting to their notion of privacy. Particularly those who traveled to Jerusalem individually rather than in groups complained about the Israeli airport security procedures. They found the questions asked by the airport security, the unrestricted inspection of their belongings, and the long interrogation and cross-examination invasive of their privacy. Travel agents who organize tour groups to Jerusalem try to spare their clients from these experiences by employing a person with special airport security clearance who mediates between the tour group and the airport security services. The apparatus is generally not bothered by the delays and the complaints about their security procedures at the airport because, as they say, they are merely doing their job. The security meta-ritual, however, required full cooperation from the incoming visitors. It required that the pilgrims understood that it was necessary for them to adjust their attitudes and behavior to the security imperative and the parameters set by the apparatus. To this end, "some 500 religious leaders and heads of Italian pilgrim groups met with El Al security officers in Rome" the media reported, "to have the airline's rigorous security checks explained to them."

The apparatus reached out to the pilgrims and their group leaders to make them shift their perception from what they otherwise deemed reasonable and necessary checking at border crossings to the security measures executed at the Israeli border crossings. "The Rome conference," the media reported, "was held to prepare community leaders for their visit to Israel and to brief them on the kinds of questions they should expect at El Al security." The shift in perception was successful, the media concluded, as "the community leaders and religious people who took part in the meeting welcomed the initiative and expressed their understanding on this sensitive topic."[12] Adjusting to the parameters set by the apparatus meant that, when the pilgrims began their journey, they adjusted their behavior according to the security imperative. The "No Joking" signs that have recently been posted in several U.S. airports are meant to achieve the same shift in perception by setting the parameters: you are now in the domain of the security apparatus—behave as expected. Once all involved have willingly adjusted to the parameters set by the apparatus, their movement to and within the reality of safety could be perfectly planned and executed. There would be no delays, no problems, no complaints, and no conflict. Everything would work smoothly. The apparatus, including the bus company, the police, and the customs authority, were now able to simply board the pilgrims on "some 800 buses" and arrange for them to be transported "from the airport without their having to pass through the airport terminal." With everyone cooperating and following instructions, security procedures were able to be "carried out on the pilgrims in their countries of origin before their departure for Israel."[13] The apparatus works under the assumption that whatever is best in the eyes of the security apparatus is best for everyone involved (see Buzan, Waever, and de Wilde 1998). Its meta-framing means that following the parameters set by the apparatus to achieve the reality of safety necessarily silences perceptions alternative to the logic of the security apparatus. Those who partake in a public event also partake in the security meta-ritual. The ritual engagement in the former is dependent on the cooperation in the latter.

## Purification of Participants and Social Spaces

Through the use of all available resources and cooperation of everyone involved, the apparatus sterilizes the social space within which the public event is to take place, and transforms that space and its people into a purified ritual space within which the reality of safety can be brought to existence. This process takes place in multiple ways. Whenever possible, the apparatus discourages people from participating in the public event. This alleviates the performance of the security meta-ritual. When a detailed road itinerary of the Pope's entourage was made public, it was provided with a prognostic course of the traffic congestion: "A sturdy pair of walking shoes will get many people in Jerusalem next week a whole lot farther than a set of wheels." As it befits the occasion, crowds should accompany the Pope's procession through the city, but continuous associations between crowds and traffic jams persuaded Jerusalemites, accustomed to driving to their destinations in the city, that they were better off staying away. "Parking along many of the capital's streets will be severely disrupted," the media predicted, and the roads on which the Pope would be traveling would be closed to traffic. Given that the Pope was to be "traveling part of the time in his open-roofed car" and that car would "be driven slowly so as to interact with the expected crowds," the media reported, traffic was "expected to be jammed for hours on some days, and parking along those streets [would] be prohibited." But there was no reason to panic. The security apparatus had everything under control. Everybody, including the emergency bilingual hotline for English and Hebrew speakers, performed as expected: "tourists will be able to receive advice in English—and Israelis in Hebrew—by calling the city's situation room."[14]

People were encouraged to remove themselves from the ritual space in other ways. With the exception of the mass on the Manger Square in the heart of the Palestinian city of Bethlehem and the open-air Mass for Youth on the rural Israeli Mount of Beatitudes, all spaces where the Pope moved were closed off to those who were not invited. Most events were invitation only. The Popemobile may have "driven slowly so as to interact with the expected crowds" as quoted earlier, but the streets were empty and void of cheering enthusiasts. Many people in Jerusalem took advantage of very attractive and affordable offers of tourist packages to Italy on the return flights that brought in the pilgrims. Others were encouraged to stay at home and participate as media audiences. An official from the Israel Ministry of Tourism related that "people don't have to see [the Pope]. People will watch TV. Even if I had an invitation I don't want to go to the [open mass in] the Galilee. I can't park. Too many people! In Yad Vashem, how many people will be there? 50? 100? It's invitation only. I will go tomorrow to greet him at the airport—again, invitation only." This official assumed that most Israelis would find it perfectly acceptable that they were being discouraged from participation. "It's good this way," he concluded, "for security. People will understand that it's for security. Believe me. It's better to watch it on TV."[15] If people stay away or watch the public ritual unfold on their television screens and if, as Dayan and Katz (1992) have suggested, through their discussion on media events, they create in the process their own family ritual out of the occasion, there is less movement to surveill, less public sociality to control, and hence less work to separate from the reality of uncertainty.

Sterilization of social spaces through which the Pope moved was achieved through processes of enclosure and purification. This meant encircling the space and removing, blocking, and redirecting the unwanted human movement away from that space. The areas in the proximity of the Pope's body were purified, cleaned, and void of pollutants from the time he landed at the airport through the time he bade farewell. The most trusted among the apparatus ensured that the areas around the Pope were not just safe but 'sterile.' Ben-Gurion International Airport security, the media reported, "which usually provides security for important visitors in and around the airport, has passed the baton" to the internal secret service known by its Hebrew initials as Shin Bet or more commonly as Shabak, which would "take the outmost precautions to ensure the Pope's safety, including the creation of 'sterile areas' around him."[16] The expression 'sterile area' first suffused the Israeli public sphere after the assassination of Yitzhak Rabin in November 1995. It denoted that for more than an hour before that fatal shot was executed, Rabin's assassin and his gun were within the safe area, the zone that was purified by the Shabak, the apparatus in charge of the prime minister's security.

Among the locals, Shabak is known to have "the mentality that a strong man can overcome two but not three." When the Pope prayed at the Cenacle, a location just outside the Old City wall of Jerusalem, associated with Jesus' last supper with his disciples, the Pope "needed breakfast which he did not eat," a local priest related. The church officials were instructed that "only one waiter" was allowed to deliver the food to the Cenacle and "we [the Shabak] will take it in" to deliver it to the Pope. The priest recounted how he delivered the food. As he walked to the entrance to the Cenacle with the breakfast tray in his hand, the Shabak "was standing there with the machinegun." The Shabak operative greeted the priest with: "No problem—but we have to taste the food." The priest replied in a very serious tone: "Oh really?" to which the Shabak responded "No, no. I am just kidding." This may sound like there was room for humor. After all, when every person has been accounted for, the process should be able to go smoothly and with less tension. More likely, however, the "just kidding" response of the security apparatus was an instance of reaffirmation on its part, at the most minute level, that every element of the public event is always subordinated to the security meta-frame. Indeed, this type of control seems to have few limits. "If he [was] somebody known to the Shabak than yes," the priest related. "For the time these three workers were inside [the Church of the Holy Sepulchre] their cell phones did not work."[17]

Throughout the visit, the sterilization process took place in phases of zoning in accordance with the Pope's day-to-day itinerary but immediately preceding his movement. Less than 24 hrs before the Pope's entourage would enter a particular area, the security apparatus first closed off all the movement in and out of that zone, completely stopping the regular movement of people and objects so that only the security-sanctioned movement could resume for the duration of the public event. So, for example, on the day when the Pope visited the Wailing Wall and the Church of the Holy Sepulchre, all the shops and restaurants along the route were ordered closed. The security apparatuses combed through all the churches, courtyards, streets, and alleys where the Pope would move. They checked every corner, turned over every object, and accounted for every resident on those streets. They put up a checkpoint at every gate along the wall of the Old City of Jerusalem and allowed only certain individuals to enter. Minutes after the Pope's entourage left the area, the checkpoints were dismantled, taking with them all the traces of the event that had just happened. As soon as the security apparatuses left the scene, movement resumed as usual.

## THE FRAMING OF PUBLIC EVENTS WITHIN THE REALITY OF SAFETY THROUGH ITS META-MESSAGE "THIS IS ORDER"

Throughout the visit, full and undivided attention was given to the protection of the Pope's body. We were reminded by the media that "the pontiff [was] an elderly man with medical problems,"[18] and an old, fragile, and ailing body that had a long, 6-day journey to sustain. The body of the Pope united the totemic powers of the ritual of reconciliation with the cosmic powers of the catastrophic uncertainty. The body that sacrificially took on the burden of the world to rescue it from the uncertain was also the body that could collapse any time and bring about a much larger catastrophe. The favorite photographic angle was one that featured the Pope's degenerated spine curvature in Atlas-like symbolism of carrying the world's problems on his shoulders. This aging body with Parkinson's disease was determined to move through the dark, narrow alleys of the unknown neighborhoods of the Old City of Jerusalem to reach "the number of sites" scattered throughout the city at which the Pope wished to pray and give himself to "the large numbers of people who want to see the pontiff."[19]

The apparatus communicates to the public the conditions necessary for the creation of the reality of safety and the media conveys to the public certain elements of the transformative practices of the security meta-ritual, but the actual operations performed by the operatives remain in the background. Even though the security apparatus is not in the media spotlight, Handelman (2004: 106) argues that it is inexorably connected to the way Israeli public events are practiced so that it shapes every single aspect of these events. The protection of the Pope's body, the use of the all-pervasive, white, trapeze-like, bulletproof vehicle with the see-through windows dubbed 'Popemobile,' and the armored vehicle of the General Security

Service designed specifically to move through the narrow alleys and walk-ways of the Old City of Jerusalem powerfully communicated the meta-message "This is Order." The Pope's unrelenting activity throughout the visit was made possible through the protective shield of the visually attractive and cute Popemobile as well as the rugged armored vehicle. These two fortresses on wheels, the fortified mobile havens of safety that are able to move fearlessly and confidently through the purified social space, communicated to those involved that the public event was unfolding within the reality of safety.

The meta-message "This is Order" was continuously highlighted as the visual symbolism of the two vehicles and the Pope as their happy passenger communicated that the performance of the security meta-ritual has enabled the creation of the reality of public safety within which the Pope can now fulfill his mission. The framing process of the security meta-ritual has successfully separated the public event from the uncertainty of the daily life in Jerusalem and enclosed the public activity within the reality of safety with the security frame. In Batesonian terms, the meta-constitution of this frame communicates as a meta-message. This means that it subordinates all the social activity within its frame to its message; that is, the people within the reality of safety orient their thinking and their activity in relation to the meta-message of the frame "This is Order." Any activity within this frame will be carried out in accordance to the meta-message of the frame. It follows that through the performance of the security meta-ritual, the form of social ordering through which the apparatus enables the bringing to existence the reality of safety, the apparatus also frames each and every aspect of the public event itself. I present two highlights of the achievement of the security meta-ritual to demonstrate how the meta-constitution of the message "This is Order" frames every subelement of the public event.

## The Open-Air Mass on the Mount of Beatitudes

Throughout the process of the security meta-ritual, the purification achieved the separation of safe from unsafe. For the open-air mass on the Mount of Beatitudes, this meant that those who were perceived as likely to follow the rules of the security apparatus were allowed in and others whose identity records may have indicated a possibility of disobedience were kept outside. The Palestinian Christians who live in Israel proper as well as those from Bethlehem and other places in the West Bank and Gaza were given the opportunity of what was to many an experience of a lifetime. After providing proper documentation, some were allowed to travel to the "northern shores of the Sea of Galilee, where the pontiff [would] officiate at one of the spectacular public masses he holds on foreign trips."[20] For the Christians in the area, this was a unique opportunity to be surrounded by tens of thousands of other Christians from around the world. Particularly for those from the West Bank and Gaza, it was also the very first possibility to leave home and see what the world might look like outside the realities of military control.

Only individuals who came in organized tour buses were allowed on the site. No access was given to personal vehicles or pedestrians. Buses are mobile physical enclosures whose movement in space is dependent on the driver. Once the driver and the passengers have been purified, the bus becomes a useful enclosure through which purified individuals can be transported through space unpolluted. The pilgrims from Jerusalem boarded the buses at 1 a.m. for a 4-hr drive to the site of the open-air mass on the Mount of Beatitudes that was scheduled to start at 10 a.m. When the media reported about the Palestinian pilgrims it also provided other details: "Preparations have also been made with the Palestinian Authority regarding the Pope's visit to Bethlehem. Some 5000 Palestinians from Gaza and the West Bank are to be transported by bus to Mount [of Beatitudes] for Friday's mass, escorted by the Israel Police."[21] As clearly stated by the media, the buses that came from the West Bank were escorted by the Israeli police in an organized convoy from their churches to the place of the mass and escorted back to their home church after the mass. I was told by the officials of the Catholic Church in Jerusalem that the group from Gaza never made it beyond the Gaza–Israeli border. It was held at the Rafah checkpoint and eventually denied permission to enter. Older Palestinians and children who could not withstand the sleepless overnight pilgrimage were also left behind as were those who, for whatever reason, did not provide proper documentation.

Not only did the security meta-ritual purify the space and the people within the reality of safety, it also spatially reordered the physicality and the aesthetics of that space. The site of the open-air Mass for Youth was the Mount of Beatitudes, an unpopulated and uncultivated peace of land, far removed from any urban area. Here, the security apparatus created spatial order out of nothingness. It first created a spatial enclosure by installing a physical barrier, a fence that encircled what was to become a place for the mass. Within that enclosure, the space was further sectioned off into smaller spaces with walking aisles between them for a free movement of the security apparatus between the subspaces. The outer fence had several openings, which became entry points for the participants who arrived in organized busses to a parking lot built several hundred meters away from the enclosure. Each bus was assigned to a specific entry point and each entry lead to a set of specific subspaces within so that after the mass, participants left their particular subspace and walked directly back to their bus that waited for them in the parking lot to take them back to where they came. In this case, the security apparatus literally created social order according to its own design: with boundaries completely sealed, entry points assigned to specific groups of pre-selected participants with appropriately assigned badges, and human movement to and within the ritual space perfectly spatially ordered.

Once the ritual space was created, the outsiders were separated from the insiders, and the access to the sterile zone took place as envisioned by the security apparatus, the group effervescence, the Turnerian communitas, and all properly ritual experiences as required by the public event were able to resume. Within the sterile subareas, united in one fortified island of safety in the midst of the unsafe and dangerous world, dancing, singing, and chanting "Viva el Papa!' erupted spontaneously. By the early morning hours before the 10 a.m. religious service, all groups had arrived at the site, each to their assigned subspace. There was great excitement and anticipation of the Pope's appearance. Music blasted out of the loudspeakers, Palestinian tunes commonly sung in Arabic in the local churches far outnumbering those in Latin and other languages. Groups displayed banners and held up posters in English, Spanish, Italian, Croatian, Arabic, Polish, and many other languages.

A Palestinian woman in her mid-30s, standing next to a man of a similar age, reflected on her experience of coming to the site: "[I came] to share with the people the happy moment," she said, because "it's nicer to come here than to sit at home and watch [it all on] TV." While the Israeli official quoted earlier suggested that watching the event on the television screens at home would be much more convenient, this Palestinian woman had a very different experience. "You see," she explained, "[for me] it's something different. This is the first time I come here to Israel and to this place [in particular]. I am from Bethlehem, but if I want to come here I should have a visa and a passport and that's not so easy to get." Control of mobility has been a fact of her everyday life. "Because of that," she continued, "it's the first time for me to come to these places . . . We have a lot of nice places and holy places that we can't go to. So, every opportunity that we have, we take."

Even though she and those who came with her have clearly passed through the purification process, their opportunity to attend the open-air mass was nevertheless micro-ordered by the apparatus. "We came by bus," she explained. "The bus that we were taking, [the security operative] did everything, he took all the names down, our identities, everything, and took care of everything by himself." All the passengers have been pre-selected and pre-approved so that the operative merely reaffirmed the order. "It was so easy," she emphasized. Unlike the reality of her daily life where passing through the checkpoints is no easy matter, this time, "[the security operatives] didn't make any problems. They check[ed] the bus at the checkpoint in Bethlehem and in Jerusalem. In Jerusalem," she clarified, "they stop[ed] the bus because there were students, guys [on the bus], because they were young." In the eyes of the apparatus, young men are a source of uncertainty. This woman understood that, in accordance of the meta-massage "This is Order," these young men had to be reconfirmed.

She had also come to accept that their pilgrimage to and from the open mass had to be micro-ordered by the apparatus. "We have succeeded to have [the] police [to follow the buses] from Bethlehem till here with us!" she exclaimed. She emphasized that "thirty-seven buses . . . from all over" came to the site, "it was very nice, you know." The meta-message "This is Order" conveys that in the hands of the apparatus and according to its design, life can be ordered and lived in certainty and safety. For this Palestinian woman, the micro-ordering of the open-air mass was in line with the meta-message. "One police car was in front, and between two buses there was another police car," she described. "Every two buses we have two police cars. And if you [could] see the view, it was very nice." But how could police escort be nice? "Yeah," she confirmed, "you know, it was like, ah, if you are inside the casino.[22] You have these lights, they are blue . . . [blinking] from all around. We were together, behind each other. It was nice. And now, if you will [be able to] see it, we will leave here at fifteen minutes before two . . . and we will go home accompanied by the police."[23] For this Palestinian pilgrim, attending the open-air Mass for Youth on the Mount of Beatitudes, orienting, adjusting, and interpreting her own pilgrimage within the reality of safety and its meta-message "This is Order" enabled a journey to places otherwise unreachable. It allowed for a freedom of movement beyond the possibilities made available in the reality of her day-to-day life. The social order of the reality of safety, made possible through the security meta-ritual and interpreted as such through its meta-message, was perceived as a common good for its participants in that it provided a protective shield within which the symbolic, the expressive, and the emotional of the public event was able to unfold.

## The Pope Goes Back to the Church of the Holy Sepulchre

The day after the Pope's departure, the chief of the Israeli Police summoned the journalists at the press center in Jerusalem for a press conference. He reported on the success of the operation, recounted the number of security personnel employed, provided detailed reports of occasions when the operation was particularly challenging, and concluded that "the Operation was extremely successful" because "absolutely nothing went wrong." The script of the security meta-ritual was perfectly executed. All uncertainty had been eliminated and kept outside the reality of safety. Within the reality of safety, the public event unfolded smoothly, without interruption, and in line with its meta-message "This is Order." The Chief was particularly pleased with how the apparatus was able to frame an event which was not listed on the schedule: "The Pope suddenly decided on Saturday that he wanted to go back to the Church of the Holy Sepulchre," the chief told the audience, and "we let him do it. It was not on the schedule but we were flexible. We accommodated him." He concluded his briefing with "I thank all the men and women who participated in this Operation. And we thank all of you [journalists] for your cooperation."[24]

The chief had rightly thanked everyone for their cooperation. In its goal to enable the bringing into existence the reality of safety, the process of security meta-ritual is indeed more pleasant and more enjoyable for everyone involved when every person orients his or her behavior in relation to the meta-message "This is Order." The unanticipated demand by the Pope to return to the Church of the Holy Sepulchre on that Saturday afternoon and how the apparatus thought of itself as being in a position to say that they would accommodate the demand of the Pope, however, makes another aspect of the security meta-ritual transparent. Not only does security frame each and every subelement of the public event, it is that whether a public event or any aspect of it will even take place at all that depends in a very large part on whether the event is able to be subjected to the meta-framing of the apparatus.

The Pope's sudden decision to return to the Church of the Holy Sepulchre is an example of how framing and ordering works under very different conditions from those at the open-air Mass for Youth discussed earlier. The open-air mass made it possible to see what a sociospatial social order would look like when the apparatus had an opportunity to create order out of nothingness. The Church of the Holy Sepulchre, on the other hand, is buried among the residences and other structures inside the densely populated Old City of Jerusalem. It is a physical place, kept alive by the pilgrims and the locals who visit the place daily, and sustained through the rituals performed around the clock by the clergy. The church houses the Calvary or Golgotha where Christ was put on the cross, the Stone of Unction on which his body was laid after being taken down from the cross, and the Tomb in which his body was buried.

For the mass inside the church that the Pope was to perform, "every single detail was done over and over again," recounted one of the priests. "The mass was planned," he recalled, with the Shabak determining every aspect of it: "They had a massive presence: one phone call and 200 came down." The mass was invitation only. "There were only some 500 tickets made available by the Shabak. There were few diplomats and non Catholics. There were no political people [present], mostly locals." The Pope wanted to visit the Calvary or Golgotha, but "he didn't go up to Calvary because the steps were to steep," recalled the priest. Everyone was under a strict timetable: "We had to role by 11:30," the priest recalled, because "the Pope had lunch at the Latin Patriarchate. All bishops were there." After lunch, the Pope took a mid-day rest and, "it had to be about 2:30 p.m.," the priest recalled, when the Pope declared "I want to go back" to the Church of the Holy Sepulchre. The priest suggested that "for the Shabak, this [was] the best situation because no one knew about it . . . The mass was planned. But going back was not. It was completely unscripted."

How the apparatus ordered and framed the Pope's return to the church has become one of the memorable tales about the visit. I present here an account as it was remembered by a local involved in the process.[25] After the mass, the local recalled, as the Pope was leaving the church, "I felt something is going to happen." This local has been observing the pilgrims come and go for a long time and he knows very well what a pilgrimage to this church entails. "As a [person] who lives here for many years, [I asked] how come the Pope is inside visiting the Tomb and not visiting Golgotha? The Popemobile came but the Pope wanted to walk through [the courtyard] not ride." Walking is an integral part of pilgrimage. Many Christians come to Jerusalem to walk in the footsteps of Jesus along the Via Dolorosa, leading into the church. "So, I told the security, but they said [the Pope] should go back because he was tired. I told them not to open the church for at least one hour after the Pope left . . . but after 40 minutes . . . they decided that the Pope was not going to come back . . . they gave up and gave order to open" the church for the public. "And in 25 minutes, we had more than 15 000 Italian, Spanish [coming along] the Via Dolorosa" on their way to the church.

After some time, he recalled, "a priest called the Latin Chapel [inside the Church] but nobody answered. So he called me and said 'in seven to ten minutes, the Pope will be here.' I said 'are you sure?' He said 'no time to argue.' It was my lucky day!" he exclaimed. "I close the phone. I call the Greek patriarch assistant because I felt the Pope would come to Golgotha. Then I called [the] head of [the] secret police. We had seven minutes. I told him the Pope was coming back. He said, 'this is order. All people out of the church in two minutes.!'" The local paused to emphasize the situation: "How can I get 15 000 out [of the way] in 15 minutes?" The Church, its courtyard, and a number of alleyways needed to be cleared. He had to be creative. "I said 'there is a bomb!' and believe me, all were out. I told them to go out this door. No one can go out that way. Then I sent seven police to the Jaffa Gate and half others to close the other side. I called the Greek patriarchate, then Sacristy to Golgotha. All in one minute." This local is very well aware of the way things work in the Church. "I called churches first, then the security chief. I can not empty the church without the church permission. They said, 'yes, empty.'" The priests were skeptical and wanted to know how this could be done. "'How will you do it?' I have my ways," he told them. He repeated "first in Italian, then Spanish, I said 'leave this place immediately. There is a suspicious object, a bag inside. They looked at me, I [looked like I] was shocked so they believed. One minute later the chief called. I said 'the church is empty.' He said, 'if one is inside you will be sorry.' I said 'it's empty.'" Not everything is always perfect so "at the last minute, some 20 or 30 people were inside [the Church]" but this was to be understood "because it was not arranged."

In recalling his story, the local also provided some sense of how the internal hierarchy may work: "Which way you need to leave?" asked the Israeli security of the Italian delegation. "Israeli security waited for answer from Italian security. The Italian security said to Israelis that [the Pope] need to leave [the Church via the street passing] the Lutheran Church toward the Jaffa Gate. The Pope's assistant to the Italian security to the Israeli security." This meant for the local that "Ok, close off part by Lutheran. [The area around the] Mooristan and the Jaffa Gate must be empty." It was indeed a lucky day for this local: "So, I stood next to the Pope and held his hand up [the steps to the Calvary]. We went up, I brought the Greek priest, took pictures, we came down, I put police in their positions, then they left." But in the world of the apparatus, it seems that, as lucky as these moments can be for those who are involved in its operations, the hierarchy is difficult to penetrate. "After the Pope said goodbye, the Italian pushed me aside [communicating that] my job is finished. But he is Italian and not from here. If it was people from here I would make sure to get my honor back."

## CONCLUSIONS

In light of cross-cultural ritual traditions as we know them from early anthropological and sociological studies of ritual, the ritual process I have been describing is a new phenomenon that speaks to how technologically advanced and globally interdependent societies respond to disorder and cope with uncertainty. For pre-modern peoples, uncertainty as much as ritual failure were understood to be integral to living and not something that could be contained or put under control. For societies with organic cosmology, everything is connected and therefore influenced by everything else. Failures, accidents, and other kinds of disorder are understood in relation to that cosmological order.[26] Today, uncertainty is seen as a threat that comes in the form of violence. Threat is collectively articulated into an expectation that uncertainty must be acted upon with clearly defined pre-emptive actions (Beck 1992). Threat and the expectation that action must be taken to prevent a possible disruption of a public event are fundamental to the continuity of existence of security meta-ritual.

Security meta-ritual is a ritual that orders—rather than represents—social life. It is performed to separate public social activity from uncertainty of the everyday life and transform that sociocultural space into a reality of safety. Following Handelman (1998), unlike the Durkheimian types of rituals whose practice is aimed at achieving solidarity, this kind of ritual is performed to facilitate change on the social world for the purpose of some social activity. Because of its exclusionary framing, this kind of ritual is in a meta-relationship to any other activity it encloses so that any social activity within its domain will unfold in relation to the meta-message of its frame.

Rituals are grounded in narratives that represent a body of thought, cultural ideas, and practices within which ritual itself makes sense. Security meta-ritual narrative is based on the belief that the security apparatus of the modern state and its use of the scientific and technological advancements can be effectively combined to impose order on conditions of uncertainty. This type of ritual is therefore rooted in science and technology and rests on the belief in the capacity of scientific and technological knowledge to make social life ever safer by controlling the vicissitudes of possible future events. Its practices exude confidence in validity and efficacy of metal detectors, fingerprinting, surveillance cameras, record checking, body searches, and alike to produce certainty within the ritual space and time. Each enactment of security meta-ritual provides a new opportunity to put these technologies to work 'in real time,' allowing for improvement of the procedures enacted in a previous security meta-ritual, and preempting one more possibility of unwanted activity.

Primary to this type of ritual are the efficaciousness and the goal-rational aim of preventing disorder and controlling uncertainty. Through the tendency to expand the notion of security to wide-reaching domains of social existence and acceptance of these processes by the ritual participants as legitimate, security meta-ritual performers are able to transcend our fragmented social existence and engage in a wide mobilization of individuals, resources, and social institutions to their end. In this process, they draw on social memory of disruptive events from the past and the technological knowledge of the present to envision how future disruptions can be pre-empted. Order is achieved through the separation of insiders from outsiders, safe space from unsafe areas, and security-sanctioned movement from other movement. This process follows the exclusive template conceived by the security apparatus. The significance of this practice is not the security meta-ritual itself. Rather, the importance of this practice is in its ability to demonstrate that reality of safety can be brought to existence when ritual participants follow the security template.

Through its own process, security meta-ritual reflects the vision of what it means to have safety and order. In the case of a public event in which the stakes are extremely high for the state, the process of security meta-ritual becomes highly visible and rigidly executed so that all available resources and all social activity within the ritual space are subordinated to this end. This visibility communicates the ability and the power of the security apparatus to channel, block, and control the movement of people and objects within that ritual space. The increasingly close coupling of security procedures with public events also exposes the normalization of the vision of social order as conceived by the security apparatus through the ritual process. Through the process of transformation of an environment that is polluted and unpredictable to a social space that is secured, ordered, and controlled, the idea of orderliness of security meta-ritual is recreated, experienced, and made known and visible to the ritual participants and the general public alike.

Rituals tend to have a capacity to be perceived as time-honored, unchanging practices that speak to legitimacy of tradition (Bell 1997). Yet, ritual is an emergent phenomenon and therefore every ritual enactment is open to a possibility of change (Handelman and Lindquist 2005). Security meta-ritual is a type of ritual adapted to absorb the risks of its own performance in that each enactment of security meta-ritual provides its performers an opportunity to put their ever-improving technologies of control to work in real time. Each security meta-ritual enactment is therefore an occasion that allows its performers to adapt to varieties of public events in different kinds of social contexts. Change is built into its very process. Whether this type of ritual will be performed depends on perceptions of fear of uncertainty. As long as the threat of disorder and violence can be made to seem plausible to the public, security meta-ritual can be justified and reenacted.

## NOTES

1. As this essay passed through multiple reincarnations, colleagues too numerous to be listed contributed to its ongoing transformation. I am, however, particularly indebted to Diana Crane, Don Handelman, Costas Nakassis, Regina Smardon, David Snow, and Charles Tilley. All footnotes referring to media reports are based on paper editions of the newspapers and are on file as research materials with the author.
2. "Biggest security blitz to guard pope here." *The Jerusalem Post*, March 12, 2000.
3. "Preparations intensify for tens of thousands expected to accompany pope on pilgrimage." *Ha'aretz,* March 9, 2000.
4. "Wind flattens stage set up for Pope." *Ha'aretz*, March 14, 2000.
5. Interview with a Catholic Church official, April 2006.
6. "Operation Old Friend set to protect Pope." *The Jerusalem Post*, March 17, 2000.
7. "Operation Old Friend set to protect Pope."
8. "Operation Old Friend set to protect Pope."
9. "Biggest security blitz to guard Pope here." *The Jerusalem Post*, March 12, 2000. The internal guide for the media distributed to journalists at the press center lists Haim Ramon as 'Coordinating Minister for His Holiness's visit.'
10. Interview with an official from the Jerusalem Municipality, March 2000.
11. "Preparations intensify for tens of thousands expected to accompany pope on pilgrimage." *Ha'aretz*, March 9, 2000.
12. "Shin Bet to protect Pope during March visit." *Ha'aretz,* February 14, 2000.
13. "Airport braces for arrival of Pope and pilgrims." *Ha'aretz*, March 5, 2000.
14. "Walk, don't ride while the pope is in town." *The Jerusalem Post*, March 17, 2000.
15. Interview with an official from the Ministry of Tourism, March 2000.
16. "Airport braces for arrival of Pope and pilgrims." *Ha'aretz*, March 5, 2000.
17. Interview with a Catholic priest, April 2006.
18. "Massive preparations begin for Pope's visit." *The Jerusalem Post,* February 16, 2000.
19. "Biggest security blitz to guard the Pope here."
20. "Preparations intensify for tens of thousands expected to accompany Pope on pilgrimage." *Ha'aretz*, March 9, 2000.
21. "Operation Old Friend set to protect Pope." *The Jerusalem Post*, March 17, 2000.
22. At the time of the Pope's visit and until the Second Intifada, there was, just outside the city of Jericho in the West Bank, a successfully run casino,

supported through local and foreign investment. Only those with a passport, including the Israelis, were allowed on the premises.

23. Interview during the open-air Mass on the Mount of Beatitudes, March 2000.
24. Media briefing at the Jerusalem press center by the chief of the Israeli police, March 2000.
25. Interview with a local, April 2006.
26. A classic anthropological study that demonstrates cultural differences regarding uncertainty and the prospects of controlling the future is that of E. E. Evans-Pritchard (1965) who studied magic among the Azande.

# Part III

# Struggle and Resistance

# When the Israeli State of Exception Meets the Exception
## The Case of Tali Fahima

*Liora Sion*[1]

*"The exception is more interesting than the regular case. The latter proves nothing, the exception proves everything"* (Carl Schmitt 1985: 22)

## INTRODUCTION

How can the West balance liberty and security over the long term? The suspension of civil liberties, detentions, and assassination of enemies—all this might be allowed as a last resort, if the life of the state were in danger. But if law must sometimes compromise with necessity, how does it influence society in the long term?

This chapter addresses these issues by studying how security in Israel shapes civil society and how society is sustained during a prolonged emergency situation. Neither Europe nor the United States is exemplar of the long-term influence of security and its consequences. Europe since the catastrophe of Weimar, the rise of fascism, the experience of communism, and the history of total wars in the 20th century is no longer considered a state of exception as an acceptable frame of response (Scheppele 2004). The United States was deeply influenced by the terrorist attacks of September 11, 2010 (9/11). The War on Terror waged by the Bush administration has witnessed a suspension of rights under the Patriot Act. Guantanamo detainees were effectively stripped of their basic legal identities (Butler 2004). However, because the United States never reformulated its guiding ideas about how to manage serious threats, the Bush administration fell back into Cold War habits, even though the present threat and the present world situation are very different (Scheppele 2004).

Since its conception, Israel made security its primary concern and, for this reason, is a prime example where securitization in Weaver's (1995) understanding has characterized the society. This has been contributed to by the reality of the Israeli-Arab conflict, exile, long years of persecution, and the Holocaust, as well as cultural codes such as ethnocentrism, anxiety, and politicized messianic religion. All of these factors mixed with the universalistic values of democracy and human rights contribute to the creation of society with militaristic characteristics, society in which security plays a major role (Kimmerling 2001). Therefore, I suggest an analysis of the Israeli society, which since its foundation in 1948 has been in a state of emergency, as an example of the ways by which security shapes society. I do so by applying three theoretical frameworks: Agamben's "state of exception," state boundaries as they are defined by bureaucratic logic and classification (Handelman 2004), and Foucault's modern forms of punishment (1979). By applying these theories, my aim is to ask how the state apparatus manages the abnormal and exception during a "state of exception"—that is, a law outside the law.

Israel is what Agamben (2005) defines as a state of exception, a provision whereby the state, having identified "crisis moments" that threaten the very continuity of the state itself, is empowered to act outside the constraints of law. It does so by permitting extreme measures, including violence against its own citizens, in its own defense. According to Agamben (2005: 87), law can be obliterated and contradicted with impunity by a governmental violence that—while ignoring international law externally and producing a permanent state of exception internally—nevertheless still claims to be applying the law. Far from being a response to a normative lacuna, the state of exception appears as the opening of a fictitious lacuna to safeguard the existence of law and its applicability to the normal situation. The lacuna is not within the law, but concerns law's relation to reality, the very possibility of its application. It is as if the juridical order contained an essential fracture between the position of the norm and its application, which, in extreme situations, can be filled only by means of the state of exception; that is, creating a zone in which application is suspended, but the law, as such, remains in force (Agamben 2005: 31). Because the state of exception is neither external nor internal to the juridical order, the problem of defining it concerns precisely a threshold or a zone of indifference, where inside and outside do not exclude each other but rather blur with each other. The suspension of the norm does not mean its abolition, and the zone of anomie that it establishes is not (or at least claims not to be) unrelated to the juridical order (Agamben 2005: 23).

The second theory analyzes internal and external through the state's bureaucratic logic; Handelman (2004) argues that a bureaucratic logic is the driving force behind expressions of nationalism in the state. He contends that bureaucratic logic has a much wider importance than simply functioning as a way of thinking only about bureaucratic institutions. This logic is crucial to how these institutions function, but more so, it is a dominant force in forming modern state social order. Bureaucratic logic is used incessantly to invent and to modify all kinds of systems of classification that often have profound consequences for individuals and groups. The modern state has a binary logic; it focuses on managing the population within its borders and maintaining territorial sovereignty in relation to other states. Internally, this means systematic gathering of information on each individual to allow for mobilization of the population for the state's purposes (Giddens 1987: 15; Desrosières 1998; Bajc 2007b). Externally, state governance is focused in part on securing its territorial sovereignty through military means and state defense policies related to the global system of modern states (Salter 2003; Torpey 2000).

Yet, Israel blurs the differences between internal and external and has no agreed geographical and social boundaries (Lustick 1993; Ron 2000). Israel struggles to maintain its blurred geographical boundaries because clarification would force either a withdrawal from the occupied territories or an extension of citizenship to the Palestinians. As a result, there is no consensus in Israel regarding the occupied territories, Palestinians, and who is entitled to citizenship. A good example of this blurring of boundaries is the activity of the General Security Service, also known as Shin Beit, which is defined as internal but operates both in Israel and the occupied territories.

To analyze how security is the dominant ordering principle of social life in Israel and how it is perceived in light of bureaucratic logic, I will analyze the exceptional case of Tali Fahima, which has captured the imagination of many. Fahima, a Jewish Israeli woman 28 years old, did what many Israelis perceive as "crossing the lines" by befriending and offering herself as a human shield to the chief of al-Aqsa Martyrs Brigades in the Palestinian town of Jenin to protect him from the Israeli military's attempts on his life. She has been accused by the General Security Service of aiding the enemy during wartime, supporting a terrorist organization, and providing information to the enemy. She was indicted by the Israeli court in December 2005, and served 26 months in jail, including more than a year in administrative detention before her conviction. After her release from jail, Fahima converted to Islam, moved to an Arab village, and joined a radical Israeli-Palestinian movement.

Analyzing the controversial case of Fahima can contribute to our understanding of the social and political dimensions of the security discourse and its symbolic boundaries. Because Fahima is what Foucault (2003) calls an abnormality (she is neither a soldier nor against military service, and she is politically unidentified), she is a curiosity in terms of the existing literature, and a new security language is needed. Her case allows us to elaborate on the relationships between security, law, and human rights in Israel and shed light on the interconnections between security, the state of exception, and the nation.

## SOURCES AND METHODS

Researching security can be a daunting task because many resources are confidential. This is especially the case when it comes to the General Security Service and the classified and clandestine nature of its activities.

Significantly, the General Security Service is accountable directly and exclusively to the office of the Israeli prime minister, which ensures that the information about its activities remains a matter discussed in very limited and exclusive circles. For these reasons, this chapter focuses only on the "open trial" of Fahima; that is, on documentation that was only partly censored or not censored at all. As with other security cases in Israel, next to any open trial that is accessible to the public there also exists a "confidential trial" that is not accessible to outsiders. In this case, however, despite the fact that it was a security trial, this trial was not classified as confidential and therefore many of the documents are open to the public.

My analysis relies on original as well as secondary data. First, I make use of the General Security Service and police interrogation protocols. These protocols, however, cannot be considered a reliable source. Because they are written by the General Security Service itself, they are one sided. Moreover, a substantial amount of data was extracted from them. For example, 10 hr of investigations could be summarized into six or seven lines. Furthermore, the setting of interrogation, even if not particularly brutal, affects what is being said in the most profound manner. Therefore, we should be skeptical of the way in which Fahima is portrayed in these protocols.

The second source I use is court protocols. Because of its public dramaturgy, this trial attracted widespread media attention. Its dramatic enactment ensured that it enjoyed ritualized attention, thus serving broader educational and moral purposes (Levy and Sznaider 2006). The court protocols are also censured to some extent and do not necessarily reflect the atmosphere in court since many comments did not find their way into its pages.

The third source is an interview with Fahima's lawyer, Smadar Ben-Natan, who gave me access to the interrogation protocols. Lastly, I make use of newspaper and Web articles about Fahima, including interviews with her, her video blog, and Web surfers' feedback and discussion groups. These articles sometimes contain some information that did not find its way into the protocols.

## TALI FAHIMA AND THE BOUNDARIES OF THE ETHNIC NATION

Two years ago, Fahima still voted Likud and advocated military solution to the conflict. Now, she considers acting as a human shield to al-Aqsa Martyrs Brigades' chief in the Jenin area, the wanted Zacharia Zbeidi, who had escaped three 'elimination' attempts. What's her story?[2]

The ways in which Fahima blurred the traditional Israeli boundaries between ethnicity, class, politics, and nationality made her into a sensation. Fahima came to the public knowledge in March 2004 when she gave an interview to *Ha'ir*, Tel-Aviv's weekend magazine. She comes from a modest Mazrachi (Jews who emigrated from Asia and Africa) blue-collar background from the impoverished southern development town of Kiryat-Gat. Her father left the family when she was an infant, and because of the difficult economic conditions at home, she was sent to a religious boarding school. Fahima's ethnic origin is important because the Israeli Jewish society is characterized by an ethnic cleavage between Jews who emigrated from Europe and America (henceforth, the Ashkenazim), and those from Asia and Africa (henceforth, the Mazrachim). There are persisting socioeconomic gaps between the two. Ashkenazim have achieved high levels of education and earnings while their Mazrachi counterparts like Fahima have not been able to catch up with them or the native-born Israelis (Khazzoom 2003; Cohen, Haberfeld and Kristal 2007).

Although Fahima came from a religious family, which as such is absolved from the responsibility of serving in the Israeli army, she insisted on joining the military and served as a low-rank clerk for 2 years. She was also different from the typical image of a political activist in Israel in that she was not middle-class Ashkenazi, had no academic education, acted on her own, and befriended Palestinians. Her activity was based neither on feminism nor on womanhood, as is the case with women activists in Israel. Even more, in the last elections, Fahima voted for the right-wing Likud party. She did not identify herself with the left, and she even reported as saying that she appreciates the settlers' actions in the occupied territories more than the rather impotent left. Furthermore, Fahima presented herself neither as pacifist nor against the military. During her stay in the Palestinian town of Jenin, for example, she practiced shooting with Zbeidi's M-16 gun. To understand why Fahima was called "the new oddity,"[3] we have to understand how citizenship has been constructed in Israel.

War and routine conflict management, as well as its construction in terms of a struggle for survival, have been central to the consolidation and enhancement of the power and autonomy of the Israeli state since its establishment in 1948. State power and its construction of conflict have shaped the boundaries of the community of citizens and defined the terms of membership and participation in it. The military is based on universal conscription for Jews, and its wars have been the main mechanisms for the construction of what Ben-Eliezer (1995) has conceptualized as the Jewish "ethnic nation."

Within the boundaries of the ethnic nation, full and effective citizenship has been constructed in republican terms; that is, with an emphasis on the individual's contribution to the fulfillment of collective goals (Peled 1993). The republican principle, however, was implemented in different terms; namely, according to how social groups were assigned to the different missions that the nation- and state-building project generated. This differential implementation gave rise to different types or forms of membership and participation that are ordered hierarchically and legitimated by different discourses (Peled and Shafir 1996).

Participation in war and military service was identified as the ultimate token of political obligation as well as the highest contribution to the enhancement of collective goals. The institutions of war making, especially the military, were instituted as the prime arenas of political integration. They are signifiers of full and effective membership in the political community (Kimmerling 2001). Thus, civic virtue was constructed in terms of, and identified with, military virtue. However, military virtue was differentially distributed, thereby reflecting the ways in which the state in Israel reshaped the links among gender, class, ethnic origins, nationality, and citizenship. In this structure, Ashkenazi Jews were highly represented in the state-formed middle classes, whereas the state shaped Mizrachi Jews as the working class. In that sense, as an uneducated Mizrachi woman, Fahima is not a part of the Israeli hegemony.

Fahima acted outside the Israeli peace movements. The Israeli peace camp comprises an array of organizations that have, since the 1970s, conducted a sustained challenge to the military policies of the state and have strived for de-escalation of the Arab–Israeli conflict. The peace camp was shaped by security, and its social composition appeals mainly to middle-class Ashkenazi (Helman 1999). Despite the fact that women have been prominent in the movement's constituency, they have been marginal in leadership positions, performing mainly administrative and technical tasks (Sasson-Levy and Rappoport 2003). The close association between the fighter's role and peace activity has pushed women to the periphery of its organizations and networks. Therefore, women's peace activity mobilizes republican motherhood and womanhood within the framework of single-gender organizations (Helman 1999). Fahima was unique in this sense because she did not act as a mother, sister, or daughter of a soldier and did not declare herself a feminist. Moreover, the Israeli peace movement is exclusively Jewish. With the exception of the very fringe, the overwhelming majority of the left refrain from cooperating with Palestinians on an ongoing basis. Yet Fahima reached out to Palestinians, not Jews.

## FAHIMA'S TRANSFORMATION

In the interview she gave to *Ha'ir*, Fahima said that she went through what she called *sobering up*, a transformation from being a voter for the right WING. . . . to a radical peace activist. This process, she said, resulted from being exposed to alternative channels of information:

> I was educated that Arabs are something that shouldn't be here. One day I understood that I have many gaps of information, things that are absent in the media. I realized that it concerns human beings, and that we have responsibility on how their lives look like. That was the day I stopped watching TV.[4]

This statement refers to multiple characteristics of Israeli society. First is the choice of the social category "Arabs." For the Israeli Jews, this is probably the most meaningful social concept, in addition to that of their own social group. It is used as a basic term to label people who live in the Middle East and who have been in protracted conflict with the Israeli Jews (Bar-Tal 1996). The concept "Arab" is acquired in the early childhood. Bar-Tal (1996), for example, found that the Israeli children begin to use the word "Arab" between the ages of 24 and 30 months.

Second, Fahima calls Palestinians "something that shouldn't be here." The psychological core of the Israeli–Palestinian conflict is the perception by both parties that this is a zero-sum conflict. This is not only with respect to the territory but, most importantly, also with respect to the national identity and national existence. This zero-sum view flows directly from the fact that the two national movements focus on the same land that both claim as their national homeland (Kelman 1999). Therefore, as is evident from Fahima's words, many Israelis have denied Palestinians' distinctiveness. These Israelis describe Palestinians as Arabs and claim that their self-definition as Palestinians, and in many cases even their residence in the country, is of recent origin. In the view of these Israelis, Palestinian nationalism is an artificial creation without authentic historical roots. The often-cited infamous statement by the former Prime Minister Golda Meir that "there are no Palestinians" is perhaps the best example of this position.

Third, Fahima states that she came to conclude that she was missing relevant information about the Palestinians. These "gaps of information," as she called them, start in school. According to Al-Haj (2005), the Israeli textbooks present a typical Zionist narrative. The aim of this narrative is to safeguard national-Zionist values and crystallize the collective memory of Jewish students on an ethno-national basis. This is an exclusivist narrative that leaves no room for dealing with the legitimacy of the Palestinian narrative.

Fourth, Fahima also came to understand that information is also "absent in the media." Indeed, the Israeli press tends to adopt the official definitions uncritically, and the reporting of extreme measures taken by Israel toward the Palestinians takes place with only little criticism. Dor (2001) argues that during the al-Aqsa Intifada, Israeli newspapers transformed the reality of a two-sided ongoing war of attrition, taking place in a continual state of occupation, to a one-dimensional story of wild, unexplainable Palestinian violence answered with calm and restrained Israeli response.

In the eyes of state agencies, the language used by the media in describing acts of political violence is of crucial importance (Schlesinger 1991). As Cohen (2001) shows, euphemisms enable their users and listeners to name things without experiencing fully their meanings. The function of euphemistic labels and jargon is to mask and sanitize cruelty or harm and give it respectable or neutral status.

The language of the Israeli–Palestinian conflict gives us ample examples. *Hissulim memukadim*—assassination or "targeted killings"—are used by the military as an effective way to eliminate without trial those responsible for terror attacks and limit collateral damage while crippling the Palestinian militia leadership. It is often the case that additional Palestinians are killed and injured alongside the "targets," most of them people who happen to be there.[5] Although this is an ongoing strategy, going back to at least 1972 when the Israeli athletes were attacked during the Munich Olympics, the sheer numbers in the current conflict (nearly 50 during the first year of fighting) was unprecedented (Gross 2003). *Mechabel*—literally, saboteur—refers specifically to a Palestinian and/or Arab terrorist. In Hebrew, there is a distinction between Palestinian or Arab terrorists and "other" terrorists (Korn 2004). *Mevukash*—literally, "wanted"—refers to a Palestinian suspected of terrorist activity. *Dam al hayadaim*—literally, blood on hands—refers to Palestinians who "spilled Jewish blood." It is a justification for "targeted killing" or listing someone as "wanted." *Ptzaza metakteket*—literally, "ticking bomb"—refers to immediate and severe threats to noncombatants and a justification to targeted killing. This special terminology enables asymmetric standards and differential consideration of the legitimacy of the measures taken as a reaction to Palestinians' insurgents.

## TALI FAHIMA TAKES ACTION

For Fahima, overcoming the denial that the "Arabs" are Palestinians with their own national aims and that Palestinians are actually "human beings" was a gradual process. She began by contacting Palestinian and Arab Internet surfers. She then invited a Palestinian man to her home out of what she called "mutual curiosity." The next step she took was to contact Zacharia Zbeidi himself. After many phone calls, she visited Zbeidi in the refugee camp in Jenin. Through this process, Fahima stopped perceiving the Palestinians as a faceless enemy and began to see them as individual human beings.

As she told *Ha'ir*, Fahima stopped believing the Israeli media and rejected her right-wing conservative education. Instead, she used English-language Web sites and started chatting with Arab Web surfers from all over the Middle East, calling herself "the Israeli girl." Although her parents were native Arab speakers, like many second-generation Mizrachi, Fahima did not speak the language. She had to use English Web sites. Although Arabic has a formal status as the second official language of Israel, it is identified with low status. Arabic language is marginalized, as are Arab citizens. To speak Arabic is to mark oneself as an outsider to the state (Brosh 1993).

After exceptionally sizeable telephone bills were noted by the General Security Services, which monitors communication between Israelis and citizens of Arab countries, Fahima was summoned to a local police station in July 2003 for a preliminary interrogation. She told her interrogator that she was too afraid to meet Palestinians or enter the occupied territories. She said that "although she has no doubt that there are also good people in the other side," they terrify her. [6] The interrogator was worried that Palestinians may use Fahima to carry a terror attack in Israel, but she promised to be alert and to contact the authorities if something like that may happen. She also promised not to enter the occupied territories.[7]

A month later, in August 2003, Fahima contacted a General Security Service agent and told him that she met a Palestinian man who told her that he initiated terror attacks against Israeli soldiers. After further persuasion, she also revealed that she had visited Zbeidi in Jenin.[8]

Fahima first heard about Zbeidi, the chief of Jenin's Al-Aqsa Martyrs Brigades, when she read an interview with him in which Zbeidi related how he became an insurgent. Twenty-eight years old at the time and married with a child, Zbeidi was a familiar face in the Israeli media. As a child, he was a protagonist of an Israeli documentary film, *Arna's Children* (2003), which followed him and his friends in their transformation from child actors to terrorists. His face, which was partly blackened by scorch marks left by a bomb that blew up when he was preparing it, his fluent Hebrew, and his terrorist activity made him into a desirable interviewee. Like many other Palestinians, Zbeidi's biography was a combination of terror and criminal activities. When he was a ninth grader, he was shot in the leg as he threw stones at Israeli soldiers during the first intifada. He was hospitalized for 6 months and underwent a series of operations on his leg, which was left permanently shortened. He never returned to school. Instead, his life alternated in and out of the Israeli military prison system. At 15 years of age, he was arrested for the first time for throwing stones and jailed for 6 months. After his release, Zbeidi graduated to Molotov cocktails and was jailed again, this time for 4 years. In prison, he learned Hebrew and became politically active, joining the Fatah.[9] After a brief stint in the Palestinian Authority police, he worked for 2 years illegally in Israel. In 1997, he was caught with a stolen car and incarcerated again. After his release, he returned to the camp and became head of the Jenin al-Aqsa Martyrs Brigades in November 2002.

Fahima told the General Security Service agent that Zbeidi wanted peace and that she did not believe that he could have initiated terror attacks. The agent reminded Fahima that by law Israeli citizens are not allowed to enter the Palestinian Authority, or what is known as zone A.[10] This law not only aims to protect Israeli citizens from endangering their lives but also to prevent them from cooperating with the Palestinians. The agent also tried to take advantage of Fahima's close relationship with Zbeidi and recruit her as an informer but Fahima refused to cooperate.[11] The closer Fahima got to Zbeidi, the more hostile she became toward the service.[12]

After her first visit to Jenin, Fahima decided to live in Zbeidi's house and act as a human shield to protect him from the military's attempts on his life. Through her actions, Fahima helped to transform Zbeidi from another rather faceless target of a *mevukash bachir* (senior wanted person) with "blood on his hands" into a human being, a man with a family and personality:

> This is a person who managed to evade the Israeli Military. It hurts their ego; I think they don't know why they are after him anymore. I am the living proof to the fact that he is not a monster . . . he shouldn't be killed for the sake of the Israeli Military honor, and on the way to kill three-four more citizens, and then to contend they were "seniors." How many seniors do these people [the Palestinians] have? If a public discourse around the liquidation attempts of Zacharia will not emerge, I will try to save him myself.[13]

Fahima defies the very basic justification for security by attributing to the General Security Service contradicting dispositions. By arguing, "I think they don't know why they are after him anymore," Fahima challenges the logic of the security bureaucracy. She suggests that being targeted by the General Security Service and the military is a bureaucratic matter of simply classifying and reclassifying of people. Through classification, argues Handelman (2004: 34), bureaucracy creates categories of people that simultaneously capture, bound, and contains them. Once a person, such as Zbeidi, is labeled by bureaucratic logic into a category, his humanness is erased together with the uniqueness of his case.

However, shortly after Fahima said that "I will try to save him myself," she lost her confidence and said that she realized that she cannot save Zbeidi.[14] Fahima was arrested on August 9, 2004, after she illegally tried to cross a checkpoint to Jenin. She was accused by the General Security Service of planning a terror attack.[15] The imprisonment may have had something to do with her extensive media coverage. Although the authorities publically ignored her actions before she gave the interview to *Ha'ir*, the media coverage may have changed that. It seems that as Fahima became public, she had to be stopped.

## THE INTERROGATION

There is a strange intimacy between the state and the people, argues Aretxaga (2003). The state excises those subjects and practices that question or threaten homogeneous models of territorial sovereignty, which are fundamental to national narratives of harmonious domesticity. This intimacy that filters and subverts modern disciplinary practices and rational technologies of control was noticed previously by Foucault (1979: 129) in his study of modern forms of punishment in which he observed that:

> The training of behavior by a full time-table, the acquisition of habits, the constraints of the body, implies a very special relation between the

individual who is punished and the individual who punishes him. . . . The agent of punishment must exercise total power which no third party can disturb; the individual to be corrected must be entirely enveloped in the power that is being exercised over him. Secrecy is imperative and so too is autonomy at least in relation to this technique of punishment (Foucault 1979: 129).

The "agent of punishment" in Fahima's case was the General Security Service as well as the police. The interrogation protocols show that Fahima was interrogated for long hours, sometimes from noon until late at night. She was held in difficult conditions in isolation and with constant artificial light, was often handcuffed, was called terrorist, and was asked to go back to be a "good Jew."[16] During her arrest, the state used psychological pressure on Fahima by feeding the media with information about her actions. Despite all this, and quite contrary to the way the Palestinian prisoners are treated, Fahima was neither tortured nor beaten. Her family and lawyer were in constant contact with her, and a woman was always present during interrogations. These sessions also usually included coffee and refreshments.

The General Security Service was established in 1948 when the state of Israel was founded. It is responsible by law to protect the Israeli democracy from terror, subversion, and espionage. The organization was initially responsible only for the internal security affairs, but this was soon extended to counterespionage and the monitoring of Israeli Arabs. After 1967, the service also became responsible for the occupied territories. Thus, the General Security Service interrogates both Jews and Palestinians and does so through its three wings. The Arab affairs department is responsible for antiterrorist operations related to alleged Palestinian and Arab terrorists. The Non-Arab affairs department is concerned with other states, including penetrating foreign intelligence services and diplomatic missions in Israel. The Protective security department is responsible for protecting the Israeli government buildings and embassies, defense industries, and the national airline. Jews are mainly interrogated through the Non-Arab affairs department, which is best known as the "Jewish wing." This department is mainly focused on Jewish extreme-right activists who threaten to hurt the Palestinians and the Israeli establishment.

According to Handelman (2004: 30), bureaucratic classification by the General Security Service is based on separation of person from person; that is, making each person into an individuated entity through administrative forces which are external to that person. This process of individuation through bureaucracy generates taxonomies within which the person is made a member of a collective in a particular social category and is isolated in this way for administrative purposes. This classification creates a hierarchy in which the Palestinians are rated beneath any Jews, even those like Fahima who are considered to be unfaithful to the state. Although a

Palestinian may be well behaved and even useful as an informer, he or she will always be an outsider and can never be trusted. On the other hand, a Jew is always an insider, even when he or she is considered to be "confused," "brainwashed," or "crazy." The Jew always has the potential to be re-educated and to be made again into a good citizen who accepts the boundaries that the state has created. The boundary enforced by the state is also supported by the *Halacha,* the Jewish law, according to which a Jew stays a Jew even if he or she converts. By definition, Jews cannot leave the collective.[17]

Fahima tried to defy her interrogators by other means. When a guard refused to light her cigarette, according to Israeli newspapers Fahima allegedly started "yelling and making a scene."[18] She did not hesitate to complain about the quality of food she received in prison,[19] something that a Palestinian detainee would not have done. Yet gradually Fahima was left in a state of powerlessness; with nothing but her body to resist institutional assault, she pretended to be pregnant to enjoy more benefits. The General Security Service used it against her and leaked to the press that she was impregnated by a Palestinian insurgent. By pretending to be pregnant, Fahima took advantage of the symbolic relations between Jewish women and the state that are established through women's very role as "mothers" (Berkovitch 1997). In an interview she explained her defiance:

> As soon as I realized that I was confronting guys from a terror organization and that there are no rules, then everything became cynical. In the interrogations I told them: I do not believe a word you say. If you tell me good morning, I would call God to ask if it's morning. I don't believe you.[20]

Fahima challenges the state by making forbidden comparisons. She compares the Israeli and Nazi bureaucratic systems by allegedly equating her interrogation to the Nazi gas chambers, [21] often called her interrogators Nazis, and compared the actions of the Israeli state in the occupied territories to the Holocaust. She also makes a comparison between Jews and Palestinians. On one occasion she threatened to arrange a terror attack against the General Security Service building and on another she allegedly called in Arabic "kill all the Jews,"[22] words which are highly symbolic for Israelis. Fahima also compares Israeli and Palestinian suffering. She said to one of the prison's commanders "I hope that your family will suffer like I suffer and [that] you'll mourn as sheik Machmud Abu Chalifa is mourned." She was referring to the deputy of Zbeidi who was assassinated by the Israeli forces. Moreover, Fahima applies Tilly's (1985) analogy of war making and state making as organized crime by applying the same language that the state uses against Palestinians and subverting the discourse on who or what is labeled a terror organization. She rejects the state apparatus labeling by arguing that the al-Aqsa Martyrs Brigade is not a terror organization while the General Security Service is. She blames her interrogators for having "blood on their hands" and reduces the service to the level of a gang that "steals and rapes,"[23] arguing that Zbeidi is "better than you."[24]

Her provocations blur yet again the Israeli boundaries and are perceived as a betrayal of the Jewish collective. In Hebrew, the word *bgida* describes both the betrayal of the state and the betrayal of a loved one. In that fashion, Fahima was perceived as betraying both her country and the Jewish collective by allegedly having a romantic affair with a Palestinian man. As Aretxaga (2003) shows, women such as Fahima who remain outside the imaginary of idealized motherhood are a reminder of what cannot be fully controlled in the nation. These women have become the embodiment of a threat, their bodies become the field through which violent statehood not only enacts but draws its power.

According to her lawyer, Fahima's loyalty to the Jewish collective, coupled with her defiance, confused her interrogators who could not figure her out and so could not classify her in any of their binary categories. For example, Fahima was asked by her interrogators if she sees herself marrying Zbeidi and allegedly answered that she will only marry a Jew and thinks that it is hard to be a Palestinian woman because they are badly treated by men.[25] When Fahima was asked why she does not move permanently to Jenin, according to the protocols she answered that she doesn't want to live there because she is part of the Jewish people. Furthermore, she allegedly admitted that she does not feel secure in the occupied territories and without Zbeidi's presence fears for her life.[26] As the only Jew, she said, she felt like an animal in a zoo.[27] She was asked about Mordechai Vanunu[28] and Elchanan Tenenbaum[29] and allegedly called them traitors, saying that, unlike her, they had obligations to the security establishment.[30] According to the protocols, she argued that she confronted Hamas militants and told them that if they attack Israel she would fight them.[31] Furthermore, Fahima supposedly justified attacks on Israeli soldiers in the occupied territories but condemned attacks on settlers and Jewish citizens.[32]

These answers are outside the binary right-left political scheme and so do not fall into the bureaucratic categories of the security apparatus. This confused the authorities because although Fahima acted in a highly political manner, she argued that not everything is political. Fahima told her interrogators that, on the contrary, for her the Palestinian issue was personal and that she was not a peace activist as many believed. The main issue, she said, was Palestinian suffering and Israeli military actions, not peace.[33]

The service did not use all the information it had to destroy Fahima's reputation. This finding, coupled with its efforts to bring her back to the Jewish collective and the fact that the protocols of her trial and interrogations were not classified as confidential, suggests that the service enjoys a degree of the state of exception within the encompassing state of exception.

## THE TRIAL

On September 5, 2004, while Fahima was still under arrest, the Minister of Defense, Shaul Mofaz, signed an administrative detention act that provided 4 months' remand. Administrative detention is an exceptional and radical measure. Quite similar to the Patriot Act of the Bush administration, it is detention without charge or trial, authorized by administrative order rather than by judicial decree. Israel inherited this law from the British Mandate but subsequently restricted the authority to arrest without trial (Hajjar 2005: 59).

According to Agamben (2005), the state of exception is a corrective for the state that cannot correct itself by its ordinary (legal) means. This probably was the initial rationale for the Israeli state of exception, keeping the mandate emergency regulations and using them as the basis for military rule imposed on the Arab population living within the boundaries of the state between 1950 and 1966. That state of exception was canceled, only to be revived after the 1967 War in the occupied territories, and since then it has become permanent. In the occupied territories, the authorities' power to detain without trial is extensive. It is allowed under international law, but, because of the serious injury to due process rights inherent in this measure and the obvious danger of abuse, international law has placed rigid restrictions on its application.

Administrative detention is intended to prevent the danger posed to state security by a particular individual.[34] It radically erases the legal status of the individual, thus producing a legally unnameable and unclassified being. According to Israeli law, those under administrative detention do not even have the status of persons charged with a crime. Neither prisoners nor accused, they are simply "detainees," the object of a pure de facto rule, of a detention that is indefinite not only in the temporal sense but in its very nature, since it is entirely removed from the law and from judicial oversight (Agamben 2005: 4).

Since the second intifada, the number of administrative detainees increased dramatically. By the beginning of March 2003, Israel held more than 1,000 Palestinians in administrative detention. In 2007, Israel held a monthly average of 830 administrative detainees, which was 100 higher than in 2006. However, this measure is rarely used against Jews. Fahima was only the second Jew who was detained, and the first and only woman.[35]

According to the General Security Service's confidential evidence, which is compiled by the apparatus using their own methods and not revealed to the public, and after Fahima's interview with *Ha'ir*, the court determined that Fahima "made up her mind to perform terror acts against Israeli targets and obtain weapon from Palestinian terror activists."[36] The court declared that "her being Jewish, a citizen of Israel may encourage her and Palestinian terror activists to perform terror acts . . . as part of an image victory in the world's public opinion and the Palestinian public." Her arrest was also justified by the argument that Fahima could not be disciplined and threatened. The court argued that "she knew that she was followed . . . Her arrest and knowledge [that she is being followed] did not stop her."[37]

Her arrest was accompanied by statements from politicians and officials and by media spinning orchestrated by the security apparatus. This included occasional leaking of strong accusations. The Minister of Security, Shaul Mofaz, told the media that Fahima posed immediate and tangible danger to the citizens of Israel: "I know perfectly all Fahima's aberrant deeds." Judge Uri Goren, who authorized her arrest and is known for his close connections with the security apparatus,[38] said: "I have reached the conclusion that Tali Fahima is determined to perpetrate a terrorist attack against Israeli targets and to obtain combat material from Palestinian terror activists."[39] It was then reported by the security services that Fahima was linked to a bomb that went off at the Qalandiyah checkpoint. The state attorney contributed to the creation of Fahima's terrorist image when he said, "The confidential evidence that was shown to me revealed a grave and immediate danger to human life."[40]

The judges' statements during the trial, their utter acceptance of the General Security Service accusations, and the discrepancies between the initial accusations and the final conviction raise questions about the involvement of the security system in the democratic legal system. The judges did not challenge the General Security Service, although there were in the past at least two cases in which the service had lied to the court. In 1984, two detained Palestinian hijackers were beaten to death by the General Security Service agents in what became known as the Bus 300 Affair. A government report later revealed that the service chief at the time had ordered the hijackers killed and then lied about it in court. In 1987, the service was found to have lied in court yet again when it extracted a false confession of espionage from an Israeli army officer, Izzat Nafsu, who had been incarcerated for 18 years.[41]

The state of exception, argues Agamben (2005: 10), is a "no man's land" that lies between "civil law and political fact." In other words, the state of exception is the political point at which the juridical stops and a sovereign unaccountability begins. In the Israeli case, the state of exception is where the court and the majority of the public are willing to believe "everything security" and credit the General Security Service despite its record of deceptions.

Because of the lack of unobstructed evidence, the persecution as well as the defense used the media as a major source, especially Fahima's interview to *Ha'ir*.[42] During the last decade, there has been an increase in use of confidential evidence during administrative detention. Customarily, the General Security Service describes the confidential evidence, but for security reasons the defense cannot view the evidence. As a result, the judge is briefed only by one side, and the suspects cannot know exactly what the allegations against them are (Saban et al. 2008). Most lawyers concur that a case in which charges are based on confidential evidence is virtually impossible to try. But in the plea-bargaining process, defense lawyers can maneuver around confidential evidence by arguing that the defendant is not a "real threat" to Israeli security (Hajjar 2005: 221).

Fahima's trial is a good example. Although she was initially accused of undertaking a terror attack, she was eventually indicted for aiding a terrorist organization. Fahima was accused of translating to Zbeidi and fellow insurgents a document that included pictures and details of wanted Palestinian insurgents and which was inadvertently left behind by a soldier during the army raid Crocodile Tears on Jenin in May 2004. However, several members of the brigade, including Zbeidi, have a good command of the Hebrew language while Fahima does not speak Arabic. Furthermore, the document contained mainly photos. Nevertheless, Fahima admitted to the accusation and was charged for assisting the enemy in a time of war by translating a confidential document. Judge Elyakim Rubinstein, who is deeply involved in the security apparatus, argued in his appeal to the supreme court[43] that:

> The accused mother tongue is Hebrew and she served in the military, even if in a minor role, and she is involved in the Israeli society . . . her translation shows a shift from humanitarian help of [establishing] a computer center to allegedly assisting the enemy . . . Together with carrying and shooting a gun we have a dangerous person who is identified with an ideological cause . . .

Judge Rubinstein states that this is not the behavior expected from a member of the collective—that is, someone who "served in the military and is involved in the Israeli society." Against the grain of the interrogation that emphasized the personal aspects of Fahima's actions, the court shifted to politics, finding her "identified with an ideological cause." Certainly, Fahima's arrest and conviction politicized her. After her release from jail, Fahima no longer defined herself as a private person but rather as a political activist. Feeling rejected by Jews, she converted to Islam, lives in a Palestinian village in Israel, stating that she "does not believe in the Israeli state and chose the Palestinian side." She "hopes to marry a Muslim and raise kids who will fight the occupation."[44]

## RE-EDUCATING FAHIMA

In his study of the prison as modern form of punishment, Foucault (1979) argued that modern forms of punishment belong to a political technology of the body aimed at the formation and transformation of "souls"; that is, of subjectivities. In this style of punishment, the subjects are bound to the state not through fear of spectacular punishment but through the production of particular states of mind, inclinations, disposition, and feelings;

that is, through the interiorization of the law. Through delicate calculations, punishment becomes "an art of effects." This art of effects is nothing other than a political art of tactical and strategic use of technologies of power such as forms of knowledge, procedures, and disciplines, applied on the body, which becomes a field of power relations, invested with the power of the state. In this section, I analyze the state's "art of effects," or how the state acted to "re-educate" Fahima.

Because of lack of evidence, the arguments in Fahima's trial were not made on facts but on their interpretation. Therefore, much of the interrogation and trial were based not on Fahima's actions but on her thoughts. It was important to the state that Fahima would accept the state-imposed boundaries by re-transforming into a "good Jew." As a result, much of the interrogation and trial focused on the right definition of "good citizen." In her appeal in September 2004, Fahima's attorney argued that her interrogation had the character of that conducted by "thought police" (*mishteret machshavot*). Fahima, she argued, was questioned about her thoughts more than about her actions. She was told by her interrogators that they would turn her into a "good Jewish woman" and that they would "re-educate her." Fahima complained that she was "brainwashed" by the service. She said that her interrogators gave her history lessons about the Israeli-Palestinian conflict.[45] In December 2, 2004, an interrogator told Fahima that he never met a Jewish Israeli woman who planned to hurt her own people. In December 6, 2004, her interrogator told her that what she was doing was not "normal" for a Jewish Israeli citizen and therefore she was required to explain her acts.

The state embraced a national security interpretation of Fahima's thoughts and actions. This interpretation is based on classifications such as insider/outsider and safe/dangerous. For example, in the beginning of her trial in December 2004, Judge Berliner ruled against moving Fahima to house arrest, because "Fahima has crossed the lines. Her ideological identity made her care for the terrorists rather than the peace of the soldiers of Israel." One journalist, perhaps cynically, aptly titled it: "Fahima is Unfaithful to the State of Israel."[46]

The defense tried to emphasize the human and private nature of the case. Fahima's attorney said, "Tali Fahima does not belong to any organization. She is a young woman who acts alone . . . her relationship with Zbeidi is totally friendly and private." Yet, at the same time, her attorney accepted the state's classification by trying to convince the court that Fahima is indeed a "good Jewish woman" and therefore does not pose a threat to state security:

> A real intention of the appealer to participate in terror acts against the Israeli people to whom she belongs, means that the appealer is willing to hurt her family and friends, who might be among the victims and suggests that she is willing to spend many years in jail and suffer being ostracized from the Israeli society for the rest of her lives.[47]

Presenting Fahima as a "good citizen" played an important role in the judges' verdict who stated that "we see a great importance in her admitting these felonies and especially her positive attitude in court, a great shift from her manner during interrogations and in court in the beginning of this trial."

There were other attempts to sway Fahima into the categories devised by the state. With time, the interrogators managed to create a rift and mistrust between Fahima and Zbeidi. They told Fahima that Zbeidi wanted to become an informer but was declined; also, that he is doing drugs and works for the Hezbullah.[48] The General Security Service convinced Fahima that Zbeidi blames her for assisting killing his people.[49]

In January 2005, Zbeidi was reported to be off the wanted list. As with Fahima, who was forced to reach a plea bargain, Zbeidi was re-educated into a "good Arab" who does not rise against the Israeli state. Ironically, Fahima adopted the rhetoric that was used against her, connecting sex and politics, and blamed Zbeidi for being a "General Security Service whore," after he reached an agreement with the Israeli security system.[50]

## THE PLEA BARGAIN

In December 2005, the court sentenced Fahima to 3 years in prison, which was reduced to 10 months for good behavior and timed served (since she had already served 16 months before her conviction). A plea bargain involves a concession on the part of the defendant to a guilty plea in exchange for reduced charges and/or the sentence being sought. According to Ben-Natan (her lawyer), Fahima regretted the way her actions were perceived but did not regret the actions themselves. She initiated a plea bargain only because she felt that the trial was an injustice.[51]

Fahima's plea bargain included her confession. A confession is usually sufficient to ensure a conviction as long as there is an additional scintilla of evidence (*dvar ma*). Hajjar (2005: 112) states that whereas in the Israeli criminal justice system a confession must pass certain logical tests, in the military court system, or in the case of Fahima in a security trial, the scintilla can be extremely tenuous. It does not have to corroborate the confession or even implicate the accused directly. All it has to show is a possible connection between the accused and the crime. The court has the option to prefer the confession over other evidence and so the practice of judges fortifies the weight and value of confessions. Explaining Fahima's confession, Ben-Natan argued that in a case of a security trial it is impossible to fight the charges because the defendant cannot prove his or her innocence, and therefore it always ends with plea bargains.

The legal definition of accusations such as "contacts with a foreign agent" or "informing the enemy" is broad and ambiguous, and therefore permits the state to decide who is an enemy and who is not. The shift between such categories can be arbitrary. Furthermore, because the state can interpret the defendant actions arbitrarily without the need to prove, the defendant's only option is signing a plea bargain as Fahima did.

Although Fahima was condemned by many Israelis, she was supported by Palestinians. In January 2005, she received an open letter from Jenin's refugee camp inhabitants. The letter praised Fahima for being a "real Palestinian man" and for serving time in jail like "men, warriors and heroes." By symbolically elevating Fahima to the status of man, she received the ultimate honor for "crossing the barrier of fear."[52] While the Israelis degraded Fahima to the level of a whore, the Palestinians upgraded her to the prestigious position of a man. Both societies failed to address the complexity of her character and actions.

## CONCLUSIONS

Let me underscore five points. First, Handelman (2004) argues that bureaucratic classification creates symbolic inclusion, exclusion, and hierarchy. As a Jewish Mizrachi woman of a working class origin with no political affiliation, Fahima was perceived as an abnormality and as "crossing the lines" of the Jewish collective and the Israeli state. Because she acted on her own, Fahima blurred the state's binary logic, which maintains that everything is ideological and in this way challenged its security rationale. The security system could not classify her as an insider or outsider. Therefore, much of the interrogation and trial focused on her thoughts and on the attempt to re-educate her as a good Jewish woman to categorize her as part of the Jewish collective.

Modern mechanisms of punishment, Foucault (1979) observed, are aimed at transforming subjectivities, at reconfiguring identity. However, sometimes this can backlash. Indeed, Fahima was not remodeled by the state apparatus into "a good Jew" as was the plan but rather into a left-wing political activist. By doing so, the state bureaucracy was now able to at last classify her. Fahima proved this classification in March 2008 when her story took another twist when she took part in a mourning ceremony for the Palestinian killer of eight yeshiva students in Jerusalem, an act one prominent publicist described as "Giving Israel the finger."[53]

The second point is methodological. Despite the fact that it was a security trial, it was not classified as confidential. Could this be as a result of the minor charges compared to the initial severe allegations? Or could it be an indication of a deliberate strategy on the part of the General Security Service to give publicity to Fahima's case and through this teach the public a lesson? After all, very few Jews in Israel have been convicted of treason. Or could it be, as Garland (1990) has noted, that neither punishment nor penal history can be wholly understood in terms of rationality?

Third, the Israeli case raises a more universal question: what are the effects of a permanent state of exception and its consequences? The Israeli state of exception, based on the Mandate emergency regulations, has existed since 1950, first against the Arab population living within the boundaries of the state, and since 1967 also against the Palestinians in the occupied territories. It seems that it is its permanence that enables so much extrajudicial activity in the occupied territories (e.g., those of the military courts, the activities of the General Security Service).

Fourth, in this light can the state maintain its integrity? The integrity of Israel has been intertwined with issues of security and, like Carl Schmitt's Germany, the security state and state of exception are braided together with the Jewish nation. Therefore, security, the state of exception, and the nation cannot be separated. The General Security Service is perceived as ubiquitous, possessing an omnipotent power. The case of Fahima is a good example, which explains why the state through the General Security Service preferred to try to bring her back into the nation rather than excommunicating her. In that sense, Israel departs from Agamben and is closer to Carl Schmitt. Rather than seeing the rule of law as something that must be followed for its own sake as a way of ensuring the integrity of the state, Schmitt argues that the rule of law may *prevent* a polity from defending itself in the event of a serious political crisis, and that the capacity of a ruler to maintain the very existence of the state may depend on that ruler *not* being bound by the rules. In fact, it is the most distinctive power of a sovereign—not simply an incidental and unusual capacity—that he has the power to suspend the law (Schmitt 1985; Scheppele 2004).

Fifth, the Israeli case is a good example not to one state of exception but to multiple degrees of states of exception within the state of exception; that is, degrees of state of exception within the encompassing state of exception (degrees to which the power of state of exception are used within the state of exception, such as the powers of the General Security Service, powers of the military, degrees to which trials are openly conducted, and the operation of military courts). In this sense, this research yields insights that transcend the Israeli context.

## NOTES

1. I thank Vida Bajc, Don Handelman, Art Stinchcombe, Ilan Saban, Smadar Ben-Natan, Christian Karner, and the anonymous reviewer for their useful comments.
2. From the interview Fahima gave to *Ha'ir* newspaper on March 18, 2004.
3. *Ha'ir* March 18, 2004. . http://www.fresh.co.il/dcforum/Scoops/97695.html. (accessed 10 November 2010).
4. *Ha'ir*, March 18, 2004. http://www.fresh.co.il/dcforum/Scoops/97695.html. (accessed 10 November 2010).

5. According to B'Tselem, since the second intifada and until October 2008, a total of 232 Palestinians were killed in this way, including 154 civilians.
6. Interrogation protocol, July 2, 2003.
7. Interrogation protocol, July 2, 2003.
8. Interrogation protocol, July 2, 2003.
9. A Palestinian political party and the largest faction of the Palestine Liberation Organization.
10. After the Oslo Accord in 1995, the West Bank was divided into three zones, called A, B, and C. Zone A is under a complete Palestinian control, and this included the towns of Jenin, Nablus, Tulkarim, Kalkilya, Ramallah, and Bethlehem. Zone B, which includes 450 Palestinian towns and villages, has a Palestinian control of civil matters, while Israel retained control over security issues. Zone C is under Israeli control, included uninhabited areas, Jewish settlements and military installations.
11. Ynet Luvitz, Vered July 28, 25: http://www.ynet.co.il/articles/0,7340, L-3119244,00.html. (accessed 10 November 2010).
12. Interrogation protocols August 26, 2003 and July 29, 2004.
13. *Ha'ir* weekly, March 18, 2004. http://www.fresh.co.il/dcforum/Scoops/97695. html. (accessed 10 November 2010).
14. Police interrogation, May 28, 2004. Also in an interview with Fahima, Galei tzahal radio station (the military radio station), May 31, 2004.
15. Ynet Luvitz, V. July 28, 25: http://www.ynet.co.il/articles/0,7340,L-3119244,00. html. (accessed 10 November 2010).
16. Interrogation protocol, August 19, 2004.
17. Therefore, the official religious authorities make an effort to bring women who married Palestinian men back to Judaism and to living within the Jewish state. See, for example, the activities of Yad le'Achim which is actively involved in the efforts to bring women who married Palestinians back to the Jewish collective. According to this organization, the Israeli police and military are often involved in these attempts. See http://www.yadleachim.co.il. (accessed 10 November 2010).
18. *Haaretz*, September 20, 2004. http://www.acri.org.il/story.aspx?id=1187. (accessed 10 November 2010).
19. *Haaretz*, February 10, 2005. http://www.acri.org.il/story.aspx?id=1187. (accessed 10 November 2010).
20. Weizz and Karn, i 2005. http://www.ynet.co.il/articles/0,7340,L-3035076,00. html. (accessed 10 November 2010).
21. Interrogation protocol, December 9, 2004.
22. *Haaretz*, September 20, 2004. http://www.acri.org.il/story.aspx?id=1187. (accessed 10 November 2010).
23. Interrogation protocol, August 18, 2004.
24. Interrogation protocol, August 17, 2004.
25. Interrogation protocol, December 24, 2004.
26. Interrogation protocol, August 31, 2004.
27. Interrogation protocol, May 25, 2004.
28. A former nuclear technician who exposed Israel's nuclear weapons program to the British press in 1986. After he was kidnapped by Mossad agents to Israel, he was convicted of treason and spent 18 years in jail, including 11 years in solitary confinement. Vanunu converted to Christianity.
29. A reserve Israeli general who was kidnapped by the Hezbollah in October 2000 during drug trafficking. He was released in January 2004 in exchange for 400 Palestinian prisoners.
30. Interrogation protocol, August 30, 2004.

31. Interrogation protocol, August 16, 2004.
32. Interrogation protocol, July 2, 2003.
33. Interrogation protocol, December 6, 2004.
34. B'Tselem, the Israeli information center for human rights in the occupied territories. http://www.btselem.org/english/about_btselem/index.asp. (accessed 10 November 2010).
35. The first detainee was the extreme right-wing activist Noam Federman, who was accused of involvement in an anti-Arab underground and was incarcerated without a trial for 9 months. Since Fahima's arrest, at least 16 more Jews were put in administrative detention, all of them men and from the extreme right-wing.
36. Weitz and Karni 2005. http://www.ynet.co.il/articles/0,7340,L-3035076,00. html. (accessed 10 November 2010).
37. Court protocol, September 5, 2004.
38. Oren, A. http://www.haaretz.com/hasite/spages/1093961.html. June 19, 2009. http://www.haaretz.com/hasite/spages/1093961.html. (accessed 10 November 2010).
39. Fahima is not the first Jewish woman who was accused of assisting a terror attack. Angelica Yosefov, a 19-year-old Jewish newcomer from the former Soviet Union, was sentenced to 18 years in jail in 2002 for assisting her Palestinian boyfriend in carrying out a terror attack.
40. Weitz and Karni 2005. http://www.ynet.co.il/articles/0,7340,L-3035076,00. html. (accessed 10 November 2010).
41. See, for example, "What happened on Bus 300?" The Jerusalem Post, December 28, 2001. http://www.jonathanpollard.org/2001/122801.htm. (accessed 10 November 2010).
    See also Gorali, M. "A dirty war at the top of the Shin Bet," Haaretz, November 7, 2002. http://www.mafhoum.com/press4/118P53.htm. (accessed 10 November 2010).
42. See, for example, court protocol, September 5, 2004.
43. Court protocol, January 24, 2005. http://www.nevo.co.il/Psika_word/elyon/050801.doc. (accessed 10 November 2010).
44. http://www.mako.co.il/news-military/security/Articleb25bae4e2f79421004. htm. (accessed 10 November 2010).
45. NRG. August 19, 2004 http://www.nrg.co.il/online/1/ART/771/081.html. (accessed 10 November 2010).
46. Shihor-Aharonson, A. July 28, 2005. http://www.nrg.co.il/online/1/ART/964/165.html.
47. Court protocol, September 2004.
48. Interrogation protocol, December 2, 2004.
49. Interrogation protocol, December 19, 2004.
50. *Haaretz*, July 24, 2008. http://www.haaretz.co.il/hasite/spages/1005267. html. (accessed 10 November 2010).
51. Interview with Smadar Ben-Natan, December 23, 2008.
52. http://www.kedma.co.il/index.php?id=458. (accessed 10 November 2010).
53. Ynet, December 3, 2008. http://www.ynetnews.com/articles/0,7340, L-3518097,00.html. (accessed 10 November 2010).

# 4 Rethinking National Security Policies and Practices in Transnational Contexts
## Border Resistance

*Kathleen Staudt*[1]

## INTRODUCTION

Since September 11, 2001 (9/11), several U.S. policy "wars" have converged—the War on Drugs, the War on Terror, and an undeclared war on immigrants—to heighten state security apparatus at the U.S.-Mexico border. In 2003, the United States consolidated major state security agencies into a mega-agency called the Department of Homeland Security (DHS). The "wars," and the fears thereby evoked, build on a long, growing tradition of security rationales to protect against external and internal threats. Tirman cites parallels between the National Security Act of 1947 that created the bureaucracy to fight the Cold War and the DHS: "a security culture evolved that emphasized worst-case scenarios, embedded secrecy, monitoring and occasionally harassed domestic dissenters, rewarded allies in Congress, and insisted on its primacy in U.S. governance" (2004: 10).

Security policies and practices are contested at the terrain of the U.S.-Mexico border. Alternative discourses claim to enhance security, one emanating from the capital city center, while the other, from an alliance of local government officials, cognizant of border people's interdependence with Mexico, and of human rights and faith-based activists at the border who call for attention to a broader approach to security that reduces poverty and enhances safety in everyday life on binational bases. Despite the well-funded, heavy state-level security practices, border people use their voices to resist in semidemocratic spaces to delay and press for changes. Activists apply principles associated with federalism, constitutionality, civil disobedience, cost-effectiveness, environmental sustainability, and human rights at subnational levels of governance to argue for human security and to challenge existing practices. In so doing, border people contest the guarded way that borders and border security have been used in classic international relations (IR), part of the political science discipline, opening the term to claim a spatial location that welcomes formal and informal cooperation across borders as a strategy for regional prosperity.

In this chapter, I analyze human rights activism at the nearly 2,000-mile-long U.S.-Mexico border, focusing primarily on the Texas-Mexico portion that makes up half of the space. This chapter is divided into two parts. In the first part, I focus on the border context, activism, and resistance. I begin with the nationwide challenges to Congressman James Sensenbrenner's harsh reform proposal of 2005 that galvanized activism in many places, including the border, and then I move to activism that challenged immigration harassment and the border wall through protests, negotiations, and electoral campaigns against the costly latitude that the U.S. legislative branch gave to the executive branch in the Secure Fence Act of 2006, which authorized the construction of 670 miles through the end of President George W. Bush's administration. In the second section of this essay, I analyze alternate conceptions of national and human security, their strategies, and levels of operation. Although little convergence exists between these conceptions, both contribute to ever-enlarging governments and ongoing securitization processes to manage globalized threat and poverty.

## UNDERSTANDING THE CONTEXT

Historically, U.S. border cities and towns developed economic interdependence with northern Mexican cities and towns. The border line divides relatives, friends and coworkers, and through most of border city history, crossing north to south and south to north has been routine and frequent. Immigrants' human faces, rather than those packaged in media portrayals, are part of the lived, ever-present reality in border locales. In Texas cities and towns like El Paso, Laredo, Brownsville, Del Rio, and Eagle Pass, Mexican-heritage people make up 80% or more of the population. Although no consensus exists among Mexican Americans about immigration, only a minority support harsh immigration policies.[2] Many border residents share Catholic religious values, which articulate a strong human rights position on immigration, grounded in faith. When Los Angeles Cardinal Roger Mahoney spoke to an open-air crowd of thousands near El Paso's Annunciation House, which has offered temporary hospitality to 90,000 migrants since 1978, he repeatedly stated that we see "Jesus in the immigrant."[3]

The border context is more complex than other locales due to its location on an international boundary line. Poverty levels are high in El Paso, like other parts of the border, and the per capita income is approximately 60% of national per capita income (Staudt 1998). Such figures make semirural areas and small towns desperate for funding, such as in Raymondville in south Texas where county government generates money for each immigrant detainee in the private detention facilities (in Staudt 2009).

With the militarization of the border (Dunn 1996), ongoing since the 1980s and augmented with the border blockades in the early 1990s, the lines of local, state, and federal and national accountability are mixed. The border economy and development strategy have long been tied to Mexico, including the export-processing zones where factories at the northern Mexican border pay minimum wage rates of US$4 daily. However, the funding associated with the Border Security Industrial Complex (BSIC) and U.S. Base Realignment and Closure (BRAC) committee, putting scores of thousands of new military families in the region, have come to represent a competing economic development paradigm. These federal government investments create jobs and deepen border stakes in state-centric security policies. The U.S. Department of Defense, under BRAC, closed some U.S. military bases and reassigned troops and their families. The transnational strategy requires relatively open borders, while the national border security strategy controls borders and delays the movement of people and goods. According to DHS annual reports, each year the El Paso ports of entry alone monitor huge numbers of northbound crossings: 40 million pedestrians, 16 million automobiles, and almost one million trucks.[4]

The federal government has been spreading resources to southwestern universities to set up "national security" and "intelligence" programs, complete with scholarships, trips, and permanent courses that connect graduates in high-unemployment, high-poverty areas with middle-class jobs in the national security complex. The University of Texas at El Paso cohosts an annual Border Security conference with Congressman Silvestre Reyes, Chairman of the House Intelligence Committee, during which scores of private contractors show their wares: high-tech surveillance equipment, heat sensors, and human detection monitoring systems. Not surprisingly, a large part of his campaign contributions come from the BSIC.[5]

## National Versus Local Perspectives

About the U.S.-Mexico border, official national security discourse paints pictures of dangerous invaders (immigrants, terrorists) and scourges (drugs) that cross the border without authorization. Border control strategies rely on militarization and criminalization, increasing national-level police and guard presence, and monitoring places where immigrants live or work for detention and deportation. Such strategies backfire in many border locales where people have been accustomed to crossing the border for work, visiting friends and relatives, shopping, and living. People's status varies from that of legal immigrant and undocumented to citizen and/or the "foreign-born" who become naturalized citizens.

Like all states in the U.S. federal system of government, locally elected and appointed law enforcement leaders develop policy and practice in cities and counties. In the state of Texas, elected city officials appoint police chiefs, while voters elect county sheriffs in partisan elections empowering border people with the potential to utilize democratic tools in a pluralist political system, albeit an unequal pluralist system with a top-heavy federal presence and national security machinery. For example, state security apparatus normalizes surveillance in federal checkpoints at interstate high-way checkpoints as people head into the interior where agents aim to inter-dict undocumented immigrants and drugs.

Before the tragic attacks of 9/11, undocumented immigrant entry had been treated as minor civil and criminal offences, only sporadically imple-mented in response to changing economic demands for labor (especially low-cost, flexible labor) in the U.S. economy since the 1930s. People migrate primary for work, safety, family, and security. Border control policies of the early 1990s, such as Operation Hold the Line (El Paso) and Operation Gatekeeper (San Diego), diverted undocumented crossers away from urban areas to unpopulated desert regions in Arizona and New Mexico where hundreds perish annually. Since 1994, a total of 4,600 immigrants have died attempting to cross the 2,000-mile U.S.-Mexico border in its treacher-ous terrain (Dunn 2009).

Large U.S. border cities are "safe," as measured by Federal Bureau of Investigation's serious crime statistics (felonies to include murder and sex-ual assault) rather than misdemeanor crimes (such as domestic violence, rampant across the U.S [Staudt 2008c]). Both El Paso and San Diego (17 miles from the border) rank in the top 10 safest big cities in the United States, as measured annually by Congressional Quarterly. El Paso is the largest U.S. city at the Mexico border. Yet at the border, the security state is virtually oblivious to violence against women, the femicide in Ciudad Juárez, and the grim poverty that grips half the population at the northern border of Mexico and a quarter of the border population on the U.S. side (Staudt 2008c). One exception is Immigration and Customs Enforcement (ICE) programming since 2003 to halt "sex tourism" with young women and girls (and boys), a practice once normalized as a right of passage or privilege to anyone with enough money to purchase sex, likely tapping only the tip of the iceberg. Overall, however, national border security has little to do with local realities.

Cities in the border region contain a heavy presence of national secu-rity personnel: U.S. Border Patrol and ICE; Bureau of Alcohol, Tobacco, Firearms, and Explosives; Drug Enforcement Agency; occasional National Guard units; and the Federal Bureau of Investigation (among others). U.S. vigilante groups, loosely identified as Minutemen, came and went, less wel-come at the Texas border than in the vast unsettled areas near the Arizona border (Doty 2009). Texas Governor Rick Perry periodically funds private contractors who provide WebCam surveillance opportunities to those who wish to augment the state security apparatus from their own homes.[6] In 1 month, the $2 million grant attracted nearly "2 million hits, 1 drug bust, 6 illegal entries."[7]

Over the last century, the majority of border residents lacked strong civic capacity. Anglo settlers, although always a minority, managed to acquire the reigns of political-economic power (Romo 2005) in the dom-inant English-language, hegemonic system into which upwardly mobile residents sought entry on mainstream assimilation terms. Texas poll taxes deterred low-income people from exercising their franchise rights. With the rising civil rights movement of the late 20th century, political opportunities opened in the 1970s with the move to district-based local elections and the emergence of social justice organizations. In the following text, I outline the transformation of muted border voices to service and legal outreach and to the more recent mobilization among youth, organized social justice activists, environmental groups, and locally elected officials who make connections with national institutions and advocacy organizations. The analysis is based on participant observation and many years of research at the border, as documented in previous books and articles.

## GROWING CIVIC CAPACITY: MOBILIZATION AND RESISTANCE

The southwestern United States, once part of Mexico, was settled by Anglos (the term for non-Hispanic white people) over the last century and a half, but most Texas border communities comprise overwhelmingly Hispanic majority populations of people with Mexican heritage. Hispanic majorities only began to exert stronger civic capacity in the 1970s and thereafter, electing more Hispanic people to public office (Staudt and Coronado 2002; Staudt and Stone 2007). Even among many Anglos, residents identify as *fronterizos y fronterizas* (borderlanders) (Martínez 1996).

In the early 1990s, the legally oriented Border Rights Coalition (BRC) allied with students of Bowie High School in El Paso over a lawsuit filed around students' daily harassment from Border Patrol agents. *The Time Has Come* is a documentary that memorializes that struggle. Literary work expanded on the everyday profiling of people who "looked Mexican," the majority of borderlanders (for example, Sáenz 1992; Nathan 1986). With support from the American Friends Service Committee, the BRC later documented human rights abuses by the Border Patrol.

Various nonprofit organizations offer legal advice to immigrants seeking naturalization, to unaccompanied minor immigrant children, and to immigrant victims of domestic violence. However worthy these efforts, the nonprofit service organizations exercise caution about open, public advocacy or the mobilization of large numbers of people at the grassroots level as a way to alter power relations.

Within the last quarter century, several grassroots organizations cultivated leaders and a wide base of support with human rights and social justice discourse as proponents of human security: everyday safety, decent-paying jobs, and freedom from arbitrary law enforcement. Here I focus on two such organizations, one set of faith-based and the other, human rights groups. Additionally, loose networking occurs along the

1,000-long Texas-Mexico border with the No Border Wall and Border Ambassadors alliances.

In El Paso, two faith-based organizations are affiliated with the Industrial Areas Foundation (IAF), an Alinsky-style social justice organization. They are linked to other Texas IAF groups, including one at the south Texas border, Valley Interfaith. The first is the El Paso Interreligious Sponsoring Organization (EPISO), a coalition of more than 20 Catholic congregations. A second sister Alinsky-style organization—Border Interfaith—represents 12 congregations, including Protestant, Catholic, Reformed Judaism, and Buddhist communities. At the Texas level, the IAF Education Fund pursues policy research and reform on several priority policy issues that percolate, bottom up, from the grassroots organizations. One priority area is immigration for which defensive postures are in place.

In the state of Texas, with its decade-long, one-party rule, Republicans have proposed harsh anti-immigrant measures; one such measure, for example, is to end birth-right citizenship, which is likely to incur costly legal challenges given U.S. Constitution's guarantees since the Civil War. Yet the moderate wing of the Texas Republican Party is attentive to business constituencies that seek low-cost labor supplies. They also want to avoid the negative consequences associated with virulent anti-immigrant measures passed in other states.

The Border Network for Human Rights (BNHR) is a grassroots mobilization organization with constituencies willing and ready to risk marching as visible forces in the region, despite the periodic atmosphere of surveillance and intimidation. An outgrowth of the smaller, narrower the BRC, the BNHR spawned the Border Task Force, consisting of elected officials and prominent community leaders, to educate state and national representatives with border voices. In late 2007, it cohosted a large conference on border immigration enforcement reforms.[8] In addition, the elected officials among Border Task Force members ally with other elected officials in the Texas Border Coalition, sharing experiences, lobbying, and filing lawsuits against the federal government such as what occurred over the border wall.

Together, these faith-based and human rights mobilization groups provide the organized capacity to engage with local officials using the power of numbers, compelling discourse, and trained leaders. The aforementioned specialized nonprofit organizations continue, focused on legal actions or public service. The Paso del Norte Civil Rights Project, affiliated with the Texas Civil Rights Project, files lawsuits for systemic change, while the nonprofit Las Americas Immigrant Advocacy Center and the Diocesan Migrant and Refugee Services provide legal services to immigrants. In most cases, organized power influences the local policies and tempers border policy enforcement but exercises more limited voice in national policy. However, BNHR leaders network both with like-minded organizations in Texas and the southwest border region and with national immigration-rights organizations and think-tanks that advocate policy change. Moreover, the Border Task Force sends local leaders and elected officials to Washington, D.C. periodically to express reality-based border voices with representatives, including those that serve on relevant congressional committees.

## The Spark to Resistance

After 9/11, with the use of threatening figures regarding 12 million "illegal aliens" in the United States, fearmongering grew, and politicians introduced immigration-control policies that would not only criminalize immigrants and their families but also those who assisted immigrants, such as teachers and clergy (best epitomized by Representative James Sensenbrenner's House Bill 4437 of 2005) passed by a majority of the Republican-controlled House of Representatives. Representative Sensenbrenner's bill provoked a groundswell nationwide reaction in March 2006, generating protest marches in large cities of up to 500,000 people in mainstream locations such as Chicago and Dallas. The groundswell also occurred at the border (CNN 2006; Watanabe & Becerra 2006).

March 31, César Chávez Day, is a state holiday in Texas, although the 2006 school calendar required attendance for public school students. On that day, high school youth "walked out" of their schools, to the surprise and shock of El Pasoans and school administrators, accustomed to a quiescent student population. Youth joined the usual cast of characters who celebrated the civil rights hero, with combined forces walking from the downtown San Jacinto Plaza (named after a Republic of Texas hero from the 19th century) to the Mexico border five blocks away. Students brought flags (Mexican and U.S.) and signs with words like "We are not Terrorists" and "These Hands are American." Soon thereafter, the BNHR organized several marches with the rallying cry "We are not the Enemy!" on April 10 and May 1, in loose coordination with other human and immigrant rights groups nationwide. Labor Day occurs on May 1 worldwide, with some national exceptions like the United States. The May 1 effort articulated multiple goals: political muscle along with consumer and work boycotts, tied to a tongue-in-cheek, humorous Hollywood film *A Day Without a Mexican* to illustrate the centrality of immigrant labor in the U.S. economy. Although Mexicans scrupulously avoid crossing the border to shop in El Paso, boycott participation was mixed and national consequences, meager. With a 3-week interval, organizers had barely enough to time to mobilize efforts; meanwhile, too, school administrators locked down campuses to avoid student "walkouts."

After May 1 events, border groups focused on local action, including attendance at a circus-like hearing by Representative Sensenbrenner, with a hostile audience and the broad spectrum of local and state elected officials denouncing his bill to a hungry press. El Paso's Sheriff Leo Samaniego and Police Chief Richard Wiles testified to opposing sides of the Sensenbrenner committee, in favor and against the bill, respectively. Human rights activists know that the power structure is rarely monolithic, even at local levels.

## Strategic Local Organizing

Failing to pass Representative Sensenbrenner's bill in its Senate version, the U.S. Congress passed and authorized other control strategies, such as the construction of euphemistically named "fences" along the border, additional high-tech surveillance technology along the border, and tripled numbers of Border Patrol officers. The federal government also made pass-through money available to states and local law enforcement at the border to monitor and help deport undocumented immigrants, in the name of eliminating the crossing of "terrorists and drug traffickers," known with a sports-like military metaphor Operation Linebacker in Texas (Staudt 2008a).

With the federal pass-through money in 2006, El Paso County Sheriff Samaniego authorized his deputies to set up automobile checkpoints in minor roads, especially in the *colonias* (unplanned settlements outside the city limits). Deputies stopped cars and asked not only for licenses and proof of insurance but also for Social Security numbers and proof of citizenship. During El Paso's checkpoint period, people worried about sending children to school. Priests reported that parishioners asked them to store food in churches so that they could avoid traveling to grocery stores. In less than a year of these enforcement practices, sheriff deputies' collaboration with DHS personnel resulted in the deportation of more than 800 people, breaking up families and increasing their insecurities, yet the deputies captured less than a kilo of marijuana and no terrorists (detailed in Staudt 2008). Faith-based activists, who couch their issue agendas in "family" terms, judged efforts to be family-threatening, poverty-evoking policies that induced insecurity. Members of EPISO, Border Interfaith, and BNHR provided testimonials of their experiences in public forums covered by the press. One Border Interfaith citizen told an electoral forum of 400 that sheriff deputies stopped him seven times in 3 months as he drove his grandchildren to school.

An alliance of human rights and social justice organizations petitioned, protested these actions, and filed lawsuits against the county sheriff's policy. Sheriff Samaniego negotiated agreements with border social justice organizations to end the practices. Given the distance that often exists between a policy and its enforcement, some sheriff deputies continued their punitive practices, violating their own department's policy, but civil society oversight continued to make these illegal practices visible.

The BNHR and IAF organizations sponsored candidate forums for El Paso's 2008 election for the new county sheriff. With hundreds present at each forum, along with local media coverage, the 12 candidates responded to pointed questions that they would no longer pursue immigration enforcement-like practices. Instead, they would follow El Paso Police Department policy to encourage victims, whether citizens or not, to report crime in a nonintimidating atmosphere. As Police Chief Wiles stated, in discourse evoking the separate functions of federal government, "If the IRS wants us to knock on doors of those who don't pay their taxes, we don't want to do that either."[9] Former Police Chief Wiles ran for sheriff, winning both the Democratic primary in March 2008 and the November 2008 election.

Local border activists reacted to human rights abuses that induced insecurities. For immigrants and some Mexican American citizens who "look like" immigrants, the atmosphere sometimes smacked of a police state. The Paso del Norte Civil Rights Project won its motion for a preliminary injunction against the nearby southern New Mexico Otero County sheriffs who stopped, searched, and seized people in relation to yet-another intriguing metaphor, Operation Stone Garden. Activists increasingly include immigration and border wall issues in their organizational work.

After Congress passed the Secure Fence Act of 2006, DHS aimed to increase fencing from the approximately 100 miles already in place to 670 miles by 2008. These barriers ranged from vehicle and fence-like mesh structures to solid wall. The costs ranged from $2 million to $3 million per mile, with outliers like parts of California to acquire land, $16 million per mile, not including subsequent maintenance costs.[10] Along the 2,000-mile U.S.-Mexico border, 370 miles of fence was built in 2008 alone, and the price tag has increased. Under the Obama administration, Homeland Security Secretary Janet Napolitano froze construction of the fence in 2010 on cost grounds.

Empowered by resolutions from locally elected bodies, including the County Commissioners Court, County Attorney José Rodríguez joined alliances with other Texas border locally elected officials in the Texas Border Coalition. Together, they filed a lawsuit in 2008 against then Secretary of the DHS, Bush administration political appointee Michael Chertoff, to halt border fence building because of the way that congressional waivers to DHS violated some 30 other hard-fought laws in place (and potentially countless other state and local laws and local ordinances, should Chertoff use his discretion). Several environmental groups and local government entities joined: local water irrigation districts (for blocking eight canals that provide water to farmland) and the Native American Tigua government (for impeding access to farms and ceremonial sites). Rodríguez claimed that Chertoff's actions represented "an unconstitutional delegation of authority" because the constitutional separation of powers was threatened in Chertoff's discretionary actions. Although U.S. District Judge Frank Montalvo dismissed the lawsuit, the judgment was appealed.[11]

The federal government pushed forward with the wall, dividing and confiscating people's land (in areas near the meandering border river, the Rio Grande). The University of Texas at Brownsville was slated for a fence/wall to run through its campus, despite university president Julieta García's outcries, like those of Brownsville's "No Border Wall" activists. She negotiated a settlement with the DHS that prohibits the fence/wall. In El Paso, environmental activist Judy Ackerman exercised civil disobedience, blocking the construction in Rio Bosque Wetlands Park for 7 hours but was arrested and charged with trespassing. As headlines proclaimed, "Ackerman trespassed, but it's Chertoff who is breaking the law."[12]

## Summary Reflection, with National Implications

Texas border communities have challenged, criticized, and resisted fence-building efforts with a surprising alliance of locally elected officials and social justice community organizations, from the eastern city of Brownsville to the far-west Texas city of El Paso. They have challenged national security discourse and practices, and defended their human security with a mix of arguments that draw on human rights, human security, federalism, constitutionality, and faith-based principles. Elected officials are also aware that local businesses depend on Mexican shoppers in the interdependent border communities. Both the El Paso City Council and the County Commissioners Court passed resolutions against stepped-up enforcement, stopping short of declaring the place a sanctuary city (as did San Francisco) but empowering officials to speak and advocate for the autonomy seemingly granted in a federal system of government and for the local law enforcement decisions to avoid involvement in federal enforcement. The city of El Paso tried but failed to prevent access permits for private contractors to lengthen the wall in the El Paso area.

At the border, binational economies and societies are interdependent, giving local government officials and nongovernmental organizations deep stakes in cooperation at local levels. Social justice activists, challenging the state-centric securitization processes, used a variety of strategies available in a democracy, from lawsuits and civil disobedience and marches, to electoral candidates and engagement with their representatives. Activists understood that national security policies run counter to human rights and security principles, perhaps best illustrated most recently with the summer 2008 ICE policy to check the documents for people in vehicles, including buses, of those who flee hurricane zones near the Texas-lined Gulf of Mexico. For the undocumented, the likely effects would be deportation, family separation, and, more chillingly, people's refusal to leave emergency zones for fear of deportation. More and more people are criminalized, netted, and deported or detained in internment camps in Arizona, New Mexico, and South Texas, under contract with private corporations.

In the 2008 Border Patrol's high-profile, stepped-up workplace raid campaigns all over the United States, working undocumented parents are deported, thus separating families from their children, many of whom, born on U.S. soil, are citizens. Deportations under the Obama administration increased in 2010. Without active human rights groups, such as those at the border, harsh policies like these go on without local monitoring that could reduce insecurity-inducing tactics like these. All over, immigration policy enforcement increases racial profiling, as personal characteristics, such as speaking English with an accent or "looking Mexican" (similar to 80% of El Paso's population), make people suspect in the eyes of authorities (Slevin 2010).

Local activism, such as that analyzed earlier, is a necessary condition for the respect of human rights and security, especially protection from family separation, the opportunity to work, and life without fear and intimidation that might lead to detention and deportation. Concurrently, local activism at the border seeks to maintain the ostensible federal system of governance and the constitutional separation of powers. Yet local activism, without national constituency support, remains a limited means to defend people from state and reform national policies involving immigration and state security. With the repetition of attack fears recalling 9/11, state security policies and practices may supersede human security. And in the semidemocracy of limited pluralism, some voices are more powerful than others, long understood at the border.

## THEORIZING STATE AND HUMAN SECURITY POLICIES AND PRACTICES

At the border, we see two kinds of security policies and practices. One is state-centric, focusing on national security and using militarist and criminalizing strategies to control people and their movement. Some of these people evoke fear from which protection is sought: drug traffickers, terrorists, and criminals. Another set of policies and practices are local, drawing on binational and international human rights and human security concerns. As analyzed earlier, these local activists also challenge central government security machinery in a federal system of governance and assert constitutional rules that authorize locally elected officials to make policy and protect their community, expecting the federal government to respect existing laws.

Human security can be conceptualized as "freedom from fear and freedom from want" (Floyd 2007: 39)—the ostensible policy agenda of good governance but one far from the practices of many governments and their spending priorities. From global or binational perspectives, poverty and the search for lives free of violence (including women's search) propel immigrants to cross borders, yet national security policies, bounded within borders, is state-centric. Human security policies address both nationals (citizens) and foreign nationals. Since 1994, a total of 4,600 immigrants have died attempting to cross the 2,000 mile U.S.-Mexico border in its treacherous terrain (Dunn 2009). U.S. security policies seem to drive these death rates by channeling immigrants to cross in deserts. This section of the essay examines the sources and levels of security policies and practices.

National security and human security principles emanate from different sources, operate at different levels, and use different strategies. National security policies, which expand and contract in different historical eras, are state-centric, operate at national levels, and utilize crime control and military tools as their weapons. Human security policies operate at individual, community, state, and global levels, using a variety of approaches: social insurance or social security, welfare, public safety, human rights, and economic redistribution. This variety of human security approaches forces analysts to 'unpack' the state and its multiple agencies and departments that implement human policies in a federal system of governance, rather than view the state as a monolithic entity guarding "us" against "others." IR discourse treats security policy as coherent within a monolithic state, albeit acting in concert with defense and homeland security agencies (elsewhere known as interior agencies).

Wars on drugs, crime, and terror have consumed U.S. security policies for decades, widening even more after 9/11 to include immigrants. Official and rhetorical wars, without doubt, induced an ominous, broadened securitization process, perhaps stronger than the 1947–1989 Cold War era. State-centric national security policies have militarized and criminalized large amounts of territory and numbers of people, resulting in growth for bureaucracy and in public contracts to private security, technology, and prison corporations with vested interests in expanded securitization. National security discourse creates insecurities in its practices, such as dividing immigrant families and inducing deaths for immigrants crossing borders (Eschbach et al. 1999; Cornelius 2001; Dunn 2009).

Official national and border security processes do not address individual and community human security. The examples on which I draw include individual women and immigrants, about whom national security measures are nearly oblivious in everyday safety and bodily integrity. In border communities, public voices have been overruled and previous laws, violated. However, the exertion of national and border security measures, paradoxically, has led to deepened democratic practices as border residents and representatives voiced concerns and actively engaged in protests, rallies, resistance, and lawsuits against the federal government. Yet *fronterizos and fronterizas* (borderlanders) hardly exert the power and authority over the security state apparatus, and their reach is local or region.

To understand these alternative views of security, I examine discursive issues in subfields of the political science discipline, particularly IR, focusing on the period when the United States strengthened and expanded its national security machinery from 1947 and thereafter. I then historicize the language of social and human security apart from the state-centric national security language and connect it with the international development approaches to human security as a policy agenda that converges with feminist IR. Coinciding with these policy discourses is a separate internal securitization process associated with the expansion of criminal penalties and incarceration in the United States that contrasts sharply with other nations. I conclude the chapter, closing with reflections on two very different security approaches—human and national—and contingencies associated with the term security. One moves toward troubling securitization based on fear, while the other augers good, but undeniably "big" governance and some redistribution of resources on global scales.

## State Versus Human Security

IR, heavily dominated by U.S. scholars, analyzes security the same way as the state political apparatus, both in foreign affairs and in internal control. IR focuses on offending enemy nations, maintaining borders, defending the homeland, and bringing order and cooperative to a near-anarchic world.

This IR language broadened its scope as the United States assumed more imperial and global power after World War II. The Cold War between the United States and U.S.S.R. led to "hot," proxy wars in many nations, colonial and independent, throughout Asia, Africa, and the Americas until the demise of the Soviet Union in 1989. Yet after the Cold War, international development advocates and economists hoped for what was called a "peace dividend" to redirect military resources into poverty reduction in ways that would address the rising global inequalities between rich and poor countries, totaling almost 200 nations at that time.

Conventional security discourse in military and foreign policy bureaucracies is a very narrow concept. From more comprehensive global perspectives, *security* refers to human health and sustenance, the seeds for which had been planted in numerous international human rights statements and resolutions since the birth of the United Nations. Human development indicators reflect these wider meanings of security: life with sufficient food, shelter, and the means to live with health and well-being. The global neoliberal economy, generating wealth for few nations, mixed growth for others, but impoverishment for many, creates insecurities in everyday life and well-being. Poverty drives migrants to journey for work and well-being in many directions, to neighboring countries and to wealthy countries to the north. People also migrate to live everyday lives free of violence.

In reconstructing the term security to include more and multiple agencies within and across states and societies, rescuing them from narrow military concerns alone, I ground the connectedness of different forms of knowledge from other disciplines such as immigration (lodged in sociology) and from the "common-sense" meanings of words like security. In the 1930s, the policy discourse of "social security" meant old-age pension and survivor support, while the defensive and offensive discourse occurs in IR as a reasonable response of national self-interest in an anarchic world.

IR and immigration scholars rarely connect, and IR theorists—with few exceptions—engage within the perspectives of official policy rather than seek social grounding in everyday lives. Among these rare exceptions are feminist theorists, of relatively recent vintage (less than 2 decades), who connect militarization to hegemonic power and/or hypermasculinity (Agathangelou and Ling 2004; Cohn and Enloe 2003; Staudt 2009). Agathangelou and Ling argue that reactionary hypermasculinity emerges when hegemonic masculinity agents "feel threatened or undermined, thereby needing to inflate, exaggerate, or otherwise distort their traditional masculinity" (2004: 519).

## Historicizing: Security Threads in U.S. Policy Perspectives

One of the best examples of nonmilitarist U.S. security policy is found in the 1930s adoption of U.S. Social Security programming to ameliorate problems for sizeable numbers of elders, their dependents, and survivors in the Depression-era economy. In that era, the leadership for this brand of security came from the U.S. Department of Labor, headed by Francis Perkins, first woman in the cabinet of President Franklin D. Roosevelt. Perkins' political background included the suffrage movement and reformism as a "social feminist."

As a relatively young nation, the United States before World War II pursued more isolationist than interventionist policies to protect itself from threats to sovereignty, given the presence of two mostly friendly neighbor nations to the north and south, and two wide oceans to the east and west (except former colony and ultimately the 50th state, Hawaii). From historical perspectives, the United States has enjoyed geography (unlike many other nations) that sheltered its borders from multiple and potential hostile neighbors, less true now in a world with high-tech weapons and free-trade policies wherein goods and people are easily moved (Naím 2005; Nordstrum 2006).

Militarist expansion spotted the U.S. history of westward expansion and colonization of and beyond its earlier frontier for which I cite a few examples, among many. Under the 1848 Treaty of Guadalupe Hidalgo, the United States took control of northern Mexico, almost half of Mexico's total territory. U.S. imperial forays occurred elsewhere in the world, mainly in the Philippines, the Caribbean, and earlier in the Americas under the U.S.-declared Monroe Doctrine of 1824 to deter additional European influence in "its" hemisphere and to protect its economic interests (see Offner 2007 for more historical analysis). The United States belatedly entered the two 20th-century world wars, well after its allies took devastating attacks. After those wars, a national security state emerged with the rise of the Cold War and the United States as a major world power after World War

II in 1947. Since then, as Bacevich analyzes, national security policy conceptualizes crisis as a permanent condition, threatening a "nation under siege" and "its very survival at risk" (2007: viii). This involves ongoing securitization.

After World War II, the United States drew lines around the U.S.S.R. and its satellites, justified through its containment policies first articulated by the ominous-sounding Mr. X (later identified as George Kennan) in the major policy journal, *Foreign Affairs*. After his analysis outlining threatening Soviet intentions and rivalry with the United States, Mr. X argued that the United States should adopt a policy of "firm containment, designed to confront the Russians with unalterable counter force at every point where they show signs of encroaching upon the interests of a peaceful and stable world."[13] According to Mr. X, at stake was the victory of communism versus capitalism (1947). With the Cold War between the world superpowers (the United States and U.S.S.R.) hot, proxy wars emerged in many nations, colonial and independent, through Asia, Africa, and the Americas until the demise of the Soviet Union in 1989. National security policy operated well outside U.S. boundaries, shoring up bulwarks against communism (or nationalists) in places such as Vietnam and Afghanistan, the latter backfiring as U.S. support for the Taliban and Osama bin Laden came back to haunt—or perhaps strengthen—securitization processes. International development advocates hoped for a "peace dividend" to address the rising global inequalities between rich and poor countries. Instead, new threats from "others" emerged with wars declared on crime and drugs. By the 1990s, a doctrine of low-intensity conflict characterized national security policy at the U.S.-Mexico border (Dunn 1996).

Internationally, the U.S. national security state morphed into a new and more global world power with a perpetual "war on terror" both within and outside U.S. society, enhanced with sophisticated technology within and across bureaucratic agencies in the security state. On September 11, 2001, with air attacks on buildings that symbolized U.S. world power in New York City and Washington D.C., killing thousands of civilians, a group of *non*-Mexican immigrants who entered the U.S. legally but overstayed their visas affirmed the risk and threat that national security discourse long warned against. The tragedy of 9/11 marked a transformation and expansion of national and border security discourse and practice. According to historian Bacevich, however, President Bush's response to 9/11 was "not a radical departure" from previous policy and practice; rather, the president exploited the "process whereby the imperial presidency and our obsessions with national security feed on one another" (2007: x).

A month after 9/11, by presidential decree, U.S. antiterrorism policy became coupled with immigration enforcement and control. Tirman argues that "much in IR has been transformed by the September 11 atrocities and the aftermath," including the "perception of threat, the global realignment of allies and 'evildoers,' and the stigmatizing of states harboring terrorists" (2004: 1). This concept is given Cold War traction in President Bush's Homeland Security Presidential Directive 2, "Combating Terrorism through Immigration Policies," issued October 29, 2001, which established the bureaucratic link for collaboration across immigration and security agencies (Tirman 2004: 2).

Sorkin argues, with the War on Terror, that the United States has taken on more aspects of a "garrison state, defended by a labyrinth of intrusions that, relying on the constantly stoked paranoia over an invisible, shape-shifting enemy, makes suspicion universal. The bugaboo is no longer 'Reds under the beds' but illegal aliens, terrorists, perverts, Muslims who legitimate the swelling Orwellian apparatus that pervades our national life" (2008: viii).

## U.N. and Feminist Human Security Approaches

From this discussion of the United States, which has just 5% of the world's population but with its lingering superpower status and dominance, including the English-language discourse of IR, I move to the United Nations, where a very different notion of security discourse emerged in the early 1990s. This discourse reinvented the language of international development in hopes to turn the Cold War military resources into a peace dividend that would invest resources into human security for "food, health, and environmental, community and personal safety."[14] The source of these human security ideas, the level of their applications, and the strategies proposed operate on very different principles than the national security state. Indeed, they operate largely outside mainstream IR.

Influential policy analyst Deborah Stone embraces broader meanings for the term security, both in theory and practice. Stone published a remarkable book, first out in 1988 but revised in a second edition in 1997, that is widely used in public policy courses but rarely in IR. The book, a response to the ascendancy of economists and rational choice theorists, restores politics and public interest (the 'polis') to its central place in the discipline rather than markets and individual choice among key criteria for policy analysis. The book also provides four theoretical frameworks within which to understand, justify, and propose policy change: equity, efficiency, liberty, and security.

Stone's chapter on security uses common-sense meanings for the word. She begins with a broad statement about human wants and needs. Attentive to both the theoretical and practical side of politics, she says "The quest for security—whether economic, physical, psychological, or military—brings a sense of urgency to politics and is one of the enduring sources of passion in policy controversies" (1988: 69). Urgency and passion become the heart of rhetoric employed in political and policy change.

Stone says that the intuitive, simplest, and most common "definition of need is what is necessary for sheer physical survival" (1998: 69). Although the neoliberal marketplace prizes cost, price, and profit factors above human need, there is a long public tradition justifying the merits of public or governmental intervention in matters of life or death, starvation, public health, natural disasters, and basic shelter.

Can we rescue words like security from its co-optation by the militaristic national security discourse in which it has been lodged since 1947 and enhanced after 9/11? IR traditionally focused on war, foreign policy, the military, national economic interests, and, more recently, peace and conflict resolution. Two decades ago, feminist IR theorists mounted a challenge to the mainstream of IR, a more sweeping challenge than what feminists posed to other subfields in the discipline of political science. Pioneering feminist scholars, such as Cynthia Enloe, J. Ann Tickner, V. Spike Peterson, and Anne Runyan, challenged the invisibility of women and gender in IR and reconceptualized the construction of women, gender, and masculinities in the field of IR.

Feminist perspectives found a welcome home within pockets of the United Nations. The United Nations Development Programme (UNDP) began to issue Human Development Reports on an annual basis, beginning in 1990, with the inspiration of economist Mahbub ul Haq. The UNDP conceptualized new ways of defining and measuring development that went beyond those of orthodox economists, including human development indicators of literacy, infant and child mortality, and longevity. Economist Amartya Sen helped promote this thinking and the human capabilities approaches that subsequently followed. His demographic analysis that "100 million women are missing" in south Asia will surely be remembered as a sharp, quantitative reminder of policies and social practices that resulted in imbalanced sex ratios and treatable death for girls and women.[15]

The UNDP's human development index was gender disaggregated from the outset in a gender development index, and the Human Development Reports ranked and compared nations, using these indices, on an annual basis. The United Nations lack sufficiently comprehensive data to measure public safety and everyday security from violence, given the massive underreporting of domestic violence and sexual assault or its nonrecognition as crime (Staudt 2008b).

Feminist IR also looks at the global economy in markedly different ways, putting women, men and the gendered power relations at the center of analysis. Enloe (2007: 39–62) problematizes *national* security actions that globalize militarization but recognizes that, in most nations, "the government-centered, militarized version of national security remains the dominant mode of policy thinking, even if today it is being challenged" (2007: 43). Enloe argues that militarization is propelled by masculinization, a process fueled by "key players' anxieties and fears of feminization" (2007: 52).

## Culture of Fear: Crime Inside the United States

By the 1990s, Glassner characterized U.S. society as a "culture of fear" (1999). In this chapter, I argue that narrow, militarized internal and external threats feed on each other, to use the verb that Bacevich employs to describe obsessive connections between the imperial presidency and national security. Both internal and external threats illustrate securitization processes.

National security agencies and agendas dovetailed with growing societal anxieties over crime amid media fascination and continuous barrages, whether through entertainment or news, of fearful threats in an era of uncertainty in the 1980s and thereafter. Whether in television crime shows or news, information is framed in crisis-laden, threatening terminology. The "politics of fear" provides leaders favoring "law and order" with a rallying cry, as is evident during elections, in the United States as well as other countries.

Ruth and Craig Gilmore provide some historical perspective on the growth of the crime-control industry and bureaucracy. From 1910 to 1975, before the official declarations of "Wars on Crime," U.S. incarceration rates were stable, at 110 per 100,000 in the population.[16] Since 1980, however, the number of people held in custody has grown 10-fold: 1 of 800 adults in 1980 compared with the most recent figures of 1 in 130; "people of color" are more heavily policed, charged, and convicted, with 70% ethnic minorities among the incarcerated (Gilmore and Gilmore 2008: 142), despite their 30% portion of the population. Crime control now jails 500,000 people with drug-related crimes but only 40,000 before 1980.[17] The United States holds 750 individuals in prison or jail for every 100,000 in the population compared with 627 in Russia, 151 in England, and 63 in Japan.[18]

In high-tuned synergy, national security policies acquire political support with what Sorkin calls a "well-cultivated climate of fear in America" (2008: x). Taxpayers devote extensive local, state, and federal government resources to crime control. With only 5% of the world's population, the United States "leads the world in producing prisoners" with a "quarter of the world's prisoners."[19] In the United States, people are imprisoned for crimes, such as using drugs and writing bad checks, that "rarely produce prison sentences in other countries" and are "kept incarcerated far longer."[20] Domestic national security policy has long been shaped by various "wars" on crime, militarist terminology that fuels local, state, and federal bureaucracy and a wide array of private contractors and related businesses from bail bonding companies to private prisons, sex-offender facilities, and detention camps for immigrants. Of course, easy access to guns and weapons contributes to crime. Glassner believes that gun accessibility is worthy of fear compared with emphasis on crime in the media and on television shows.

## CONCLUSIONS

Historical state securitization processes are connected with immigration enforcement, in ways that resemble former President Dwight D. Eisenhower's warnings about the "military-industrial complex" in 1961. Securitization at the border uses official national security discourse and militarized, criminalization strategies against immigrants; this creates a serious backlash in the border population, which is long accustomed to interdependency with Mexican border cities and towns and made up of a population with friends, relatives, and coworkers on both sides of the border, citizens, legal permanent residents, and Mexican nationals.

Drawing on the vantage points of border voices, human and feminist theory, and critiques of mainstream IR, I argue the necessity of differentiating between state-centric national security and local-to-global human security conceptions. Each conception emerges from different sources, operates at different levels, and utilizes different strategies to accomplish their objectives. One of them uses threats to provoke securitization processes: national security, complete with wall-building. Yet threats to life and well-being pose equally troubling concerns.

In this chapter, I discussed mainstream, state-centric IR, attentive to national security apparatus that in the United States has strengthened after World War II and 9/11. The culture of fear within the United States, evinced in criminalization and incarceration rates that surpass other nations in the world, augments and deepens the securitization process.

My chapter contrasted national security discourse with human security conceptions that emerged from both international development advocates, expecting a 'peace dividend' after the Cold War, and from feminist challenges to traditional IR. Human security discourse focuses on poverty reduction within and across borders in global perspectives. Some of its roots can be found in early 20th century Social Security. From my border vantage point, I show that social justice advocates adopted human rights and security principles in their challenges to heavy and hard national security practices that disrupted the interdependent border regions and the citizens and Mexican nationals who lived on either side of the border. The Border Wall symbolizes the excesses of control and militarization in the state-centric model.

Despite the border security apparatus, border people challenge and resist the ways those policies aim to shape lives. Both the city council and county commissioners court in El Paso have passed pro-immigrant resolutions. An amazing alliance of community human rights activists and locally elected officials have delayed or "outlawed" the immigrant harassment through checkpoint practices. Locally elected officials have sued the federal government over the way it has broken other laws in attempts to build the border wall/fence, undermine federalism and the constitutional separation of powers, and confiscate property in the process.

Whether border activists and elected officials will be able to use democratic practices and tools to counter the hard, militarized security state, or a security state garbed in possibly softer guise with a new U.S. president in 2009, has yet to be seen. Moreover, whether human security principles will take hold at national and global levels is even more uncertain in our unequal world. Strong forces protect neoliberal economies and many corresponding neoliberal states from engaging in the sort of policies that redistribute wealth and opportunities within and across nations, using big governments. Were countervailing forces ascendant instead, the discourse and practice of human rights and human security policies would promote social reforms and transformation in democratic and good but big governance across a variety of agencies in non-monolithic states further unpacked in federalism. I have contrasted security discourses and practices but, from a long-term perspective, they are joined at the hip if examined from multilateral, North American perspectives to include Mexico and nonmilitarist, non-walled strategies to reduce immigration for shared prosperity.

## NOTES

1. I thank Jane Jaquette, the outside reviewer, and the editors for their comments on earlier drafts.
2. Nevins, J., and Dunn, T. "Barricading the Border." *Counterpunch,* November 14/16, 2008, pp. 5. Downloaded 11/21/2008. See also Pew Hispanic Center. 2008. "Immigration." http://pewhispanic.org/topics/?TopicID=16.
3. Personal observation, El Paso, TX. April 14, 2007. Accessed 11/21/2008.
4. U.S. Department of Homeland Security/Customers and Border Protection. 2008. Press release, El Paso, TX, Ports of Entry.
5. On campaign funding, see Tom Barry. 2009. National Security Business on the Border: Former Border Patrol Chief Silvestre Reyes Now a Major Player in New Military, Intelligence and Homeland Security Complex. *Americas Policy Program.* http://newspapertree.com/politics/4230-reyes-the-rainmaker-building-the-paso-del-norte-security-system-from-academics-to-economics. BSIC comes from Staudt, Payan, and Dunn (2009).
6. See www.blueservo.net.
7. Grissom, B. 2008. "Cameras net 2 million hits, 1 drug bus, 6 illegal entries." *El Paso Times,* December 17, 1–2A.
8. Building a New Vision of the Border: A Conference on Border Policy. November 29–30, 2007. Border Human Rights Collective and U.S.-Mexico Bi-national Task Force.
9. Personal observation, El Paso, TX, February 19, 2008.
10. Nevins, J., and Dunn, T. "Barricading the Border." *Counterpunch,* November 14/16, 2008. Downloaded November 21, 2008, pp. 3, 5.
11. Grissom, B. "County wants high court to rule on fence lawsuit." *El Paso Times,* September 24, 1–2A, 2008. The effort ultimately failed.
12. Herweck, S. "Ackerman trespassed, but it's Chertoff who is breaking the law." December 18, 2008. *Rio Grande Guardian* (electronic subscriber news service) reprinted in www.newspapertree.com. Accessed 11/21/2008.
13. "X" (Kennan, George). 1947. "The sources of Soviet conduct." *Foreign Policy.*

14. Jolly, R. and Ray, D. B. 2006. "The Human Security Framework and National Human Development Reports." NY: UNDP Human Development Report Office Occasional Paper 5, p. 5. See also, United Nations Development Programme (UNDP). 1994. *Human Development Report*. NY: Oxford University Press.
15. Sen, A. 1990. "100 Million Women are Missing." *New York Review of Books*.
16. Liptak, A. "Inmate count in U.S. dwarfs other nations'." *New York Times*, April 23, 2008. A1, A14.
17. Ibid.
18. Ibid.
19. Ibid.
20. Ibid.

# Part V
# Law, Citizenship, and the State

# 5    A Note on Security Modulation

*Willem de Lint*

> *"You name the agency, they were told to stand down . . . The interest from the middle bureaucracy was not that there had been a security breach but that someone had bothered to investigate the breach.* That was where the terror was."
>
> Veteran CIA/NSA Intelligence Operative to Christopher Ketcham, *Counterpunch*, March 3, 2007

## INTRODUCTION

In previous articles (de Lint, Virta and Deukmedjian 2007; de Lint 2008b), colleagues and I advanced the idea that security simulations are next generation to what had appeared as a policy modus for crime control; that is, of a crime policy that needed more than anything else to be seen to be done according to the contemporaneous culture of control (Garland 2000). We argued that security simulations are events that demonstrated competence in marshalling the optics of security even in the absence of a danger independent of the security control apparatus. As illustrated by the quote above, the policy question involves the finessing of uncertainty and risk and the attribution of terror as the absence of a controlled response within the coordination of a culture of control.

Here, I would like to stipulate some features of security modulation as the reflexive, anticipatory, measured, and normalized application of crisis response against a danger or threat that is subject to replication or control by 'our own forces.' The notion of modulation suggests that there is an agent which triggers or sets the dosage of security information that is maintained or released, so I will begin with a brief comment on agency. In the last segment, I will provide an illustration.

## AGENCY IN AGENCIES

How agents and agencies protect or defend us from internal and external threats and dangers is among the starkest symbols of our liberal democratic virtues. However, we often avert our gaze precisely to avoid too deep a probe of the settled binaries that distinguish 'us' and 'them.' One of the defining acts of social order and organization is the ritual application of the criminal label or the public ceremony of official sanction (Garfinkel 1956).

This application is directly tied to trust in government and leaders. In carrying out this function, social and political leaders are often confronted with a stark choice: they can simplify the functional binary (us/them, good/evil) and divide a social problem into a matter of strong leadership (us) against dangerous threat (them) or they can attempt to bridge social and political ruptures. If they do the latter, for example, by offering to reframe a crisis or problem in the context of complex historical grievances, 'self-help' (Black and Baumgartner 1987), or as an issue that must be deferred to the courts, they appear to relinquish decision-making authority and risk the charge that they are 'weak on security.'

This is a good portion of the institutional backdrop against which agents and agencies operate. Its implications are often underestimated. That threat is dependent on beliefs and that we depend on security officials to distinguish the 'real' from the 'fanciful' most often produces unremarkable results. On the other hand, it also stimulates the self-fulfilling prophecy that crime or insecurity will be found where you look for it. Crime and threat will be more predictable and manageable if you look for it by planting informants and feeding and growing criminal networks, a practice that over time corrupts and extinguishes the moral distinction that is the putative basis of the intervention. It may even be understood as a product[1] that can be rolled out to serve or mollify, at pivotal junctures, the appetite of agents or agencies, the maintenance of security networks and apparatuses, and the continuities of politics. This is not postideological (Fukayama 1989). What emerges is the domestication of the 'away' politics of necessity and realism, one that overlays, undermines, and supplants consent structures with assemblages of coercive control.

There are three or four postulates at the back of this thesis. The first is that the modern liberal-democratic regime of self-government and citizen-subjects as the basis for a social order is being overturned. As Foucault has demonstrated, the individual responds as a basis or root of institutions of governance to the needs of the sovereign. Where populations and beyond (societies of control) form the postulates of the power grid, natural law and principles of justice are shunted aside as the armor of a redundant entity. This is not to say that there is not a clash of regimes of truth and that classic liberal ideas do not still interpolate the free rights-bearing citizen-subject but only to point out that as the singular basis of governance this is an increasingly weak agency.

The second postulate regards the objection that there must be a coordinated organization among a cadre of privileged knowers who share the singular aim to achieve the desired social and political consequence.[2] On the contrary, and referring also to Foucault, the production of effects only requires the will to power, or that careerism within agencies takes place against a background of rewards or incentives that fosters, as per some criminological work (Lyng 1990), 'edgework.' For agents and agencies populated by individuals seeking to advance their careers, the discovery of crime or threat will match the postulates about crime and threat, and the bigger the match the more useful (provided that the wheels don't come off) and lucrative the reward for those agents and agencies. Where operational edgework is matched to aggressive careerism that places security over justice (as per risk attributions), the term can at once refer to a deviant and normalized subculture. These actors are stimulated by a higher yet subaltern organizational imperative.

On the other hand, what has been called the "manufacture of consent" (Hermann and Chomsky 1988) and has been referred to in terms of "legitimacy crisis" or the "trust gap" between official positions on matters of public policy and public belief is a matter of profound and concerted governmental activity. If, as according to Lippmann (1922: 17), security actionable information is made ready for 'sound public opinion' through the public relations of government agencies and the management of mass media sources and distributions, the effect of agency is through the simplification of the message.[3] As most recently presented in Wilford's *The Mighty Wurlitzer: How the CIA Played America*, Lippmann's traditionalist view of public opinion management is shared sufficiently by establishment corporate media and government agencies (*New York Times*, CENTRAL Intelligence Agency, Rendon Group) that there may be few who are in a position to decipher when and where the 'mighty Wurlitzer' is being played.

Although crime and security productions originate in and feed back into popular cultural beliefs, they are also decoupled from the principles and rules of liberal democracy and from the popular will. This is because it is understood that it can be both counterproductive and dangerous to engage politics strictly by the rules, a view that becomes stronger the closer one gets to defense of the sovereign (as Agamben 2003, for instance, shows). The knowledge of the executive sovereign is a strategic knowledge, deployed through tradecraft and statecraft, including the use of disclosures, secrets, and other information control tactics. If one has accepted the argument that the threat is 'real' and existential, one is likely to accept that the means to counter it may allowably extend beyond the requirements of transparency and visibility in the 'just society.'

There is one final piece regarding the view of agency that is an important backstop to this thesis of security modulation, and it evinces intelligence tactics. Despite research that supports the organizational efficiency of what is known as 'political action'[4] and its utilities in security agencies' mandates, the term 'conspiracy theory' is used as a wide brush to tarnish those who look for relatively powerful and coordinated agents of action (or agencies) within rather than without the established corporate–state nexus.[5] The power of this rebuke stems from the influence of Karl Popper, among others, who have discredited the popular desire to attribute complex events to human agency rather than unintended consequences. Thus, for example, 9/11 can be a terrorism conspiracy of great sophistication only where the agency is exogenous. This technique of neutralization (external nonstate organizations share interests and values and deploy practices making them capable of secret conspiracies, internal state-based organizations do not) distorts the contention that there can be two tracks of policy (as per Strauss) and that information control practices serve exclusive elite interests.[6]

Governments act on widespread beliefs and, as we are increasingly aware, these may be stimulated or directed by fear, which, in turn, is stoked by an absence of credible information. As has been demonstrated,[7] where information and trust gaps are wide, belief in a conspiratorial agency is likely to prosper. The result is not necessarily a condition that absents itself from (further) manipulation, nor ought it to be assumed that many agents and agencies within what has been called a 'security apparatus' do not 'mind the gap.' As illustrated by a recent high-profile paper on 'conspiracy theories' (Sunstein and Vermeule, 1998) that concludes that the U.S. government ought to take steps to "cognitively infiltrate" "fringe" groups and counter the message of a "harmful" government conspiracy (citing several examples of the U.S. government having done just that), the security apparatus is already involved in minding the gap. *Playing* the gap is the analytical object of what follows.

## COMPONENTS OF SECURITY MODULATION

### Exceptionalist Foundation, Risk Reflexive Modernity

The postideological era that Fukayama (1989) perceived produced a problem for the realist foundation of Western democracies, particularly its existentialist and decisionist politics. In the absence of a strong, capable enemy after the collapse of the Berlin Wall and the Soviet Union, the covert tail that wagged the overt dog of democratic politics—particularly in Europe, Asia, and Central and South America—was in danger of being snipped. However, as a matter of foreign affairs, there was, in fact, almost a seamless transition to a new counter-ideology. What could not be seamless is the substitution of 'home' order making for 'away' order making. Within liberal democracies, such a transition would necessarily be more irruptive, requiring, as Klein (2008) has pointed out, "shock therapy." Indeed, after 9/11, the enemy/friend binary of national security and realist foreign affairs become the hypothetical center of domestic social order, decentering and displacing delocalized, deterritorialized, or reglobalized constitutional tenets and values (Aradau and van Munster 2007; Hornquist 2004; Neocleous 2006; and de Lint 2008a).

As elaborated by Huysmans (2004), exceptionalism reconfigures political communities through a redistribution of fear and trust, a reconsideration of inclusions and exclusions, and the institution of a predisposition toward violence. By exceptionalism, we mean the limits of law in the necessity of sovereign decision making, where the sovereign, according to Schmitt, is "he who decides the exception"[8] or where the final say is not subject to law or rule but is "wholly original to the power in question" (Lazar 2006: 257). A foundational postulate here is the friend/enemy distinction or the idea that a proper grounding of sovereignty is in the hard binary that also permits correspondingly hard or exclusionary policy responses. As nicely encapsulated in Brighenti (2006), the norm is a constitutive moment that is exceptional and may also be a "dirty birth," dirty by necessity where risks and dangers are existential or perceived as such. Although exceptionalism has been newly rediscovered in criminological texts (de Lint and Virta 2004; Aradau and van Munster 2007), it has not been absent from political science, especially with the repopularization of Schmitt in academic and policy circles since the declaration of the "War on Terror" (Walker 2006: 77).

How does this foundation in a revivified exceptionalism mesh with the somewhat oppositional condition of a risk reflexive modernity? According to numerous analysts, the first element of risk reflexive modernity is a condition in which there are major catastrophic threats and risks that might at any time cripple critical infrastructures and governments (Beck 1992; Giddens 1991). These threats are characterized by unpredictability and scale. Response to these threats and risks has challenged societies and governments to develop population-wide measures, such as is witnessed recently in the regulatory response to the H1N1 threat.

The second element is reflexivity within institutions, both cultural and organizational. Responses to catastrophic risks by critically reflexive institutions will auger the widespread transformation toward a reflexive modernity that questions or undermines the liberal foundations of the first phase of modernity, including its constitutional and parliamentary foundations (van Loon 2003; Adam, Beck, and van Loon 2000). Pre-occupation with and popularization of imminent danger and catastrophic threat sets up the condition for a scalar response by government, which may be viewed in military jargon as 'means other than war' (i.e., follow the logic of the response of war without having to depend on the legal conditions of a state of war). These are viewed not through the lens of the first phase as deconstructive of the modern impulse but through the lived experience of the second phase as responsive to the pace and scope of current 'reality.'

Reflexivity is not limited to the interaction between legal and political institutions and the unpredictable character of catastrophic risk. Modernity also incorporates the 'detraditionalizing' impulse, the 'setting free' of individuals through the undermining of pre-existing sociocultural coordinates in its own 'universalisms.' Consequently, it is not surprising that the location or arena for threat or risk must also be the purported antecedent to the first phase of modernity in the 'barbarism' of the pre-modern.[9]

Together, these comprise a dynamic frame of reference: exceptionalism reconfigures the 'detraditionalizing' impulse to 'set free' certain dangerous sociocultural coordinates, those, especially, still perceived with 'barbaric nationalism' or the enemy of modernism.[10] Well-popularized catastrophes pound the first phase of modernity and produce a risk reflexive modernity and institutions that look out over the lived environment as a proliferation of known and unknown threat. The consequence is a precautionary risk management where the "decision on the enemy is expanded into decisions on catastrophic contingency" (Aradau and van Munster 2007: 697) and posits the necessity of precautionary action in the avoidance of risks that "exceed the limits of the insurable" (Ewald 1991: 222 in Aradua and van Munster: 697). Evidence of this approach in support of a hybrid of networked centralized information control is everywhere to be found. The discourse of precaution and risk management has become almost a prerequisite of policy discussions and this discourse has further pushed exceptionalist information control imperatives and the enemy/friend binary into the heart of political articulations.

## Responsiveness to the Optics of Control: Government Seen to be Doing Security

There is a great deal of criminological literature that has advanced Garland's hypotheses regarding the emergence of a 'culture of control' predicated on shifts in social practice and cultural sensibility (Garland 2000) or in an adaptive strategy that stresses partnership and prevention and a sovereign state strategy that enhances control and expressive punishment (Garland 2000: 348). In adapting policy, policy makers in 'high-crime societies' work through civil society partnerships in the provision of security emphasizing proactive prevention. However, they also reserve a strategy of 'punitive segregation' that carries forward the 'old myth of the sovereign state' in more 'expressive and intensive forms of policing and punishment' (Garland 2000: 349).

Consistent with the cultural and social trends identified by Garland, governments have become increasingly responsive to the optics of policing and security and have been adapting practices that seek to layer official responses more discretely or more boldly, depending on the expected audience or reception (de Lint and Hall 2009). The first requirement remains, as Garland pointed out, that government is seen to be acting or forging and implementing policy to address the 'crisis.' We would add that the response today, unlike that of the 1980s and 1990s, is not the problem of crime as per 'doing crime control,' 'the war on crime,' or the 'war on drugs,' but the merging of external and internal, existential and quotidian security in the countering of asymmetrical threat. The result is a precautionary exceptionalism, a safety/security amalgam where government redrafts crime into existential threat and pre-emptive response as 'doing security.' In being seen to be 'doing security,' governments have taken extraordinary measures, many of which are inconsistent with the liberal democratic state. These include the public order measures in precautionary risk management (Levi 2009) and can be seen "to span the whole realm between exceptional measures and the immediacy of action on the one hand and the ordinary administrative, police, and insurance measures on the other" (Aradau and van Munster 2007: 696).

In the double-context of risk reflexive modernity, it is not simply that risks are identified and understood as "bads" (Beck 1992) to be avoided. Given the requisites of institutional growth or the requirement that budgets are justified and mandates maintained or augmented, the security-intelligence infrastructure of government is growing risk at least as much as an opportunity not to be missed as a bad to be avoided. A simple institutional instrumentalism determines that catastrophes, whether natural (Hurricane Katrina) or a product of human systems (September 2009 world financial crisis), will be played up, if not invited, as necessary and functional to test system readiness. As elaborated by one significant body of economic analysts (Milton Freidman and the Chicago School), even catastrophic economic disasters are viewed favorably, if not planned, as harbingers of radical "shock therapy" (Klein 2008). As Klein documents, seismic ruptures—including, as President Richard Nixon famously said of Chile, "making the economy scream" when the radical therapies of the Washington consensus are contested—are the precursors to the evacuation of the social and to economic recolonization by transnational corporate elites (which are positioned to maximize windfall dividends from such catastrophes). It need not be added that intelligence czars regularly rotate between private multinational corporations invested in the disruption of peaceful resolutions to conflict and the hallowed halls of political chief executives whose constituencies regularly audit politicians on their readiness to pull the trigger.

The double-context of risk reflexivity (i.e., inclusive of elite and specialized institutional instrumentalities) has dovetailed with the need for governments to be more concerned with the appearances of doing security and the collapse of the exceptional and the quotidian to produce a variety of bold measures that have been rolled out recently, one of which colleagues and I discussed previously in an analysis of the police "surge" (de Lint, Virta, and Deukmedjian 2007). The surge is a purposefully aggressive and dramatic police training exercise involving sometimes dozens of police officers in a reaction to a mock terrorist attack or threat on critical infrastructure. In one sense, surges are under the radar because they zero in at a very particularistic level of social interaction, usually a limited geographical area. In another sense, they are explosive, demanding their publics to accept that a new order or 'new normal' necessitates that rights will subside to police sovereignty, even where there is no real threat present. This new kind of order making or policy management has captured themes that are derived not from the ideal foundation of liberal democracies but rather from its antithesis in the authoritarian, preventative regulatory state (see Ashworth and Zedner 2008).

Finally, to be seen 'doing security' is now also to be seen acting reflexively, recursively, and playing to multiple constituencies. Security policy is derived out of an overlap of narratives, technology, interests, ideologies (rationalities), and—as we are stressing here—the collection, analysis, and selective dissemination of information written to be read by a plurality of audiences or constituencies. As an answer to discrete and sometimes antagonistic questions about government direction and utilities, the security policy text is multidimensional, offering cues, code words, and palliatives to assuage those constituencies. It can also be announced in the event, as by an act of war or surprise attack, a kind of decision that is not necessarily expected to be the result of public debate. Governments can provide a multitude of narratives about actions that are launched under the auspices of the state, and these will be targeted at specific audiences in the reconciling of interests and politics.

For example, a compelling reading of Canada's participation in extraordinary rendition is that Canada wanted to signal strongly to an audience of the U.S. security intelligence establishment and its political authorities that it, too, was willing to make a straightforward sacrifice of justice or human rights for security. One of the leading lines for this is that Canada is trade and intelligence dependent on the United States and must therefore take a line of appeasement. At the same time, for a large constituency of the Canadian public, Canada wanted to send a contradictory signal: that it was not willing to sacrifice human rights or justice for security. Canada took a line against participation in Desert Storm. But note the timing of the former (see the following) and the fact as per the latter (as of the time that this is written) that Omar Khadr is not being repatriated by Canadian authorities. The lesson that is quite likely learnt from this when it comes to Canadian security policy is not that the Canadian democracy trumps American security intelligence, but rather that the separation of the two tracks of discourse (and two discrete audiences) must be better managed. Hence, the importance again of the dissemination dimension of information control.[11]

This idea that policy is codified can be taken further. It may well be the case, as several analysts have suggested, that a sizeable segment of the U.S. political elite has accepted an inversion of Gramsci's organic intellectual in the Straussian idea of a division between the exoteric and esoteric (represented by the intelligence agent of any recent John Le Carré novel). According to Strauss, the value and purchase of classical political philosophy may be rescued for current politics, rather than for a nonrealizable utopian liberal ideal, only by a conversion. It requires a division of meaning from the same event-text, one to be inferred by a general audience and another by a special few, the latter being the purists with the capacity to convert ideas into action.[12] Strauss and his followers suggested that a commitment to liberal politics requires the provision of an external bogey to prevent the collapse of liberal democracy as an organizing principle, especially given the fall of an alternative grand ideology.[13]

## The Normalization of Intelligence (in the Compartmented Substitution of Individual or Quotidian Security for [Elite] Institutional or [Trans]national Securities and in the Substitution of Dangers and Risks for 'Control' Simulations)

It is a mainstay of domestic policing that it is now or ought to be intelligence based or intelligence led (de Lint 2006; Radcliffe 2007; etc.). What this means in practice is that many commonplace occurrences are threaded through an intelligence registration. This infusion of intelligence and the intelligence cycle has a specific consequence: the adaptation of local routines and ordering practices to a particular tenor of extra-local institutional interests in security, guaranteed by the ORCON (originator control) and 'need to know' stipulations. This includes, for example, the popularization of the idea of 'mosaic,' so that there is now an avoidance of activities among otherwise 'innocent' people of a sequence of connections that would approximate those of 'known terrorists.'

Government agency control over information is deployed against a shifting institutional context that might be called an intelligencized bureaucracy—one that is restructured not according to the traditional modernist hierarchies based on clear lines of accountability and discrete mandates but on a network of "new governance" (Salamon 2002) dynamic flows and fusions where the locus of command is mobile and amorphous. Whereas under that modernist bureaucratic accountability, the paper trail was a means and protection from improper state action ensuring a system of monitoring and access to people and testimony, once decisions and knowledge are generated within fluid, flexible, and makeshift networks, often struck up around projects or problems, traditional forms of inquiry and oversight prove less effective.

The assumption is that intelligence, as information that can make a political difference (de Lint 2008a),[14] offers even liberal constitutional democracies a preferred means of political and social control. A combination of factors has made this so, including the efficiency and competition of states' arguments (state governments need a position from which to bargain for resources that provides them with their own secure informational sources), the necessity argument (the security of the state of necessity requires that discretion to suspend the law rests with the sovereign), and the exceptionalist argument (external security is first order, internal security [and justice] is second order). Each of these may be contested (see, for instance, Lustgarten and Leigh 1994) as a matter of argument about what is truly efficient, necessary, and secure, but secret state empowerments continue relatively unabated, and the historical evidence shows us that where there are challenges to democratic states, liberal democracies often retreat from the polyarchic to the national security or garrison type (Tapia-Valdes 1982) as governments deploy intelligence and security resources against internal and external opposition.

Given the importance of presentation or form, the time-constrained political term, and the necessity to look both 'smart' and 'right' in innovating policy options, politics has become the art of finessing the limited workable territory between antagonism[15]: it requires the exploitation and launch of bold executive action with the grain of liberal democratic aspirations. In this field of play, security intelligence represents an opportunity. It provides a policy escape hatch by way of constitutional joker or blind. The bias of policy production in the impossible context of homage to (efficient, exceptional) elites and (visible, foundational) democratic institutions may be finessed as a stop-gap or one-time measure. This may be realistic about citizenship and rights and attaches qualifiers and exclusions to the ambit of the rule of law; it is expansive about the security of the state and pushes the existential into the quotidian, substituting justice for security, rights for risk.

## Timing: Deploying the Fact of Necessity, Responsiveness, and Visibility When Maximally Suited for Policy Roll-outs

Timing is, of course, a crucial element of any kind of politics or policy. The test of policy is that it is rolled out to maximum effect and limited negative feedback. Political timing is the anticipation of conditions for policy and bold action and the readiness to announce a position in ideal conditions. This requires a "rehearsal of the sovereign" (Chappell 2006), or the priming of the political well that may include trial balloons, live training exercises, and hoaxes—each launched to append a consent dividend (of nonresisting witnesses) to an initiative.

Because the autocratic impulse is understood of necessity to belong with the immediacy of the moment, whereas the polyarchic impulse follows by way of mopping up, the timing of bold decisions even within liberal democratic traditions incorporates the Schmittian position. In this regard, the 9/11 event is popularly and expertly criticized as a deviation from 'shoot first, ask questions later.' Indeed, this presumption that immediate and, of course, pre-emptory action belongs with the free sovereign and that deliberation belongs with the republic or parliament dovetails with the conditions of catastrophe and asymmetry that are said to characterize the 'threat landscape.'

A further element of timing is visibility. The ground is readied for action long before the decision to act is made. There is official policy versus unofficial practice or bureaucratic policy. Also significant, there are official budgetary versus 'black' allocations; again, a feature of governments designed to maintain economic and strategic advantages in the 'international system.' Finally, there are matters of public information versus those claimed as state secrets or otherwise manufactured in the ebb and flow of black information available for leaks or disclosures (according to the principle that distribution of information obtains a clear objective, and knowledge advantages are often proprietary and finessed for market or political gain).

The logic of political timing, including the privilege of coercion and release of information, is observable in the popularization of pre-emption and precaution. This is also a further iteration of the longstanding bureaucratic necessity of 'ready roll-outs' from the warehouse of commissioned reports. What I would like to stress here is that the interaction between the ready infrastructure of police and security capacities and operations, the executive 'right' to push 'go,' and the cultural expectation and anticipation of a 'go event,' are now a matter of *modulation* or *precisely considered manipulation*.

In sum, security modulation is the operation of policy (governing through security) on the basis of four discrete elements: one is the exceptionalist foundation and the straightforward necessity of major policy responsiveness to catastrophes or 'big,' 'major' risks in the context of reflexive modernization (risk reflexive modernity); the second is responsiveness to the optics of control (meeting the challenge that government is seen to be doing security); the third is the normalization of intelligence (in the compartmented substitution of individual or quotidian security for [elite] institutional or [trans]national securities and of real-world dangers and risks for 'control' simulations); and the fourth is timing (deploying the fact of necessity, responsiveness, and visibility to maximally suit policy roll-outs).

## SNIPPET OF SPECTACLE, OWNERSHIP OF CHAOS

"The match is about to begin."

Khalid Shaikh Muhammad (to Mohamed Atta)

Melding our earlier remarks on agency with our outline of the constituent parts of security modulation, we are in a position to query the fascinating cross-fertilization of live training exercises and spectacular security events. Security modulation is a matter (to reverse our previous order) of timing, optics, intelligence compartmentalization, and (exceptional, decisionist) necessity. Live training exercises, including war games, are launched to test force readiness, resolve, and planning. Security mega-events offer spectacle and announce policy in taking sovereign ownership of chaos.

The reflexivity, recursivity, and blurring of the 'real' and the 'apparent' in the security modulations will be a matter of contestation because it involves claims-making about the authority of sovereignty itself, as previously noted. In places where the territorial or nationalistic base of claims-making is deeply contested, pre-emptive decisionism is understood to be more strategic, if not necessary. In Israel and occupied Palestine, we may see it in its fullest contours. Israeli journalist Amira Hass, with Israel's *Ha'aretz* newspaper, said the following about the incursion into Gaza in 2008:

> There was no war between two symmetric parties. [. . . .] What Breaking the Silence people noticed from the—when they spoke to soldiers, a massive, wet—what we call wet training exercise of the Israeli forces. [. . . .] With live ammunition. So a massive exercise. And I see it as a massive exercise for wars to come, not for wars that were, but for wars to come, using all the sophisticated, almost science fiction weapons, weaponry that Israel has against, what I see, Native Americans with their arrows (Hass 2009).

Is 9/11 a security mega-event that collapses agency, optics, compartmentalization, and necessity? More than 41 U.S. intelligence and counterterrorism veterans challenge the official account of the 9/11 Commission, with Robert Baer (veteran Middle East specialist) stating that Bin Laden and al Qaeda could not have accomplished it, and the evidence pointing to a U.S. government cover-up, a conclusion shared by Melvin Goodman, a former senior Central Intelligence Administration (CIA) official. A former U.S. Navy Intelligence officer, Wayne Madsen, called the event the result of "a highly compartmentalized covert operation." If 9/11 cannot be fully known, it is not only because evidence was suppressed (World Trade Center steel immediately shipped to China), but because it implicates the command of the U.S. government, which is 'too big to fail.'

On 9/11, 5 classified training exercises were probably being carried out by the CIA, the National Reconnaissance Office (NRO), US Space Command, North American Aerospace Defense Command (NORAD), and the U.S. Air Force. These included simulation exercises (or simex) that involved diverting fighter planes to ward off a Russian incursion in the north (Vigilant Guadian), a 'plane into building' scenerio (NRO headquarters in Washington), and live-flys, including hijackings of airlines

(Vigilant Warrior). The exercises were under the command of an 'exercise maestro' and a communications hub of the Secret Service, which has the legal authority to command all agencies in a national emergency Ruppert 2004: 133–156). According to some of the participants, including the Northeast Air Defense Sector (NEADS) mission crew, there was a good deal of confusion and delay caused by the contemporaneous drills, which led air traffic controllers to believe first, that the hijackings were exercises, and second, that some of the exercise were real, probably from 'injects' or false-positive radar trails injected onto the screens.[16] A further postulate, inasmuch as the reference to 'warrior' may have involved a red team versus blue team, enemy-friend contest, is that the combination of 'hijacked plane' and 'plane into building' invited participants into a cover story. Nonetheless, in addition to being classified, the drills were significantly compartmentalized on the argument that limited knowledge of the whole exercise made it a better test of command decision making. NORAD's commander for the continental United States was not read into all its component parts (Spencer 2008: 38).

A continuity of government program was activated coincidentally with the events of 9/11 and these drills (Gellman and Schmidt 2002), a phenomenon that "helps explain the thinking and behavior of the second Bush Administration in the hours, days, and months after the terrorist attacks on September 11, 2001" (Mann 2004a: 139). This program, which is intended to counter a decapitation of government by creating executive redundancy, emerged in the 1980s under the Ford administration, and creates three teams of representatives from the State Department, Defense Department, CIA, and other agencies and is run by the National Program Office and according to James Mann, read James Woolsey, Dick Cheney, and Donald Rumsfeld, among others, into a "permanent, though hidden, national security apparatus of the United States" (Mann, 2004b).

Both exercises were highly classified, and this permitted much of the documentary evidence pertaining to communications between various agencies to be destroyed or heavily redacted before or during the investigation, although reference to Vigilant Warrior is given by Richard Clarke in response to his question about the scrambling of jet fighters: "Not a pretty picture, Dick. We are in the middle of Vigilant Warrior, a NORAD exercise" (Clarke, 2004). The official 9/11 Commission Report made mention of the drills in a single note: chapter 11, note 116 (United States, 2004). The continuity of government exercise itself was a sensible continuation of one of the other drills, Global Guardian, which had started the previous week, involving US Strategic Command, US Space Command, and NORAD, and was based on the premise that the United States may be under attack by a foreign power (Associated Press, February 21, 2002).

The official 9/11 conspiracy theory is disbelieved by detractors possessing impressive credentials, including security, policing and intelligence professionals, engineers, architects, physicists, and academics. As noted earlier, that disbelief is countered variously, including reference to the improbability of its agency and means. However, both agency and means ought to be reviewed in light of our remarks on necessity, intelligence (compartmentalization), policy optics, and timing. There is little need to repeat what has been noted on the question of timing, both with respect to the particular event and its utility in streamlining geostrategic policy (into the 'War on Terror'). As is evident here, decision making takes place within a "highly compartmentalized" working environment (Giraldi 2008).[17] On policy optics, it is to be noted that when political operations involving covert actions are launched against foreign enemies (eg. Gladio), they often involve what is sometimes described as a 'riddle wrapped inside an enigma,' with multiple layers of cover obscuring the true objective and means. It is unknown if on 9/11 the presence of the many drills and potentially the blue team/red team conflict would have offered a worst-case cover if the al Qaeda story-line began to unravel. That provisional or alternative narrative might have been that, yes, there were exercises and they went awry.

These are (necessarily) speculative examples of precautionary risk mitigation exercises that exploit exceptional, intelligenicized (compartmentalized) policy optics and choices. They appear against a backdrop of the institutional necessity for security product edgework and the means of security production within a putatively open and democratic society, perhaps as an object lesson so outrageous and existential that it cannot be too closely analyzed for its authenticity. In addition, if we view security modulation in the terms of Foucault's biopolitics and biosecurity—that is, as management of population or governance through danger and life production—the effort is conceived and delivered as a manageable training operation, it predicts a response to positive and deliberate encouragement, it is a double exercise, staged, ambiguous, existential.

If the hypothesis outlined is confirmed and security modulations are exercises of irruptive policy making organized through decisionist, intelligencized methods and optics, then this genre of order making relies upon a variation of reflexive modernity, one in which the pre-emptive logic and the dissolution between real and imaginary is complete. The problem or policy root for the reflexive interaction between a polity and government is not the modern, objective, discovered 'social fact' (catastrophic risk or threat) but a controlled real-time exercise that features real-world cut-ins. Risk, danger, threat: these are partial circumlocutions that cover the deployment of measured policy in the tradition of 'means other than war.'

## CONCLUSION

> *An investigator close to the matter says it reminds him of the Anto-*
> *nioni film "Blow-Up", a movie about a photographer who discov-*
> *ers the evidence of a covered-up murder hidden before his very eyes*
> *in the frame of an enlarged photograph. It's a mystery that no one*
> *appears eager to solve.*
>
> Christopher Ketcham, *Counterpunch*, March 3, 2007

The horrific events of 9/11 have generated an avalanche of popular and scholarly reports of a new security and policy paradigm; it is Cofer Black, who served as director of the CIA's Counterterrorism Center between 1999 and 2002, whose pithy testimony on the subject of operational flexibility to the 9/11 Commission is often used to encapsulate the paradigm shift: "All I want to say is that there was a 'before' 911 and 'after' 911. After 911 the gloves came off" (in Priest and Gellman, 2002). 9/11 is message and spectacle, order and chaos, signal and noise, and those in a position to distinguish and prioritize these terms, it is contended here, are by design few and far between.

To invert the preferred and official doctrine with respect to authorship, order, and signal is to criminalize the agency of the sovereign, a measure that, as pithily phrased by Ruppert (2004), is akin to crossing the Rubicon, or the point of no return. Consequently, that sovereignty trumps law is one explanation for the nonapplication of the rule of law and the mistreatment of 9/11 as a crime scene investigation. As popularly contended and indicated by Black's comment, where the paradigm shift intended is already a systemic adaptation of governmentality from rule of law auspices as the dominant paradigm, the signal event still carries the intended message, albeit more blatantly and baldly. Indeed, and following much of the recent literature on securitization (e.g., Bigo 2002; Waever 1995; Stritzel 2007), in which claims-making involves valued referent objects that are so existential that exceptional means and politics are advanced as legitimate, the question becomes how far, in the reflexive postmodern, has the signal event been advanced as pre-emptive, compartmentalized, policy optics?

In the meantime, for lesser policy objectives the style of information control is still iterative with the field or culture of politics of liberal democracies, particularly the legacy of rights and the rule of law. The function of transparency, of review and exposure, and the spotlight of moral and ethical examination, particularly of the collective actions of the state, has been and continues to be a mechanism of correction in the direction of the still-dominant political expectation of the governed for democracy and the rule of law. Thus, in liberal democracies there is a separation between intelligence and policy: intelligence 'fixed around policy' is the exception rather than the rule, and intelligence can speak truth to power. However, this is true up to the point at which the sovereign no longer supports intelligence independence. As information becomes intelligence and intelligence intersects with policy interests, it is politicized in the narrow sense of the term.

## NOTES

1. As discovered by Richard Pape (2003), suicide bombers (like those of September 11, 2001) are 'blowback' and their blowback is a boon to security intelligence in a continuous feedback loop.
2. This harkens back to the elite theorists, including W. Pareto, G. Mosca, and R. Michels.
3. Lippman proposed three elements to public opinion formation, including the subsumption of political communication under the economics of mass media, the creation of a culture of 'objectivity' in the journalistic profession, and the construction of a system of organized intelligence in elite administrative cycles (1922: 16). The news editor is an intermediary between mass opinion (and mass hysteria) and corporate government objectives, and the better the organization of information by security and police organizations or agencies, the greater the precision the reporting to the public and the clearer the message regarding the requisite political choices.
4. According to Prados (2006: 19), mechanisms of political action by covert operatives includes propaganda; subsidizing political parties, labor organizations, cultural groups, print and broadcast media, and other agents of influence; and sowing disinformation to discredit contrary messages.
5. One may define conspiracy as the attribution of agency without sufficient information. The importance of agency attribution stems from the proximity of the issue at the center of the conspiracy, particularly as a threat to people or peoples.
6. Consequently, serious debate on 'secret government' conspiracies is relegated to fringe media or countered by a 'not malevolent but incompetent' argument, suggesting that the effect, while appearing convenient, is the product of several overlapping bureaucratic snafus or by a rogue disgruntled malcontent, a 'lone gunman' acting alone. It is also tarnished by overexposure in splinter tabloid media. The alternative, as per Wendt and Duvall (2008: 607), is akin to a serious exploration of the UFO: it is a nonstarter inasmuch as modern sovereignty is 'constituted and organized by reference to human beings alone. Like the UFO, secret government conspiracy is understood as a taboo of scientific inquiry because the 'functional imperative' of sovereignty cannot decide the conspiracy exception 'while preserving the ability to make such a decision' (607).
7. See, for example, *Conspiracy Theories: The Philosophical Debate* (David Coady, ed., 2006) and *Changing Conceptions of Conspiracy* (Carl F. Graumann and Serge Moscovici, eds.,1988).
8. Schmitt was particularly keen on rescuing the ultimate authority of the sovereign because Weimar Germany was so comprehensively neutralized by its constitution.
9. Thus, according to Habermas (2001: 103), 'successful forms of integration have shaped the normative self-understanding of European modernity into an egalitarian universalism that can ease the transition to postnational

democracy's demanding contexts of mutual recognition for all of us—we, the sons, daughters and grandchildren of a barbaric nationalism.' Derrida (in Birnbaum 2004) comments on the relationship between deconstruction and the 'legacy of perfectibility' that belongs with Europe by attempting to avoid the idea that detraditionalizing impulse is inconsistent with the meaning of Europe: 'What I call "deconstruction," even when it's directed against something European, is European; it's a product; it's a European relationship to oneself like the experience of radical otherness. Ever since the Enlightenment, Europe has continuously criticized itself, and within this legacy of perfectibility, there is a chance for a future. At least, I'd like to hope so, and that's what feeds my indignation when I hear Europe definitively condemned, as though it were nothing but a crime scene.'

10. Note here that Derrida's deconstruction is not Schmitt's exceptionalism because the relationship to oneself is linked to an effort of 'perfectibility' that incorporates or assumes the experience of radical otherness in a condition of possibility rather than the privilege of radical sovereignty in a condition of anarchy or war. However, Derrida is indignant where the European cultural project identified with the first phase of modernization is dismissed 'as a crime scene.'

11. An illustration is provided in the policy decision to attack Iraq. To the United Nations and the American people, the invasion was sold or 'fixed' for the exocentric audience around 'weapons of mass destruction' (later substituted with the overthrow of rogue regimes, the 'export of democracy,' the need to 'drain the swamp'): modern democracies, it was being said, needed to take the offense to the enemy before the enemy could take the offense to them. This take offered a means–ends sleight-of-hand inasmuch as security is a process in the same way as the march toward democracy, and thus security, is for democracy and justice. To a more esoteric audience what was signaled is a new strategic policy of pre-emption (internally referred to as "full spectrum domination") and the consolidation of security discourse on counterterrorism, discourses that find immediate support in interests that would be bolstered by the control of strategically central oil fields and by creating new military outposts in the Middle East. To an even narrower audience, Wolfowitz could make the off-hand suggestion that Iraq was something of a stop-gap in the hop-scotching from bogey to bogey as the Project for a New American Century unfurled.

12. Strauss held this view because he wanted to reconcile classical political philosophy with the politics of liberal modernity but not its essence, which he saw as too problematic, and likely to lead the United States into relativism and nihilism.

13. It was its value for organizing political thinking post–Soviet Union that attracted many ambitious young liberals and conservatives alike to Strauss.

14. Intelligence may be defined as information that is exclusively actionable. It is information that is fed through the intelligence cycle by agencies that mutually recognize one another with respect to their intelligence capabilities. If intelligence is information that can make a political difference or that may be actionable to the political realities of the day (to borrow from the quote opening this chapter), security intelligence is intelligence about national security that may possess this actionability.

15. The foundational antagonism of liberal democratic rule continually rejuvenates itself. On the one side, frustration with democratic decision making, on the other, alarm with executive authority.

16. Major Kevin Nasypany, the NEADS mission crew commander who helped design the day's exercise, responded at one point, "The hijack's not supposed to be for another hour" (Bronner 2006). When NEADS Commander Robert Marr saw his personnel reacting to the news of the hijacking, he reportedly thought that the day's exercise was "kicking off with a lively, unexpected twist" (Spencer 2008: 26).

17. Gladio was stay-behind program established WWII that deployed participating countries secret services in counter-communist actions extending, according to some accounts, to an infiltration, radicalizing and criminalizing of communist groups (see Ganser 2005).

# 6 *Before the Law*
## Creeping Lawlessness in Canadian National Security

*Reem Bahdi*[1]

> Before the law sits a gatekeeper. To this gatekeeper comes a man from the country who asks to gain entry into the law. But the gatekeeper says that he cannot grant him entry at the moment. The man thinks about it and then asks if he will be allowed to come in later on. "It is possible," says the gatekeeper, "but not now."
>
> Franz Kafka, *Before The Law* (2003)

## INTRODUCTION

Exceptionalism scholars largely focused on post–September 11, 2001 (9/11) derogations from established rights invoke the camp metaphor to highlight the collective and systematic migration toward lawlessness (Agamben 1998; Calarco and DeCaroli 2007). The camp represents a space of suspended rights marked by the direct exercise of arbitrary sovereign power over physical, bodily life. Arabs and Muslims who have come under national security scrutiny in Canada have been banished to the edges of the camp (Razack 2008). Much like their U.S. equivalents, Canada's camps function as sites of lawlessness, spaces where individual rights are denied to subjects who seek but are refused legal protection. Security in the everyday lives of Arabs and Muslims in Canada betrays an arbitrariness that cannot be dismissed as the product of unrelated episodes perpetrated by isolated individuals. On the contrary, the lawlessness that marks post-9/11 national security cases and investigations in Canada derives from systemic and specific institutional practices that combine to threaten accountability, reduce the effectiveness of oversight, and ultimately pave a path to the camp in Canada.

This chapter chronicles the response of Canadian national security agencies, government lawyers, and elected officials to particular legal aspects of several high-profile national security cases in Canada. Specifically, it sets out how official responses to rights-claiming by investigative targets combined with official information control tactics tend toward lawlessness and undermine individual rights by thwarting accountability while simultaneously maintaining the façade of human rights protection. Although human rights protection and access to justice remains possible in Canada, the collective stories of several Arab and Muslim national security targets demonstrate the extent to which Canada has drifted toward lawlessness in its counterterrorism practices despite laws that purport to restrain arbitrariness and abuse of power.

In the wake of 9/11, we risk becoming Kafka's antihero: the man who gave up everything to access the law and died while passively accepting the authority of those who stand outside the law. We risk resigning ownership over the law to institutional gatekeepers without sufficiently questioning their authority or the consequences of our own resignation for human rights and due process in Canada. As a result, lawlessness may colonize the core of law itself, collectively moving us toward the state of exception, that "*fictio iuris* par excellence, which claims to maintain the law in its very suspension" (Agamben 2005:59).

## ANTITERRORISM IN EVERYDAY LIFE

While the Bush Administration carved out legal "black holes" and established Guantanamo Bay to facilitate the torture of terrorist suspects,[2] created the concept of "unlawful enemy combatant" to defeat the application of the Geneva Conventions[3] (Sands 2009), sought to redefined the legal meaning of torture (Jaffer 2007), exempted national security investigations from the prohibition on racial profiling in law enforcement[4] and limited access to information under the Presidential Records Act,[5] Canada publicly rejected the U.S. strategy of explicitly exempting national security targets from the protection of human rights norms and due process. Rather than calling on the War Measures Act to altogether suspend rights, Canadian officials responded to al- Qaeda's attacks by enacting Bill C-36, the Anti-Terrorism Act (Diab 2008), which purportedly "was carefully developed to combat terrorism, while ensuring that fundamental interests, such as privacy and other human rights, are respected."[6] In many respects, human rights find greater protection in Canada than in the United States (Jenkins 2003; Alden 2008). However, a close reading of the stories of Arabs and Muslims caught by Canadian national security investigations reveals that, contrary to the official rhetoric, a balance has not been struck between individual rights and national security agendas.

Canada's war against terrorism hits Arab and Muslim communities hard; their rights have been diluted in full view of the Charter of Rights and Freedoms (Aiken 2007; Diab 2008; Roach 2001; Bahdi 2003). Since 9/11, Canadian officials acting in the name of national security have imposed significant suffering and humiliation upon members of these communities. Officials have exposed targets of national security investigations to torture, facilitated their disappearance, compromised their physical health, undermined their mental well-being, and shattered their dreams. Through both action and inaction, officials have also heaped traumas upon the families of investigative targets.

Two commissions of inquiry determined that Canadian officials contributed to the overseas torture of four Canadian, Arab-Muslim men. National security agencies, government lawyers, and Canadian diplomats betrayed the rule of law and helped deliver Maher Arar, Abdullah Almalki, Ahmad El Maati, and Muayyed Nurredin into the hands of torturers. Canadian officials labeled the men as terrorists without evidence, improperly shared misleading and harmful information with foreign states, arranged for questions to be put to the men by intelligence agencies of states known to torture without regard for the men's well-being, and failed to come to the aid of the men when they had the opportunity to do so[7] (O'Connor 2006).

Although both the O'Connor and Iacobucci Inquiries documented the suffering imposed upon Arar, Almalki, El Maati, and Nurredin, Pither's description of the dehumanization of El Maati best conveys the range and depth of suffering the men endured in part as a consequence of Canadian action and inaction. The food came once or twice a day, usually a piece of pita bread with rice or beans on top. The guard would throw the food through the bars onto the floor of the cell. Unless the food happened to be delivered during the 10 min his handcuffs were switched to the front, El Maati had to kneel and eat off the floor like an animal. Rats the size of his hand could come out from the toilet and sometimes beat him to the food. In addition, the toilet was home to huge cockroaches (Pither 2008: 139).

Other Arab and Muslim men also claim that Canadian officials facilitated their overseas detention and torture. Abousfian Abdelrazik, a Canadian citizen, was arrested in the Sudan in 2003 while visiting his ailing mother, and was tortured in detention. Publicly available government documents indicate that Sudanese officials arrested him at the request of Canadian officials. The Canadian Security Intelligence Service (CSIS) and the Royal Canadian Mounted Police (RCMP) cleared Abdelrazik of connections to terrorism. Yet, Foreign Affairs Minister Cannon effectively exiled Abdelrazik by refusing to issue a travel document that would have allowed Abdelrazik to return to Canada. Minister Canon indicated that Abdelrazik must remove himself from U.S. and U.N. terrorist lists before he would be allowed to have a Canadian passport, an unprecedented and virtually impossible criteria.[8]

Nicole Chrolavicius, Benamar Benatta's lawyer, observes that Benatta "is the first and only known case of Canada effecting an extraordinary rendition—an illegal transfer of a person from one legal jurisdiction to another outside the scope of law" (Teotonio 2008). Benatta alleges that Canadian officials handed him over to the United States at the request of U.S. officials without regard for the possibility that he would be abused and tortured. An Algerian refugee claimant who arrived in Canada via the United States on September 5, 2001, Benatta was detained in Canada while officials confirmed his true identity. On September 12, he was brought before a Canadian immigration adjudicator who ordered his further detention in Canada until his identity could be verified. Instead, Canadian officials hustled Benatta into the back of a car and, without his knowledge or consent, handed him over to American officials as a "suspicious traveller." In the United States, Benatta was imprisoned and held in conditions that the United Nations recognized could be considered tortured.[9] He was cleared of any connection to 9/11 events by the Federal Bureau of Investigation within a few weeks of his arrest.[10] However, he remained in detention for several years on trumped-up immigration charges.[11] Canada has since recognized Benatta as a convention refugee but refuses to bear any responsibility for his pain and suffering.

While Benatta, Arar, Almalki, El Maati, Nurredin, and Abdelrazik endured torture and mistreatment in foreign jails, members of the 'Toronto 18'—a purportedly "homegrown" terrorist cell—claim mistreatment by Canadian officials in Canadian jails. As their trials winds their way through the courts, the question of whether homegrown terrorism had developed into a serious threat has dominated much of the public discussion of the case. Yet, few appear interested in allegations of mistreatment by the men. Zakaria Amara, one of the accused, gives a glimpse into his mistreatment: "When I was first brought to cell 1 unit 1K, I was slammed face first on the floor, a huge shield was then pressed against my back while a guard smeared my face with his boots because I dared lift my head."[12] Corrections officials deny allegations of abuse and at least one newspaper labeled them a "typical" ploy invoked by terrorist suspects as a form of "judicial jihad."[13] However, some of the prisoners were held in solitary confinement for more than 2 years.[14] International law recognizes extended solitary confinement as a form of psychological abuse,[15] which can shade into torture.[16] Moreover, lawyer Faisal Kutty's report to the U.N. Human Rights Council details other serious violations of the prisoners' rights, including inadequate medical services; lack of exercise; lack of respect for religious expression; exposure to harassment, abuse, and insensitive comments about their religious views and beliefs; and excessive force and humiliation at the hands of prison guards.[17]

Canadian officials have also imposed psychological suffering and hardship on refugee claimants through their administrative control over refugee lives. Tortured in Syria for writing in support of the Palestinian Liberation Organization, Nawal Haj Khalil came to Canada in March 1993 with her two children, hoping for a new life. Born and raised in Syria, her political activities brought her in conflict with the regime of President Hafez al-Assad. In 1978, she was detained, beaten, and tortured for 4 months for distributing pamphlets deemed insurgent by the Syrian government. Although immigration officials recognized Haj Khalil as a convention refugee and acknowledge that she poses no risk to Canadian national security, they have nonetheless denied her application for permanent residency, along with her children's applications, on the basis that her writing in support of the PLO rendered her a member of a terrorist organization. Haj Khalil sought a ministerial exemption from the finding that she should be excluded from Canada on this basis, but, after more than 16 years since her arrival in Canada, Haj Khalil awaits resolution of her claim.

Throughout her years in Canada, Haj Khalil has had trouble finding employment and, because she did not qualify for financial aid, she could not attend college to improve her skills and better herself. She eventually developed dysthymia or "chronic sadness" and experiences episodes of major depressive disorder that render her suicidal.[18] She conveyed her despair over her uncertain state of affairs during her hearing before the federal court.

> I didn't want anyone to know what is my status in the country, how long I been have in the country. I don't want to tell anybody. How I live, I don't want to tell anybody. Why I'm there, I don't want to tell anybody. I can't. I feel if I will be questioned one more time I will kill myself.[19]

Hassan Almrei, Mohammad Mahjoub, Mahmoud Jaballah, Adil Charkaoui, and Mohamed Harkat similarly live in varying degrees of limbo. All were subject to security certificates under the Immigration and Refugee Protection Act. These certificates permit the indefinite detention of noncitizens deemed national security threats pending deportation. All the men were eventually released subject to "control orders" that required, among other things, strict surveillance by family members, permission to receive friends, curfews, wearing an electronic tracking bracelet, surveillance of family mail and conversations, seizure of possessions at the discretion of officials, and surveillance by officials.[20] In March 2009, Mahjoub requested to return to detention for the sake of his family because the court-sanctioned control orders proved so harsh and humiliating that one of his young children threatened to run away from home while another spoke of suicide.[21] A federal court judge found that a Canada Border Services Agency raid on Harkat's that involved dogs and more than 16 officers was intrusive and violated his dignity.[22] Because Harkat, like the other detainees on control orders, has to be supervised by family members, his family was forced onto welfare when Sophie Harkat quit her civil service position to stay home with her husband.[23] Omar Khadr, for his part, remains in Guantanamo Bay despite a Supreme Court of Canada ruling that Khadr's constitutional rights had been violated by Canadian officials,[24] the executive which failed to seek Khadr's repatriation.[25]

Not one of the individuals who have come under security scrutiny since 9/11 has fully secured justice. Although the security certificates against Almrei and Charkaoui were deemed unreasonable by the federal court,[26] the men remain under a cloud of controversy, tarnished with the terrorist label. While the Canadian government settled with Arar, reportedly for defamation, he remains on U.S. terrorism lists.[27] The government has refused to compensate or otherwise offer remedy for the suffering of other victims of the war against terrorism. Abousfian Abdelrazik, a widower, returned home to Montreal after years of languishing in the Canadian embassy in Khartoum, too afraid of Sudanese authorities to leave the compound but unable to return to his children in Montreal. The federal court issued a strong judgment, effectively ordering the Conservative Party government to bring him home but Abdelrazik`s quest for justice has likely only begun. The federal court found on the basis of evidence before it that CSIS had facilitated Abdelrazik`s detention. But Abdelrazik's claim for compensation will likely be mired in court as the Conservative government appears steadfast in its unwillingness to pay him damages. Moreover, Abdelrazik remains on the UN Security Council's 1267 list of terrorists, which prevents him from receiving money, working, or maintaining a bank account. The Canadian government has not reported any effort to have Abdelrazik removed from the list even though the federal court stressed that the listing provisions violate the principles of natural justice.

Similarly, Haj Khalil, Benatta, Almalki, El Maati, and Nurredin have sought to litigate their claims in the face of staunch opposition from the Department of Justice. Two levels of court have rejected Haj Khalil`s right to sue and in an ironic twist, the federal court attributed her suffering to her quest to litigate her rights.[28] She awaits consideration from the Supreme Court of Canada, which may refuse to hear her claim altogether. Her limbo continues. The claims of Almalki, El Maati, Nurredin and Benatta have been mired under motions and have yet to advance on the merits. Not surprisingly, years of legal proceedings have taken a toll on the justice seekers. Almalki equates his experiences before the Iacobucci Inquiry with torture, a perfectly comprehensible claim once one understands that torture is marked by a loss of control over one's life and is perpetrated not without special torture tools but with instruments that ordinarily play a beneficial role in society (Scarry 1985). National security agency continue to target Almalki, El Maati, Nurredin, the men held under security certificates, and those associated with them for investigation.

Those charged under the Criminal Code of Canada have arguably fared better than those pursued under other statutory authorities; however, one cannot claim that justice has been done or seen to be done under the Criminal Code. Charges against seven members of the "Toronto 18" were stayed, but those caught in the criminal sweep remain tainted by the accusations made against them. The youngest of the accused was found guilty of plotting to detonate an explosive, although his lawyers argued that the RCMP informant had entrapped the young man and the very same informant indicated in court that the youth was innocent of all charges and knew nothing of the alleged plot. Nonetheless, the youth was sentenced to 2.5 years and released after his sentencing hearing because of time already served.[29] In the meantime, Mohammad Momin Khawaja, the first person found guilty under the antiterrorism provisions of Canada`s Criminal Code, filed an appeal of his conviction in April 2009, arguing that the presiding judge made serious errors in law in both convicting and sentencing.[30]

Cognizant of the harm generated by Canadian national security efforts, legal scholars critical of Canada's national security strategies argue that the Canadian legislative response is flawed because it fails to protect fundamental rights, superfluous because Canadian law already addresses national security threats, and dangerous because it spawns abuse without advancing national security (Diab 2008; Pue 2003; Bahdi 2003; Aiken 2007). The next two sections of this paper extend this critical tradition. Rather than focusing on the legal texts or critiquing mistakes made by national security, however, these sections focus on the techniques adopted by Canadian officials to justify the harms inflicted upon national security targets. These techniques fall into two general categories: first, the rights-claims of national security targets are delegitimized, and second, information concerning national security investigations is manipulated to the benefit of officials over investigative targets. These dual strategies ultimately thwart accountability of government officials by frustrating effective oversight and disenfranchise rights claimants while simultaneously maintaining the illusion that justice for national security targets remains accessible.

## SILENCING RIGHTS-CLAIMS

Legal theoreticians often articulate rights-claims as the public demand for recognition as a person of equal dignity. Rights-claims convert private experiences of pain, tragedy, and trauma into public narratives that demand respect, recognition, explanation, and accounting. As Freedman notes, rights-claims are both declarative and constitutive of "the right to be seen, to be heard, to be listened to" (Freedman 2000: 434). In the same vein, Williams contends that invoking the language of rights "elevates one's status from human body to social being" (Williams 1991: 153). Arab/Muslim and rights, however, maintain an uneasy relationship with the rights-claiming paradigm. Rights-claims in the national security context are stood on their heads, as Arabs and Muslims face a barrage of challenges from Canadian officials that aim to eliminate specific rights claims while at the same time positing the very act of rights-claiming as violence. These challenges generate several interdependent consequences. First, they undermine the possibility of invoking rights as a symbol of social respect or the "right to be seen, heard and listened to" and reduce Arab and Muslim rights claimants from social being to human body. Second, they create the illusion of rights protection, thereby collapsing the divide between law and lawlessness. Third, they conceptualize Arab and Muslim rights-claiming as threatening to national security, which in turn justifies violence against the rights claimant by Canadian officials. The point, in short, is not simply that Arabs and Muslims are ultimately denied their rights but that officials refuse to recognize Arabs and Muslims as legitimate rights claimants in the first place.

This strategy of delegitimizing rights while purporting to protect them and the attendant justification of official violence and lawlessness through the fracturing of rights-claims emerges starkly in political rhetoric surrounding the security certificate regime. Officials justify the indefinite detention permitted under security certificates on the basis that the detainee is held in "a prison with three walls" from which he can escape at anytime simply by agreeing to leave Canada. Ministers Anne McLellan and Irwin Cotler, for example, implicitly invoked the three walls metaphor in a joint statement which illustrates how officials purport to protect rights while effectively denouncing the very act of rights-claiming. Emphasizing that the detainees present a risk to Canada and maintaining that their lack of freedom arises only because they challenge their deportations, the ministers stressed that the detainees "can, and always have been able, to leave the country at any time. They are detained solely by virtue of their refusal to leave Canada."[31]

Ministers McLellan and Cotler's contention that the detainees can end their own suffering trivializes the rights-claims at issue in several ways. By describing the security certificate regime as a choice between detention and freedom, the ministers misrepresent the issues at stake. Security certificates do not represent a choice between detention and freedom. The certificates are issued against noncitizens who often risk torture if deported. The three walls argument implicitly invoked by the ministers remarkably altogether ignores the risk of torture and thereby belittles the right to be free from torture. The ministers' invitation to imagine that stepping beyond the three walls means stepping into freedom, represents an invitation to erase the detainees' identity as refugees and construct them instead as people who have nothing to fear but who likely should be feared—sleeper cell agents determined to remain in Canada for the sake of their terrorist cause. Ultimately, the ministers' reliance on the three walls metaphor proves significant not because they seek to justify violations of the detainees' rights, but because it posits that the detainees are not entitled to be free from torture and have that right be taken seriously by Canadian officials in the first place. The security certificate detainees are made to stand outside the legal order through misleading juxtapositions and false choices that silence and privatize their harm in a way that is all too familiar to racialized rights claimants in Canada.[32] (Aiken 2007) The three walls argument also belittles the challenge to fundamental legal principles posed by security certificates.

Canadian law generally abhors indefinite detention. Individuals held under security certificates, however, do not know how long they will be confined—they can technically be held for the rest of their lives if they are not deported.[33] A security certificate is issued simply where the government can establish "reasonable grounds" to "believe" that an individual may be linked to terrorism.[34] The proceedings can take place *in camera* and *ex parte*. Given the low threshold of proof and restricted disclosure allowed by the law, it is perfectly conceivable that innocent individuals—people who legitimately fear persecution and torture—will be caught in the security certificate net. The detainees would, ironically, be better off convicted of terrorist-related offenses under the Criminal Code rather than merely being suspected of terrorism under immigration legislation. Not only does the Criminal Code requires proof beyond a reasonable doubt while the Immigration Act permits detention using reasonableness as the standard of proof, a convicted terrorist is sentenced to a specific term in jail while a security certificate detainee can be held for an indefinite period of time in abhorrent conditions.[35] Given this context, the contention that the detainees can end their incarceration by leaving their three walls and Canada renders fundamental violations of Canadian legal principles, the detainees' suffering, and their rights claims irrelevant and illegitimate.

Once Arabs and Muslims are imagined as illegitimate rights claimants, the very act of rights-claiming becomes a threat, an act bordering on and suggesting violence. Law morphs into lawlessness and, in the process, Arabs and Muslims are reduced from social beings to human bodies who can be tortured, abused, tormented, kidnapped, isolated, defamed, exiled, or indefinitely detained. Indeed, national security agencies have demonstrated a propensity to regard Arab and Muslim demands for rights and justice not as the request for recognition as person worthy of equal rights and respect but as evidence that the claimant is a national security risk. Perhaps Arar's story best illustrates the extent to which rights-claiming can be interpreted as a threat which helps justify violence by and for the nation.

Lawlessness entered Arar's life exactly at the moment he asked for his rights and precisely because of his rights-claiming. When the RCMP first contacted him, Arar agreed to be interviewed without a lawyer on the condition that information from the interview not be used in any legal proceedings.[36] The RCMP deemed Arar's conditions too strict and decided against the interview. But, they also drew an unsubstantiated negative inference about Arar. They characterized Arar's request as a refusal to be interviewed and presumed that he had something to hide. Translating Arar's "yes" into a "no," the RCMP informed U.S. officials that Arar had refused to be interviewed. They added that Arar had "suddenly" left Canada after the interview request when, in fact, 5 months had passed between the interview request and Arar's departure from Canada with his family.[37] The negative inference drawn about Arar's attempts to protect his legal rights subsequently formed the basis of yet another unreasonable inference made by the RCMP; they labeled Arar and his family "Islamic Extremists" with suspected al-Qaeda links. Arar's quest to protect his rights was thus transformed into violent, terrorist intent.[38]

Why did rights-claiming lead the RCMP to draw a negative inference about Arar and his family? Perhaps Arar's attempts to protect his rights flew in the face of an unstated assumption: national security is better served when Arabs and Muslims submit to agency sovereignty and do not ask for their rights. Indeed, members of the RCMP have expressed general frustration with policing Arabs and Muslims in the context of a system of legal rules and legal scrutiny. This frustration reveals itself in the phrase "judicial jihad," a phrase that has become part of the parlance in at least some RCMP circles.[39] RCMP references to judicial jihad neatly conveys the Agamben's observation that the state of exception operates as "the force of law without law" or what Razack identifies as "the idea that only an unfettered state power can properly confront threats to the nation" (Agamben 2005: 39; Razack 2008: 28). RCMP officers understood Arar's rights-claims as an illegitimate limits on their power. Razack argues that "race thinking becomes embedded in law and bureaucracy so that the suspension of rights appears not as violence but as the law itself" (Razack 2008: 9). To the extent that asking for rights in the context of national security fetters the power and discretion of the investigators and decision maker, the request for rights is heard as a potential but real threat to the nation, a 'jihad.' In Arar's case, the threat was grafted onto his person, and morphed with his identity as an Arab Muslim man, leading investigators to the conclusion that Arar had links to al-Qaeda. In this way, rights-claims were turned against the claimant and the quest for rights opened the path to lawlessness, punishment, torture, and despair rather than, as expected, protection from lawlessness and despair.

Government lawyers also expressed exasperation with rights-claims in the national security context. Serving its liaison role and drawing from the experience of its members, the Council on American-Islamic Relations (CAIR-Can) advises members of the Arab and Muslim communities not to meet with national security officials in the absence of a lawyer. Government lawyers at the Arar inquiry questioned Dr. Sheema Khan, president of CAIR-Can, about the efficacy of such advice.

> I am wondering if you would agree with me that from a policing perspective, if it were the case that no citizen would ever speak to them without a lawyer present, it would in fact be very difficult for them to do their job? They make hundreds of inquiries in the course of any given day, and if there is a whole population that refuses to meet with them without a lawyer present, that actually makes it very difficult for them to do their job.[40]

This line of questioning not only suggested that Canadian Muslims should resign ownership over their rights, it posited the very act of Arab and Muslim rights-claiming as threatening to the nation. Although it is not doubt true that police would find it difficult to do their jobs if every citizen insisted on a lawyer before speaking, the Department of Justice ignored that the Arab and Muslim interaction with police has historically been marked by intimidation and fear (CAIR-CAN Annual Review 2003–2004). In the direct context and immediate aftermath of what Canadian government officials did to Arar, government lawyers were pressing for a leap of faith by members of the very community from which Arar was taken and tortured.

Once they regard national security investigative targets as unworthy of rights-claiming, Canadian officials have adopted procedural and substantive techniques to strip Arabs and Muslims of rights. The first technique is procedural: render rights-claiming utterly impractical by creating insurmountable financial barriers for the justice seeker. The Minister of Citizenship and Immigration employed this technique against Haj Khalil when she sought to sue immigration officials for financial and psychological harm arising from the unreasonable delay in processing her landing application. Her story reinforces that Arab and Muslim rights-claiming will not only prove difficult to realize in the national security context but that the very attempt to claim rights in the first place can be turned into a negative factor that will weigh against the claimant. Although the federal court found that immigration officials had inordinately delayed Haj Khalil's application for permanent residency, it concluded that immigration officers do not owe a duty of care to Haj Khalil because recognizing such a duty would create a chilling effect on national security investigations.[41] The Department of Justice then asked for and received a $305,000 cost order against Haj Khalil.[42] Such a staggering award sends an indirect but clear message: beware asking for rights and trying to hold governments accountable for their unreasonable acts when national security is at issue.

Government lawyers also seek to defeat rights claimed of national security targets by constructing substantive legal arguments that promote lawlessness. This is achieved either by denying the application of established legal norms to the national security context or redefining existing laws so that they further—rather than limit—the power of the state to act arbitrarily. Denial and redefinition play an obvious role in thwarting both rights and government accountability because if there are no relevant legal norms, then scrutiny and analysis of government acts and decisions prove not only futile but absurd. Although scholarly attention has focused on the Bush administration's use of denial and redefinition in the now infamous 'torture memos' crafted by lawyers in the administration to justify official torture policies and practices (Sands 2009), similar reliance on denial and redefinition by Canadian government officials has virtually escaped scrutiny.

Justice lawyers wielded denial as an instrument before the Iacobucci Inquiry, for example. As part of his deliberations, Commissioner Iacobucci invited the Department of Justice to present its position about the legal standards against which the conduct of Canadian officials should be measured. In its submissions, the Department of Justice argued that even if Ottawa did share information with torturing states and thus helped facilitate the men's arrest and detention abroad, this would not put Canada in breach of its obligations under the International Convention Against Torture (CAT) ("Hearings on Standards of Conduct" 2008). The CAT, according to the Department of Justice, simply requires Canadian officials to prevent torture on its own soil, but creates no obligation for Canadian officials vis-à-vis events that take place in foreign countries. Such a reading of the convention proves overly formalistic, defies national and international human rights principles, and provides justification for the contracting out of torture (Bahdi 2009). Even more astounding, the Department of Justice denied knowledge that Almalki was tortured in Syria, even though a report by fact-finder Stephen Toope held that Almalki gave credible accounts of his treatment in Syria and noted that he was "especially badly treated, and for an extended period."[43] The Iacobucci Report also stressed that government officials must be sophisticated in their assessment of risks of torture and that they had concrete evidence of the torture of Almalki and other citizens abroad but failed to act appropriately.[44]

The Department of Justice turned to redefinition in its justification of the treatment of Benatta by Canadian officials. Benatta filed a $35 million claim for compensation against the Canadian government, alleging that officials, through their illegal acts, placed him at risk. The government denies Benatta's allegations and refutes all responsibility by contending that they simply returned Benatta to the United States under a routine 'direct back' procedure.[45] A 'direct back' is an administrative procedure whereby an individual who appears at a Canadian point of entry can be directed back to the United States, and vice versa, if space or other resource considerations determine that the individual cannot have his or her claim processed at that particular point in time.[46] When he was allegedly directed back to the United States as government lawyers contend, Benatta had already been in Canadian detention for 7 days and had appeared before an immigration adjudicator who ordered his further detention until his identity could be verified.[47] He had made a refugee claim, which entitled him to positive protection from persecution pending final determination of his claim and which required the government of Canada to respect his rights as noted in the Canadian Charter of Rights and Freedoms.[48]

One can imagine the fear and uncertainty that gripped Canadian officials shortly after 9/11. However, if they had concerns about Benatta, Canadian officials might have acted with clear legal authority by, for example, continuing to detain Benatta while U.S. officials sought his extradition. Benatta's surreptitious transfer to the United States—effected without his consent and without a paper trail—perhaps lent Canadian officials the conviction that they no longer had any responsibility for Benatta. Removing him from Canadian soil, it seemed, erased the possibility of rights-claiming. Immigration officials, claiming that they were too busy to complete any paperwork to document what happened to Benatta (2008), exercised full sovereignty over Benatta's body but felt no obligation toward him as a rights-bearing individual. He simply disappeared from their consciousness.

We may learn more about Benatta's saga as the court hears his claim. It appears that Canadian officials collaborated with their U.S. counterparts to suppress due process in the past.[49] If Benatta's allegations prove founded,

they mean that Canada had a hand in violating international law's prohibition on forced disappearances. This prohibition is as strong as the prohibition on torture because forced disappearances and torture go hand in
hand—people disappear while in government custody precisely so that they
can be abused or tortured (Ratner 2001: 123–124). If Benatta's allegations
prove founded, moreover, then Canadian officials, like their U.S. counterparts, manipulated immigration procedures to cover up what was at best a
negligent investigation of Benatta and at worse a conspiracy with U.S. officials to effect Benatta's disappearance using nefarious and illegal methods.
Until we learn more, however, the Department of Justice's invocation of the
direct back provisions to explain Benatta's undocumented transfer to U.S.
authorities in bizarre circumstances smacks of ex post facto justification
and redefinition of the law to justify lawlessness.

False juxtapositions, unreasonable cost demands, denial, and redefinition delegitimize the rights-claims of national security targets and limit
their access to justice. These strategies collectively rely on a metalogic for
their credibility: in the national security context, exceptional measures
prove necessary. Every high-profile national security case is shot through
with the claim that exceptional times demand exceptional measures, and
national security agencies should not, in times of emergency, be limited by
laws that might unduly restrict their powers to defend the nation. In other
words, lawlessness constitutes the necessary corollary of national security
(Dyzenhaus 2006).

In Canada, however, arguments about necessity and lawlessness are
rarely made expressly. On the contrary, they are bundled up and packaged
along with claims about the importance of individual rights. While Americans derogate, Canadians balance. The logic of necessity in the United
States takes the form of express exemptions to rights. In Canada, the logic
of necessity proceeds through the balancing of individual versus collective
rights. But, faced with the necessity calculus, individual rights hardly stand
a chance. If the battle is between the one and the many, and if individual
rights threaten the many, then individual rights must always give way to
collective well-being. Even after the O'Connor and Iacobucci Inquiries,
CSIS refuses to unequivocally renounce torture and continues to invoke a
simplified Raskolnikovian logic of utilitarian necessity to justify reliance on
torture confessions.[50] The recurring debate about the efficacy of torture in
Canada demonstrates that as we move further from 9/11, the logic of necessity deepens its roots rather than withering away (Sands 2009).

The balancing rhetoric proved highly convenient for Ministers seeking
to justify the antiterrorism legislation in the face of almost unanimous criticism from Canadian academics and rights groups.[51] Balancing captured the
political and social imagination; however, the purported balance between
collective versus individual rights has morphed into lawlessness. This invitation to balance proves convincing in the abstract (Ruddock 2004). Upon
scrutiny, however, the individual versus collective rights paradigm radically

alters the foundations of Canadian jurisprudence by sweeping away the sophisticated balancing techniques fashioned by our courts in favor of political expediency and misleadingly simple formulas. The balancing act too-often proposed by government officials distorts legal principles and doctrines (Roach 2003; Stuart 2005). Indeed, the European Court of Human Rights has rejected the proposition that the risk of torture should be balanced against national security.[52] In Canada, however, balancing became a favored trope for government officials after 9/11. Ministers McLellan and Cotler joined forces to invoke Supreme Court jurisprudence and justify deportation to torture on the logic of balancing individual rights versus collective or national security.

> [W]ith regards to the issue of non-removal of security certificate cases based upon a substantial risk of torture in their country of origin the Supreme Court of Canada articulated its position in the *Suresh* case. As a government, we carefully balance the rights of the individual with the interest of national security.[53]

Ministers McLellan and Cotler cite Suresh to justify the balance of individual rights with national security, but they fail to indicate that the Supreme Court of Canada had not countenanced an unqualified balancing of individual versus collective rights as the framework within which national security analysis should proceed (Suresh v. Canada 2002: at para. 51). On the contrary, using the sophisticated balancing techniques developed under section one of the charter, the court had recognized the possibility of deportation to torture but had also ordered a stay of Suresh's deportation and had underscored its abhorrence for torture. However, the decision ushered in a simplistic political discourse of necessity shorn of the court's nuances and express limits on deportation to torture.

Anything becomes justifiable within both law and politics through simple balances. This is the new *normal*. The political and social consolidation of the new normal in Canada exhibited a remarkable coherence to the conditions precedent identified by Agamben's state of exception; it is the product of democracy, and it adopts the metaphor of war to support and maintain its internal lawlessness (Agamben 2005). "The legal category of the emergency, then, extends or completes law's empire" (Humphreys 2006). It is, as Pue so aptly described, "constitutional governance in a state of permanent warfare" (Pue 2003). In the state of permanent warfare, Canada's intricate web of laws, policies, and practices create the illusion of rights but ultimately carve out spaces where rights often proved a chimera because Arabs and Muslims rights claims are delegitimized through procedural and substantive techniques, while government officials advance simplistic arguments of necessity and balance to justify a regime of internal lawlessness.

The first section of this chapter surveys the harm generated by the 'war against terrorism' for members of Canada's Arab and Muslim communities and illustrates how government officials exercise sovereignty over Arab and Muslim bodies. The section immediately preceding this identified the legal and rhetorical techniques advanced by government officials to delegitimize Arab and Muslim rights-claiming and to deny access to justice. Ultimately, the delegitimizing of rights-claiming combines with securitization to perpetuate sovereignty over Arab and Muslim bodies. The next section turns to the problem of securitization in Canada. Securitization refers to the process whereby national security agencies seek to maximize control over information while minimizing accountability. These two ends prove intimately connected, as control over information both underscores the need for accountability and simultaneously thwarts it.

## SECURITIZATION

Securitization in Canada manifests itself in various ways as national security agencies have gained virtually unfettered freedom to determine how much information they are permitted to cultivate about a suspect while also determining in significant measure how much information can be released about their own conduct.[54] Information control has taken on its own dynamic and become an end unto itself. It is now beyond doubt that national security agencies circulate in-house fabrications as truth via national and international information-sharing networks. Perhaps the best-known example of such in-house fabrications is the RCMP labelling of Arar and his wife as members of a "group of Islamic Extremist individuals suspected of being linked to Al Qaeda" (Pither 2008: 163). Arar was tortured because the RCMP falsely created the impression that they held evidence of his al-Qaeda connections. In reality, all they had was information that Arar associated with other Syrian Canadians in Ottawa, vacationed in Malaysia, and occasionally walked and talked in the rain. Rather than circulating this information throughout global national security information-sharing networks, the RCMP circulated the unjustifiable conclusion that Arar represented a threat. As an added ironic and tragic twist, the RCMP became even more interested in Arar as a potential terrorist when the Americans sent Arar to Syria to be questioned, although U.S. interest in Arar was derived from information received from the RCMP.[55] (O'Connor, 2005: 147; Pither 2008: 218). Similarly, El Maati, Almalki, and Nurredin also faced torture as a result of national security agencies across jurisdictions secretly sharing secretly false information.[56] It took two public inquiries and several years to help illustrate to the Canadian public how the RCMP recycled their own echo as evidence against the men whom they wrongly deemed to be national security risks.

National security agencies have also strategically withheld information during legal proceedings. Justice O'Connor, in his final report, characterized the government's claiming of national security confidentiality as a "bargaining position" rather than a measured need to keep certain information out of the public eye for legitimate national security reasons.[57] RCMP officers obtained search warrants while failing to disclose that the justification they put before the presiding judge might be the product of torture.[58] A federal court judge recently questioned whether CSIS had violated its obligation to act in good faith by failing to disclose information that might undermine its case for holding Harkat under a security certificate. The judge also raised concerns about 'possible prevarication' by a CSIS witness.[59] National security agencies also revealed their propensity to strategically withhold information before the Iacobucci Inquiry. The RCMP explained before the inquiry that they "had no evidence indicating that Syria was a 'human rights violator' and therefore to comment on that in an application for a warrant would have been expressing an opinion on a political issue."[60]

Agencies also manipulate the media through selective information leaks, feeding the public penchant for sensational antiterrorism stories. When the Toronto 18 plot was uncovered, "almost five thousand articles reported on the arrest and allegations"[61] before a publication ban was imposed approximately 2 weeks after the arrests. Commissioner O'Connor thoroughly analyzed the media leaks around Arar's case and observed that the leaks were timed to discredit Arar or deflect away from the commission's findings.[62] Selective media leaks were also used against El Maati. In October 2001, media reports had surfaced that Canadian officials had detained a man in possession of government maps, which helped linked him to a terrorist plot.[63] Several years later, CSIS officials testified at the Iacobucci Inquiry that the map held no particular significance. But, it was left to an investigative reporter to uncover and inform the public that the map in El Maati's possession was nothing more than an outdated tourist guide distributed by the Canadian government. One of those investigative reports, Jeff Sallot speculated that officials manipulated the media. "I realized that nobody in the government or the security agencies had bothered to check out the map, or if they did—and this is even worse—they realized that there was nothing to the map, but it was a good story to have out there" (Pither 2008).

The highest level of government officials also resort to media manipulation. Kalajdzic analyzes the inaccurate and incomplete information Minister of Public Safety Stockwell Day pressed in the media after the release of the Iacobucci Report to reassert Almalki as a threat and simultaneously deflect criticism from Canadian officials (Kalajdzic, 2009). More recently, the government of Prime Minister Stephen Harper again resorted to selective media leaks when it released statements labeling Abousfian Abdelrazik as a senior al-Qaeda operative. The new round of allegations was released to the press on April 29, 2009, on the eve of an anticipated motion by Member of Parliament Paul Dewar requiring Abdelrazik to appear before the Standing Committee on Foreign Affairs. The media reports also noted that the government had labeled Abdelrazik an al-Qaeda operative because he was listed by the United Nations and because of information provided by Zayn al-Abidin Muhammad Husayn, the Palestinian man commonly known as Abu Zubaydah whom former President Bush had identified as an al-Qaeda leader. The Canadian media reports, however, failed to include that the most recent information questions whether Zubaydah was an important al-Qaeda figure and stresses that the information he gave at Guantanamo Bay about other purported al-Qaeda leaders was fabricated for the purpose of ending torture, which reportedly included 83 rounds of waterboarding.[64] The media also failed to observe, and the government sources on which they relied presumably failed to note, that the U.N. listing procedure violates the principles of fundamental justice in part because the United Nations offers no effective procedure to permit one to remove one's name from the list.[65]

Agency sovereignty and control over investigative targets are strongest under the prevention side of the mandate; hence, agencies have tended toward prevention over enforcement (van Munster 2007). Testimony at the Arar inquiry revealed that CSIS wanted the RCMP to lay charges against Almalki while he was held in Syria so that he could be brought home. But, the RCMP did not have enough against Almalki to charge him so their strategy shifted to prevention rather than enforcement. In the RCMP framework, prevention included seeking access to the information that Abdullah might provide under torture and threat of torture by the Syrians. "We may have to take and be satisfied with the prevention side of the mandate and hope that additional information can be gleaned with respect to his plans . . ." wrote Corporal Rick Flewelling, the man tasked with overseeing Project A-O Canada.[66]

Agency appetite for information about investigative targets appears insatiable and unchecked. Almalki has been followed, tortured, and examined by a commission of inquiry yet government officials appear still unable or unwilling to charge him with any offense. Still, Almalki remains under investigation. Given the deference courts show to administrative agencies in the enforcement of their mandates, he will unlikely secure judgement from a court that he should be left alone. Indeed, no effective mechanism exists to hold national security agencies accountable for their decision to initiate or continue a particular investigation.[67] Even the Arar inquiry, the most comprehensive post-9/11 review of national security investigations, refused to second-guess the efficacy of investigating Arar. Agencies have historically proven overwhelmingly successful in seeking surveillance warrants.[68] The prevention side of the mandate, which also frees national security agencies from making a case against investigative targets while seeking charges under the Criminal Code of Canada, requires national security agencies to demonstrate their case beyond a reasonable doubt, a standard which they have only occasionally been able to meet.[69] National security agencies remain virtually unaccountable in determining when too much information is enough.

Agencies also regulate the flow of information that is released about them. Mechanisms introduced to take the near monopoly over information flow away from national security agencies have achieved only limited success. Commissioner O'Connor and his counsel had full access to information throughout the Arar inquiry; however, they fought a constant disclosure battle with government lawyers who overclaimed national security confidentially and invoked national security to prevent embarrassment and government accountability (Pither 2008). For example, the government withdrew its claims to confidentiality over the fact that the RCMP had falsely linked Arar to al-Qaeda only at the end of the Arar inquiry.[70] The commissioner fought the government in federal court over national security confidentiality claims and ultimately won but only after the release of his report. Perhaps learning a lesson from the tenacity of Commissioner O'Connor and his team in seeking public disclosure of information, the Harper government defined the Iacobucci Inquiry as an "internal inquiry." As a result, the inquiry was held almost entirely in secret. It allowed minimal participation of the very men whose torture defined its mandate. It also restricted the participation of their lawyers.

Critics of securitization and national security confidentiality appeared to win partial victory when the Supreme Court of Canada determined that the *ex parte, in camera* security certificate proceedings violated the Charter. The government responded to the court's ruling by, inter alia, introducing the special advocate regime.[71] Shortly after their appointment, the special advocates themselves indicated that they cannot fully fulfill their responsibilities because of the restrictions placed upon them in communicating with their client and others.[72] Although the special advocates have proven remarkably effective despite the limitations placed upon them, the problem of misinformation by agencies remains a concern. For example, proceedings before the federal court reveals that CSIS edits documents before it places them before the court. The Federal Court rightly expressed its concern by noting "the failure of CSIS, and of its witnesses, to act in accordance with the obligation of utmost good faith recognized in Charkaoui v. Canada" and noted that CSIS's conduct "undermined the integrity of [the] Court's process."[73] The court reinforced that "filtering evidence, even with the best of intentions, is unacceptable. Failing to properly fulfill undertakings made to a Court of law is equally unacceptable."[74] The reliability of CSIS' entire investigative framework also came under scrutiny in court when one expert referred to CSIS intelligence reports as "wiki-intelligence."[75]

Other oversight mechanisms heralded as measures to protect Canadians from abuse of information by national security agencies have proven less ineffective. Shirley Heafey, in her capacity as chair of the Commission for Public Complaints Against the RCMP (The CPC), repeatedly stressed that the CPC lacks the resources and legal authority to oversee the work of the RCMP.[76] The CPC, unlike the Security Intelligence

Review Committee that oversees CSIS, does not have the clear statutory authority to compel testimony or require the production of documents or impose change upon the RCMP[77] (Task Force on Governance and Cultural Change Within the RCMP 2007: 11–13). Heafey bluntly summed up the situation: "We can't investigate unless there's a complaint and even if there is a complaint, we can't see the information," she said. "So for all practical purposes, there's no civilian oversight" (CAIR-CAN Annual Review 2003–2004). Even the Security Intelligence Review Committee, often heralded as the best model for oversight and accountability, can only make recommendations, not binding decisions, and has limited jurisdiction over CSIS when responsibility for national security investigations has perforated well beyond CSIS.[78]

In the wake of the Arar fiasco, Justice O'Connor made extensive recommendations aimed at overhauling oversight mechanisms.[79] Minister of Public Safety Day contended that these recommendations have been implemented, but critics charge that little has changed. CSIS has also promised to overhaul its policies and procedures after revelations that the agency had been either negligent or duplicitous in document disclosure before the federal court in June 2009.[80] Policy and procedural reviews will no doubt prove important; however, they do not address the main problem, which is the apparent willingness of at least some national security agents to deliberately deceive and manipulate information to conform to desired ends (Kalajdzic 2010). No wonder that the federal court worried about the prevarication of CSIS agents. It was not the first time that national security agencies exhibited a willingness to adopt strategies to thwart the release of information and thereby frustrate oversight. Lack of oversight is thus both constitutive and declarative of securitization; continued agency control over information gathering and release both reinforces the urgent need for accountability and undercuts its realization.

It was not supposed to be this way. To help allay public concerns while also dampening criticism about the Anti-Terrorism Act, Canadian officials stressed that sophisticated and reliable oversight mechanisms, including ministerial oversight, would protect individual rights. Indeed, Anne McLellan, Deputy Prime Minister and Minister of Public Safety and Emergency Preparedness, and Irwin Cotler, Minister of Justice and Attorney General of Canada, advised aggrieved individuals and communities in a chastising tone to avail themselves of available mechanisms if they had concerns about national security investigations; "we have robust independent review and accountability mechanisms in place," claim the ministers. "They are there to be used" (McLellan and Cotler 2005).

But, oversight proves only as good as the information provided to the oversight bodies by the very agencies the bodies are expected to watch. Canadian ministers were expected to play an oversight role, yet soon after Justice Dennis O'Connor exonerated Arar and exposed the extent to which Canadian officials had stereotyped, mislabeled, and misrepresented Arar to their U.S. counterparts, Minister McLellan acknowledged that she could not effectively oversee national security agencies. In response to a question about whether she regretted her own lack of attention to Arar's ordeal, McLellan explained that she learned about RCMP's activities from Justice O'Connor's Report.

> . . . I think that Mr. Justice O'Connor's report, uh, raises, um, some important questions around, um, what was told to various officials in the government at various times . . . members of the government, should have serious concerns in relation to that part of Mr. Justice O'Connor's report that speaks to the fact that perhaps certain information was left out of certain timelines that was provided to PCO and . . . and to others.[81]

Former Solicitor General, Wayne Easter, whose portfolio included the RCMP, also claimed that he was kept in the dark.[82] Despite assurances that rights would be protected through effective oversight, including political oversight, the very ministers entrusted with oversight admitted that the promised protections proved meaningless.


## CONCLUSION

Canada has determined that the best route to national security lies not in suspending rights-claims through a state of emergency but "governing constitutionally in a state of permanent warfare." Careful attention to stories of the people whose lives have been torn asunder by the "war against terrorism" reveals the extent to which they are marked by lawlessness even as they appear protected by the rule of law. We may not yet fully understand the collective and individual impact of Canada's decision to respond to the "war against terrorism" through a legal regime that has pulled lawlessness into itself.

Unable to clear their names, national security targets and their family members remain susceptible to being detained and once again abused by foreign governments. In their state of suspended rights, they embody "bare life," a person whose fate is effectively abandoned to the "sovereign police who temporarily act as sovereign" (Agamben 1998: 174). They remain in both the law and the public consciousness neither charged nor exonerated, neither accused nor innocent, neither detained nor free. Their existence in a state of perpetual investigation coupled with their inability to fully clear their names "[r]adically erases any legal status of the individual thus producing a legally un-namable and unclassifiable human being" (Agamben 1998: 3).

Exceptions to equal and just treatment in Canada have increasingly been justified by necessity, emergency, and collective rights. If the drift toward exceptionalism and lawlessness remains unaddressed, we may find ourselves, like Kafka's tragic antihero, waiting in vain before law's gate.

## NOTES

1. I benefited from a grant from The Law Foundation of Ontario and hours of exchange and discussion with Dr. Willem de Lint and Professor Jasminka Kalajdzic, along with invaluable research assistance from University of Windsor Faculty of Law students Megan Mossip and Juliet Mohammed.
2. American Civil Liberties Association. April 22, 2009. *Bush-Era OLC Memoranda Relating to Interrogation, Detention, Rendition and/or Surveillance.* Online. Available HTTP: <http://www.aclu.org/safefree/general/olcmemos_chart.pfd> June 9, 2009.
3. Executive Order 13440. *Interpretation of the Geneva Conventions Common Article 3 as Applied to a Program of Detention and Interrogation Operated by the Central Intelligence Agency.* 20.6.2007. *Military Commissions Act, 2006.* Publ. L. No. 109–336.
4. Department of Justice (2003). "Policy Guidance to Ban Racial Profiling." Canada. Online. Available HTTP: < http://www.usdoj.gov/opa/pr/2003/June/03_crt_355.htm> June 7, 2009.
5. *The Presidential Records Act* (PRA) of 1978, 44 U.S.C. ß2201–2207.
6. Department of Justice (2001). "Checks and Balances in the Proposed Anti-Terrorism Act," Canada. Online. Available HTTP: < http://www.justice.gc.ca/eng/news-nouv/nr-cp/2001/doc_27789.html> June 8, 2009.
7. Iacobucci, The Hon. F (2008). "Transcript, Hearing On Standards of Conduct," "Internal Inquiry into the Actions of Canadian Officials In Relation to Abdullah Almalki, Ahmad Abou-Elmaati and Muayyad Nurredin." Ottawa: The Queen's Printer.
8. *Abdelrazik v. Canada (Foreign Affairs)* 2009 FC 580. Mr. Abdelrazik's has proceeded to sue the federal government in tort on various grounds. See *Abdelrazik v. Canada* (Attorney General) [2010] F.C.J. No. 1028.
9. UN Commission on Human Rights (2004). "Civil and political rights, including questions of torture and detention: Opinions adopted by the Working Group on Arbitrary Detention," *United Nations Working Group on Arbitrary Detention,*19 November. Online. Available HTTP: < http://www.unhcr.org/refworld/country,,UNCHR,,PAK,,470b77b10,0.html> March 18, 2010.
10. United States of America v. Benamar Benatta, 200301-CR-247E (United States District Court (W.D. New York) September 25, 2003.
11. UN Commission on Human Rights (2004). "Civil and political rights, including questions of torture and detention: Opinions adopted by the Working Group on Arbitrary Detention", *United Nations Working Group on Arbitrary Detention*, November 19. Online. Available at http://www.unhcr.org/refworld/country,,UNCHR,,PAK,,470b77b10,0.html.    March 18, 2010.
12. Amara, Z. (2008) "An Unjust Law is No Law at All Toronto 18," *Toronto 18.* Online. Available HTTP: <http://toronto18.com/index.php?option=com_content&task=view&id=140&Itemid=1> June 9, 2009.
13. Bell, S. (2006). "Suspects' Torture Claims Predictable, Experts Say" *National Post*, 14 June. Online. Available HTTP: http://canadiancoalition.com/forum/messages/17059.shtml June 8, 2009.Error! Hyperlink reference not valid.

14. *Toronto 18* (2008)"Presumption of Innocence Project Press Conference". *Toronto 18 Website* Online. Available HTTP: <http://toronto18.com/index. php?option=com_content&task=view&id=165&Itemid=1> June 8, 2009.

15. *Effects of Psychological Torture.*Center for Victims of Torture Online. Available HTTP: http://www.cvt.org/main.php/Advocacy/TortureisUn-American/EffectsofPsychologicalTorture. June 9, 2009

16. Ayan, A., et al. (participants) (2007) "The Istanbul Statement on the Use and Effects of Solitary Confinement". *International Psychology Trauma Symposium.* December 9. Online. Available HTTP: http://www.solitaryconfinement. org/uploads/Istanbul_expert_statement_on_sc.pdf 16.3.2010; Smith, P. S. (2008) "Solitary confinement, An introduction to The Istanbul Statement on the Use and Effects of Solitary Confinement," *Danish Institute for Human Rights,* Online. Available HTTP: <http://www.humanrights.dk/files/pdf/Engelsk/International/Solitary_confinement.pdf> June 15, 2009; Special Rapporteur on torture and other cruel, inhuman or degrading treatment or punishment, *Interim report of the Special Rapporteur on torture and other cruel, inhuman or degrading treatment or punishment,* UN GAOR, 63d Sess., UN Doc. A/63/175 (2008) at para 77; Istanbul Statement on the Use and Effects of Solitary Confinement, UN GAOR, 63d Sess., Annex, Agenda Item 67(a), UN Doc. A/63/175(2008).

17. There have been some developments with the Toronto 18 cases since this paper was written. At the end, charges against 7 of the original Toronto 18 were stayed, 7 pleaded guilty to various charges and 4 were found guilty at trial. Appeals are pending in some of the cases. Zacharia Amara, the man identified as the ringleader, has appealed his indeterminate life sentence for knowingly participating in a terrorist group. Kutty, F. (2008) "Submission of the Canadian Coalition for Peace and Justice", *Submissions to the United Nations Human Rights Council,* Fourth Universal Periodic Review, Canada. Online. Available HTTP: < http://lib.ohchr.org/HRBodies/UPR/ Documents/Session4/CA/CCPJ_CAN_UPR_S4_2009_CanadianCoalitionforPeaceandJustice.pdf> March 18, 2010.

18. Haj Khalil v. Canada, 2007 FC 923 at para. 215. Haj Khalil lost her appeal at the Federal Court of Appeal and has sought leave to appeal to the Supreme Court of Canada. See *Haj Khalil v. Canada,* 2009 FAC 66.

19. Haj Khalil v. Canada, 2007 FC 923 at para. 227.

20. Almrei (Re), 2009 FC 3, Canada (Citizenship and Immigration) v. Jaballah, 2009 FC 284, Canada (Citizenship and Immigration) v. Mahjoub 2009 FC 439, Charkaoui, (Re), 2009 CF 175, Harakat (Re), 2009 FC 53.

21. Canada (Citizenship and Immigration) v. Mahjoub 2009 FC 248, Homes Note Bombs (2009) "Mahjoub Forced Back to Jail by Devastating House Arrest Conditions," *Homes Not Bombs Blogspot.* 19 March. Online. Available HTTP: <http://homesnotbombs.blogspot.com/2009/03/mahjoub-forced-back-to-jail-by.html> June 15, 2009.

22. Re. Harkat, 2009 FC 553 at para. 57, 66.

23. Ottawa Citizen (2008). "Harakat's wife ready to explode." *Ottawa Citizen.* Online. Available HTTP: <www.canada.com/deltaoptimist/story.html? id=989637d8–001e-491a-83d6-ec8a9a25660c> June 9, 2009.

24. *Canada (Justice) v. Khadr,* 2008 SCC 28, at para. 37–39.

25. *Canada (Prime Minister) v. Khadr,* 2010 SCC 3, at para. 7. In *Khadr v. Canada* (Prime Minister), 2010 FC 901, the Chief Justice of the Federal Court of Appeal issued a stay of an enforcement of a judgment of the Federal Court which had found that Khadr was entitled to an effective remedy. Khadr has since struck a deal with American, and it would seem Canadian officials, that would allow him to return home to Canada to serve out a sentence in exchange for pleading guilty for killing an American soldier.

26. Almrei (Re), 2009 FC 1263, Charkaoui, (Re), 2009 FC 1030. please add: On May 4, 2010, Hassan Almrei filed a civil claim against the federal government following a finding by the Federal Court that the "the defendants breached their duty of utmost good faith and candour to Mr. Almrei and to the Court in failing to conduct a thorough review of the information in their possession and in failing to make representations based on all the information, including that which was unfavourable to their case." See the statement of claim filed in the Ontario Superior Court of Justice available at HTTP: <http://jurist.org/pdf/securitycertclaim.pdf>. October 30, 2010. A reasonableness decision in Harakat's case is expected late in 2010 while Jaballah's and Mahjoub's reasonableness hearings have, at the time of writing, yet to be completed.

27. Blanchfield, M. (2009) "Arar Still Unwelcome In The U.S.", *Times Colonist*, 17 April. Online. Available HTTP: http://www.timescolonist.com/news/Arar+still+unwelcome/1505044/story.html. June 5, 2009.

28. Haj Khalil v. Canada, 2009 FCA 66, at para. 12.

29. The Canadian Press (2009), "Toronto 18 Video Evidence Released" 2009—CBC—October 20, 2009 http://www.cbc.ca/canada/toronto/story/2009/10/20/toronto-18-amara-video963.html. March 15, 2010.

30. R. v. Khawaja, [2008] O.J. No. 4244; R. v. Khawaja, [2008] O.J. No. 4244, R v. Khawaja, (2009) Court File No. 04–630282 (Notice of Appeal). A decision from the Ontario Court of Appeal remains pending at the time of writing.

31. McLellan, A and Cotler, I. (2005) "Joint Statement by the Hon. Anne McLellan, Deputy Prime Minister and Minister of Public Safety and Emergency Preparedness & the Hon. Irwin Cotler, Minister of Justice and Attorney General of Canada" Department of Justice: Emergency Preparedness. Online. Available: HTTP: <http://www.justice.gc.ca/eng/news>. March 15, 2010. The three walls metaphor has also been invoked under Stephen Harper's Conservative government to justify the security certificate regime. See for example the debate over Bill C-3, An Act to amend the Immigration and Refugee Protection Act (certificate and special advocate) and to make a consequential amendment to another Act, 39th Parliament, 2nd Session, Edited Hansard, Number 044, Tuesday, February 5, 2008 HTTP: <http://www2.parl.gc.ca/HousePublications/Publication.aspx?DocId=3249159&Language=E&Mode=1&Parl=39&Ses=2>

32. Christie v. York (1939), [1940] S.C.R. 139.

33. Almrei (Re), 2009 FC 3, at para. 275.

34. *Immigration and Refugee Protection Act*, 2001, c.27, s. 34(1)(c).

35. House of Commons Debates (2008). House of Commons Debates 3. P. (ed.), 5 February(2008, February 5)., 39th Parliament, 2nd Session. Online. Available HTTP: *<http://www2.parl.gc.ca/HousePublications/Publication.aspx?DocId=3249159&Language=E&Mode=1&Parl=39&Ses=2>* June 10, 2009.

36. The O'Connor Commission p. 100.

37. The O'Connor Commission.

38. The O'Connor Commission.

39. Shephard, M. (2007) "Exclusive Interview: Ex-Top Spy Breaks Silence," *The Toronto Star*, March 26. Online. Available HTTP: <http://www.thestar.com/Unassigned/article/217952> June 15, 2009.

40. O'Connor, The Honourable Denis (2005) *Commission of Inquiry into the Actions of Canadian Officials in relation to Maher Arar*, Vol. 25. Ottawa: Canadian Government Publishing. Online. Available HTTP: http://www.stenotran.com/commission/maherarar/2005–06–09%20volume%2025.pdf. April 9, 2010, p. 6300.

41. Haj Khalil v. Canada, 2007 FC 923 at para. 191.

42. Haj Khalil v. Canada, 2009 FCA 66, at para. 15.
43. Report of Professor Stephen J. Toope Fact Finder: Commission of Inquiry into the Actions of Canadian Officials in Relation to Maher Arar. Canada. 14 October 2005. Online. Available HTTP: http://www.abdullahalmalki.ca/ToopeReport_final.pdf. April 8, 2010.
44. 432–433 at para. 120–122.
45. *Immigration and Refugee Protection Act*, 2001, c.27, s. 20(2) and 23(5). United States of America v. Benamar Benatta, 200301-CR-247E (United States District Court (W.D. New York). September 25, 2003.
46. Citizenship and Immigration Canada (2006), "A Partnership For Protection: Year One in Review", *Citizenship and Immigration Canada*. Online. Available HTTP: <http://www.cic.gc.ca/english/department/laws-policy/partnership/chapter5.asp> 15.6.2009; Wilkinson, R. (2002). "After The Terror... The Fall Out", *United Nations High Commissioner for Refugees,* 1 January.Online. Available HTTP: http://www.unhcr.org/publ/PUBL/3ccd58429.html. June 15, 2009.
47. Benatta v. Attorney General of Canada, (2008) 07-CV-336613PD3 (Statement of Defence).
48. Charkaoui v. Canada (Citizenship and Immigration), 2007 SCC 9).
49. The Canadian Press (2008) "Canadian gets life in embassy bomb plot", *The Ottawa Citizen*, 14 June.: Online. Available: HTTP: <http://www.canada.com/ottawacitizen/story.html?id=448b4ead-8e29–4747-befd-a8fff7654273&k=77983&p=1> June 14, 2009.
50. O'Brian, G. (2009), "Testimony of Mr. Geoffrey O'Brian (Advisor, Operations and Legislation, Canadian Security Intelligence Service (CSIS))" *Standing Committee on Public Safety and National Security: House of Commons*, 31 March. Online. Available HTTP: ).<http://www2.parl.gc.ca/HousePublications/Publication.aspx?DocId=3787859&Language=E&Mode=1&Parl=40&Ses=2> June 15, 2009.
51. Cotler, I. (2001). "Does the Antiterror bill go too far?", *Globe & Mail*, 20 November. Available. Online via *Interdisciplinary Studies in Law: University of Ottawa*. HTTP: <http://www.cdp-hrc.uottawa.ca/eng/education/courses/CML4112D/cotler.html> March 23, 2010.
52. *Saadi v. Italy* (Fed) no. 37201/06 ECHR 2008 at para. 27.
53. McLellan, A., and Cotler, I. (2005) "Joint Statement by the Hon. Anne McLellan, Deputy Prime Minister and Minister of Public Safety and Emergency Preparedness & the Hon. Irwin Cotler, Minister of Justice and Attorney General of Canada" Department of Justice: Emergency Preparedness. Online. Available: HTTP: <http://www.justice.gc.ca/eng/news. March 15, 2010.
54. Forcese, C. (2009) "Canada's National Security "Complex": Assessing the Secrecy Rules", *IRPP Choices*, June 15(5), Online. Available HTTP: <http://www.irpp.org/choices/archive/vol15no5.pdf> March 18, 2010.
55. The O'Connor Commission.
56. Iacobucci, The Hon. F (2008). "Transcript, Hearing On Standards of Conduct", "Internal Inquiry into the Actions of Canadian Officials In Relation to Abdullah Almalki, Ahmad Abou-Elmaati and Muayyad Nurredin." Ottawa: Queen's Printer.
57. The O'Connor Commission,
58. The O'Connor Commission, p. 138.
59. Harkat, (Re) 2009 FC 553 at para. 12.
60. Iacobucci, The Hon. F (2008). "Transcript, Hearing On Standards of Conduct", "Internal Inquiry into the Actions of Canadian Officials In Relation to Abdullah Almalki, Ahmad Abou-Elmaati and Muayyad Nurredin." Ottawa: The Queen's Printer.at para. 127.

61. Toronto Star Newspaper Ltd. v. Canada, 2009 ONCA 59, per Rosenberg JA (dissenting) at para. 4.
62. The O'Connor Commission.
63. The O'Connor Commission, 116, para. 28.
64. Mickum, B. (2009). "The truth about Abu Zubaydah" *The Guardian*, 30 March. Online. Available HTTP: <http://www.guardian.co.uk/commentisfree/cifamerica/2009/mar/30/guantanamo-abu-zubaydah-torture> 18.3.2010; Tate, B. P. (2009) "CIA Mistaken on 'High-Value' Detainee, Document Shows" *Washington Post*, 16 June. Online Available HTTP: <http://www.encyclopedia.com/doc/1P2-20418535.html> March 18, 2010.
65. *Abdelrazik v. Canada (Foreign Affairs)* 2009 FC 580.
66. The O'Connor Commission, p. 21–22.
67. The O'Connor Commission. See Recommendation 2 at 317–342 for details of its proposed role.
68. Freeze, C. (2004) "CSIS Spy-Warrant Requests Meet With Little Opposition, Documents Reveal", 15 November *Globe and Mail* . Online. Available HTTP: http://circ.jmellon.com/docs/view.asp?id=737. March 16, 2010.
69. Attaran, Amir (2010), "Amir Attaran: Terrorism isn't Special" (full comment), *National Post,* 19 February. Online. Available HTTP: http://network.nationalpost.com/NP/blogs/fullcomment/archive/2010/02/19/amir-attaran-terrorism-isn-t-special.aspx. March 23, 2010.
70. Fadden, Richard B. (2009) *"National Post:* Letter-to-the-Editor to the Director", *Canadian National Intellegence Service.* Online. Available HTTP: http://www.csis-scrs.gc.ca/cmmn/dr_ntpst_lttr-eng.asp April 8, 2010.
71. Bill C-3, An Act to amend the Immigration and Refugee Protection Act (certificate and Special Advocate) and to make a consequential amendment to another Act. Passed by the House of Commons, February 6, 2008: 2nd Session, 39th Parliament.
72. Schmitz, C. (2008) "Special Advocates Decry Gag Order", *Lawyer's Weekly*, 12 September. Online. Available HTTP: <http://www.lawyersweekly.ca/index.php?section=article&articleid=755> March 18, 2010.
73. Re. Harkat, 2009 FC 241 at para. 59.
74. Re. Harkat, 2009 FC 241 at para. 66.
75. Re. Almrei, 2009 FC 1263, at para. 199.
76. Commission for Public Complaints Against the RCMP (2005) "Submissions of the Commission for Public Complaints Against the RCMP Regarding the Policy Review of the Commission of Inquiry into the Actions of Canadian Officials in Relation to Maher Arar", Public Hearing, 9 June 2005. Online. Available HTTP: http://www.stenotran.com/commission/maherarar/2005–06–09%20volume%2025.pdf.
77. *Canada (Royal Canadian Mounted Police) v. Canada (Attorney General)*, 2005 FCA 213.
78. The O'Connor Commission,
79. The O'Connor Commission.
80. Federal Court Communication (2009) "Communication in the Matter of Mohamed Harkat. S. 77(1) of the IRPA".Ottawa: Federal Court. Online. Available HTTP: http://www.justiceforharkat.com/e107_files/downloads/DES-5–08-Communication-June5–2009.pdf. March 15, 2010.
81. *The House, CBC-Radio* (2006) intervier K. Petty, 7 October, Toronto.
82. Sallot, J. (2006) "Former Minister Says He Was Kept in the Dark On Arar", *Globe and Mail*, 24 October Online. Available HTTP: <http://www.rcmp-watch.com/former-minister-says-he-was-kept-in-the-dark-on-arar/> 2010.

# 7 The Pre-emptive Mode of Regulation

## Terrorism, Law, and Security

*Gabe Mythen*

## INTRODUCTION

In the first decade of the 21st century, security institutions in Western nation-states have been preoccupied with attempting to limit and reduce the terrorist threat. After the September 11, 2001 (9/11), attacks, national security issues have ascended the political agenda, embedding terrorism as an axial political concern (Furedi 2005; Mythen and Walklate 2008; Ould Mohamedou 2007). Given that terrorist acts effectively undermine the neoliberal premise that the state is able to secure order, governance, and control over its territory, it is easy to see why the regulation of terrorism has become a focal topic. Post-9/11, political elites, intelligence experts, and establishment academics have posited that the extraordinary nature of the terrorist threat requires extensive legal and military measures, alongside intensified modes of policing and surveillance[1] (Clarke 2007; Lesser at al. 1999). In defining the actions of 'new' Islamist terrorist organizations as a radical departure from the past, a political narrative bound up with future threats demands that legal, military, and security responses be pre-emptive and embracing.

It is my intention in this chapter to broadly unpack and scrutinize the assorted modes of political and legal regulation that have emerged in response to 'new terrorism,' both in the United Kingdom and globally. I wish to contend that the sociopolitical construction of new terrorism has catalyzed a changing set of security discourses that permit draconian legislation and sanction unacceptable modes of surveillance and state violence. I will argue that the constellation of dominant ideologies that constitute new terrorism and the aligned 'War on Terror' are based around a future-centric calculus of risk. In a nutshell, a discernible shift is taking place in strategies of risk regulation around national security from retrospective probabilistic estimations of harm to a pre-emptive approach that is based on futurity. This revised calculus of risk involves a motion away from the past and present questions of 'What was?' and 'What is?' toward the future framed 'What if?' (see Mythen and Walklate 2008). Given the potential scope of such an inquiry, I want to highlight just two *problematiques*. First,

I wish to argue that the preventative mode of regulating new terrorism is erroneously based around worst-case scenarios that promote a form of a pre-emptive delirium among securocrats responsible for national security. The construction of worst imaginable scenarios—such as the use of weapons of mass destruction (WMD)—have also been used by the British state as a lever for the war on terror. The absurd quest to 'win' such a war by vanquishing 'global terrorism' has sanctioned ruinous pre-emptive military interventions and led to loss of life for countless innocent civilians. Second, focusing primarily on counterterrorism measures introduced in the United Kingdom, I go on to illumine the coercive capacity of pre-imaginings of harm as a prop for hegemonic control. It is my contention that dominant security discourses around new terrorism, alongside the resultant forms of undemocratic legislation that they seek to make permissible, are led by catastrophic visions of harm that have the potential to foster an unhealthy climate of fear.

It needs to be recognized from the outset that the institutions and areas of policy that have been affected by the new security agenda associated with the terrorist threat are diffuse and include education, religion, immigration, welfare, policing, and law (see McCulloch and Pickering 2009; McGhee 2008; Mythen and Walklate 2006a). This granted, for analytical purposes I wish to focus relatively tightly on counterterrorism legislation in the United Kingdom as a means of establishing the links between political desires, pre-imaginings of harm, and the use of pre-emptive regulation. A comprehensive review of the impacts of antiterrorism legislation on civil liberties is beyond the ambit of this chapter. However, I do want to elucidate that counterterrorism legislation in the United Kingdom is being dangerously driven by dystopic imagined futures, leading to a skewing of the balance between collective security and civil liberties. Before evaluating some of the key domestic security policies that have emerged in response to the terrorist threat over the last decade, it is first necessary to identify the ideological drivers of these policies and sketch out a conceptual apparatus that can help us understand the motion towards pre-emptive law and the broader securitization of everyday life. With this objective in mind, it is worth considering what discrete social theories of risk have to say the contemporary context in and through which such exceptional security measures have taken root and flourished.

## TERRORISM, RISK, AND HUMAN SECURITY: CONCEPTUALIZING THE PRESENT

Political violence has been a ubiquitous feature in the histories of many Western countries, including the United Kingdom, the United States, Germany, France, and Spain. Yet in recent times, the nature and scope of terrorism have been redrafted in political and media discourse, with the contemporary terrorist threat being cast as unprecedented and cataclysmic (see Aradau and van Munster 2007; Lambert 2008). The events of 9/11 have been earmarked as both a historical watershed and a catalyst for a new phase of political struggle, legal transformation, and military expansion (Kellner 2002; Welch 2006). Making staggeringly simple sense of 9/11, assorted politicians, academics, military personnel, and security experts have sought solace in classification, hailing a new type of terrorism, typified by the actions of Islamic terrorist networks such as al-Qaeda, Jemaah Islamiyah, and Lashkar-e-Toiba. Due to an amalgam of their geographical reach, fluid organizational formation, and weapons capability, these groups are said to represent a unique type of terrorism (Laquer 2003; Morgan 2004). The narrative of 'new terrorism' suggests that it can be readily distinguished from traditional terrorism with recourse to a range of novel features, including the scale of attacks launched, the use of high-lethality weapons, and the magnitude of human harm intended. Rather than working under well-defined hierarchical structures, new terrorist groups are said to have disparate aims, scattered organizational cells, and possess the capacity to strike with alacrity across the globe (Clark 2007; Hoffman 1999: 9; Lesser et al. 1999).

Through a process of ideological construction, the rather ahistoric dominant discourse of new terrorism has been solidified by politicians and in the mass media. Although it is expectable that modes of political violence will be subject to transformations (see Vedby Rasmussen 2006), there are a host of reasons to be skeptical about the tidy and uniform narrative of new terrorism (see McGhee 2008: 5; Burnett and Whyte 2005). Years after terrorist attacks attributed to al-Qaeda, including the Bali and London bombings, it remains unclear whether those undertaking such acts belonged to or were directed by the network in any concrete sense. Furthermore, amidst feverish speculation over future terrorist attacks involving WMD, we would do well to remind ourselves that the 9/11 attacks were executed without weaponry sophistication using low-tech facilities (Furedi 2002: 17). I am less interested here in the dubious deployment of the new terrorism moniker and more exercised by the effects that its assembly and usage has had on the regulation of security. Putting aside institutional myth making around new terrorism, we can locate a clear command for citizens to 'think security' in the years that have passed since 9/11 (de Lint and Virta 2004: 466). The invitation to think security produces ripples that extend beyond the cultural and symbolic, with the discourse of (in)security being drawn upon to vindicate actions with wide-ranging economic and material effects. Post-9/11, the U.K. government has dramatically increased the amount spent on national security, restructured domestic security measures, passed through extensive antiterrorist legislation, and orchestrated a national campaign to inform the public about the terrorist threat (see Mythen and Walklate 2006a; Kearon et al. 2007; Spalek 2008). Outside the United Kingdom, a range of counterterrorism measures have been introduced in countries perceived by their political leaders to be at threat (see Diprose et al. 2008; Patane 2006; Safferling 2006). At a geopolitical level, a 'coalition of the willing' spearheaded by U.S. and U.K. governments have adopted an 'activist' approach to dealing with international terrorism, assuming aggressive militaristic policies against 'aberrant regimes.' Although the violent invasions and occupations of Afghanistan and Iraq have constituted the apex of this formation, the War on Terror as an assemblage of processes and practices is designed to puncture opposition and direct conduct through a vortex of coercive deeds, including punishing nation-states that are deemed to harbor terrorist groups and attempting to depose political leaders considered undesirable.

Insofar as it is axiomatic to state that risk has become an integral feature in the mapping of human security in Western cultures, the processes and practices clustering around new terrorism must be understood in appropriate social and cultural context. Responding to this challenge, a range of theorists have sought to grasp the essence of a world that appears to be increasingly bound up with and directed by issues of safety and security. Much has been made of the cultural ubiquity of risk and the ways in which security issues penetrate lived experiences across a range of spheres, including health, employment, relationships, and consumption. Beck's (1992; 1995; 1999; 2009) risk society thesis famously recounts the emergence and escalation of dangers that threaten the planet as a whole, rather than individuals, groups, or regions. The humanly generated risks that emerge as unwanted side effects of unfettered economic and technoscientific development undo previous conceptions of safety and present irresolvable difficulties for institutions tasked with the management of human security. For Beck, manufactured risks are debounded entities that are temporarily and spatially mobile. By way of example, Beck (2002) refers to the climate of uncertainty generated by "transnational terror networks." Given the global geographic in which terrorist networks operate, the risk of harm is general and universal. In Beck's risk society narrative, such a political rotation occurs away from the positive pursuit of acquiring 'goods' (e.g., income, health care, education, housing) toward the negative mission of avoiding 'bads' (e.g., terrorism, environmental pollution, AIDS). While the distribution of goods is sectoral—some win and some lose—the distribution of 'bads' produces universally deleterious effects. Everybody loses. Consequently, Beck's "terroristic world risk society" is one of political disorientation, individual insecurity, and perpetual uncertainty. For expert systems, the net result of de-territorialized risks is the unraveling and undermining of regulation and control. Institutional power holders are rendered accountable for making decisions in a miasma of imperfect information and incomplete knowledge (Beck, 1999: 78). As we shall see, so far as regulating terrorism is concerned, one perceptible response to such radical uncertainty has been a shift toward futurity in both practices of risk analysis and the language of governance. Beck posits that the volatility of manufactured risks, coupled with the antiquated nature of legal, political, and welfare systems in the West, means that extant structures are not equipped or able to manage contemporary threats. The somewhat farcical result of a mismatch between manufactured risks and the regulatory capacities of security institutions is a process of 'organized irresponsibility' through which institutions cosmetically treat risks and simulate attempts at control to reduce public concerns (Beck 1995: 107). As such, the fundamental institutional occupation in the world risk society is not so much managing risks per se. Given that manufactured risks are essentially unmanageable, the task of government, law, politics, and science focuses more on perfecting a bluff of controlling the uncontrollable while simultaneously trying to convince fearful citizens that public safety is achievable (Beck 2009).

In contrast to Beck's focus on uncontainable global harms, Furedi's (2002; 2005; 2007) culture of fear perspective suggests that our preoccupation with issues of risk and security is symptomatic of a tendency to focus on the destructive features of social life. For Furedi, a burgeoning climate of fear is prevalent, promoted by state institutions and exacerbated by those working within the media and security industries. This culture of fear entails the embedding of risk as a recognizable and omnipresent feature of everyday life (Furedi 2002: 5). The frequency and acceptability of risk across diverse cultural domains turns a range of lived experiences into safety situations. Furedi posits that our preoccupation with risk is dangerous in a number of ways. First, so far as scientific, technological, and social developments are concerned, the balance between constructive outcomes and negative consequences becomes distorted, with the latter assuming precedence. Second, media emphasis on high-consequence, low-probability harms incites people to become more inward-looking and fearful. Applying his approach to the problem of terrorism, in recent work Furedi (2007) has argued that what we ought to concern ourselves with is not so much the harm caused by terrorist attacks, but more the way in which the media constructs danger and the ways in which political and military responses to terrorism serve to escalate, not reduce, further acts of violence.

Both Furedi and Beck's work have been important in explaining why risk has become a common cultural referent and accounting for the ways in which risk is mobilized in attempts to regulate society. Through a process of what we might call 'risk creep,' a host of expert systems have been influenced and directed by the logic of risk in the endeavor of social regulation. The institutional drivers of risk creep—whom Bigo (2002) fittingly dubs the "managers of unease"—have sought to raise awareness of risk and intensify the security responsibilities of citizens. As Dean (1999) suggests, individuals have become "multiply responsibilized" around a span of health, security, and welfare risks. At a macro level, at the same time as institutions commit to governing the future, they also become stakeholders in the safekeeping of citizens through security policy, policing, and legal regulation. There are a number of ways in which theories of risk can be put to work to read both the sociocultural impacts of terrorism and political attempts to stage-manage it (Beck 2002; Mythen and Walklate 2006b; Mythen 2008). Although such applications are outliers to this chapter, what is critical for my purposes is the entrenchment of three trends. First, that security has become one of the structuring principles of politics. Second, that a fixation with the terrorist threat is symptomatic of a society in which citizens are incited to be more risk averse and self-surveying. Third, that the number of areas of public life open to risk assessment has extended considerably in the last 2 decades. I wish to revisit these issues later, but let us first delve more deeply into the discourse of new terrorism and the associated strategies of risk regulation that it permits.

## STATE VIOLENCE AND THE 'WAR ON TERROR': IMAGINING THE FUTURE

Perhaps the most dramatic responses to the 9/11 terrorist attacks have been the military invasions of Afghanistan and Iraq that have acted as the apex of the War on Terror. Despite the avowed objectives of security seeking, these military incursions do not appear to have reduced the threat of political violence—either in the occupied countries themselves where security has arguably diminished, or abroad by those objecting to the use of military force by occupying armies[2] (see Diprose et al. 2008). Nonetheless, the solidification of a cycle of violence has not deterred supporters of the War on Terror, who continue to believe that terrorism can be expunged by a mix of aggression and disciplinary measures that punish so-called 'rogue states.' The vow to 'take the fight to the terrorists' has been central to alarming and brutal acts of statecraft, including the detention of 'enemy combatants' at Guantanamo Bay, torture of terrorist suspects, and the shadowy practice of 'extraordinary rendition.'

As Beck (1999) avers, the problem of not knowing—and, moreover, knowing about not knowing enough—has visibly dented the authority of security institutions. In response to pervasive indeterminacy about terrorist attacks, an array of methodological tools of imagining the future have emerged, including horizon-scanning exercises, scenario testing, and simulated disasters (de Goede 2008: 156). Engaging with security threats that stretch the boundaries of calculability effectively reverses the use of probability estimates based on previous incidents and feeds speculation about future unknowns (Salter 2008). Although there is some logic in casting out to possible threats to improve preparedness in the event of terrorist attacks, the presentation of nightmare scenarios has been one of the principal ideological strategies invoked by those calling for stricter terrorism laws. Safety-centric political appeals have sought to play upon public fears by conjuring up a ruinous future in which benign nations are victimized by malevolent terrorist aggressors. The much-maligned doctrinal discourse of the war on terror mimes a pantomime battle between good and evil that denies complexity, ambiguity, and motive. Elemental in the discourse of the war on terror is a power-play around risk production, definition, and responsibility. This power-play involves the use of 'What if?' scenarios to cast inaction (nonviolence) rather than action (violence) as dangerous. Accordingly, pre-emptive military assaults put in train under the auspices of the War on Terror have been vindicated as attempts to secure a safe future:

> America must not ignore the threat gathering against us . . . we cannot wait for the final proof, the smoking gun that could come in the form of a mushroom cloud.[3]
> We are in mortal danger of mistaking the nature of the new world in which we live. This is not a time to err on the side of caution, not a time to weigh the risks to an infinite balance.[4]

It is easy to make associations between 'What if?' modes of risk assessment, military ventures, and the governance of terrorism. Post-9/11, the United States and the United Kingdom have chosen to bypass international law and threatened to attack without warning any state considered to be a threat to (inter)national security. Although Bush and Blair's successors have shied away from directly using the term 'War on Terror,' the narrative of a future dystopic remains and plays to a reformed calculus of risk that focuses on hypothetical events. Drawing on the work of Grusin (2004), critical security thinkers have usefully deployed the term "premediation" to describe the ways in which politicians have used the media to bring a risky future in to view in the present. Premediations are linguistic and visual representations created by a scattered band of performers, including journalists, film makers, cultural intermediaries, government, and security practitioners. Premediations do not so much represent what *has* happened, but what *may* happen next. The melding of existing intelligence with dark fantasies and collective fears makes worst-case scenarios thinkable. Amoore (2007) alludes to these future oriented ways of seeing (in) security as "vigilant visualities." Through the lens of vigilant visualities, responsibility for guarding against the terrorist risk in the future depends on assertive action in the present. In such a present, critical reflection, dialogue and maintaining peace are tantamount to the recklessness of inviting victimization. Although this contorted discourse has been common among senior politicians seeking to gain support for restrictive surveillance and legislation, there are reasons to be believe that such a worldview is not universally shared. The Joint Terrorism Analysis Centre (JTAC) and an influential Chatham House group of security experts have publicly stated that the conflict in Iraq is serving as a pivot point for international terrorist activities (ISP[5]/NSC Briefing Paper, 2005). Furthermore, an ICM poll found that 64% of Britons blamed the government's decision to go to war in Iraq for the July 7, 2005, bombings in London.

The various forms of risk regulation that make up the quest to predict the unpredictable are locked into a governmental compulsion to 'discipline the future' (see Ewald 1991: 207). Of course, risk intrinsically involves prospect. Risk assessments pledge to calculate probabilities with the aim of reducing future harms (Aradau et al. 2008: 149). Although there is nothing new in this, it is the extent and intensity of attempts to govern the future in the present that is remarkable. The 'What if?' question has been central in orchestrating a movement away from regulation through deterrent toward pre-emptive interventions against individuals, groups, and nation-states suspected of involvement with terrorism. The rationale underpinning pre-emption is that threats do not need to be imminent, so long as they are potentially catastrophic (Zedner 2007, 2008). Yet if security strategies are determined by so called 'ticking-bomb' scenarios, the only thinkable end point is paranoiac doomsday, as the Iraq imbroglio vividly illustrates. The rationale for the occupation of Iraq was based on two ill-founded assertions. First, that Saddam Hussein was developing WMD and seeking to use them against Western nations. Second, that Iraq had established links and was planning to operate with Islamic Fundamentalist terror networks. As became apparent after the invasion, the intelligence on which these claims were based was highly dubious. More recently, the 'What if?' question has resurfaced in political language as a means of issuing threats of military action against Iran and North Korea for suspected development of nuclear weapons (see Mythen and Walklate 2008).

## THE PRE-EMPTIVE TURN AND COUNTERTERRORISM

Central to the configuration of security around the global War on Terror has been a combination of imagined extraordinariness of threat and institutional fearfulness of losing public confidence. These contemporary frighteners are also ever-present in political narratives that seek to legitimate exceptional domestic security measures designed to combat terrorism. What Vedby Rasmussen (2004) has dubbed the "presence of the future" slants the regulation of the terrorist risk toward the projective. In relation to domestic terrorist attacks, a plethora of cataclysmic possibilities have been raised, including the use of radiological dispersal devices, biological and chemical attacks, contamination of water supplies, and air strikes against nuclear facilities. Whatever the purported value of premediations in raising risk consciousness, such nightmare scenarios are likely to raise rather than reduce public anxieties (see Aradau et al. 2008: 149). The net result of the creeping presence of the future in domestic security assessments in the United Kingdom is that imagined forthcoming events have come to direct contemporary policies. Thus, we can trace a familiar discursive formation of catastrophic future attacks at play in calls for more restrictive counterterrorism laws in the United Kingdom. The day before announcing plans to further extend the period of detention without charge in the 2008 Terrorism Bill, Security Minister Tony McNulty prompted the public to "imagine two or three 9/11s. Imagine two 7/7s. Given the evidence we've got such scenarios aren't fanciful" (Roberts 2008). Ironically, the cultivation of a climate of fear has perhaps had the effect of destabilizing rather than enhancing public trust in security institutions. The production of a climate of fear around terrorism—whether it be intentional or incidental—is connected to adjustments in methods of risk assessment and also to changes in governmental strategy. As Amoore and de Goede (2008: 11) describe it: "a desire for zero risk joins a vision of worst case scenarios in order to enable pre-emptive action against perceived terrorist threats." Clearly such pre-emptive action is itself not without risks. Regrettably, over-reliance on worst-case scenario thinking has served as a propeller for inordinate counterterrorism legislation and overzealous surveillance and policing. There are numerous examples to draw upon. In 2005, Jean Charles de Menezes, a Brazillian citizen living in the United Kingdom, was mistaken for a suicide bomber at Stockwell underground station and shot dead by officers acting under the Metropolitan Police Service's 'shoot-to-kill' policy, operationalized in response to the terrorist threat (see Tulloch 2006: 71). In 2006, more than 250 police officers were involved in a raid on a house in Forest Gate in East London, apparently in pursuit of a chemical weapon. In the subsequent arrest, Mohammed Kahar was shot in the chest while being detained with his brother Abul. After being held and questioned for 8 days, both men were later released without charge. More recently, in a series of spectacular raids undertaken as part of Operation Pathway, 12 men were arrested under counterterrorism legislation. Despite the media highlighting specific targets of attack and the prime minister suggesting that the security services had foiled a plot that was "very big," after 13 days of questioning all those arrested were released without charge.

Supporting the deployment of pre-emptive policing, in the last decade, the U.K. government has introduced unprecedented rafts of counterterrorism legislation. During its tenure, New Labour has redrawn the legal governance of terrorism through an assemblage of measures, including the Terrorism Act (2000); the Anti-Terrorism, Crime and Security Act (2001); the Prevention of Terrorism Act (2005); the Terrorism Act (2006); and the Counter-Terrorism Act (2008). Insofar as these forms of legislation have been formally imposed to reduce the degree of threat to the public, justifiable concerns have been raised about the ways in which certain elements of new terrorism laws infringe civil liberties. The 2005 Prevention of Terrorism Act, for example, includes offenses that have proved difficult to define in a court of law, such as incitement to terrorism, acts preparatory to terrorism, and giving and receiving terrorist training. Although loosely defined laws have lengthened the specter of surveillance that hangs over Muslim minority groups, the incitement to self-surveillance has been typified by the U.K. government's CONTEST strategy and its establishment of

Muslim Contact Units instigated to proactively seek out intelligence about suspicious activity (see McGhee 2008: 48). The continued identification of Muslim minority groups as 'suspect communities,' alongside the criminalization and marginalization of young male Muslims, is serving to alienate an already materially disadvantaged and politically disaffected group (Mythen, Walklate, and Khan, 2009). The stereotyping of risky ethnicities under conditions of uncertainty can lead to suspicion and distrust between those defined as fearful and those that are to be feared.

The logic of anticipatory risk has featured heavily in U.K. counterterrorism legislation through the implementation of procedures that are preventative, such as indefinite imprisonment of terrorist suspects, extending periods of detention without charge, and control orders. These new strategies of risk control form part of a deeper trend of developing regulatory methods of 'pre-crime' (see McCulloch and Pickering 2009; Zedner 2007). The controversial use of control orders affords the Home Secretary personal power to tag and track suspects and to keep them under virtual house arrest without formal charges being levied. Control orders are sanctioned in situations in which a person is suspected of being involved with terrorism, but the evidence is such that a case against cannot be made public. Before the acceptance of control orders, Section 23 of the Anti-Terrorism, Crime and Security Act (2001) afforded the home secretary the power to incarcerate without charge foreign nationals suspected of being involved in terrorism. In 2004, this practice was duly declared as illegal and in breach of the European Convention on Human Rights. Following on from this, the U.K. government introduced control orders as part of the Prevention of Terrorism Act (2005). In their attempts to limit future dangers, control orders are exemplars of the pre-emptive mode of risk management. In effect, those subject to control orders are punished and incarcerated in the present for their suspected capability to generate harm in the future. Control orders place a string of invasive requirements on the individual that make it impossible for them to live the life of a normal citizen, including strict curfews on association and communication, confinement, and complying with monitoring systems which disrupt sleeping patterns (see Saner 2009: 28; Travis 2009).[6] The imposition of control orders sanctions the keeping of a suspect under house arrest for up to 16 hours with basic legal rights such as privacy, asylum, and free movement being curtailed. Such efforts to restrict the movements of terrorist suspects have caused widespread disquiet among libertarians and human rights campaigners. The imposition of control orders effectively leaves those bound by them in ignorance of the allegations against them, jeopardizing the democratic right of the accused to hear charges or defend themselves. It is thus unsurprising that the House of Lords has rejected the state's use of control orders, ruling unanimously that they violate Article 6 of the Human Rights Act, which protects the right to a fair trial (see Booth[7] 2009: 17).

The pre-emptive modus operandi is also embodied in cumulative extensions of the period of detention without charge for terrorism suspects. In less than 10 years, the permissible period for detaining terrorist suspects without charge in the United Kingdom has incrementally risen from 7 to 28 days. While former Prime Minister Tony Blair had campaigned for the introduction of 90-day detention without charges, in the 2008 Terrorism Act, Gordon Brown proposed a lesser figure of 42 days. The rationale for a further extension to 42 days is twofold.[8] First, there is the much dramatized 'ticking-bomb' situation in which a detainee may know about an imminent terrorist attack and where the police need to extract the information necessary to prevent the attack. Second, it has been claimed that the complexity of terrorism plots involving individuals based in many countries may take long periods of time to unravel. Both of these explanations err toward the hypothetical and usher in pressing questions. Do technologies such as computers and mobile phones not leave a deeper evidence trail and make gathering primary evidence easier? Given that it is already possible for the police to hold a suspect for up to 28 days and charge them with a low-threshold terrorism offense, is an extension reasonable? A convincing case is yet to be made as to why the United Kingdom is at greater risk than other nations threatened by political violence. For example, the maximum permissible period of detainment without charge in the United States is 48 hours and in Spain it is 5 days.

Before revisiting interpretations of the securitization process that might be made through the prisms of risk theories, it is worth stressing the connectivity between the logic of anticipatory risk, the pre-emptive turn in security management, and political attempts to harness fear. Incitements to public fear that mock up the horrors of the future are invariably cranked up at times when government seeks public support for law and order legislation (see Burkitt 2005; Walklate and Mythen 2008). Following de Goede (2008: 159), we need to recognize that premediations are thus not only speculative, but moreover *creative* enterprises. When it comes to the material formation of security policies, it is sagacious to ask whether fictional future possibilities are a firm and sound basis for producing legislation in the present. If the regulation of terrorism is driven by deleterious imaginings, the introduction of pre-emptive measures that threaten civil liberties becomes nothing short of logical. Yet unwarrantable gravitation toward the 'What if?' question means that the basis of evidence mutates under the penumbra of new terrorism. Once a projective 'What if?' position is normalized, presumption of innocence is replaced by presumption of guilt. Evidence is required in refutation, not prosecution. Silence equals culpability.

To return to risk theory, the future-mania that has taken hold around terrorism can be interpreted in several ways. Furedi's thesis enables us to tap straight into the heart of the state's fixation with security and aptly describes a society that has become unable to accept risk as an integral feature of human experience. Furedi describes the ways and means by which

Bigo's "managers of unease" are able to profit politically, culturally, and economically through the production of fear. This provokes the rhetorical question of whether it is the terrorist threat that has grown so dramatically or the manufactured culture of fearfulness. Meanwhile, Beck provides a way in to the catastrophic possibilities and novel uncertainties that global terrorism ushers in. The risk society thesis neatly melds to fit with dominant discourses around global human security in light of the terrorist threat. In many ways, terrorism is an archetypal risk society issue, bearing all the hallmarks of a manufactured risk (Beck 2002; Mythen 2008). Clearly, the kinds of attacks launched by groups such as Jemaah Islamiyah and Lashkar-e-Toiba are anthropogenic, unpredictable, and not amenable to limitation or control. This said, there are also ways of replenishing and extending risk society theory. Although Beck's organized irresponsibility serves as a valuable cautionary concept in explaining the inability of institutions to reduce environmental harms, in the field of national security a sister concept can perhaps be suggested, that of 'organized overresponsibility.' Whereas organized irresponsibility involves a toothless performance of risk regulation, forms of organized overresponsibility around terrorism—including invasive surveillance, pre-emptive intervention, and draconian legislation—have biting material effects. The irony of the situation is that, despite the polarities of meaningful action (overresponsibility) and performative inaction (irresponsibility), the outcome at the level of risk production remains unknown and uncontrollable. Attempts to control terrorism through coercive foreign policy, military force, and mounds of counterterrorism legislation have not reduced the threat of harm from terrorist attacks, nor have they stabilized international relations (Aradau et al. 2007; Vedby Rasmussen 2006).

## CONCLUSION

It must be recognized that sociopolitical and legal regulations have long involved governance through risk (see McCulloch and Pickering 2009; O'Malley, 2009). Although this is indisputable, what is new about contemporary modes of risk management around national security is the extent to which future gazing and the associated utilization of hypothetical scenarios is being deployed as an acceptable foundation for the induction of regulatory measures, policies, and sanctions in the present. Although Aradau et al. (2008: 149) are correct in their observation that dominant constructions of security futures draw heavily on the catastrophic, it seems that the idea of the future catastrophic is shading into a perilous hyperreal situation in which the present is actually subsumed by the future catastrophic. In light of managers of unease being forced to concede the inevitability of future terrorist attacks, the inevitable further waves of counterterrorism legislation may appear constitutive of a gesture of security. Yet beneath the shrugs and motions, the pre-emptive turn is constitutive of a calculated attempt at governance. It represents a determined effort to resolve a frightening fictional future in the present. By resolving imagined security catastrophes in advance, state institutions are able to symbolically act out their vigilance and competence (see Amoore 2007).

Given the current trend toward organized overresponsibility in the regulation of terrorism, coupled with the political harnessing of fear, it is probable that pre-emptive risk management strategies will continue to proliferate. The pre-emptive turn in security management—around terrorism but also in other areas of crime control—is likely to lead to the further expansion of the surveillant assemblage and a widening of the public spaces in which security operates. I have argued here that the pre-emptive turn very much requires the ideological practice of premediation to make both the cultivation of fear and the initiation of repressive measures appear reasonable. Counterterrorism legislation, coercive foreign policy, and military violence all depend upon the cultural undergirding that pre-imaginings of harm allow. I have argued here that the presentation of imaginary threats as real, and the treatment of these threats as real at the level of regulation, is deeply problematic. Hypothetical scenarios may be useful in training police and emergency services to be prepared to respond to unusual attacks, but they do not make a sound basis for modifying law. Although premediations are performative entities, they can be wielded to justify coercive practices. Through the projector of catastrophic pre-imaginings of harm, a rationality can be provided for the securitization of more or less anything and everything (Salter 2008: 251). All of this is not to pretend that in seeking to maintain national security, clear-cut distinctions can be made between sensible precautions and institutional overreactions. As Beck muses, "it is increasingly difficult to make a clear and binding distinction between hysteria and deliberate fear-mongering, on the one hand, and appropriate fear and precaution, on the other" (Beck 2009: 12). This point notwithstanding, amidst the febrile atmosphere around (inter)national security, legislation is fixing and being fixed around premediations of risk and associated metanarratives of (in)security. As the political offering of a safe future, good life is replaced by a vision of dystopic insecurity; it is imperative that critical social scientists seek to deconstruct both the logic of preimaginings of harm and their substantive outcomes at the level of risk regulation. This task necessarily involves challenging and interrupting coercive law that is made based on imaginings or predictions rather than evidence.

Although the international formation of security policy promulgated by the United States and the United Kingdom constitutes an attempt to produce order in a chaotic world, the drive to simply expunge terrorism is akin to nailing water to a wall. Casting 'terrorism' as a protean foe crudely ascribes a homogeneous identity to a plethora of conflicts that have unique national and regional histories. The 'global terrorist enemy' looks very different in Chechnya than it does in Spain, in Istanbul than in Palestine. To reduce terrorism to a universal disease that can only be vanquished by force represents the failure of powerful states to come to grips with some of the drivers of political violence, including colonial exploitation, poverty, economic imperialism, religious bias, and geopolitical exclusion. The current neo-isolationalist vogue is regrettably symptomatic of a countermodern security strategy that papers over complexities to provide false certainty. At the level of domestic security, it is critical that those in government pause long enough to think through the root causes of terrorism, not simply the ways in which citizens can be pre-emptively surveyed or perpetrators punished (see Lambert 2008). If the pursuit of security comes at the expense of human rights, then not only is the quality of that security compromised, but the very principles of democracy are undermined. To ensure that social justice is upheld, it is imperative that pre-imaginings of harm and the emergent security regimes taking shape through the 'What if?' prism are scrutinized evidentially and contested politically. The palette of pre-imaginings of harm around terrorism denote not only attempts to persuade the public about the legitimacy of state violence but also act as forms of dramaturgy that simulate resolution of the future in the present. The contemporary definitional struggle over terrorism is thus not only about the immediacy of the here and now, but also over how the future is imagined, by whom, and with which ideological objectives.

## NOTES

1. P. Wilkinson. (2003) 'Observations on the New Terrorism', Foreign Affairs Committee of the House of Commons, London: HMSO.
2. Sturcke, J. (2005) "Intelligence warned of Iraq terror link." *The Guardian*, July 19.
3. Bush, G.W. (2002) Speech delivered at Cincinnati Union Terminal, Cincinnati, OH.
4. Blair, T. (2004) Speech delivered to Sedgefield Community, Sedgefield, UK, p.7.
5. ISP/NSC Briefing Paper 05/01, (2005) *Security, Terrorism and the UK*. London: Chatham House.
6. Saner, E. (2009) "A day in the life of a terror suspect," *The Guardian*, June 13.
   Travis, A. (2009) "Law Lords outlaw control orders' evidence," *The Guardian*, June 11.
7. Booth, R. (2009) "Court revokes control order that forced man to leave London," *The Guardian*, July 4.
8. Anderson, B. (2008) "The Government is pursuing the 42-day law for the basest of party," *The Independent*, June 9.

# Part IV

# Global Agendas, Local Transformations

# 8 Re/Building the European Union
## Governing through Counterterrorism

*Sirpa Virta*

## INTRODUCTION

This chapter deals with the main European Union (EU) security and policing strategies and the ways they have been translated into action in national and local-level security and policing strategies in three EU member states: Great Britain, the Netherlands, and Finland. Through the EU and national strategies, internal policy is giving way to an expansive logic of security. This is seen in the reconciliation of national security and counterterrorism, with community policing, local crime prevention, and community safety policies. The new politics of community policing, The Community Policing on Terrorism with an ILP approach, brings the state to neighborhoods. In terms of the organized nature of power (Hörnqvist 2007), the strategies are seen as organized forms of exercising power: programmatic attempts to shape policing, especially local policing, in member states. Therefore, it is suggested that the political viability of these strategies should be evaluated at national and local levels, as a part of translation and implementation processes.

The basic structure of the EU consists of three "Pillars." The so-called third Pillar of the EU (originally "justice and home affairs") refers to steps to ensure the interoperability or cooperation of police and justice in criminal matters, also in terrorism, and extends to the "communitarization" of visa, asylum, and immigration practices and the free movement of people between EU countries. The proposed Reform Treaty (the Treaty of Lisbon) will abolish the pillar structure, and once the treaty is ratified, there will be other important changes as well concerning the area of freedom, security, and justice. As the European Parliament gets the power of codecision in police and judicial measures, the third Pillar will disappear. Nonetheless, the special history of the third Pillar means that the agencies, bodies, and the leading role of the council will remain in place, enhanced by the creation of the Standing Committee on Internal Security. A well-recognized democratic deficit of the EU remains unsolved. When the area of freedom, security and justice in the EU was established in a special European Council summit in Tampere, Finland, in 1999, the cornerstone for enlarging the union was to be a shared commitment to freedom based on human rights, democratic institutions, and the rule of law. With terrorism and its threat becoming powerful determinants of strategies and politics, these principles seem to have lost their prominence. In the Treaty of Lisbon, "EU state building" is evident in both the creation of bodies and agencies to act on an EU-wide basis and the creation of administrative and operational cooperation centrally organized by the EU

The threats in Europe are global in nature, from environmental and climate threats to terrorist threats and extremism. The security environment has especially changed in this respect. The post–Cold War environment is one of increasingly open borders in which the internal and external aspects of security are indissolubly linked. The counterterrorism discourse is connected with the "new terrorism," but several European countries already had a longer tradition of combating regional terrorism (e.g., Spain, France, Germany, Great Britain). Yet the new terrorism was defined differently, having an international dimension and being inspired by a radical interpretation of Islam. A specific European dimension to the new terrorism was its definition as "home grown terrorism" (Kleemans 2008: 6).

The growing sense of uncertainty surrounding the terrorism issue has resulted in a new mood of prevention, pre-emption, and precaution that can readily result in restrictive, even oppressive and discriminatory outcomes. The policy-making processes follow the "Precautionary Principle." Terrorism has made the precautionary logic obvious, and politics in general have taken a dramatic turn aimed at making precautionary logic part of everyday life. Counterterrorist policy and strategies also increasingly draw upon a transnational policy community (Goldsmith 2008: 143, Ericson 2007: 38, see also Hörnqvist 2007: 40). In terrorism research, September 11, 2001 (9/11) has refocused the issue of pre-emption and introduced the notion of "preventive war," but there is also a dichotomy between the criminal justice and the war models of countering terrorism (Ranstorp 2007: 15). The Hague[1] Programme (2004), the EU Strategy for Combating Radicalisation and Recruitment (2005), and the EU Counter Terrorism Strategy (2005) and its Action Plan on Combating Terrorism (2006), as well as some other common security and policing strategies, are results of such policy-making processes in the EU policy community. They rely on policing, and especially community policing, as a vital tool for local-level counterterrorism, and prevention is their key element and objective.

It has been argued that there is a basic philosophical difference between the U.S. and the European approach to counterterrorism, the former representing the war model and the latter the criminal justice model. European governments consider terrorism to be a tactic, and therefore it is impossible to declare "war" against a tactic. Military incursions can deter attacks, save lives, and change regimes, but they cannot promote or improve public ethics, social and political education, acceptable behavior, or civic institutions. After 9/11, the United States posited that a democratic Iraq would pave the way for more democracy in the Middle East and thereby undermine terrorism, while some European states argued that war in Iraq would in fact do more to enhance the appeal and swell the ranks of al-Qaeda. For Europe, the focus was not on regime change but rather on a number of socioeconomic reforms in developing states. Although the U.S. government officially joined this part of the effort in the National Strategy for Combating Terrorism (2003), it has been argued that the strategy has been inconsistent with U.S. behavior since the start of the Bush administration (Von Hippel 2007: 94–95). However, as Crelinsten (2009: 13) argues, the war model in the United States represents "September 12 thinking."

According to Jones and Wiseman,[2] neither soldiers nor private security guards are trained to those tasks, but the public police forces are increasingly being educated to achieve them, and therefore the Europeans have chosen to expand and educate police forces and community policing officers to fight terrorism. "Community policing as a working philosophy builds confidence in the civic governance structure. European insistence on strengthening community policing in human intelligence gathering, data sharing, interagency and international cooperation, efficient centralization of police efforts, coordinated deployment of tactical units, and EU-wide arrest warrants, is a complex, progressive and sophisticated process" (Jones and Wiseman 2005: 2–9.) However, it is still very unclear what concrete measures are expected from the police in EU member states in this respect. Initial experiences from the Netherlands about the reconciliation of community policing and counterterrorism show that it may become an "unhappy marriage" in practice (de Kool 2008).

It is difficult to get a proper picture about the EU as a security actor, especially in the counterterrorism arena that has become a crowded policy space with a considerable number of actors and interactions that operate at different levels of governance, from local to international, from public to private. In addition to formal institutions, there are a lot of informal, horizontal, and networked types of governance, such as secret communities and ad hoc investigations (den Boer, Hillebrand and Nölke 2008: 66–67). The security field of the EU is today even more "always-in-motion bricolage of networks, processes and institutions" such as characterized in Loader's 2002 article "Policing, securitization and democratization in Europe" (129). Therefore, the organizational context of organized forms of power is very complex. Strategies are prepared and formulated by various EU expert and working groups and networks, coordinated, for instance, by the EU counterterrorism coordinator and ratified through formal EU decision-making processes.

This chapter examines how national security strategies and local policing strategies respond to the common EU strategies. The main focus is on counterterrorism and especially on strategies combating radicalization and recruitment. Once implemented nationally and translated into community policing practices and measures, they will become a part of our everyday life in many ways. It is argued that combating and preventing radicalization and recruitment will change drastically the value, purpose, and contents of community policing. The processes of translating the strategies into implementation and action may not be very transparent or politicized, open to discussion and alternatives. They are rather bureaucratic and administrative processes, mainly dominated by police, intelligence organizations, and secret services. These processes also often begin before the common strategies even take place because of policing policy transfer, informal police cooperation, and police training and education business.[3]

Three countries, Great Britain, the Netherlands, and Finland, represent the frontline of the localized development and all have new national security strategies and community policing strategies that follow the EU strategies guidelines. Great Britain has experienced terrorist attacks (the 2005 London bombings being the most serious). In the Netherlands, there have been politically motivated violent attacks (e.g., the murder of Theo van Gogh in 2004). Finland is not, according to the EU-wide threat assessments, a known target of any terrorist group, but its membership in the EU is seen as a potential threat factor. All three countries have been advanced in developing community policing models and practices. The strong unifying powers of the EU strategies can be seen throughout the Europe; for example, in Germany and Belgium, who have federal state structures (SIAK 2007).[4] The EU Commission–supported European Forum for Urban Safety Secu-CITIES project ("Cities Against Terrorism") has strengthened the localization development.[5] Terrorist threat is seen today primarily as a European problem: "Europe is the focus of a clear threat" (SIAK 2007: 28) *and* a local problem of the capitals like London, Madrid, or Paris, and therefore the EU countries call for local-level solutions, especially in tackling homegrown terrorism. Even national and centralized police organizations have started to develop community policing, or at least local policing, according to the EU counterterrorism strategies' guidelines. Even in countries where community policing has not been a success story, such as in France (Brogden and Nijhar 2005: 114), the new politics of community policing together with domestic pressures such as urban riots in Paris have brought it back to the agendas of policing strategy makers and local police organizations.[6] However, this is a developing field of enquiry that still lacks truly comparative data. The main EU strategies and programs are from 2004 through 2007, and the processes of implementation and translation of the strategies into action are in some member states faster than in others.

To sustain, guarantee, or improve legitimacy of implementation of the strategies, and legitimacy of the institutions implementing them, it is suggested that the political viability of the strategies should be evaluated at national and local levels. Political evaluation is often lacking in policy transfer processes even if the strategies were formally ratified or signed in the member states' parliaments. Political evaluation, originally a concept of Arendt, is by definition contextual, it has no prejudices, it includes ethical aspects, concentrates on specific problems, and takes account of various perspectives of stakeholders (Lappalainen 2002: 63–67) and is or should be conducted *before,* for instance, adoption and implementation of strategies. Methodologically, political evaluation requires political reading of strategies; reopening the political and repoliticization of translation processes. As a method of critique, repoliticization is an interpretative action, opening new playgrounds in showing that there are chances for action, alternatives, and choices to be made, and a possible opposition against some generally accepted truths. It is argued that security should be politicized instead of continuous securitization of the political (de Lint and Virta: 2004).

Political viability criteria measure strategy or program outcomes in terms of impact on relevant power groups such as decision makers, administrators, citizen coalitions, neighborhood groups, and other alliances. Political insight, understanding of organizational and administrative preferences and procedures, and knowledge of the motivation of actors enable these criteria to be used. The evaluation criteria for political viability of a strategy or program are acceptability, appropriateness, responsiveness, legality, and equity. Administrative operability refers, for example, to administrative structures and operability, social and political circumstances, performance regime, or local police organizational and other conditions, including resources. Patton and Sawicki do not include it in the category of political viability, but in this context it could be seen as an integral part of it. Acceptability refers both to the determination of whether a strategy is acceptable to actors in the policy-making and implementation process, and to the determination of whether citizens, residents, and other actors are receptive to it. As a criterion, acceptability means that values, ideologies, and politics behind the strategy are recognized as worthy of being accepted nationally and locally. Appropriateness is related to acceptability in that it addresses the issue of whether policy objectives mesh with the values of the community or society. It involves issues of human values and rights. Responsiveness is related to acceptability and appropriateness and involves the target group's perception of whether the strategy or program will meet its needs. Legal criteria can be considered within the category of political viability since laws can be changed through political action. Equity as a criterion arises when the differential impact of a strategy or program is important. It is related to fairness and involves moral and ethical issues (Patton and Sawicki 1993: 215–217).

## COUNTERTERRORISM AND THE POWER OF SECURITY

The relationship between counterterrorism and security is complex and ambivalent. Security is a justification for counterterrorism strategies and measures. The context for counterterrorism is "a complex security environment," and there are many kinds of security: societal, economic, human, and environmental—all of which demand attention alongside, and often intertwined with, the demands of international security (Crelinsten 2009: 23). Counterterrorism is included in the EU and many national security strategies, and it is included in security politics, foreign politics, defense politics, and internal politics or home affairs. Counterterrorism, as a phenomenon and a policy, exists because terrorism is seen as the major security threat or risk for people, states, and societies, cities, and neighborhoods.

Neocleous argues in his book *Critique of Security* (2008) that security is the supreme concept of liberal ideology, and that security is a political technology and a technique of power. In his view, liberalism should be read less as a philosophy of liberty and more as a technique of security. Neocleous analyzes the ways security is used as an ideological and political tool. Within the counterterrorism context, it is argued that perhaps the key date for our times is September 14, 2001, for this was the day President Bush declared a state of emergency. Emergency became permanent, and the exception became the rule (Neocleous 2008: 31–41). This is the manifestation of the power of security.

According to Schmitt's concept of sovereignty, sovereign is he who decides on the exception (Neocleous 2008: 40). It could be argued that the EU itself has in fact "decided on the exception" by building and broadening counterterrorism complex (institutions, networks, strategies, and measures) in the name of security. Counterterrorism has become the rule. Ambivalence lies in counterterrorism practices and measures that can, in turn, constitute security threats themselves.

## THE EU COUNTERTERRORISM STRATEGIES: GOVERNING THROUGH COUNTERTERRORISM

"Power is organised in strategies" (Hörnqvist 2007: 221). The strategies that will be analyzed are all part of the EU organization. The main component of particular interest in the EU strategies is counterterrorism. Governing through counterterrorism is in many ways a political project; it is not just about prevention of terrorist attacks or recruitment but also about prevention of radicalization and therefore the effort of the strategies is, or "should be[,] to win the battle of ideas," as argued by Wilkinson (2007: 320). It is very common nowadays to hear calls for a "comprehensive approach" to countering terrorism, and it is viewed almost as axiomatic that the only way to combat terrorism is to promote international cooperation. Counterterrorism means the responses to terrorism and the efforts to prevent it. Presently, the main EU security and policing strategies and programs are mainly counterterrorism in nature, and it could be argued that instead of (or in addition to) governing through security, the EU is governing through counterterrorism. Therefore, it is interesting to analyze how strategies and programs are implemented and translated into action in national and local security and policing strategies and practices, and the interaction between the global, national, and local.

Governance refers to the set of rules, decision-making procedures, and programmatic activity that serve to define practices and to guide the interaction of those participating in these practices. Counterterrorism could be seen as global governance, referring to the global rules and programs that typically are institutionalized as legal regimes within international organizations such as the EU A common theme in counterterrorism is the need to harmonize policies and strategies between countries across a wide range of policy domains (Crelinsten 2007: 216–222). The various counterterrorism strategies, as well as legislation, are important instruments of the EU agencies. The whole arena of the EU counterterrorism governance includes, for instance, bodies and network arrangements such as the Counter Terrorism Group and the Police Working Group on Terrorism and institutions and intelligence networks such as Europol, Eurojust, the European Police Chiefs Task Force, and the Joint Situation Centre. Security governance in the EU is increasingly provided in network-like structures that allow a high degree of flexibility and speed, but there have been concerns about the legitimacy and accountability of network governance in the field of law enforcement and counterterrorism (den Boer et al. 2008: 69). In recent communication from the EU Commission to the Council and the European Parliaments[7] regarding the implementation of the Hague Programme, there are suggestions about the establishment of several new networks.

Crelinsten describes the complexity of the geography of counterterrorism by classifying the strategies and measures according to their nature: coercive, proactive, persuasive, defensive, and long-term counterterrorism, and according to the dimensions of time (short-term vs. long-term), space (unilateralism vs. multilateralism, local vs. global, or "glocal"), type of power (hard power vs. soft power), and type of intervention (tactical vs. strategic) (Crelinsten 2009: 39–47). The EU counterterrorism strategies are proactive, persuasive, and long term. In Crelinsten's matrix (2009: 241), countering radicalization through community policing is seen as counterterrorism politics exercising soft power.

In many countries, there have emerged counterterrorist law reforms and the need for new legislation, but democratic processes tend to be too slow for national security decisions that have historically been dominated by the executive and lacked transparency. Governments attempt to persuade legislative bodies of the appropriateness of the measures, and there has been comparatively little room for parliamentary input (Goldsmith 2008: 142). In counterterrorism phenomena and strategies, there are problems that pose clear dangers for democracy; for example, a lack of openness and accountability that are a direct result of the nature of proactive policing and security intelligence, and infringement of individual rights and freedoms by discrimination due to selective targeting and the identification of dangerous classes of people (Crelinsten 2009: 109).

The EU cannot intervene in national and local politics or policing directly. Therefore, the Council of the EU strategies and policy programs are guidelines for the member states' police forces, and because terrorism is a common concern many governments and police forces take these strategies seriously. Common European police training and education (mainly by the European Police College [CEPOL], with assistance of other EU bodies such as Europol) support the adoption and implementation of the strategies, for example, by organizing courses and awareness seminars all over the EU The most important strategies for the development of policing and police cooperation in Europe are European Security Strategy,[8] the Hague Programme (2004) and its Action Plan (2005), the EU Strategy on Counter Terrorism (2005) and its Action Plan (2006), and the EU Strategy on Combating Radicalisation and Recruitment (2005). The strategies are introduced in this chapter, and the main focus is on the parts that have been most influential in national and local policies.

The point of departure of the European Security Strategy ("A Secure Europe in a better world") (2003), is that no single country is able to tackle today's complex problems on its own. Although large-scale aggression against any member state is improbable according to the strategy, Europe faces new threats that are more diverse, less visible, and less predictable. The five key threats defined in the strategy are terrorism, proliferation of weapons of mass destruction, regional conflicts, state failure, and organized crime that can have links with terrorism. Terrorism is the first of the five key threats and it is argued to be also the main reason why concerted European action is indispensable. It is linked to violent extremism and arises out of complex causes. These include the pressures of modernization; cultural, social, and political crises; and the alienation of young people living in foreign societies. The policy implications include development of common threat assessments that are seen to be the basis for common action. This requires improved sharing of intelligence among member states and with partners. According to the strategy, policies and action should also be more coherent. Better coordination between external action and Justice and Home Affairs policies is crucial in the fight both against terrorism and organized crime (European Security Strategy 2003: 3–13). The European Security Strategy aimed to transform the EU into a conscious security actor, but one question has not yet been answered today: should the EU be considered a "civilian only" security actor, using mainly soft power means, or is it capable and ready to use also its hard power, commencing with military? The current strategy development of the European Security Strategy seems that it will be closer to the development of the European Security and Defence Policy and the Common Foreign and Security Policy.[9]

The European Council of November 4–5, 2004, endorsed The Hague Multiannual Programme for Strengthening the Area of Freedom, Security and Justice (The Hague Programme). It is the successor of the Tampere Programme, which was endorsed by the European Council of October 15–16, 1999. The political mandate of The Hague Programme is that it reaffirms the importance that the EU attaches to the areas of freedom, security, and justice, placing it as a high priority on the Union's agenda "not only because it figures among the fundamental objectives of the Union, but in particular because it is at the heart of citizens' interests." The Hague Programme and its Action Plan (The Hague Programme— Ten Priorities for the Next Five Years) (2005)[10] are the most important strategies in development of policing and police cooperation in Europe; in the context of counterterrorism and prevention of radicalization and recruitment The Hague Programme is seen as a "European framework" for more effective intelligence exchange, improved police cooperation, and also for common policing strategies and police training. It puts strong emphasis on developing Europol, Eurojust, and CEPOL to enhance the counterterrorism capability in the EU

To enhance more effective intelligence exchange, The Hague Programme adopts an intelligence-led policing (ILP) model, which has been developed by Europol named the European Criminal Intelligence Model and which is based on the British National Intelligence Model.[11] Europol had a special project of education and implementation of ILP in all EU member states' police organizations in 2006. CEPOL has had and have 2 or 3 courses per year about the best practices of ILP. The police in many countries have developed national versions of ILP (e.g., in Belgium and Finland, ILP; in Norway, "knowledge-based policing"; in Sweden, the "Swedish Intelligence Model") (Virta 2008: 28–29).

According to the Hague Programme, the security of the EU and its member states has acquired a new urgency, especially in the light of the terrorist attacks in the United States in 2001 and in Madrid, Spain, in 2004 (the Hague Programme 2004: 12.) These were followed by the London bombings by radical Muslims, three of whom were British born, and the killing of the Dutch filmmaker by a young Dutch Muslim. The phenomenon called homegrown terrorism was explicitly linked with problems that have deeper roots in modern Western societies (Kleemans 2008: 7).

According to The Hague Programme, the fight against terrorism calls for an integrated and coherent approach, and the key element in the near future will be the prevention and suppression of terrorism. A common approach in this area is based on the principle that when preserving national security, the member states should take full account of the security of the union as a whole. This way the EU strategies are used as responsibilization instruments. National security and local "community safety" are part of a larger entity, and also local police and community policing policy makers are made responsible for counterterrorism and prevention of radicalization and recruitment. Governments and police forces report to the EU about the implementation of the strategies.

In December 2005, the European Council adopted the European Counter Terrorism Strategy, which groups all actions under four headings: prevent, protect, pursue, and respond. The first objective of the strategy is to prevent people from turning to terrorism by tackling the factors that can lead to radicalization and recruitment, in Europe and internationally. *The EU Action Plan on Combating Terrorism* (2006) of the strategy includes detailed measures for each of the four objectives. The prevention measures include: disrupting the activities of the networks or individuals who draw people into terrorism (under it as a more detailed measure "to promote *community policing* through improved training; task undertaken by CEPOL"), and ensuring that voices of mainstream opinion prevail over those of extremism, thus promoting security, justice, democracy, and opportunity for all. The measures under the title *protect* include, for example, threat and risk assessments, protection of critical infrastructure, and transport security. The measures for *pursue* are information gathering, analysis and exchange, impeding terrorists' movements and activities, and police cooperation. Responding means civilian and military rapid EU response capability to deal with the aftermath of a terrorist attack and assistance to victims.

The EU Strategy for Combating Radicalisation and Recruitment to Terrorism (2005) is complementary to the counterterrorism strategy. According to it, Europe has experienced different types of terrorism in its history, but the terrorism perpetrated by al-Qaida and extremists inspired by al-Qaida has become the main terrorist threat to the EU Although other types of terrorism continue to pose a serious threat to EU citizens, the EU's response to radicalization and recruitment focuses on this type of terrorism. To counter radicalization and recruitment, the EU resolves to disrupt the activities of the networks and individuals who draw people into terrorism, and ensure that voices of mainstream opinion prevail over those of extremism. The strategy has a broad approach to the problems and challenges. According to it, there is a range of conditions in society that may create an environment in which people can more easily be radicalized. Such factors do not necessarily lead to radicalization but may make the radical message more appealing. Therefore, the structural factors supporting radicalization should be eliminated, inequalities and discrimination should be targeted where they exist, and intercultural dialogue, debate, and long-term integration should be promoted.

The strategy on combating radicalization and recruitment is not primarily a police strategy but rather a political program addressing root causes. However, because it is not possible for the EU to change social and political conditions (to eliminate inequalities, discrimination, and structural factors) in the member states, what is left is police and policing. Therefore, when trying to disrupt the activities of the networks and individuals who draw people into terrorism, the strategy relies on policing; we need to spot such behavior by, for example, *community policing*.

## Implementation

Monitoring the implementation of the strategies at the EU level is an ongoing process. The latest report on *Implementation of the Hague Programme* and its *Action Plan* (2007) from July 2008[12] concludes, for instance, that "As in 2005 and 2006 insufficient progress has been made, especially in areas mainly related to the Third Pillar" but "The only area under the Third Pillar in which good progress has been made is the fight against terrorism, which continues to be one of the main political priorities in the Justice and Home Affairs area."

The counterterrorism coordinator's duty is to report every 6 months to the Council of the EU on the implementation of the EU Counter Terrorism Strategy and Action Plan, and to suggest priorities for further action. Information for the reports is collected from member states' governments and police forces. The coordinator's report from May 19, 2008,[13] lists initiatives regarding each of the four objectives (prevent, pursue, protect, and respond). For instance, with regard to the objective of prevention, in April 2008 the council agreed on a general approach to a revised framework decision on combating terrorism, the aim of which is to encompass three new crimes in EU legislation (public provocation to commit terrorist offences, recruitment for terrorism, and training for terrorism). Additionally, the *Working Party on Terrorism* has finalized draft council conclusions on enhancing cooperation in the area of countering radicalization and recruitment to terrorism. The main objectives are the prevention of radicalization and recruitment through increasing the quality and quantity of information gathered and shared between member states, implementing joint initiatives, sharing best practices, and studying the possibility of elaborating a methodology to assess the effectiveness of counter radicalization and recruitment measures, as well as exchanging analysis and government assessments among officials with competence in these areas across the EU

In April 2008, the council reached political agreement on a decision transforming Europol into an EU agency. The decision extends Europol's mandate to cover organized crime, terrorism, and all other forms of serious cross-border crime. The coordinator's report's priorities for further actions[14] include improvement of systematic transmission of information to Europol and Eurojust. National authorities are not always willing to report to Europol, which reduces reliability of Europol's Terrorism Situation and Trend Report, for example. The objective of the *Strategy of Europol* (2008)[15] is to enhance the role of Europol in intelligence exchange so that, for example, it will be involved in 90% of all intelligence exchange concerning terrorism in Europe.

In an informal meeting of the counterterrorism coordinator and "a number of high-ranking civil servants" from member states on March 5, 2008, the participants agreed that the EU needs to do more in the area of prevention of radicalization and recruitment. Proposals in preparation will deal with ways to counter terrorist propaganda, ideas to counter radicalization through better dialogue with religious denominations, means to prevent radicalization on the Internet, best practices on the role of local authorities, and innovative development of community policing (The Report of Counter Terrorism Coordinator: Implementation of the EU Counter Terrorism Strategy—Priorities for Further Action. 2008: 6).[16]

The EU security and counterterrorism strategies count on local policing and especially on community policing and the formal and informal networks of local police. The new politics of community policing means that community policing is not just a matter of local policing and local priorities but also a matter of the EU and national security. However, it is not very clear what concrete measures are expected from the police and what is possible for the police to deliver. There are also many open and delicate issues, such as cooperation between local police and security services in the field of counterterrorism and prevention of radicalization and recruitment. National security and policing strategies tend to be quite general in nature, but most of the main objectives of the EU strategies have been adopted in them.

## NATIONAL SECURITY STRATEGIES— TRANSLATING SECURITY INTO ACTION

Security politics in many countries have traditionally been about foreign and defense politics, thus focusing on national external security. In new national security strategies that emerged in the counterterrorism era post-9/11, the meaning and definition of "national security" have changed. In the past, the state was the traditional focus on foreign, defense, and security policies, and national security was understood as dealing with the protection of the state. Today, national security has broadened to include numerous additional threats to individual citizens and to the way of life, including climate change, flooding, pandemics, and social vulnerability, or exclusion and domestic accidents, as well as terrorism, international organized crime, and chemical, biological, radiological, and nuclear weapons threats. Although few strategies are named as internal security strategies as in Finland, at least some of the threats are global and international in nature. The national security strategies and counterterrorism strategies examined in this chapter are from Great Britain, the Netherlands, and Finland.[17]

The need for national security strategies (of a new kind) derives from the changed security environment in general and particularly from the common EU security and counterterrorism politics. The broad scope of national security strategies means that they focus on underlying drivers of security and root causes of insecurity and are preventive in nature. There is also a strong ethos of responsibilization of citizens and local communities in national security strategies. On a policy-making level, the development is a two-way street; there is a lot of interaction between the member states and the EU For instance, it could be argued that the influence of strategic development in Great Britain to the EU Counter Terrorism Strategy (2005) has been significant. The EU strategy was endorsed by the European Council in December 2005, during Great Britain's presidency of the EU The CONTEST (the Counterterrorism Strategy of Great Britain, 2006) looks like a perfect implementation strategy of the EU strategy (same structure and the same, although more detailed, content), but the first version of the CONTEST is from 2003 so it is more likely that the EU strategy is built upon it.[18]

In Great Britain, the CONTEST strategy is divided into four principal strands that are almost identical to the EU Counter Terrorism Strategy: prevent, pursue, protect, and prepare. The prevent strand is concerned with tackling the radicalization of individuals. The main methods are tackling disadvantage and supporting reform (i.e., structural problems that may contribute to radicalization), deterring those who facilitate terrorism and "the battle of ideas" (challenging the ideological motivations of extremists). The pursue strand is about reducing the terrorist threat by means of intelligence, disruption, and working with communities. The Security Service, the Secret Intelligence Service, and the Government Communications Headquarters are critical to the work on pursue, as is the work of police, both special branches and *neighborhood policing* alike. Involving local communities in counterterrorism means that they should be provided as much information as possible, while maintaining the balance with the integrity of the ongoing counterterrorist operations (including protecting the source of any intelligence). The police should engage with local communities through local partnerships, and through regular contacts with community representatives informally. The other parts of the strategy are about protecting the public, key national services, and U.K. interests overseas, and preparing for the consequences of a terrorist attack.

The first National Security Strategy of the United Kingdom: Security in an interdependent world (March 2008) aims to address and manage the diverse, interconnected set of security challenges and underlying drivers. The point of departure is prevention by "early engagement." Terrorism is mentioned first in the list of threats and risks, but the strategy includes also many elements from international relations and foreign policy; for instance, nuclear weapons, global instability and conflict, failed and fragile states, climate change, competition for energy, poverty, inequality, and poor governance. Regarding terrorism and counterterrorism, the National Security Strategy reintroduces CONTEST adding nothing to it.

The first National Security Strategy (2007–2008) of the Netherlands is more an internal security strategy by nature than the British strategy. The need for the strategy arises from "vulnerability of the society, which is confronted with threats like bird flu, climate change, and terrorism." The definition of national security stipulates: "National security is under threat when vital interests of the Dutch state and society are harmed to the extent that society can become destabilised." These vital interests are territorial security, economic security, ecological safety, physical safety, and social and political stability (which include tensions between ethnic groups). Security is seen as everyone's concern. As a member state of the EU, the Netherlands is aligned with and agrees with the security strategies of the EU, which are seen as important guidelines for national strategies.

There is no special counterterrorism strategy in the Netherlands, but counterterrorism is included in the *National Security Strategy*, and the *National Coordinator for Counter Terrorism* post has been established. In the *National Security Strategy*, terrorism is classified as a "classic" threat and divided to catastrophic terrorism and radicalization. Radicalization is mentioned also under social-economic threats as one dimension of social vulnerability. The explanation to this is the Dutch definition of consequences of radicalization: "radicalisation in its most extreme form can lead to terrorism, but also threatens social cohesion in Dutch society without an act of terrorism being required" (2007–2008). Radicalization is therefore treated as a type of antisocial thinking.

The first Internal Security Programme[19] of Finland was a part of the government's strategy package. The purpose was to highlight the importance of internal security. Finland has traditionally had national security and defense strategies concentrating mainly on foreign policy, international relations, and defense issues. The concept of national security has been earlier connected with these issues only. The second Internal Security Programme[20] has more of a criminological and welfare policy approach: the aims are to prevent social exclusion, to reduce the amount of violent crime, to reduce the number of accidents, to prevent crime and public disturbances, improve the status of victims, maintain border and customs security, tackle organized crime, and combat terrorism and violent radicalization. Although Finland is not a known target of terrorism (according to the EU and domestic threat assessments), terrorism has been included into the strategy due to the fact that the EU security and counterterrorism strategies should be implemented nationally. Being a member state of the EU is also seen as a possible threat as such, if the EU itself is treated as an enemy. The main principle in counterterrorism and preventing radicalization is cooperation between the authorities and other sectors of the society and integration of the immigrants. Following the guidelines of the EU counterterrorism policy, and as a part of the implementation process of the second *Internal Security Programme* 2008, the first *National Counter Terrorism* strategy of Finland was completed in February 2010.

The objectives of the EU security and counterterrorism strategies have been adopted in national security objectives in all three national strategies. Regional and local-level policing strategies are built to meet these new national security challenges and targets too, in addition to conventional local policing and community safety issues. This is more visible in Great Britain and the Netherlands than in Finland, where there has been no urgent need yet for local-level counterterrorism measures. However, in the national strategies, approaches to radicalization and recruitment are similar in all three countries and follow the EU guidelines and definitions.

## THE COMMUNITY POLICING ON TERRORISM

Community policing seems to be seen at the moment as an elixir to solve the ills of societies or as an antidote to a very wide range of political, social, criminal, educational, security, and safety problems (Brogden and Nijhaar 2005). This is seen especially in the EU security and counterterrorism strategies but also in various international organizations' efforts and projects. For instance, Organisation for Security and Co-operation in Europe has several ongoing police assistance programs, in Kosovo and elsewhere, to educate and to some extent also to facilitate community policing. Community policing has been a part of many EU civilian crisis management initiatives as well.

By the 1980s and 1990s, community policing was introduced as the main policing strategy in many European countries. One decade later it seemed to be out of fashion, partly because it had not always delivered what the most optimistic missionaries promised. Specific strategies of problem-solving policing, of reassurance policing, and of ILP replaced community policing in policy development in many countries. The concept of the new politics of community policing ("The Community Policing on Terrorism") refers to the situation today; the newest "wave" of community policing derives from the needs to respond to global and national security threats, notably to terrorism. Community policing is seen as a vital tool for local counterterrorism and prevention of radicalization and recruitment (Virta 2008).

The Hague Programme and the other EU security and counterterrorism strategies stress the importance of intelligence exchange and suggest that the ILP policing model be implemented in all member states' police forces. In criminological literature, there is confusion over whether there has been a paradigm shift from community policing to ILP: are they separate strategies (e.g., Ratcliffe 2008; Deukmedjian 2006) or should they be seen as complementary, with ILP a tool to support community policing (e.g., Hughes and Rowe 2007; Virta 2008)? In practice, in many European police forces, ILP policing has been adopted as an intelligence management model, to improve processes of intelligence gathering, intelligence analysis, and strategic management. Community policing, together with effective community intelligence management and information exchange not just at local level but between local police and security services, and internationally (e.g., through Europol), is seen as a promising counterterrorism vision in the EU strategies. This vision has been realized in local policing strategies and practices.

National Policing Plans in Britain determine strategic policing priorities for the police forces. For 2008–2009, there were six strategic policing priorities for Wales, one of them an implementation of CONTEST counterterrorism strategy. North Wales Police, for instance, include preventing terrorism and extremism in its strategic priorities for 2008–2011, under the title Partnership. Although neighborhood policing and preventing terrorism are both partnership issues, they have not been reconciled in other ways. Preventing terrorism means working toward the CONTEST strategy, and the force is also a part of the new Wales Extremism and Counter Terrorism Unit.[21] The Association of Chief Police Officers National Community Tension Team started in 2006, and its main areas of businesses are tension monitoring and prevention part of the CONTEST strategy. It provides weekly national community tension assessments (which are based on information from each police force), collects community intelligence and introduces it into the National Intelligence Model processes, and has produced a special Basic Command Units (BCU) Commanders Guide for Counter Terrorist Operations.[22] BCU of police forces are closest to the citizens and, therefore, the guide stresses the importance of gathering community intelligence and engagement of communities for local-level counterterrorism. For instance, in London, Metropolitan Police Commissioner Sir Ian Blair introduced in 2006 "the new paradigms of community policing," which meant investments in community policing and new procedures for local counterterrorism.[23] The Government's Green Paper[24] reconciles neighborhood policing and national security strategies, and is the newest indication of localization of national security.

In the Netherlands, the police have played an important role in local counterterrorism since 2005. The police, having an indispensable local network of contacts, are of "major importance for investigating and identifying radicalism, radicalization and recruitment. The role of the local police as an information source must not be ignored."[25] *Counter Terrorism at Local Level*–Guide[26] by the National Coordinator for Counter Terrorism follows the principles of the EU strategies. The aim of the guide is to provide local authorities with a basis for developing a local approach to counterterrorism. There are not many evaluations or research yet about the effectiveness of local counterterrorism initiatives, but the pioneer study of de Kool about the signaling of Islamist radicalism and terrorism by Dutch local police officers show that although police leaders are convinced of the need for recognizing Islamist radicalism and terrorism by community policing methods and local police officers, the ability of the local police officer to identify and signal signs of radicalism and terrorism is questionable (de Kool 2008: 95).

The community policing strategy[27] of the police in Finland is a response to the need for community policing reform. Community policing had got a new status of one of the main methods to implement the governments' Internal Security Programme (2002) which meant also more pressures (but no resources) for the police from the government. Local safety planning has been institutionalized; most of the municipalities have a local safety plan, as a result of cooperation between the police, rescue services, local authorities, and the voluntary sector. Furthermore, the external pressures from the EU have led to the adoption of an ILP model as well as acknowledgement of prevention of radicalization and recruitment. *The Hague Programme* (2004) has been one powerful driver behind the new community policing strategy. At the local level, counterterrorism is not yet included in safety plans, but local policing, especially community policing initiatives in Helsinki and Tampere, is working on ethnic relations and integration to prevent social exclusion of the immigrants (Virta and Hukkanen 2008: 127.)

Community policing has philosophical elements, and its objectives according to an influential account of Alderson (in Tilley, 2003: 314) from 1979 are "to contribute to liberty and equality, to help reconcile freedom with security and to uphold the law, to protect human rights, to help create trust in communities and to strengthen security and feelings of security." ILP operates at other levels; it is a way of doing business and a management tool. However, it has no value in itself or fundamental philosophical elements such as community policing (Tilley 2003: 311–315). Reconciliation of community policing and ILP for national security and counterterrorism purposes may not respect the philosophical elements and objectives of community policing, notably, trust in communities and protection of human rights. There is already some evidence that trust and confidence in the police can be seriously undermined in situations in which communities feel that they have been overpoliced, defined as suspect communities, and alienated. The treatment of people and communities as informants rather than true partners in intelligence gathering and negotiating conflicting values of community policing and national security policing are examples of potentially harmful practices. According to research results, there have been emerging tensions between the police and communities, between the police departments and individual officers, and between the police and security services, especially in the sensitive field of intelligence gathering, sharing, and dissemination (de Kool 2008).[28]

## Radicalization and Recruitment—Beyond Crime Prevention?

Local counterterrorism initiatives have been government-driven in the Netherlands, Great Britain, and Finland. They have been like crime prevention partnerships by structure. There has been a strong ethos of engaging communities into the processes of sharing and gathering community intelligence, for early recognition of radicalization processes within. The EU strategies are not very concrete and clear in their demands regarding community policing strategies concerning prevention of radicalization and recruitment. There should be deep understanding and knowledge of the phenomena of radicalization and recruitment if prevention is expected to be successful. However, there is not much academic research either yet. One exception, for instance, is Silke's article "Holy warriors: exploring the psychological processes of jihadi radicalisation" (2008) about the phenomena.

According to the definition of the Dutch National counterterrorism coordinator "two key processes pave the way towards actual terrorism: radicalisation and recruitment. Radicalisation is a social process, while recruitment is a form of direction that taps into radicalization and seeks to channel it in the direction of violence" (Radicalism and Radicalization. Addressing radicalism and radicalization at local and judicial levels. The Memorandum to the House of Representatives of the States General. 2005). Explanations of how individuals become radicalized and recruited into terrorist groups are psychological, social, political, or religious (see Sinai 2007: 39–41), which makes prevention efforts very complicated. In the EU strategies, terrorism is seen as a crime to be prevented and terrorists as criminals. However, as in the Security Strategy of the Netherlands for 2008–2011, radicalization is also seen as a threat to social cohesion in Dutch society, without an act of terrorism being required.

If radicalization is separated from recruitment it would be very problematic to tackle radicalization through crime prevention or community policing methods. Radicalization is not a crime; it is a social and individual, psychological, process. Radicalization means that once radicalized, a person thinks in a certain way (which is seen as unacceptable), and he or she must be prevented from thinking and acting further in the direction of recruitment. In the strategies, there are no separations made whether the suspected radicalized target has any contacts with terrorist groups or whether he or she is an individual thinker (in danger of becoming potential suicide bomber alone, or without any intentions at all). To win the battle of ideas, objectives in the counterterrorism strategies operate at a collective level, but policing unacceptable forms of individual thought may lead to *thought police*. An individual's internal life, thoughts, has become a legitimate subject for public concern (Furedi 2005: 155).

When trying to prevent radicalization, which may lead to homegrown terrorism, the police have to assess local community context and the state of the society, keeping in mind national security threat assessments and priorities, as well as European and global terrorism threat assessments. The police have to act locally and think globally. Intelligence requirements are endless. In Great Britain, neighborhood policing teams have community engagement strategies that define the methods of capturing accurate community intelligence and building an accurate community profile (BCU Commanders Guide for Counter Terrorist Operations, 2008). Community profiling and community impact assessments are innovations in local counterterrorism; profiling is for preventing terrorism and impact assessments are made for effective organization of the services after an attack. There are only few studies yet about the response of communities or community police officers to the new strategies, or about the community counterterrorism partnerships; Wouter de Kool (the Netherlands) and Basia Spalek et al (Great Britain) are working on the themes. The preliminary results of both of these studies, however, indicate that preventing radicalization and recruitment is something beyond crime prevention.

The Dutch counterterrorism coordinator has differentiated between three indicators that "can prove helpful in recognising processes of radicalisation." These are ideology, behavior, and appearance. Indicators relating to ideology refer to changes in social, political, or religious convictions (a change in a person's ideology). Indicators relating to behavior involve a change in the way a person acts and reacts (e.g., someone refuses to shake a woman's hand). Indicators relating to appearance, then, involve a change in outward appearance (different clothing or a new beard). For police training, additional indicators have been developed: cash, accommodation, preparation, objects, transport and forged documents, connections, and changes in behavior (de Kool 2008: 98).

According to the research results of de Kool, there have been numerous problems with police efforts to prevent radicalization by community policing methods. The police lack skills and knowledge about the cultural differences and backgrounds of ethnic groups and also about the nature of terrorism and radicalization. The ethnic communities are insular, and the language barrier is a significant problem. At the organizational level, there are failures in sharing information between departments at the local level and between the local police and intelligence services. Community police officers feel uncomfortable approaching people in their new role, and they have experiences of losing trust, which is the most important precondition to get community intelligence. Once lost, the trust is very difficult to re-build. The changing role of local police in this respect has reduced trust between the officers themselves too, between departments and individuals (de Kool 2008: 104–107). Sloggett has also warned recently that counterterrorism and radicalism prevention measures of the police—especially in the area of the chemical, biological, radiological, and nuclear weapons threat—may have unintentionally driven people into the radicalization processes. There should be more understanding of the processes, and the fact that once started it is difficult to provide legitimate exit routes from radicalization processes (Sloggett 2008a).

The ongoing research project (Police-Muslim Engagement and Partnerships for the Purposes of Counter Terrorism, Spalek et al. from University of Birmingham [United Kingdom]) focuses on the enhanced community aspect of counterterrorism and the central role of policing. The Muslim Contact Unit of the London Metropolitan Police, which builds upon community policing, is one of the main partners in local level counterterrorism. The research study highlights the tensions for policing in a counterterrorism context in having to negotiate adopting a pragmatic "what works" approach within a highly politicized arena. The pathologizing of Muslim youth increases the sense of alienation in "suspect communities." The preliminary results also tell that it is harmful for trust building that people feel it uncomfortable to live in suspect communities, and they feel pressurized to explain the construction of their Muslim identities, particularly in relation to Britishness (Spalek et al 2008).

The role of local police and community policing strategies in counterterrorism is very problematic as they are organizationally in-between the EU (and its growing intelligence requirements), national security agencies and intelligence services, and local authorities, community safety partnerships and local communities. They should be able to balance tensions between secrecy, repression, and national security priorities and openness, transparency, and local needs and priorities. The new politics of community policing brings the state to neighbourhoods, but there should still be room for local strategic priorities also regarding of *how* to translate counterterrorism strategies into action; political evaluation could be a part of environmental scanning and intelligence management, local safety planning, neighborhood management, and partnerships. Security and prevention of radicalization and recruitment are political and democratic problems that pertain to everyone and are linked to local conditions, and therefore there cannot be one solution for all.

## POLITICAL VIABILITY OF THE STRATEGIES?

### The Future Strategic Development

The proposed future of European Home Affairs and Justice Police can be gleaned from two recent reports of informal high-level advisory groups, so-called "Future Groups": Freedom, Security, Privacy—European Home Affairs in an Open World (June 2008) [29] and Proposed Solutions for the Future EU Justice Programme (June 2008). [30] The reports were discussed in the Council of the EU meeting on Justice and Home Affairs in Brussels, July 24–25, 2008. [31] Both reports formulate the Post-Hague Programme, and the proposals have been decided to forward (by the Council) to the Commission so that it could take them into account when drawing up the program to succeed the Hague Programme for the period from 2010 to 2014.

The point of departure in the reports is that the major challenges for citizens' security today include organized crime and terrorism, both of which constitute not only a direct threat to the people in Europe but also to the values on which the EU is founded—democracy, peace, and

fundamental rights. The proposed solutions for the new justice program include, therefore, enhancing judicial cooperation and increasing the effectiveness of day-to-day police cooperation within the EU The Future of European Home Affairs Report lists numerous proposals regarding counterterrorism and police cooperation; for example, improvement of the information flow between member states' law enforcement authorities, Europol and Eurojust; better political, technical, and operational cooperation with the United States and Russia; and focusing on mid- and long-term prevention, especially in terms of radicalization and recruitment. As terrorism is often accompanied by political propaganda, the EU must develop a positive countersystem based on its values: the rule of law, fundamental rights, peace, and liberty. To win the battle of ideas requires improvements in communication with civil society.

According to the Statewatch analysis of Bunyan ("The Shape of Things to Come: EU Future Group"),[32] there is a clear change in terminology and ideology in EU state building. For instance, the shift from references to "law enforcement agencies" as requiring this and that power to "public security organizations" (including but limited to law enforcement agencies) would mean strengthening the powers of all security agencies, not just those dealing with terrorism and organized crime. Bunyan sees also the discussion about common shared European values and the idea of "winning the battle of ideas" very problematic; the EU values are neither common nor shared but rather those of the ruling elite who assume they can define and propagate as a "consensus" where there is none.

With regard to police cooperation, the report on the future of Home Affairs stresses more effectiveness and efficiency, and recommends deepening law enforcement cooperation as a whole. Methods for getting member states' police forces closer to each other and developing a common culture for all police forces include, for example, systematic common European police training. The Post-Hague Programme 2010–2014 would therefore continue the responsibilization of national and local police forces for combating terrorism and radicalization and recruitment.

The European counterterrorism strategies have some common themes with European civil crisis management initiatives and contingency planning (see Drennan and McConnell 2007), but they ignore strategies and development of the human security field. Human security, as a conception and a strategy, seeks to decouple security from questions of war and peace and deploy it as a device aimed at urging governments to treat as emergencies such chronic threats as hunger, homelessness, disease, and ecological degradation (Loader and Walker 2007: 15). It has been argued that there is the tendency today to emphasize the importance of human security as a guiding principle of the European Security and Defence Policy, as a new kind of nonviolent intervention, but there is also an opposition to this view (Silvestri 2008: 8). The human security approach is politically contestable, and in the European Parliament especially the Greens are working for it (see, for instance, Green Security Strategy for Europe).[33] However, the tone of the Internal Security Strategy of Finland (2008) is similar to the human security approach: prevention of social exclusion is its main objective. Human security as a concept is not mentioned in it, however, and the counterterrorism part of the strategy follows the EU strategy almost literally.

## Political Evaluation

Governing through counterterrorism refers to the EU security and counterterrorism strategies and how they shape national and local-level security and policing strategies, policing practices, and local counterterrorism measures. "Governing through" has been used frequently in research to describe the current ideology or politics of governance; governing through security (e.g., Loader 2002) and governing through terrorism (Ericson 2007) are examples, but the problem with these expressions is often that they do not tell *who* governs and exactly *how*. The state, the EU, or security network may be the actor, but the processes of governing through counterterrorism, for example, may not be very easily identified. Counterterrorism strategy as a broader concept consists of written and ratified documents (strategies, action plans, and program), policy transfer and implementation processes, and translation into action processes. Strategy is seen as an organized form of exercising power by nature. According to Hörnqvist (2007), a strategy is a process made up of three stages, each of which is crucial in the exercise of power: setting the target, targeting, and staying on target. Features of the organizational context constitute part of the business of exercising power as much as the interventions themselves. The deployment of interventions is connected to available information, performance targets, policy goals, selected risks, threat assessments, legal powers, administrative guidelines, and organizational routines. Strategies are grounded on interventions directed at a particular target group, to change the behavior of the target group. One important element of a strategy is also that all parts of it are visible; the policy goals are publicly stated, the interventions are observable social practices and described in action plans, evaluations are published in reports, and common visions are articulated in educational and other materials (Hörnqvist 2007: 35–37).

In repressive strategies such as counterterrorism strategies, the overall targets are set by threat assessments. In the EU the most influential threat assessment today is the Terrorism Situation and Trend Report, the intelligence product of Europol. In the targeting process, interventions are directed by operationalizations of the selected threats. For example, in combating radicalization and recruitment, personal history, physical appearance, and behavior have been translated into indicators of threat and thus guide the interventions. Considerations of threat constitute the main vehicle for ensuring staying on target. Information flows and common visions are articulated in terms of an identical set of threats. Although the organizational context is the EU and not the state, like in Hörnqvist's analysis of the organized nature of power, the methodology of reading the strategy politically and politicizing the translation and implementation processes leads us to the claim for political evaluation of the strategy.

Politicization as a political science concept means re-interpretation of a phenomenon from a political point of view. It refers to opening new aspects of contingency in the situations and thus expanding the presence of the political in it (Palonen 1993: 11–13). In its everyday use, the term politicization has long carried a merely negative meaning. There has always been concern about politicization of the judiciary and of the police, and in this respect there has been a battle against it—a battle to ensure that certain things are not made in the party sense political (Connelly 2001: 154). It has been argued that we live today in postpolitical times (Furedi 2005; Boutellier 2005 and many others), especially due to the current governing through security strategy. In the counterterrorism research context, politicization has been suggested also in terms of "institutionalization of pluralism" whereby different assessments of the problem as well as what should be done can be more openly investigated and discussed (Goldsmith 2008; 163).

Politicization as a precondition for evaluation of political viability of the strategies needs future-oriented perspectives, choices, and alternatives. There are still many obstacles in re-thinking the relationship between security and politics. These include the tendency to see people as the object rather than as the agent of change (Furedi 2005: 3), the idea that in the risk society the aim is not to achieve good but to prevent evil (Boutellier 2005: 38), and the role of expert knowledge under uncertainty (Goldsmith 2008: 145), just to mention a few. However, it could be argued that the need to balance counterterrorism strategies and measures with legitimacy requirements will lead to changes in thinking toward understanding of "security in ambiguity" and the significance of embracing the political (de Lint and Virta 2004) or even to abandon security and concentrate on politics (Neocleous 2008: 186).

## CONCLUSIONS

"The safety utopia does not have to assume the form of a culture of control where a strong state promotes the interests of the well-to-do in the name of safety. It implies a definite call for moral reflection, for a renewed formation of local communities, a strengthening of the capacity for empathy, and a reconsideration of impassive market thinking." (Boutellier 2005: 132).

Mary Kaldor, who has been involved in the EU Human Security Doctrine development, has suggested the term "cosmopolitan law enforcement" as an alternative to the War on Terror (Kaldor 2006: 191). The *Community Policing on Terrorism* could also be seen as an alternative to the war on terror, on a local level.

The EU security and counterterrorism strategies, relying on community policing, look like they were promoting what Nye (2004) calls soft power. Especially "the battle of ideas" part of the strategy, which requires more and better strategic communication with societies, seems to rest on the ability to shape the preferences of people in Europe (see also Crelinsten 2009). By definition, soft power rests on shared values (Nye 2004: 111). The EU Area of Freedom, Security and Justice is named according to the basic values of the integration of the EU, but these values are not very visible in counterterrorism strategies, except that security is used as a justification for counterterrorism measures. It is problematic to discuss soft power in this context, but it is argued that rather than new soft power investments, the new politics of community policing means that national security and counterterrorism bring hard power to community policing. Counterterrorism strategy will change community policing (values and methods) because they are based on different kind of ideology and measures: secrecy and suspiciousness against openness and trust. Soft power means also manipulation of agenda, which means that soft power may produce hard power measures as well. In other words, strategies are organized forms of exercising soft and hard power. Power is hence both productive and destructive (Hörnqvist 2007: 217).

In the future, Europe will integrate much of its policing, intelligence gathering, and policy making to tackle terrorism, and start new networks of antiterrorism centers. The powerful reports of the future of Home Affairs and Justice include also development of a Euro-Atlantic area of cooperation with the United States to combat terrorism, sharing vast amounts of intelligence and information on citizens of the EU The current criminal justice model of counterterrorism in Europe is, however, different from the war model of the United States.

The EU monitors implementation, results, and outcome of the security and counterterrorism strategies. The European level threat assessments, conducted by Europol, will guide member states' security and policing strategies in the future even more than today. Concerted European strategy and its implementation are supported, for example, by common European police training and education. The concept of national security has changed in the last few years in many countries. In addition, many local-level security and policing strategies have recently adopted the EU-level and national security targets.

The Hague Programme failed to propose the improvement of the legitimacy of the multitude of old and newly created bodies and related information systems. Hence, large corners of the EU internal security governance are murky areas as they remain unaccountable and are only marginally legitimate. Counterterrorism has become a vibrant area of policy initiation, strategic partnerships, and intelligence exchange, infusing the growth of transnational policy webs or even global epistemic communities that escape the probing eye of parliamentarians, judges, and citizens. (den Boer, Hillebrand, and Nölke 2008: 76–77.) Although suggesting assessments of democratic, legal, and social legitimacy of counterterrorism networks and initiatives, the authors conclude that these criteria are of only limited applicability. The proposed Post-Hague Programme has no improvement initiatives in this respect.

As argued by Boutellier, the safety issue also has the potential to give society and communities new moral impulses. The call for *safe freedom* for the people puts a great deal of pressure on the local government and communities. A comprehensive preventive policy, based on solidarity, is called for that more emphatically connects social policy to the safety issues (Boutellier 2005: 127). In the analysis of Boutellier, on the way toward the safety utopia, politics and morality are reconciled. The method could also follow the ideas of French political scientist Pierre Rosanvallon about counterdemocracy, which would involve re-politicization of security, resistance, and citizens' control of how organized forms of power operate (Rosanvallon

2006; see also de Lint and Virta 2004). Resistance could also take the form of "counter-politics" against the permanent emergency and exception (Neocleous 2008: 75), which means that "We need a new way of thinking and talking about social being and politics that moves us beyond security" (186). To oppose the power of security would mean thus refusal and anti-power, rather than counterpower, because as Holloway (2002: 17) argues "once the logic of power is adopted, the struggle against power is already lost" (in de Lint and Virta 2004: 477).

In this chapter, the EU strategies are treated as organized forms of exercising power, and therefore it is suggested that evaluation of political viability of the strategies is an important counterpower strategy or a form of resistance. The political evaluation criteria, especially acceptability, appropriateness, and equity, are about values, ideologies, fairness, and equal distribution. Equity involves moral and ethical issues. It is possible to assess political viability of a strategy before its translation into action and implementation; political evaluation could be included in policy transfer, strategic planning, and management processes at national and local levels. This will produce and increase legitimacy of the EU strategies and the authorities implementing them. If there were no evaluation of the political viability of the strategies in the translation process, one could argue that instead of policy transfer the process is more like policy laundering by nature.

## NOTES

1. The Hague Multiannual Programme for strengthening the Area of Freedom Security and Justice. 4–5 November 2004. Available. Online HTTP://ec.europa.eu/justice_home/doc_centre/doc/hague_programme_en-pdf.
2. Jones, A. and Wiseman, R. (2005) *Terrorism and community policing in the 21st century, the USA and Europe compared*. Paper. Los Angeles Community Policing. HTTP://www.lacp.org/. 30.4.2007.
3. The author has been involved in common European police training and education as a lecturer, supporting country representative and course manager in several community policing and other courses and seminars since the establishment of CEPOL (European Police Academy) in 2000. The courses are meant for senior police officers from all EU Member States, and they are organized by national police colleges (usually 3–5 countries together). The Headquarters / Secretariat of CEPOL is located in Bramshill, Great Britain.
4. Federal Police Belgium (2008) *Community Policing and the prevention of radicalisation and recruitment of terrorists*, Belgian Approach. SIAK (2007) Scientific Series: *Islamic Extremism—Ideology and Modes of Dissemination*. Sicherheitsakademie, Austria: Federal Ministry of the Interior.
5. SecuCITIES (2007) *Cities against terrorism*. European Forum of Urban Security. Report Written by F.Esposito: Lalo.
6. The author has discussed with several high-ranking French senior police officers during the last 12 months in 4 CEPOL Community Policing seminars (in Riga, Athens, Tampere and Stockholm) and their message has been that there are strong pressures from below, from residents and local authorities, to re-build community policing in France.

7. Communication from the Commission to the Council and the European Parliament. Report on Implementation of the Hague Programme for 2007. Commission of the European Communities. Brussels. July 2, 2008.
8. European Security Strategy (2003), "A Secure Europe in a Better World", Brussels. December 12, 2003. Online. Available HTTP: http://www.consilium.europa.eu/uedocs/cmsUpload/78367.pdf (Accessed March 10, 2010).
9. Silvestri, S. (2008) "Revising the European Security Strategy", paper presented in the international conference "European Interests and Strategic Options," Paris, May 2008, p. 8.
10. The Action Plan of the Hague Programme: Ten priorities for the next five years. Online. Available HTTP://ec.europa.eu/justice_home/news/information_dossiers/the_hague_priorities/ (accessed 6 October 2008).
11. About the development of ILP models and concepts, see for instance Ratcliffe 2004 and 2008.
12. Communication from the Commission to the Council and the European Parliament. Report on Implementation of the Hague Programme for 2007. Commission of the European Communities. Brussels. July 2,2008.
13. The Report of Counter Terrorism Coordinator: CTC report—Implementation of the Strategy and Action Plan to Combat Terrorism. Council of the European Union. Brussels. 19 May 2008. 9416/08.
14. The Report of Counter Terrorism Coordinator: Implementation of the EU Counter Terrorism Strategy—Priorities for further action. Council of the European Union. Brussels. 19 May 2008. 9417/08
15. Strategy of Europol (2008) Europol Publications. The Hague, the Netherlands.
16. The Report of Counter Terrorism Coordinator: Implementation of the EU Counter Terrorism strategy—Priorities for further action. Council of the European Union. Brussels. May 19, 2008. 9417/08.
17. The National Security Strategy of the United Kingdom. Cabinet Office. UK. March 2008; Countering International Terrorism: the United Kindom's Strategy (CONTEST), HM Government, UK. July 2006; National Security Strategy and Work Programme 2007–2008. National Security Program Office of the Netherlands, June 2007; Internal Security Program 2004 and 2008, Ministry of the Interior, Finland.
18. This policy transfer especially from Great Britain to the EU (as a whole) is seen also in the way The Hague Programme adopts the ILP model, a model based on the British National Intelligence Model and developed for the EU by National Criminal Intelligence Service).
19. *Internal Security Programme (2004).* The Ministry of the Interior, Finland.
20. *Internal Security Programme (2008).* The Ministry of the Interior, Finland.
21. North Wales Police Authority and North Wales Police: Three year strategic plan 2008–2011. www.north-wales.police.uk. (accessed 7 April 2008).
22. BCU Commanders Guide for Counter Terrorist Operations. ACPO, NCCT Paper, London, 2008.
23. Blair, I. (2006) Commissioner's Urban Age Summit speech, 12 November. Online. Available HPPT: <http://cms.met.police.uk/news> January 15,.2007.
24. *From the neighbourhood to the national: policing our communities together.* (2008) Government's Green Paper. Home Office. UK. Published July 17, 2008.
25. Radicalism and Radicalization. Addressing radicalism and radicalization at local and judicial levels. The Memorandum to the House of Representatives of the States General. The Hague. 2005.
26. Counter Terrorism at Local Level–Guide (2007) published by the National Coordinator for Counter Terrorism , the Netherlands.

27. Community policing strategy (2007) The Ministry of the Interior, Police Department publications. Finland.
28. Spalek, B. et al (2008) *Police-Muslim Engagement and Partnerships for the Purposes of Counter Terrorism: an examination.* Summary report, November 18.
29. Freedom, Security, Privacy—European Home Affairs in an open world. Report of the Informal High Level Advisory Group on the Future of European Home Affairs Policy. June 2008.
30. Proposed Solutions for the Future EU Justice Programme. High-Level Advisory Group on the Future of European Justice Policy. June 2008.
31. Council of the European Union. Press Release; 2887th Council meeting on Justice and Home Affairs, Brussels 24 and 25 July 2008. Provisional version. http://www.consilium.europa.eu/Newsroom.
32. Tony Bunyan (2008) "The Shape of Things to Come: EU Future Group" Statewarch Analysis. On line HTTP://www.statewatch.org/analysis/the-shape-of-things-to-come.pdf. February 15, 2009.
33. Green Security Strategy for Europe. The Greens/ European Free Alliance in the European Parliament. January 15, 2008. www.greens-efa.org. (accessed 6 October 2008).

# 9    Transnational Media Corporations and National Culture as a Security Concern in China

*Jiang Fei and Huang Kuo*

## INTRODUCTION

Security, especially within the nation and state political framework, has gained a worldwide acceptance. Focusing on theories of national security in China, Liu (2001) divides the notion of security into two dimensions: sovereignty-related concerns and nonsovereignty concerns. Sovereignty includes the concepts of a nation's right to state survival, multilateral political relationships with other countries, opportunity for development, and the definition of national boundaries. The nonsovereignty dimension includes the balance of the natural environment, the guarantee of energy supplies, the health of the financial sector, the harmony within the nation's society, and all aspects of culture as well as their related "industries" and activities.

In the People's Republic of China (PRC), the phrase "national security" was popularized with Lipmann's *U.S. Foreign Policy: Shield of the Republic* in the 1940s (Liu 2001). The Chinese Communist Party is the ruling power in the PRC. The central government under the Chinese Communist Party is the single legal force to control the military. This institution is also responsible for national safety. Furthermore, most of the main cultural materials are controlled by the central government. In this case, it is the policy maker in the central government who decides the keynote or the mainstream of the national culture. Other social forces, including the democratic parties, such as the Revolutionary Committee of the Chinese Kuomintang, China Democratic League, and China Democratic National Construction Association (9 parties in total), are incorporated within the Chinese People's Political Consultative Conference and act as cooperator, political consulter, and democratic supervisor for the Chinese Communist Party in power. They represent a different social stratum of China. They are important components of the national government. They also have duties of national safety on their shoulders. Because nongovernmental organizations (NGOs) in China are not yet well established, the central government of the PRC can be seen as the only, and perhaps the most, suitable figure to ensure not only state security but also cultural security. Regarding the nonsovereignty security framework, such as cultural security, we suggest that culture has two facets. The first facet takes place in an international context. It infers international respect for a nation's cultural traditions. The second facet occurs within the national context such as balancing the domestic cultural market among its multiethnic divisions. This facet demands positive cooperation and harmonious coexistence among varied ethnic groups within the nation-state.

Although "security studies" as a new label has replaced "national security studies" (Wyn Jones 1999: 94), the issues in China still remain state-centric. Falk (2004: 325) writes that "the state-centric world order of the Westphalian era, roughly from 1648–1990s, embodied a clear conception of world order." Falk continues: "The guiding idea of sovereignty legitimized territorial governance as the exclusive prerogative of a central government that represented the state in its external diplomatic relation." In conclusion, Falk explains that "a map of the world incorporated these spatial notions, which also made concerns about boundary-management and territorial aggression central to notions of security." In light of this world order, the central government in the PRC, together with other parties and interest groups, sees itself as legally bound to ensure the safety of the state.

The meaning of national security changes as the context shifts. We argue in this chapter that with the diminishing of the Cold War, Western-based globalization promoted the communication of the Western culture and propelled a shift in "security" concerns from states' physical boundaries to cultural boundaries. The two world wars were fighting for and about territory and profits; therefore, the security issues were located within the field of sovereignty. The subsequent Cold War added ideological concerns to the traditional concept of security, and increased the awareness in cultural impacts and ramifications. The Cold War was interplay between sovereignty and nonsovereignty security dimensions, and it dismantled the traditional notion of "security," rebuilding it into ever-changing perceptions. Although it is time to "roll up the map of the Cold War, and travel without maps for a while" (Thompson 1982: 34), the boundaries of the old perceptions have become totally blurred, and previously discrete components have become increasingly interdependent and interconnected.

To build "a better security system" (Barnett and Adler 1998: 417), the concept of "societal security" is introduced to security studies to link the international, national, and individual facets. Individuals are studied as members of a social group or community, and "the security of people, either as individuals or as a global or international collectivity" are studied with a focus on everyday issues such as "economic welfare, environmental concerns, cultural identity, and political rights" (Waever 1995). In the case of China, the nation-state is a "unified political community," and the assumption that "there exists such homogeneity of interests and identification within that community" makes it possible to reduce security into a minimal conception of strategies for state security, which is "synonymous with aggregate individual security" (Reus-Smit 1992: 17).

In this chapter, we explore security issues from cultural perspectives and argue how the policies of the transnational media corporations (TNMCs) and the responses of the Chinese state have affected the lives of the Chinese people. In the case of China, cultural security was and continues to remain a key focus of the nation's security concerns. Cultural security is influenced by the culture industry and vice versa. The commercialization of Chinese cultural industry started with the establishment of China's first newspaper group (Guangzhou Daily News Group) in January 1996. Over the next 10 years, 85 media groups were founded in China. The blooming of China's media groups is the outcome of commercialization of the Chinese media system. This commercialization has significant Chinese characteristics, which means cultural industries operate independently in economics but still take the responsibility for promoting the government's policy and ideology, as well as governing the cultural market. Therefore, the development of the Chinese culture industry is not simply a shift of its role from a deputy of ideology to a share of the market.

In the context of media globalization, cultural security has become more complex. Cultural events are disseminated internationally; therefore, it is necessary to understand the substance of cultural events from two perspectives. On the one hand, abstract cultural conceptions were invented and used as universal ideas as if they could cover all cultural issues from different cultural backgrounds, such as "value." Most of the time, these concepts were used as ideology to deconstruct the indigenous culture directly. On the other hand, culture was defined by cultural products, and audiences could identify themselves with cultural products but not culture itself. However, most of the cultural products are generated in the Western countries. The new kind of audience was invented through the consuming of cultural products. As Friedman (1999: 127) suggests, "the world has become one place, structured by multinational capital whose project is to surpass the nation-state and create a world society, or at least a world working class." We suggest that this so-called new world working class is the new audience who are, following Anderson (1983), imagined communities that commonly share knowledge and messages provided by the global media. The anxiety of the Chinese state is that the cultural industry will re-map the world under the new framework and with the help of the "new" audience.

When the central government of China sees this trend from the perspective of security, they think that China is facing both the traditional problems of national boundary, such as Taiwan, and the new conception of cultural boundary. In the eyes of the government, this is the competition between the Chinese traditional values and the Western modernization. The collapse of the Soviet Union has turned China into the biggest socialist country, a state that struggles for its dreams of both socialism and modernization. At first flush, these two dreams do not conflict with each other, but observing the colonization history in China by some Western countries[1] for almost a century, the Chinese government tends to see the Western culture-oriented modernization as a security-related issue. Modernization is a broad concept. The industry system modernization can help China become wealthier. However, the state fears that those cultural discourses behind the products could overthrow the traditional values and the values of communism as well.

These anxieties of the Chinese state in the wake of what it sees as the work of the TNMCs in the former Soviet Union, France, Germany, and Canada have aroused the enthusiasm of Chinese scholars to study the TNMCs. For example, researchers in China found that one of the main reasons for the collapse of the Soviet Union was the neglect of cultural value construction that related to the socialist system (Zhang and Qi 2003). In response, Hui-lin hu, a scholar of cultural industry studies, wrote in a popular weekly paper arguing that to promote cultural industry in China was not only an approach to developing the national economy but also an approach to survive in a new culture.[2]

Likewise, a scholar of communication (Zhu 1999) states that since the Americans claimed the construction of the information highway in 1993, we are facing a new world based on the use of the Internet. The U.S. government has made full use of the Internet to export American values, culture, and ideology. Most of this work, Zhu suggests, has been done with the help of those transnational media groups from the United States. In terms of cultural security in China, Cui-ran (2003) suggests that what is needed is to "build up the new World Order through the promotion of Chinese traditional cultural value to conquer the Cultural Imperialism from America." Another Chinese scholar supports the agenda of the Chinese government, stating that China should make cultural security a "key element in influencing the national security, a deep subject in deciding the structure of national security" (Lin 1999).

Scholarly discussion on the topic of cultural security, however, took place in other countries long before the current discourse in China. It was the launching of Sputnik 1 by the U.S.S.R. in 1957 that prompted a wide-ranging discussion on the topic. The world's first Earth-orbiting artificial satellite opened the so-called Space Age, which immersed the world in modern instantaneous communication technology, such as mobile phones and satellite television. This development stimulated the idea of a global village raised by McLuhan in 1964. At the time, scholars drew attention to the potential of the satellite and television to accelerate social change (Ferguson 1976: 121–129). This discussion gained momentum after the dissolution of the U.S.S.R. In 1993, France introduced the policy of cultural exception, a new concept, to the General Agreement on Tariffs and Trade. The policy states that cultural exports should be treated differently than other goods in trade negotiations because national cultures should be protected. This policy allowed France to use tariffs and quotas to protect its cultural market from other cultural products, most notably U.S. films and television. Through this concept, France was granted cultural exception. In October 2005, UNESCO's *Convention on the Protection and Promotion of the Diversity of Cultural Expressions* enshrined cultural exception as a method of protecting local cultures. The United States opposed the provision, claiming that cultural exception is a form of protectionism that harms global trade and that the provision outlined in the United Nations Educational, Scientific, and Cultural Organization convention allowed for oppressive governments to suppress minority cultural voices.[3]

In summary, in this global world, the impact of TNMCs on a nation such as China can be viewed from two perspectives. From the macroscopic view, it shows us the interaction and shifting of different culture. From the microscopic view, it shows us the influence on the target audiences and the challenge to the local and national traditional communication model. In such a context, the issue of cultural security in China has special meanings: 1. Sustainable development of the national sovereignty and political/cultural system; 2. Successiveness of traditional values to distinguish China from other civilizations; and 3. Protection of cultural industry for the sake of national interests.

Instead of paying attention to the first aspect, as is often done among the scholars in international relations or political science, this chapter focuses on the third point. We analyze the effects of transnational cultural influences and the reaction of the PRC state in combating what it sees as an issue of cultural security. We suggest that these policies also influence the lives of the Chinese people. First, we analyze how the Chinese state perceives cultural impacts from abroad on Chinese traditional values, cultural industry, social life, and cultural system. Second, we analyze the strategies the Chinese state has implemented to counteract these influences in its mission to ensure what the state sees as a vision of how the Chinese cultures should develop. Finally, we suggest ways in which the strategies of the Chinese state, put in place to ensure the state's vision of the Chinese culture, effect the actual people in China.

The chapter is focused on examples of the U.S. TNMCs for two reasons. First, most of the TNMCs in China are headquartered in the United States. Second, the U.S. TNMCs seem to have absolute hegemony in the world cultural product market—they have "world ambitions" and the power to determine international cultural ecology.[4] We also see a shift in U.S. policy after the September 11, 2001 (9/11) attacks. For example, the White House Office of Global Communications, founded in January 2003, was granted $200 million a year toward the coordination of U.S. state propaganda efforts. This included funding overseas advertisements, magazines, libraries, educational programs, and other initiatives targeted mostly at Middle Eastern and Islamic populations. According to an updated Final Report of the National Commission on Terrorist Attacks Upon the United States ("The 9/11 Commission"), the U.S. "has to . . . defeat an ideology, not just a group of people."[5]

## THE INFLUENCE OF THE TRANSNATIONAL
## MEDIA CORPORATIONS IN CHINA

The influence of the TNMCs on China's national cultural security is a double-edged sword; they inspire as much as they threaten the existence of the Chinese cultural industry. The importance of the TNMCs has been viewed by some Chinese scholars in the following way: "Ever since the 1990's, the development of media technology such as satellites, Internet and wireless phone, together with political goals in global scale and international cultural conflicts, have facilitated national media groups going overseas" (Jiang 2005). Given this structure, "TNMCs should be studied as an important political and cultural figure besides their economic influences on multi-disciplines and from multi-dimensions" (Jiang 2005).

China has long been targeted as a big media market with potential development due to its mass audience and underdeveloped current situation caused by conservative media policy. China's reform and opening-up policy and its World Trade Organization (WTO) membership have opened the door for international groups to enter China. Tom Goddard, the CEO of Viacom Outdoor International, foresaw big opportunities in 2005 and expressed them in the following way: "The best way to enter Asian Pacific market is through the gateway of Beijing—the capital city of China and the host of 2008 Olympics."[6]

TNMCs started stepping into China in the 1970s. After International Data Group (IDG) published *Computer World*, a professional technological journal, in Chinese in 1989, most of the top global media corporations, such as the News Corporation, Viacom, Disney, AOL, Warner, and Bertelsmann, all found ways to enter the Chinese media market. The following paragraphs attempt to sketch a panoramic view of the game between the Chinese government and TNMCs from strategic and practical perspectives. We analyze positive as well as negative aspects of TNMCs' influences on Chinese culture and raise questions about the role of the TNMCs in cultural security on a global scale.

Driven by economical, cultural, or political interests, TNMCs run businesses in different media fields in China.[7] For example, there are magazines, book publishing, advertisements, broadcasting, television programs, Web sites, and video productions. In terms of IDG alone, it publishes 12 Chinese magazines. There is an unbalance between China's import and export of cultural products. In book publishing, for example, the number of books China imported between 1997 and 2002 was 40,980, while it exported only 3,967. This ratio is approximately 10:1. Table 9.1 illustrates China's book copyright business deals in 2005.

Foreign media groups rushed to be involved in the Chinese media industry after China joined the WTO on December 11, 2001. In 2002, the Chinese government started to invite foreign media groups to invest in the retail market of books, newspapers, and magazines in Beijing,

*Table 9.1*   China's Book Copyright Business Deals in 2005

| Book Copyrights Import | | Book Copyrights Export | |
|---|---|---|---|
| *Country and Zone* | *No. of Titles* | *Country and Zone* | *No. of Titles* |
| United States | 3932 | Taiwan | 673 |
| United Kingdom | 1647 | Republic of Korea | 304 |
| Germany | 366 | Hong Kong | 169 |
| France | 320 | United Kingdom | 74 |
| Russia | 49 | Singapore | 43 |

Source: General Administration of Press and Publication, People's Republic of China, 2007

Shanghai, and six other big cities (Tianjin, Guangzhou, Dalian, Qingdao, Zhengzhou, and Wuhan), as well as in five special economic districts (Shenzhen, Zhuhai, Shantou, Xiamen, and Hainan provinces). By the end of 2004, with the approval of the Chinese Bureau of Broadcasting and Television, 33 foreign satellite television channels had access to Chinese TV industries. All big international media corporations have established their business in China. Table 9.2 shows that the news corporations in China, owned by Rupert Murdoch, have reached almost all fields of the Chinese media industry.

## Bertelsmann AG

In February 1995, Shanghai Bertelsmann Cultural Industry Co. Ltd. came into existence in terms of a joint venture between Bertelsmann Corporation and China Science and Technology Book Co. under the administration of Shanghai News Publishing Bureau. At the end of 1998, the Bertelsmann Book Club website (www.bol.com.cn) was set up. In early 2000, Shanghai Bertelsmann Information Technology (SBIT) was established as a platform for e-commerce for developing digitalized products. In December 2000, BOL China (www.bolchina.com), completely owned by Bertelsmann, was launched as an online mega-store for media products. By the end of 2000, the membership of Bertelsmann's book club reached more than 1.5 million, which makes more than $80 million in books and video sales. To reinforce his management in the Chinese market, Bertelsmann established Bertelsmann Business Service Co. Ltd. in Shanghai in December 2000 (Jiang 2005: 35).

Bertelsmann's strategy of inserting a local presence started in July 2002. Chinese Bertelsmann Book Club allied with two subcorporations of Chinese Sun Culture Media Co. Ltd. in the Great China district (including the mainland, Taiwan, Hong Kong, and Macao), "ing Wen Recording Company" and "Sun Cross-Media Industry Development Company," to cooperate in publication. Bertelsmann's first step out of the Shanghai district

*Table 9.2*   News Corporations Owned by Rupert Murdoch

| Fields | Production |
| --- | --- |
| Newspaper | Online network of *People's Daily*[8] |
| Television | STAR TV, Phoenix satellite television (Hong Kong), CHANNEL [V][9] |
| Interactive television | NDS cooperated with Sichuan Provincial Network Co. Ltd, provided NDS Open VideoGuard conditional access and an interactive television stock information service and electronic program guide for the cable television network's digital broadcasting infrastructure; this was a significant win for NDS in China, which demonstrates their unique ability to offer the end-to-end digital broadcasting solution.[10] |
| Internet | Purchased the stock of CNC[11] and was sold out to Telefonic (Spain) in July 2005 at the price of $110 million. Its retained profit is $50 million. |
| Others | Chinese wireless service market[12], sold scientific programs such as Fantastic Earth and Crazy Weekend |

in China was marked by the establishment of a Beijing service center in Cyber Digital Square in the Haidian district on December 29, 2002. On June 23, 2003, Bertelsmann combined the users of www.bbc.com.cn and www.bolchina.com to a new online platform called www.bol.com.cn. In the following years, the Chinese Translation Publishing House Yilin cooperated with Liaoning Publishing House Company to import foreign books to China and be involved in book wholesale market.

Bertelsmann Book Club and BOL China, subsidiaries of Direct Group, are active in both traditional and digital retail markets for books and audiovisual products. Christian Unger, president of Direct Group Bertelsmann, reveals Bertelsmann's strategy to *Beijing Review* with the following words: "The key strategy is to build up a far-reaching platform based on both traditional sources and digital technologies, and to provide customers with more direct and convenient access to all Bertelsmann media products and services."[13] The club is now the largest book club in terms of joint ventures in China, providing up-to-date selections of books, CDs, video CDs, DVDs, and computer games to more than 1.5 million members nationwide through mailing catalogs and online service.

Bertelsmann adjusted its strategy according to the Chinese media environment. In 2008, fierce online competition and changing reader habits led Bertelsmann to shut all Chinese bookstores. However, this has not influenced its long-term commitment to the Chinese market because, as Bertelsmann was quoted in a Chinese daily, "We will put the investment in the book sector to other sectors of Bertelsmann in China."[14]

## Disney

Disney began to sell the series of 30-minute cartoons "Mickey Mouse and Donald Duck" to the Chinese Central Television station (CCTV) in 1980. The two figures soon became popular stars in China. In 1994, Disney sold a children's program, "Little Mythic Dragon Club> (in Chinese pinyin: Xiao Shen Long Ju Le Bu), to the Hinterland CATV of China. Now the program covers 49 cable television channels in 31 provinces and attracts an audience of almost 160 million. It is one of the most influential teenage programs in China. Another achievement of ESPN in 1994 was to cooperate with Shanghai CATV. In 2001, Disney Net Company and Chinese Haihong Company built up www.disney.com.cn, linking 16 Web sites of Haihong's. In 2003, they began building the first Disneyland in China. On its opening day (September 12, 2005), 16,000 people visited Hong Kong Disneyland.[15]

In 2003, Disney Net Company cooperated with the Japanese company INDEX to produce a Disney brand mobile phone and promote content service in China. The same year, cooperation with Sohu.com, one of the top three online portals in China, was set up to promote Disney products and service. It is reported that the Shanghai Disneyland project received permission from the Chinese government in November 2009[16] and, according to Chinese News Net of August 2008, Disneyland in Shanghai will open in 2012.[17]

## Viacom Inc.

In 1995, MTV Mandarin took initial steps to start MTV programming in China. "The long-term goal is 24-hour programming," said Harry Hui, managing director of MTV Mandarin. "We look forward to bringing our passion and energy to the China market." MTV Mandarin currently runs 1 to 3 hr per day in China, and reaches 40 million mainland homes daily via 38 television stations (Jiang 2005: 58).

MTV's local programs include Tianlaicun (literally: 'natural sounds village'), which is shown on hundreds of Chinese television stations; Shanghai-based MTV English, teaching viewers English via the lyrics of international pop songs; and the upcoming Sprite Know-How, a short-segment program featuring fashion and pop culture news and interviews. MTV Mandarin's video jockeys are unique to its viewers,[18] and the "CCTV—MTV Music Celebration" has been an annual event since 1999. By 2002, "MTV-Lai'ka Fashion Celebration" was held in Shanghai while "Development of Media in 21 Century" conference, sponsored by Viacom and Chinese State Administration of Radio, Film, and Television, was held in Beijing.

On March 24, 2004, in cooperation with Shanghai Media Group, Viacom started Chinese children program production. This was the first TNMC to gain program permission in China. Redstone, the president of Viacom, sated that "Partnerships with Chinese companies are central to our long-term strategy, and Viacom's alliances with the two leading regional TV players—Shanghai Media Group and now Beijing Television—represents a significant commitment to producing high-quality, locally produced content for audiences in China and around the world."[19] On March 20, 2005, Viacom signed an agreement with Tsinghua Tongfang Company to work together on digital television programs. MTV China launched the first HIV/AIDS awareness and prevention campaign in China, called "Ninja: The Enduring Master," which was locally produced. At the same time, the Mandarin-language version of MTV International's confidential HIV/AIDS information Web site (www.staying-alive.org) was set up. The partnership between Viacom and China's search engine Baidu.com started on October 9, 2006. It is said that "China may be ripe for Viacom,"[20] and the "tentative" talk between Sumner Redstone and Chinese officials on building theme parks in Shanghai in July 2007 further proves this statement.[21] Given the fierce competition from the Disney Land, Viacom has failed to build the theme park in Shanghai. Nevertheless, Viacom has not given up the initiative. What looks like a change of strategy, Viacom has recently began negotiations with the government of Tianjin City for a possible theme park there. At the same time, Viacom had been looking for a new director for its Chinese business, someone who was familiar with the rules of both, traditional media and new media. In 2008, this position was taken on by Wang'hai, formerly a vice director for PPLive, a live platform for P2P streaming media.

## Hachette Filipacchi

*The World Fashions: ELLE* in Chinese was permitted to circulate in mainland China in 1988. By 2003, it reached the circulation of 348,738 and shared 45.5% of the magazine market in Beijing, Shanghai, and Guangzhou. Being a dominant top magazine for white-collar women in Mainland China, *ELLE* has more than 1.5 million readers. It became the founder of the First Magazine Readers' Club in China, with more than 260,000 members. Soon, following *ELLE*, was the successful circulation of the sport magazine *Bo* (in 1994), *Famous Cars* (in 1995), and *Health* (in 1997). In 2001, *ELLE* launched its Chinese website (www.ellechina.com).

Based on *Elle's* successful market strategy and loyal readership, *XIN LI YUE KAN* (pinyin, literally: *Psychology Monthly*) was launched in June 2006 by CSPC. One million copies of the first issue were circulated together with *ELLE, Marie Claire,* and *Woman's Day*. Its advertising is managed by Beijing Hachette Advertising, of which Hachette Filipacchi Media is the majority shareholder.[22] The goal of the magazine, as expressed by Tu Xiaodong, the magazine's editor-in-chief, is to " . . . help Chinese women seek personal development in a booming modern society. Like many Western women, Chinese women have an intense professional and family life and are looking for the right balance between their desire for independence, determination to succeed in their relationships and be part of the tremendous development of their country" (Jiang 2005: 73).

## Reuters Co. Ltd.

One-hundred-fifty-year-old Reuters Co. Ltd. is the first foreign news agency in China permitted to take photos for First National Division Football League. Since 1980, Reuter has had offices in Beijing, Shanghai, Dalian, Shenzhen, Chengdu, and other big cities in China.

Qing Niao Web is a China-based exclusive investment technology project of Reuters Group. It is a top global service of information, journalism, and technology. Based on Reuters' worldwide information-collecting terminals, the Web site provides integrated authoritative information in various fields to industries doing business-to-business e-commerce. Currently, Reuters Group's Qing Niao B2B business and Shanghai Xinliduo Company's data-collecting business are both under the administration of the Xinhua News Agency and the Ministry of Information Industry.[23] Its cooperation with the Xinhua News Agency also includes using www.xinhuaonline.com as a platform to provide information on finance, sports, and the stock market with the exception of political and ideological issues.

The scope of the TNMCs in China is provided in Table 9.3. TNMCs in China do not consider their current achievements noteworthy. What they have done is to achieve a foothold in China's media market. By popularizing their brands and images unceasingly during the process of localization, they are waiting for the golden opportunity of complete victory in China. TNMCs have predominant advantages compared with their Chinese partners in terms of capital, administration system, mechanics, and technologies. What is more, they possess valuable experiences of running international business. All of these factors make them superior to their Chinese allies who may well become their potential competitors in the context of what is still an immature Chinese media market.

## The State Response Toward the Transnational Media Corporations

The impact of the TNMCs in China and the response of the Chinese state toward the TNMCs repeat the history of the Warring States Period[24] in China. The two eras are both characterized by separate regimes—namely, political and military power of warlords, and cultural and economic power of media corporations, as well as sharp conflicts and strategies for achieving goals. The Chinese and TNMCs interact through competition and convergence. In doing so, they adopt the strategies used by the warlords in the Warring States period, *He-Zong* and *Lian-Heng*. We suggest that this is because the situations are similar and follow the logic of war used in theories of security studies. Waever (1995), for example, writes that "the inner logic of war follows from its basic character as an *unconstrained* situation, in which the combatants each try to function at maximum efficiency in relation to a clearly defined aim." TNMCs and Chinese media industries play the roles of *Wang* in the Warring States Period in China. *Wang* (the King) was the title for the ruler of China before the Qin Dynasty (221 B.C.–206

*Table 9.3* The scope of the TNMCs in China

| TNMC | Newspapers/ magazines | Book | Video | Broadcast/ Television | Internet | Others |
|---|---|---|---|---|---|---|
| News Corp (USA) | | | | Phenix satellite television (1996). STAR satellite television Channel [V]. Discovery | NetEase.com (2000) Peopledaily. com; Phenix.com Phenix SMS; CNC | Wireless service |
| Bertelsmann (Germany) | National Geography (Chinese version). *Car Fans, Parents* | Reader Club | Explore (Series) | | www. bolchina .com (2000) www.bbc. com.cn (1998) | |
| Disney (USA) | | | | Mickey Mouse and Donald Duck (1978). Xiaoshenlong Club (1994) ESPN | www.disney. com.cn, short message www.sohu .com (Chinese channels) | Mobile phone of Disney band and content service (MICKEY UNLIMITED) Disney garden (11, HK 2003) |
| Time Warner (USA) | *Fortune eCompany Now China* | | Warner Music | Huyu satellite television (CETV 2001) (sold to TOM 2003) | Legend's Fm365.com | Yongle cinema Shanghai (2003) |
| Viacom (USA) | | | Nick- elodion DVD/ VCD | CCTV–MTV music chan- nel (1995) Nickelodeon knowledge garden (2001) | Baidu.com | Theme parks |
| Reader's Digest (USA) | Puzhi Topics on China (copyright) | | | | | |
| Hachette Filipacchi (France) | *ELLE* (Hong Kong 1987; Taiwan 1991) *Car & Driver* (Hong Kong 1989; Taiwan 1991) | | | | | |
| Policy of China now | Unlimited on retailing and circulation investment from 2006 | | | Program cooperation Channel and frequency are controlled by government | Joint venture, 49% invest- ment ratio ISP | Unlimited network service for mobile phone |

B.C.). Below him were local warlords called *Zhuhou* (nobles, pinyin: zhū hóu) whose responsibility was to support *Wang* in an emergency. In the *Spring and Autumn Period* (between 722 B.C. and 481 B.C.), *Zhou Wang* (King of Zhou Dynasty) lost most of his power and the most powerful *Zhuhou* became the de facto ruler of China. Subsequently, in the Warring States period (from 5th century B.C. to 221 B.C.), most *Zhuhou* declared themselves *Wang* or kings, and regarded themselves equals to *Zhou Wang*. After *Qin Wang* Ying Zheng (King of the state of Qin), later known as Qin Shi Huangdi, defeated all other *Wang* and unified China, the new title *Huangdi* (emperor) was initiated. The unification of China in 221 B.C. by the First Emperor *Qin Shi Huangdi* (or *Shih Hwang-Tih*) marked the beginning of Imperial China.

As every Chinese student learns, the process through which the state Qin defeated the other six states (Qi, Chu, Yan, Han, Zhao, and Wei) and united China into an empire is the practice of the strategies called *He-Zong* and *Lian-Heng*. The representative works on war and strategies during this period are *Strategies of the Warring States* (pinyin: Zhang Guo Ce) and *The Art of War* (pinyin: Sunzi Bingfa). This genre of military strategies represents a philosophy of war for managing conflicts and winning battles, and it has been seen as a prime example of Taoist thinking. *The Art of War*, still today an influential ancient Chinese work on military strategy as well as international relations, has been translated into more than 10 languages, including English, Russian, French, and German. In fact, the book is so important that it is also on the U.S. House Armed Services Committee Chairman's recommended national security reading list.[25] The history of the Warring States period is a part of the obligatory curriculum in junior and senior high school in China. Sun Tzu and other philosophers and strategists, such as Confucius and Lao Tzu, are a part of the so-called Hundred Schools of Thought in China (pinyin: zhuzi baijia).[26]

The literal meaning of *Zong* in Chinese is "north-south" while *Heng* is "east-west." *Zong-Heng* is a phrase referring to the alliances formed among the Warring States. *He-Zong* means "forming the alliance among the six states" to stand ground with state Qin and emphasizes the unity of "the less-powerful." *Lian-Heng*, on the other hand, means to ally with state Qin to benefit from its strength and prosperity; in other words, to "join the Syndicate."[27] State Qin applied *Lian-Heng* strategy to break up the alliance (*He-Zong*) and finally conquered the six states one by one.

We suggest that the ancient Chinese strategies of *He-Zong* and *Lian-Heng* are also applied in the Chinese media market by the TNMCs and Chinese media industries. The Chinese media has been centralized since 1949, which means that the central government of China has been absolutely in charge. The implementation of reforming and of opening up policies in 1978, however, began to undermine the centralization. The entrance of TNMCs into China as new players in the mid-1980s further destroyed the centralization and the balance of the Chinese media market. In 1994, China started its application for re-joining what was formerly General Agreement on Tariffs and Trade (changed into WTO in 1995). This roused Chinese policy makers, media practitioners, and scholars alike to reflect on the situation of Chinese media industry, to investigate the development of TNMCs, and to discuss strategy toward the transformation and competition. After long-standing centralization, Chinese media industries faced many problems. For example, as Jiang (2005) reports, media practitioners lack professionalism, which puts them under pressure to meet the needs of the audiences. Similarly, lack of operation skills cause media facilities to close. As a result, media technology and facilities are underdeveloped. Another problem, according to Jiang (2005), is that Chinese media industries are used to depending upon government funding, which makes self-sufficiency very difficult. Compared with the developed transnational media giants, Chinese media industries were like "naïve children under overprotection" with no experiences of self-support and competition. The situations of TNMCs and Chinese media industries in 1990s were similar to that in the Warring States period: the TNMCs have the advantages in funds, technology, facility, management, and experiences. For these reasons, they play the role of the strong state of Qin. The Chinese media industries, on the other hand, have the advantages in policies, culture, language, and audience share, but they are inexperienced in market economy, and weak and small in terms of scale and scope. Therefore, they play the roles of the weak states (e.g., Qi, Chu, Yan). In such a situation, the Chinese media groups are applying the strategy of alliances with each other to compete against the expansion of the strong states, *He-Zong*, while the TNMCs create alliances to participate in this expansion (i.e. *Lian-Heng)*.

In 1996, the *He-Zong* of the Chinese media groups started to form. The strategy has been to create an alliance between the integrated provincial and county media companies, and to be able to compete with the coming foreign media groups. This changed the landscape of the Chinese media (Figure 9.1). As mentioned in Figure 9.2, China Media Group (CMG) is the largest media group in China. CMG united five major subsidiaries: CCTV, China Radio International, China National Radio, China Film Group Corporation, and the China Radio and Television Transmission Network Corporation Limited (China Broadcast Network). CMG also has three professional performance troupes: China Broadcasting Performing Arts Troupe, China Philharmonic Orchestra, and China Film Orchestra; seven newspapers; 17 magazines; two publishing houses; and nine audio-visual publication and program production enterprises.

The TNMCs used the *Lian-Heng* strategy (see Figure 9.3). As presented in detail in Figure 9.4, the first stage of the strategy was to cooperate with the local media since no direct investment in China was permitted. Through the international licensing agreements, TNMCs cooperated with local media companies in terms of management contracts and joint ventures with the

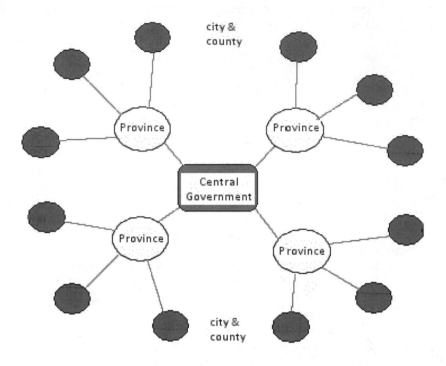

*Figure 9.1*    Framework of media market in China before 1996.

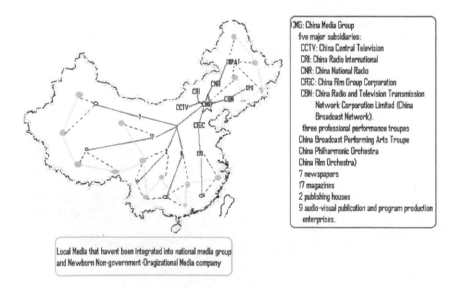

*Figure 9.2*    Media groups in China.

promise of a win–win relationship. From 1978 to 2001, TNMCs took decisive actions to enter the Chinese media market, similar to warships going ashore before the dawn (in Chinese pinyin: *Duo Dian Qiang Tan*), as we have attempted to illustrate with the cases of IDG, Disney, Viacom, News Corporation, and Bertelsmann.

TNMCs' second stage strategy was to cooperate with one another. After building a stable relationship with the Chinese media companies and establishing their own local presence, the TNMCs started to enlarge their sphere of activity. They took advantage of one another to invest in different fields in China; however, in the process, the Chinese local media groups were left with little space to grow.

The final-stage strategy of the TNMCs is for long-term benefits. After adapting to China's environment, the TNMCs have directed their efforts to change the Chinese media market. Their strategies include not only economic but also cultural aspects. The Chinese traditional culture has long been a barrier to the TNMCs grand prospect in China. To express it again in Chinese cultural terms, the TNMCs' strategy is to stop water from boiling by taking away the firewood from under the cauldron rather than scooping and cooling the water and then pouring it back (in Chinese pinyin: *Yang Tang Zhi Fei Bu Ru Fu Di Chou Xin*). It appears from the actions of the TNMCs that the ultimate goal of their local presence is to create new audiences for their programming. The Chinese state is concerned that such audiences would give up Chinese indigenous programs to the preference of those of the TNMCs' because their tastes would have changed. The state fears that this would mean their renunciation of the Chinese traditional cultures. Indeed, Viacom has successfully practiced this strategy. For example, when MTV first broadcast in China, few Chinese youth knew about it. After MTV created their own local program by integrating Chinese elements into American formats, millions of

*Figure 9.3*   Three-stage strategy of the TNMCs in China.

| step | time | policy | China | TNMC | characteristics/strategy | examples |
|---|---|---|---|---|---|---|
| 1 | 1978–2000 | Opening policy in 1978 | **H E** | **L I A N** | *Duo Dian Qiang Tan* (literally: [Military] Land the beach of China from multipoint randomly. In Chinese: 多点抢滩 ) | IDG (1988), Disney(1994) Viacom(1995) Newscorp (1995) Bertelsmann (1998) |
| 2 | 2001–2005 | WTO membership in 2001 | | | *Fen Jin He Ji* ( literally: [Military] concerted attack by converging columns. In Chinese: 分进合击 ) | Time-Warner (2001)¹ Newscorp-Star(2002)² Vivendi Universal SA (2002)³ |
| 3 | 2005–now | promise of WTO and promotion from Olympic 2008 | **Z O N G** | **H E N G** | *Fu Di Chou Xin* ( literally: to take away the firewood from under the caldron; or to remove the ultimate cause of trouble. In Chinese: 釜底抽薪 ) | Hachette Filipacchi (create new audiences of white collar) Viacom (raise new audience of young generation); Bertelsmann (change the habit of reading) |

*Figure 9.4*   Implementation of the TNMCs' three stage strategies.

Chinese youth became avid viewers. The same is true of Viacom's children's program—Nickelodeon.

This strategy has broken the balance of the Chinese media market. *He-Zong* strategy is implemented by the Chinese government. This can be expressed as "cooperation on command: rather than "cooperation on demand." Chinese media groups were formed more for the political purpose than for an economic one. The subsidiaries in media groups need time to fit together. This, however, seems like a "mission impossible," because integrating subsidiaries into one organic unit under the rules of the market is very difficult due to the Chinese administration system.

By the end of 2003, there were 69 media groups in China, including a number of corporations: 8 newspapers, 13 radio and television stations, 1 magazine, 9 press, 5 circulation, and 3 film. These groups were still too weak in terms of capital to compete with TNMCs.[28] For example, the total assets of all Chinese newspaper media groups in 2006 was $13.33 billion. In contrast, one single American News corporation had $ 42 billion of assets in 2002 and its annual income was $15 billion.

Figure 9.5 maps the current Chinese media capital market in a triangle composed of media capital from Chinese government (G-media, with local branches), TNMCs, and NGOs. The straight lines (1 through 4) represent the relationship of *He-Zong*, which means alliance of the weak to repel the strong. The lines refer to the *He-Zong* strategy applied by the Chinese government toward the domestic media branches/groups (lines 1, 2, and 3) and NGOs (line 4). The dotted lines (A to E) represent the relationship of *Lian-Heng*, which means TNMCs offer benefits (in terms of funds, technology, facilities, management, and international market) to gain cooperation from Chinese local media groups (dotted lines A, B, and D), NGOs (dotted line E), and the government media groups (dotted

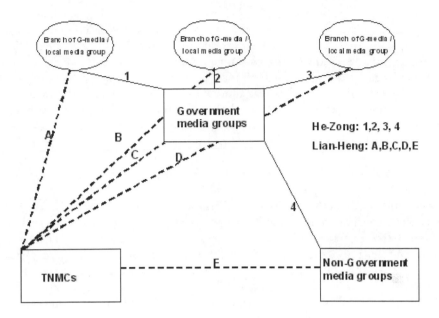

*Figure 9.5*   Triangular media market and competition strategies in mainland China.[29]

line C). TNMCs' *Lian-Heng* strategies create a successfully crisscrossed network of alliance with different players of the Chinese media market. Equipped with a huge amount of capital, flexible policies, and worldwide resources, TNMCs have broken up the Chinese media market and so the strategies of the Warring States in Chinese history reappear in the current Chinese media market.

## The Changes to the Lives of Chinese Audiences

The state promotes the reforms on media technology and production in China, which result in wider choices for audiences. The TNMCs use sophisticated technology and so, in contrast to most of the programs of local television, their products are more attractive to the Chinese audiences. Chinese media groups, in turn, have to improve their productive ability to meet the challenges from programs of the TNMCs. For example, Chinese cartoon corporations learn from Disney to produce more attractive figures to favor the young audiences. Creative Power Entertaining[30] has been producing the series "Pleasant Goat and Big Big Wolf" since June 2005, and its television animations were aired on approximately 50 local stations with the top audience rating at 17%; the box-office receipts of two *Pleasant Goat* movies released in 2009 and 2010 amounted to nearly 200 million RMB.

This is the success of the *He-Zong* strategy of the Chinese government to congregate media corporations and encourage local media companies so that they are more competitive in producing better products to meet the needs and wants of the changing audience. In this way, the audiences are being shaped by the TNMCs in China.

There are indications that this dynamic is also influencing the taste of the audience and the society as a whole. "I want my MTV!"—the simple cry of a spoiled child who wants his eye-candy is regarded as one of the most successful slogans ever devised. MTV Mandarin's slogan, however, is not "I want my MTV" (wo yao wo de MTV!) but "We are MTV," which means "We're unique and no one else can claim it!" Being one of the most brand-conscious companies in the world, MTV is, of course, experiencing an identity crisis in China. Few Chinese heed the fact that "MTV" is actually a specific company and not just a strange foreign term for "music video."[31] To reiterate, MTV in China is seen simply as a format of music programs with video instead of a symbol of the company Viacom. The other side of the coin is that MTV has become so popular that it not only stands for a certain kind of music but also represents a new kind of lifestyle through novel and fashionable behaviors never shown in traditional Chinese music programs. With the popularity of MTV, a new style of dressing, singing, dancing, and even behavior is welcome by the Chinese audiences. The state is concerned that it is not only the behavior but also the taste of the people that has been changed. To the state, this is particularly significant because the changes happen mostly among young viewers who will be Chinese mainstream audiences in the future.

The TNMCs' youth programs also seem to play an educational role after school. Although not as dull as the description by a British journalist, who described Chinese education as consisting "mostly of quiz shows, team competitions and endless lineups of youngsters, dressed uniformly, standing erect and answering questions,"[32] there remains a popular view in China that the Chinese youth programs used to be dry, conservative, and pedantic. It has been suggested that the deficiency of the Chinese programs leaves a vacuum for the TNMCs and Viacom to bring their playful, antiauthoritarian programs to Chinese youngsters. Traditional Chinese culture requires children to behave well at any moment of their life. Respecting parents and authority is a Chinese tradition promoted by Confucianism with thousands of years of history. In the eyes of the Chinese state, this is the cornerstone of a harmonious society. The Chinese government reasons that, after 6 to 7 hr of education in classrooms, children's programs, which are full of fun and antiauthoritative images, are surely taking over the students and turning them into consumers. According to many foreign journalists writing about China, "fun" has evidently become a desperately needed element in the Chinese youth culture. Young audiences may well be attracted by fun without the pressure of knowledge acquisition. The idea of getting rid of responsibility to chase fun may indeed flatter the youth. In this, however, there is a contradiction between school education and the TNMCs' programs for children because, in the eyes of the Chinese state, children's programs provided by the TNMCs can never turn them into qualified citizens. The TNMCs' products are produced in local language and custom with Western values embedded in. The Chinese state is concerned that the audiences accept the messages at face value, which creates anxiety on the part of the state that the Chinese with Western values may no longer be Chinese. Therefore, cultural barriers are placed by the government to protect the identity of the Chinese.

## DISCUSSION AND CONCLUSION

This study adopts the new framework (Buzan, Waever, and de Wilde 1998: 195) for security analysis, which expands the security agenda from the military and the political onto the economic, the environmental, and the societal with a focus on cultural issues. China is emerging as a major economic and political power in the global world. From the standpoint of the Chinese state, the state does not present a threat to other countries because it follows the ideas of Confucius and Mencius "which place non-violence and accommodation before violent defense or offence in ranking strategic choices" (Fierke 2007: 41). In this light, China will resist any threats toward its state and people strategically.

The competition and transformation between the TNMCs and the Chinese media industries turns the Chinese media environment into "unstructured situations," which are "novel, unknown, surprising, different from usual" (Milnes 2008: 151) for Chinese audiences. This uncertainty creates a concern for the state, namely "being and feeling safe from harm or danger" (Fierke 2007: 13) because the strategies and acts of the TNMCs and the Chinese government media have led Chinese media environment into another Warring State period.

In this war, TNMCs play the role of strong state of Qin, and their aims are economy oriented. They apply the strategy of *Lian-Heng* to ally with other players so that they may survive in a foreign land, expand the business, fight for audience share, and increase influences and control. The Chinese government media adopt the *He-Zong* strategy to develop themselves in scale and scope to compete with the TNMCs. The challenges for Chinese media are not only the competitions for media market and audience share but also the responsibility of maintaining the Chinese cultural identity. In addition, China is not only concerned with maintaining its cultural identity but also cares about its image in the world. Besides implementing the strategy of *He-Zong* to strengthen the Chinese media industries and setting policies and regulations, the government believes that "the best defense is to offence."[33] Since then, China has increased its financial input in the cultural industry, encouraged Chinese nongovernmental capital to be involved in the culture industries inside and outside of China,[34] and supported the globalization of the Chinese government media.

The Chinese people as an audience are given the right to choose from more and better media content due to the competition, but their tastes, lifestyles, and world views seem to have changed as a result of their consumption of foreign media products. The Chinese government believes there is a need to set up policies and regulations for cultural products to protect the Chinese cultural identity, and this raises the question of "the relationship between receiving protection and the liberty of those who are protected" (Fierke 2007: 14).

The Chinese government's strategies for securitization of the Chinese cultural identity are based on the premise that PRC, as a state, is a "unified political community," in which "the homogeneity of interests and identification" actually exist (Reus-Smit 1992: 17). The securitization of everyday life is a practice that is "internally complex and involves reference to several dimensions" (Fierke, 2007:34). Therefore, it is associated with power, control, domination, and surveillance. As Waever (1995:55) writes, the benefit of uttering *security* makes it possible for "a state-representative [to] move a particular development into a specific area, and thereby claims a special right to use whatever means are necessary to block it." This chapter contributes to our understanding of securitization by analyzing China as a nation-state playing the role of the guardian of national culture. The government is convinced that the national security is "synonymous with aggregate individual security" (Reus-Smit 1992: 17) and, therefore, sees itself as the protector of the Chinese people. Perhaps we can say, using again the metaphors from a recent Chinese animation titled "Pleasant Goat and the Big Big Wolf," that the Chinese state sees itself as the protector of the "pleasant goats" from the violence of "big big wolves."

## NOTES

1. After the two Opium Wars (1839–1842, 1856–1860), China was colonized by the United Kingdom, France, Germany, Japan, the United States, Russia, and other countries. China entered upon a new historical stage after the founding of the PRC in 1949.
2. Hu, H.-L. (October 10, 2002). "Keep the Chinese national cultural security in positive developing policy." *Literature and Art Weekly* (in Chinese).
3. http://portal.unesco.org/en/ev.php-URL_ID=31038&URL_DO=DO_TOPIC&URL_SECTION=201.html. (accessed 7 Nov 2010).
4. "Human Development Report 2000: Human Rights and Human Development" http://hdr.undp.org/en/reports/global/hdr2000/.
5. The National Commission on Terrorist Attacks 2004: 376. Available online at: http://govinfo.library.unt.edu/911/report/index.htm. (accessed 7 Nov 2010).

6. "Viacom Outdoor announces strategic acquisition in China." http://www.cbsoutdoor.co.uk/web/Current-news/Newspage-UK/Viacom-Outdoor-announces-strategic-acquisition-in-China.htm (accessed 7 November 2010). See also http://www.cbspressexpress.com/div.php/cbs_outdoor/release?id=13517 (accessed 7 Nov 2010).

7. Please Note: All the numbers and figures in this chapter on TNMCs in China are from the *Foreign Media in China*. I am the main author and editor-in-chief of the book, published by the Chinese Federation of Literary & Arts Circles Publishing House in 2005, Beijing, China.

8. In June, 1995, the News Corporation announced a deal with *The People's Daily*, run by the Communist Party's Central Committee, to invest jointly $5.4 million in an information and technology business—a deal that seemed more of a door opener than a money maker. News Corporation executives said the business would involve projects in electronic publishing, digital mapping, and an online database. Drawn as a 20-year venture, the new company, Beijing PDN Xinren Information Technology Company, is half-owned by *The People's Daily* and by News Corporation. Source: *The New York Times*, June 19, 1995. http://query.nytimes.com/gst/fullpage.html?res=990CE4D6153AF93AA25755C0A963958260&n=Top/News/World/Countries%20and%20Territories/China).

9. In 1995, in Asia, STAR TV cemented its place as the number one media brand in the region, reaching more than 300 million viewers in 53 countries. Taking advantage of its leadership in the traditional pay-television business, STAR started building Asia's leading multiservice, multiplatform group to exploit the business opportunities of the broadband Internet in Asia.

   Long-term exclusive deals with U.S. film studios ensure STAR's leadership in entertainment for years to come. To satisfy demands for Chinese programming content, STAR owns the world's largest contemporary Chinese movie library and has entered into exclusive output agreements with prominent Hong Kong film companies such as Media Asia, China Star, Teamwork, FBI, and BOB. STAR is also dramatically increasing its own production of original drama series and films.

   In China, the Phoenix Chinese Channel, a 4-year-old joint venture, remains the most widely watched foreign television channel. Phoenix registered year-on-year advertising revenue growth with primetime slots almost fully booked. On June 30, 1995 Phoenix was listed on the Growth Enterprise Market of the Hong Kong Stock Exchange.

   Channel [V] and joint venture channel ESPN STAR Sports are also listed in the top 15 most popular channels among the more than 100 available in China. During the year, STAR moved to 74% ownership of Channel [V].

10. News Digital Systems (NDC) is a DRM and conditional access firm. It is listed on the NASDAQ as NDS but its major shareholder is News Corporation. (Source: http://en.wikipedia.org/wiki/NDS_Group). Sichuan Provincial Network, China's second largest provincial cable network with more than 7 million subscribers, expects to launch its new digital service at the end of 2001. (Source: *Business Wire*, July 10, 2001. http://findarticles.com/p/articles/mi_m0EIN/is_2001_July_10/ai_76418888. )

11. China Netcom (Group) Corporation Ltd. (CNC): a state-owned enterprise established under the laws of PRC and the ultimate controlling shareholder of the company and its subsidiaries. (For more details on CNC, please go to: http://64.233.169.104/search?q=cache:zH5Qa7ADeLQJ:www.china-netcom.com/english/inv/FAQ_E.pdf+New+corporation+%E4%B8%AD%E5%9B%BDCNC&hl=en&ct=clnk&cd=8&gl=us).

12. "Rupert Murdoch said on Tuesday that his wife, Wendy Deng, was working with senior News Corp executives to help bring the company's popular MySpace social networking site to China. Murdoch said MySpace in China was likely to have local partners, who would own around 50 per cent. This would ensure the content was more suitable for a Chinese audience, and Murdoch also said it would mean his local partners could deal with complaints." (Source: News Corp plans MySpace in China; van Duyn, A., and Chaffin, J., in New York, *Financial News*, September 19, 2006).

13. Liu, Y. (September 8, 2005). "Distribution rights to fight." *Beijing Review.*

14. JIANG Yan, "Bertelsmann closes bookstores nationwide", http://news.xinhuanet.com/book/2008-06/17/content_8384468.htm. (accessed 7 Nov 2010).

15. "Tens of Thousands of People expecting the opening of Disney land in Hongkong," (in Chinese: Wan Zong Qi Dai Di Si Ni Kai Yuan), http://news.sina.com.cn/c/2005–09–10/21097732728.shtml.

16. Iger, R. "Shanghai Disneyland will be a Milestone for Disney Corp" (in Chinese: Di Si Ni Zong Cai: Di Si Ni Le Yuan Luo Hu Shanghai Shi Yi Ge Li Cheng Bei), http://news.xinhuanet.com/society/2009–11/04/content_12385822.htm. http://finance.qq.com/a/20091105/000874.htm. (accessed 5 Nov 2009).

17. http://www.chinanews.com.cn/cj/cytx/news/2008/06–28/1295922.shtml.

18. Barden, C. "I Want My MTV . . . In Mandarin!" *Beijing Scene.* http://journeyeast.tripod.com/mtv.html. (accessed 7 Nov 2010).

19. Brennan, S. "Viacom expands in China," *The Hollywood Reporter*, September 27, 2004. http://www.allbusiness.com/services/motion-pictures/4911081–1.html ).

20. Macklin, W. "Viacom signs deal with China's Baidu," *BizReport* October 19, 2006 . (http://www.bizreport.com/2006/10/viacom_signs_deal_with_chinas_baidu.html)

21. Li, K. *Reuters,* July 13, 2007. "Viacom explores China theme parks, movies." http://uk.reuters.com/article/industryNews/idUKN1341233620070715.

22. Psychologies magazine in China, June 12, 2006. http://www.hfmasia.com/news.php?newsid=13.

23. People's Daily Online (http://english.peopledaily.com.cn/200109/27/eng20010927_81198.html).

24. The Warring States period (pinyin: Zhànguó Shídài), also known as the Era of Warring States, covers the period from 475 B.C. to the unification of China under the Qin Dynasty in 221 B.C. During the Warring States period, regional warlords annexed smaller states around them and consolidated their power, and finally developed into seven major states. The most famous strategies during this period are called *He-Zong* and *Liang-Heng.*

25. Retrieved from http://www.navytimes.com/news/2009/07/military_skelton_recommendedreading_073109w/, accessed on March 27, 2010.

26. The Hundred Schools of Thought refers to philosophers and schools that flourished from 770 to 221 B.C. in China, which is the period in *Spring and Autumn* and *Warring States*. It is the Golden Age of Chinese philosophy. A broad range of thoughts and ideas were developed and discussed freely, and further influence lifestyles and social consciousness in East Asian countries even today.

27. Pozzi, D. C. , and Wickersham, J.M. (1991). *Knowing Words: Wisdom and Cunning in the Classical Traditions of China and Greece.* Cornell University Press. pp. 117.

28. http://news.xinhuanet.com/newmedia/2005–04/12/content_2818122_1. htm. (In Chinese.)
29. Here we use "nongovernment media groups" to represent those individually run media enterprise (in pinyin: *Min Ying Chuan Mei Ye*) as distinct from NGO.
30. Creative Power Entertaining is a Chinese cartoon and film production house based in Guangdong, aiming to produce China's new generation of original cartoon animations, television programs and series, and movies. Website: http://www.22dm.com/about/index.aspx.
31. Barden, C. "I Want My MTV . . . In Mandarin", *Beijing Scene*, http://journeyeast.tripod.com/mtv.html.
32. Barboza, D. (January 10, 2006 ). "Viacom testing limits of youth TV in China 'sliming' accepted, but not other antics." *International Herald Tribune.*
33. "The Chinese Ministry of Culture Hold A Conference on How to Promote Chinese Cultural Industry to Compete Globally" (in Chinese: Wen Hua Bu Zhao Kai Zhongguo Wen Hua Qi Ye Zou Chu Qu Yan Tao Hui), http://www.sccm.gov.cn/Culture_Exchange/show.asp?id=1530. The conference suggested that the Chinese government should take care of the image of China in the world. The Chinese media industries should improve their competitive power and enter the global stage.
34. CHEN Jianwen, director of Jin Hua You Dian Gong Cheng An Zhuang You Xian Gong Si, a field engineering corporation in Zhejiang Province of China, bought the stocks and turned to be the director of DOLON TV in Bishkek, capital of Kyrghizstan in October 2005 (source: http://fec.mofcom. gov.cn/xwdt/gn/261889.shtml); WANG Weisheng and LIU Haitao, businessman from Wenzhou, Zhejiang Province of China, bought a national TV of UAE (United Arab Emirates) and transformed it into an Aisa Arab Bussiness TV (AABTV) of the end of 2005, (source; http://www.hangzhou.com. cn/20080505/ca1493949.htm);YE Maoxi, also a businessman from Wenzhou, Zhejiang province of China, who does press business, bought a satellite Television named as PROPELLER in London in August 2009. (Source: http://www.prfax.com.cn/a-show-20090728095126823044.aspx).

# 10 Security Metamorphosis in Latin America

*Nelson Arteaga Botello*

## INTRODUCTION

During the decade of the 1990s, it was possible to observe in Latin America a significant increase in criminal violence. The eventuality of suffering some type of assault in public or the possibility of being a victim of a kidnapping has turned into one of the most widespread fears in societies in this region of the world. In this sense, it is not surprising that the latter part of the past century saw an increase in the demand for public and private security services, the extended use of different types of electronic surveillance and security technologies, and the proliferation of closed neighborhoods, as well as the comprehensive use of citizen watchdog bodies such as "Neighborhood Watch" or the "culture of filing complaints," each strategy more extensive than the preceding one. In the same way, during those years, one could also see the creation of institutions defined as "intelligence" specific, supposedly to create databases for monitoring criminal information; at the same time, within the government realm, reforms were initiated by police and judicial forces (Frühling 2005; Duce and Pérez 2005), many of which were inspired by the policies of "zero tolerance" (Wacquant 1999; 2008).

In this context of securitization, in the next decade and shortly after September 11, 2001 (9/11), another altogether different scenario directed toward the fight against terrorism and organized crime can be connected. In this sense, what was considered on other occasions as a common offense can today be judged as an act of terrorism or as a product of organized criminal activity, whose aim is the generalized destabilization of society. Since 9/11, an expansion in the use of electronic surveillance equipment in distinct spaces of everyday life can be seen, one which allows for the collection, organization, and analysis of specific information relating to specific population groups. However, this process is not only a result of the exportation to Latin America of certain security practices established in the United States after the attacks on the World Trade Center in New York City. More so, this event has come to accelerate and reinforce a process that in a significant number of the Latin American countries is consolidating the implementation of control devices over those sectors that are thought to be responsible for criminal violence; namely, of those excluded and marginalized within the urban spaces.

Thus, it is not surprising that one can begin to observe a fusion between security strategies oriented toward reducing crime and the security logic promoted by the United States; the Merida Initiative, approved by the U.S. Congress, and Plan Colombia, could be used as examples of this process. With this, it can be noted that not only is there a real increase in the use of different security devices along the different spaces and social spheres but also a stronger connection between them, establishing with it "archipelagos of security" that function as dikes that allow a maintenance and a control of social groups considered dangerous—social groups evidently identified with certain sectors of the excluded and marginalized. In the majority of cases, the security policies meant to diminish the presence of criminal violence instead seem to increase the violence, reinforcing the hatred and the rejection of symbols of wealth, the consumer and social well-being, which excludes large bands of the population.

This chapter attempts to show how the appearance of certain security measures has been possible, and how these measures that have been put in place, are defined from a metamorphosis in the countries; internal organization (generating specific state public policies, as well as particular forms of civil society organizations). First, the conditions of certain transformations of the social, political, cultural, and economic spheres faced by the countries in the region during the last years will be explored, including those which have caused the notion of security permeating everyday life. Second, based on the transformations mentioned, distinct strategies and various security devices established and linked in Latin America will be analyzed, and how the formation of "archipelagos of security" are being created. In the third part, how the events of 9/11 accelerated the consolidation of securitization strategies (public and private) as a security issue will be examined, as well as how security strategies such as the Merida Initiative and Plan Colombia have been conceived with the goal of not only reinforcing the security policies in countries where they apply but also to guarantee the so-called hemispheric security of the American continent. The last part includes a reflection about the implications registered in the securitization strategies projected for the Latin American region, in particular about the effects which these transformation processes cause in the formation of spaces of exception (Agamben 2003; Diken and Bagge Laustsen 2005), and which notably weaken even young democratic institutions of the region.

## THE EMERGENCY OF SECURITY: CRIME, VIOLENCE, AND SOCIAL EXCLUSION

Toward the end of the 1980s, Latin American experienced a significant increase in criminal violence. Next decade, between 1990 and 1995, 60%

of its population was a victim of some type of criminal offense (Del Olmo 2000). In Argentina, for instance, the number of offenders has doubled between 1990 and 1999 (Pegoraro 2000), while the rate of delinquent acts for each 10,000 inhabitants in 2004 reached 343.0; in 2005, it reached 332.0.[1] In Mexico, the criminal rate totaled 1,000 crimes for each 100,000 inhabitants in 1990 and reached 2,500 crimes for each 100,000 inhabitants (Ruiz 1998) in 1998; the rate per 100,000 inhabitants recorded an increase in crimes to 1,391.5[2] in 2000. For its part, in Guatemala, criminal offenses rose almost 100% between 1995 and 1998 (De León, Ogaldes, and López 1999), reaching in the year 2000, 239.63 recorded crimes per 100,000 inhabitants.[3] In Nicaragua, crime against people and property doubled between 1992 and 1996 (Saldomando 1999). With regard to the perception of crime[4] in Latin American countries, in 2005 the percentage increased to 82.68%. During the same year, in Argentina, this same indicator rose to 84.75%; in Mexico, it reached 77.76%; and in Nicaragua it reached 92.49%.[5]

According to Londoño and Guerrero (1999), urban violence in Latin America represents a net cost on the order of 12.1% of the gross domestic product (GDP), making up $145 billion dollars a year. Furthermore, for the year 2007, the lost product, due to violent deaths, was 10,133 USD million, approximately 32% of the GDP[6] of lost product due to violent death. Even in Central American countries, which existed in a state of armed conflict during the Cold War, the rate of death caused by criminal activity is actually higher than during periods of armed conflict (Chinchilla 2005).[7] In this region, the patterns of violence preceding internal conflicts have multiplied due to drugs and arms trafficking, youth gangs, kidnappings, money laundering, and homicide. In Central America in 2004, the homicide rate rose to 20 for every 100,000 people; 77% of these offenses were committed with firearms.[8] In this region of America, until 2005, the most violent countries were as follows: El Salvador with 3,778 homicides, 11.5 per 100,000; Guatemala, with 5,338 homicides, 8.0 per 100,000; Honduras, with 2,417 homicides, 5.0 per 100,000; and Nicaragua, with 729 homicides, 2.2 per 100,000.[9]

In fact, toward the mid-1990s, when expressions of criminal violence in the region reached their peak, the rate of homicides reached 28.4 for each 100,000 people, second only to Sub-Saharan Africa, which reached a rate of 40.1 (Morrison, Buvinic, and Shifter 2005). For 2004, the rate for Central and South America moved between 25 and 30 homicides for every 100,000 persons, while in South Africa, the rate reached close to 35 (Geneva Declaration Secretariat 2008). Accordingly, the five countries of Latin America with the highest rate of homicide are Colombia, Venezuela, Bolivia, Ecuador, and Brazil; the three with the lowest homicide rate are Chile, Peru, and Panama (Hinton 2006). The data on victimization are only a sample of the level of increase in criminal violence and, offers—in a majority of cases—valuable information that could allow the problem of "black figures" of criminality to be resolved. According to the most recent data from the region, all of the countries of Latin America showed rates of victimization above 20%, a majority above 30% and 40%, and five of those between 40% and 60%: Guatemala, El Salvador, Venezuela, Mexico, and Ecuador (Rico and Chinchila 2002). As indicated by the report of Latinobarómetro of 2008, the rate of victimization in the region is 33%.[10]

This scenario, which shows a significant increase in criminal acts, coincides in a large way with the economic changes happening since the introduction of free-change policies, especially since the decade of the 1980s (Concha-Eastman 2000), which concluded a period of economic growth flourishing in the region against a backdrop in which the substitution model of imports was established shortly after World War II (Székely 1994). The re-setting and economic crisis of the 1980s and 1990s, brought about to a large extent by the policies of economic adjustment, had as a consequence that the increase of the region was no larger than 3.6% on average (Pastor and Wise, 1999). In fact, these effects still remain. In the region during the 2000–2005 period, the GDP at purchasing power parity (PPP) passed 6,822.46 USD to 6,686.63 USD, having a lower rate in 2004, with 6,392.48 USD (Inter-American Development Bank). But the crisis can also be seen in another example. According to recent data, between 2000 and 2004, the urban unemployment rate in Latin America oscillated between 10 and 8 points.[11] Meanwhile, between 2001 and 2003, the gross national income per capita was an average of 7,200 dollars (World Bank, World Development Indicators). Informal employment, has in the same way, assumed an important role in the economies of other countries, as workers are increasingly engaged in the world of self-employment and flexible work. In Latin America between 2002 and 2006, the informal sector averaged between 20% and 40% of the economy in the region.

On the other hand, the obligations of these countries with respect to external debt reached 1.94 billion dollars in the decade of the 1980s (Martin and Schuman 1998). This context has been fertile ground for an increase in social inequality and for the fall of the index of human development in the region in the last two decades (Huang 1995), thereby affecting social policies in the region during the decade of the 1980s, when nine of every 10 countries experienced significant cuts in social spending and which, measured in terms of income per capita, meant that public spending in real terms on social programs declined in eight of them (Ward 1993). Even during the first decade of the 1990s, the annual increase of the GDP in Latin American countries was below 6%, a rate required to observe a significant increase in places of employment and the achieving of social equality (Pastor and Wise 1999). About this point, it is worth mentioning a study conducted in six Latin American countries (Argentina, Brazil, Colombia, Guatemala, Mexico, and Peru), which shows—following the index of Gini—that inequality, in regards to home income and access to health services, has increased significantly between the years 1990 and 2000 (Koonings and Kruijt 2007).

This type of impoverishment process and social exclusion can be seen with better clarity in Latin American urban spaces. The outward manifestations of this trend are less obvious since the urban population of the region has increased significantly in the last 50 years. A number of cities have experienced rapid population growth: Mexico City has gone from 2.4 to 22.1 million; São Paulo, 2.4 to 19.0 million; Buenos Aires, 4.6 to 12.6 million; Rio de Janeiro, 3 to 11.9 million; Lima, 0.6 to 8.2 million; and Bogota, 0.7 to 8 million (Davis 2006). As some figures show, during the middle of the 1990s, poor settlements in metropolitan zones covered at least 50% of Lima, 35% of Rio de Janeiro, and 40% of Caracas. Notably, the population in these cities grew 60% between 1973 and 1987, while the poor populations (or shantytowns) rose more than 100% (Neira 1995). Some data indicate that 65% of the total poor population in Latin America inhabits urban zones. In fact, it can be estimated that in these areas, 50 million people are found to be living in extreme poverty (Koonings and Kruijt 2007). Davis (2006), in a study of marginal urban populations on a worldwide scale, shows that the four largest centers of extreme poverty are located in Latin America (Mexico City, Caracas, Bogota, and Lima).

These data on marginalization and violence have been related to an increase in the rates of criminal acts, many of which have been highlighted in different studies in Latin American countries (Velho 1996; Ruiz 1998; Brugués, Cortez, and Fuentes 1998; Teutli 2000; De Andrade 2002; Santana 2002; Novaes 2002; Carranza 2004; Sosa 2007). Such studies confirm that the relationship between poverty and delinquency delineates a perspective, which according to Caldeira (2000), underlines a number of important studies of Latin America, whose results also support the existence in the Latin American region of a correlation between unemployment and delinquency, as well as between inequality and delinquency (Carranza 2004).

In a majority of the countries in Latin America, armed violence—as perpetrated for example, by armed groups and gangs—has occurred where political institutions and public security providers suffer from weak governance, alternative forms of political authority and security delivery, social crisis or malaise, macroeconomic distortions and political disorder, inequity, and a growing urban population, particularly in Central and South American countries.[12] According to data from recent years, in a large part of Latin America the incidence of criminal violence has been accompanied by a medium human development index, with inequity close to the median, an exponential increase in the urban population, and an average life expectancy index, while the number of homicides has increased and the citizen compliance with the law diminished.

As Wacquant (2008) points out, the conjunction of abysmal inequality with grossly inefficient or sometimes nonexistent public services and massive unemployment in the context of a polarized urban economy has been converted into the scourge of countries and cities in Latin America, a condition that only exacerbates delinquency. However, poverty in and of itself does not generate delinquency; rather its increase is also related to at least two other factors. The first refers to a dynamic expansion of the forms of urban life and a secularization of values, along with rules that regularly accompany this process (Romero 2000; Binford 1999; Vilas 2001; Handy 2004) and is linked with the emergence of a series of new cultural and symbolic forms, as well as with the construction of new subjectivities with regard to crime and violence. These situations in certain occasions have come to be regarded as so-called "expressions of popular culture" (Aparecida 1996) and are connected with very concrete cultural expressions, through music such as funk or samba in the case of Brazil (Vianna 1996), the music known as "narcocorridos" in Mexico (Simonett 2001), the cumbia "villera" in Argentina, rap in some other Latin American cities (Castells 1998), and punk or *ska* in almost all of the countries of the region.[13]

The second factor deals with the processes of political change as characterized by scenarios of "democratic transition." Evidently, the authoritarian systems, which worsened in the region—in some cases with military dictatorships such as Argentina, or in other cases with single-party governments as in Mexico—foundered until they formed democratic institutions. However, this transition, far from being exempt from difficulties, has generated a scenario of institutional emptiness, where the old practices have not disappeared and the new ones have not quite consolidated, thereby impacting directly the regulation and control of crime; democracy, paradoxically, appears to take away the capacity of coercion of the state (Hinton 2006), often leading to a scenario in which a "firm hand" is needed to end the high rates of criminal activity, typically by using the military and employing "zero tolerance" policies (Peralva 2001; Bodemer, Kurtenbach, and Meschkat 2001).

As a result, the increase in levels of criminal violence, which sometimes accompanies it, has generated a process of social dismantling, crystallized in the fragmentation and fracture of the urban spaces in Latin America (Schteingart 2001; Prévôt 2001; García and Villá 2001; Lacarrieu and Thullier 2001). Thus, the middle classes and social sectors that appear better located in the social scale are entrenched in urban or suburban "bunkers" (Davis 1992). Generally surrounded by a wall, these bunkers are architecturally homogenous, socially nondifferent, protected with private guards and surveillance systems (Caldeira 1996, 2000), reproducing exactly the landscape and excluding urbanism in the United States during the 1980s. These housing zones, or islands of well-being, keep away the so-called "dangerous classes," thereby excluding and marginalizing them in the process of economic globalization of Latin American cities.

These dangerous groups are exactly the ones who live in what Buck-Morss (2003) calls "wild power zones," characterized by the junction of violence and poverty, where the most violent crimes are registered, uniting high rates of infant death, interfamily violence, and malnutrition—an existence carried out under a climate of profound racism, where police violence prevails, and where acquiring a weapon is the best option of security. In both areas of the city—the bunkers of the middle and upper classes, as well as in the wild power zones where social fragmentation is reflected—a culture of fear is constructed day by day (Pascual 2007), one that can only bring about the construction of borders to limit, surround, and contain that which is considered representative of the danger: insecurity and crime. The borders, as stated by Duclos (1995), are designed to contain people, and for that reason are porous and ephemeral, needing updating constantly with the goal of guaranteeing the protection of specific spaces. In this way, the culture of fear intertwines with the issue of security, in such a manner that it shapes and refines the state's capacity to manage fear (Deleuze and Guattari 1989), and thereby putting at risk the "normal" development of things.

Thus, the meaning of security in Latin America must, out of necessity, be anchored in the idea of control, specifically as it relates delinquency and violent crime. This belief has led to the formation of a variety of spaces of management of fear—neighborhoods, commercial centers, private and government buildings, parks, business districts, streets, and avenues—as well as the implementation of security policies in zones considered "dangerous," typically shanties and marginal neighborhoods, where policies are established to reduce the apparent risk of being a victim of any kind of offense or crime. Although a group of countries in Latin America appear to have consolidated policies and reforms to the political and judicial system, in the same way, it is still possible to observe processes in neighborhoods and communities, which tend to establish and to perfect their own security mechanisms. In general, the problem of inequality, poverty, and social exclusion are considered causes of offences and criminal violence. However, the policy makes the governments of the region believe that society cannot wait for this transformation to occur of its own accord. On the other hand, criminality should be contained and punished immediately and expeditiously. In this way, as pointed out by Wacquant (2004), security strategies appear as a new form of government applied to social insecurity, in the context of the turbulence of economic deregulation, unstable employment, marginalization, and urban exclusion. This vision of Wacquant resembles Foucault's later lectures on security as a synonym for governmentality: the security and surveillance dispositifs would be inserted within the control of a series of probable events, in which the state intervenes in all the cases where everyday life is threatened by a singular and exceptional event (Foucault 2004).

## THE ARCHIPELAGOS OF SECURITY

In the 1990s, in various Latin American countries, there began a metamorphosis in security issues, modifying the role of the states in the articulation of securitization strategies. The presence of democratic institutions in consolidation—having to face authoritarian practices—may have influenced one of the main decisions to re-evaluate policies of security (in particular, public security) that were not sufficiently effective. For this reason, perhaps, the first measures of security organized in large part in urban and rural communities took the form of neighborhood protection strategies.

The upper and middle classes of Latin American societies were the first to establish this strategy—certainly not planned—of isolation of large urban centers in fortress cities (Caldeira 1996, 2000). Neighborhood spaces such as the residential zones in Mexico, or the so-called "countryside" in Argentina, are characterized by being closed in and having mechanisms of access control based on video surveillance systems, fingerprint-reading technology, and identification cards (Arizaga 2000; Giglia 2001). Moreover, the architecture of the houses is homogenous and responds to the model of North American suburbs (Ellin 1997). The middle class, for its part incapable of having access to this type of housing, has opted for the closing of streets to traffic in their neighborhoods, even though it goes against the laws of vehicle traffic in many cities. Far from establishing indiscreetly physical borders for maintaining the security of their neighbors, between them they have put in play the idea of insecurity in open spaces, without walls, vulnerable to criminal activity, provoking at the same time the sensation of shared lives and expectations (García and Villá 2001). In this way, the closure of housing zones represents a political manifestation within such social sectors, one intended to defend a position of privilege that is being threatened not only by the increase of delinquency, but also by the economic transformations that began to occur during the 1980s and the first half of the 1990s.

Along with the construction of physical borders and the use of surveillance technologies to control the entrance to these neighborhoods, other strategies have been developed, largely inspired by "neighborhood watch" policies established in various developed countries in the 1970s. The objective of this approach is to involve the general population in surveillance strategies within their neighborhood, to detect suspects, illicit activities, or behaviors considered "deviant" or potentially dangerous (Arriagada and Godoy 1999). In general, these strategies suggest that a community of neighborhoods has been instrumental in forming an integral process of anticriminal planning. Its development is directed, above all, to satisfy the demand of security in certain sectors of the middle class, and in a large way, of the marginal zones on the outskirts of urban centers of Latin American cities. The system, in other words, is intended not only to organize mechanisms of cooperation between the community and the police, but to re-establish the social integration in those zones considered to have strong organizational problems, as highlighted by the presence of single-parent families and addictions (alcohol and drug abuse), as well as the presence of gangs and other forms of organized youth.

The aim of these policies in Latin America is to increase contact between the police and the community by setting up continuous meetings, in which the police collect information on what the community considers to be dangerous for the neighborhood, and at the same time to identify people and groups who may commit crimes (Rico and Chinchilla 2002; Jarrín 2004; Smulovitz 2005; Mesquita and Loche 2005; Chinchilla 2005). Normally, these meetings set out to inform the neighbors of recommendations to increase security in their houses, through the strengthening of locks on doors and windows or outside of that, establishing routes considered secured (illuminated and well-traveled) to work and to shopping areas (Capano and Feleci 1999). Generally, these types of strategies have encouraged the construction and socialization of stereotypes that relate to people considered "suspicious," which basically translates into anyone who does not share the customs, attitudes, or the neighborhood attire of the local community.

In addition, a mechanism of exclusion based upon the principle of security has been established along the commercial and business districts within the globalization nodes of Latin American cities. Zones such as Santa Fe in Mexico City (Mexico), Puerto Madero in Buenos Aires (Argentina), Miraflores in La Paz (Bolivia), Centro Comercial Leste Aricanduva in São Paolo (Brazil), Larcomar in Lima (Peru), and Sanhattan in Santiago (Chile) are examples of spaces whose objective is to organize services, the construction of buildings, streets, and avenues in a way that guarantees the optimum development of business and commercial operations carried out by the middle- and upper-class sectors. These spaces are protected by police, both uniformed and undercover, as well as by closed-circuit television (CCTV) and, in some buildings, by private police. In the same way, as stated by Zukin (1995), these spaces appear to conform as a kind of aseptic urbanization, whose model is taken from Disneyworld-type urbanizations. A similar phenomenon has occurred with the proliferation of malls built to the style of those in the United States in the 1970s. Intended for the consumption of products that tend to strengthen the identity of the middle and upper classes, these malls have started to damage little by little the diversity of the city's downtown areas, a situation that could already be observed in Latin American cities during the 1980s.

Between closed or regulated habitation zones and business or commercial center districts, as well as workplaces, the streets and avenues that connect them are found, and are away from the environment of security created by them. Gradually, the logic of security has been expanded to include the main avenues of communication within the cities, especially through the installation of CCTV, but also through intrusive forms of surveillance: the checkpoints set up by local and national police, including the army as seen, for example, in Mexico and Brazil (Arteaga 2006; Wacquant 2008). The purpose of setting up checkpoints on the population is to find possible suspects, wanted criminals, drunk drivers, or those consuming some type of drug (as it happens in Brazil [Leeds, 2007]); to check the legal status of automobiles; and to detain adolescents or youngsters under the legal age to drive. The intention, in the last instance, is to consolidate the idea that human traffic is required to be under surveillance, thereby, guaranteeing that those who enter any closed place or other area (such as a commercial center, school, or neighborhood) can travel without fear. In regards to this scenario, society has generated the "secured routes" toward work or places for leisure or consumption (Rotker 2000). In Latin America, it is common in everyday life to hear conversation about the safest routes to use to cross the city, at different hours and days, since one route may be safe on one day at a specific time, but it may not be a few minutes later, as well as hearing how people begin to stop visiting public spaces due to the fear of insecurity in the city. This was illustrated in an interesting study on the theme developed by Briceño-Leon (2007) in the case of Caracas, Venezuela.

In the same way, in these years, it is possible to observe an exponential increase of private security organisms or, as Volkov (1999) would state, of business corporations that generate profit, legally, from the administration of certain violence in specific places. Currently, private security services cover not only aspects related to the job of guarding but are also linked to activities that include alarm installation and maintenance, investigations, handling of goods and valuables, consultations, and provision of electronic surveillance and security systems (Newburn 2001). At this point it is worth noting that the main businesses in Latin America divide their activities into three large sectors.[14] The first sector is directed to the security of the information in businesses and public entities, with the aim of safeguarding its integrity and availability through the administration systems of database security, guaranteed protection of computer systems, and electronic transactions, as well as the backup and recovery of information, particularly electronic and multimedia. These companies offer industrial counterespionage services, detection of compromised telephone lines, and electronic monitoring systems, as well as "electronic checkups" to detect information leaks, analysis of telephone calls, and satellite monitoring (GPS). A second group of companies installs electronic surveillance devices that allow control over access to businesses, private houses, and factories, such as electronic lock keypads, hand biometric readers, proximity detectors, cards with magnetic bands, iris and fingerprint readers, movement detectors, and video doormen.

The third vector of this activity is directed at the installation and commercialization of systems of armor in different types of vehicles. A large number of these companies argue that an inordinate emphasis on security tends, ironically, to intensify the feeling of insecurity, having as an effect the perception of the necessity to use such services.

Recent data point out that in 2003, there were 1,630,000 private security guards in Latin America (Abelson 2006). In the region, a majority of the executives of private security businesses are active or retired police officers. The reality is that those who directly provide security services work in precarious conditions, without preparation and with low salaries; it is even possible to find active police who work as private agents at certain periods during their workday. Even though in some countries this is sanctioned (such as in Uruguay), in other countries sanctions do not exist, even though regulated, as in Brazil. In Central America, for example, providing the services of personal police to private security firms is only allowed in El Salvador and Panama (FLACSO 2007).

As a fourth factor, and a perspective that has also proven effective in mitigating criminality and violence, comes from police reforms, vis-à-vis the judicial and penal systems in Latin America (Frühling 2005). In fact, from the founding of democratic systems in the region, police institutions have had to redefine and transform, in the first case, its organization by deviating from the doctrines of national security that dominated the 1970s and 1980s. The initial idea that delinquency is a problem that requires the optimization of the police's capacity of performance has been brought about in a majority of the countries in the region (except for the Dominican Republic, Paraguay, and Bolivia) by the activation of training policies of the police forces and the redefining of their organic structure. Even though this process has been put in practice in a different way, according to the Report on the Security Sector in Latin America and the Caribbean, developed by the Latin American Social Science School (FLACSO, in Spanish), the countries that have conducted more profound reforms in their police organizations are Jamaica, El Salvador, Honduras, Nicaragua, Panama, Argentina, and Paraguay, while the countries lagging behind the most are Mexico, Brazil, Chile, and Bolivia. In contrast with an unequal process in the transformation of the organization and the functioning of the police, it is necessary to point out that—notwithstanding Honduras, Paraguay, and Bolivia—meaningful technological changes have been promoted, specifically software, computers, and electronic surveillance devices. The colonization of technology in police activity has enabled the consolidation of an actuary language applied to societies, based on probability calculations and statistical distributions, with the principal objective of identifying and controlling groups considered to be dangerous. The crossing of the infinite amount of data in matrixes facilitates the detection of behaviors, uses, and social spaces susceptible to be placed under police and judicial control.[15] In this way, it is possible to observe how on different levels and in different social and institutional spheres, security issues are transformed from public policies pushed by the state into policies of assurance of everyday life events, thus allowing the securitization of public, residential, and commercial spaces through the use of population surveillance systems but directed toward the construction of borders that constrain those events that may alter distinct activities happening in everyday life. This class of securitization strategies based on electronic surveillance harmonized with international incentives is then constituted as a particular form of government, to conduct the population, aiming to contain groups that it believes to crystallize criminal violence—namely, the large marginalized and excluded groups that inhabit Latin American societies. The objective would be to control possible adverse behaviors of these groups over the different forms of everyday life, in neighborhoods and business and consumer spaces, as well as the trajectory between them.

However, the different expressions of security in the societies of the region do not necessarily function alone. It is possible to observe that they connect and articulate, forming "archipelagos of security" (Lyotard 1986). Following this idea, each space or social sphere maintains its own territory, its own objective of attention and of restraint of danger. In the same way, these securitization strategies have also allowed the establishment of bridges, which communicate each one of these islands, and constitute a certain logic of transaction and communication between them. Such bridges can be built by public or private institutions, generating surveillance networks that allow the administration of risk, harmonizing this way the closed enclaves with a series of governmentality devices, and stopping and controlling insecure flows of people or objects. Therefore, it is relevant to point out that current hemispheric surveillance strategies—such as the Merida Initiative or Plan Colombia—have favored the consolidation of these archipelagos of security, making the law and surveillance structures work, and leaving aside the problems that are the core of criminal violence: poverty, inequity, exclusion, and unemployment.

## EVERYDAY LIFE AND HEMISPHERIC RISKS: THE LINKS OF SECURITY

As it could be observed, the increase of offenses and criminal violence in the decade of the 1990s allowed the possibility of the emergence of securitization strategies in various Latin American countries. The actions of 9/11 made it possible that in the next decade this logic would be accelerated. The emergence in different countries of Latin America of a series of legal reforms tending to establish a legal framework against terrorism has allowed the realization of this process, especially in Argentina, Colombia, Costa Rica, El Salvador, Guatemala, Honduras, Nicaragua, Panama, Peru, the Dominican Republic, and Mexico. The logic that is known as terrorism is clearly connected with the fight against what is known as organized crime, particularly against activities linked to the trafficking of drugs.

Drug trafficking in that sense, has been turned into "narco-terrorism." Its presence has resulted in, according to the government of the United States (U.S. House of Representatives, 2003), murders, kidnappings, and attacks to the population in countries such as Panama, Venezuela, Ecuador, Colombia, Paraguay, Brazil, Mexico, Peru, and Bolivia. In general, narco-terrorism implies the trafficking of people, smuggled goods, and money laundering. However, the problem of security in Latin America has not been defined only in terms of the war against narco-terrorism. In 2003, the Organization of American States (OAS) adopted the concept of hemispheric security based upon the strengthening of citizen's protection, appealing to the concept of human security, reaching further than national security, based on the notion of sovereignty. According to the Declaration on Security in the Americas, the concept of security in the region would be multidimensional in scope, by traditional and new threats, as well as concerns and other challenges to the security of the countries as determined by political, economical, social, health, and environmental aspects such as democracy, poverty, youth gang violence, and natural disasters, respectively.[16]

This way, between 2004 and 2009 in the police and military budget, the help to the region by the United States (the main financial provider for the control of these risks) has been 5.9 billion USD.[17] Of this investment in the stated period, 55.3% was assigned to Colombia, 15.4% to Mexico, 5.5% to Peru, and 4.0% to Bolivia, which means that 80.2% of the military and police financing in Latin America is oriented to these four countries. In an effort to confront social and economic risks, an investment of 7.2 billion USD[18] was made during the same period. In this case, the investment was aimed at Haiti (16%), Colombia (13%), Bolivia (7.2%), Peru (7.1%), Honduras (6.8%), and Mexico (5.8%), concentrating in these countries 55.9% of the social and economical help. As can be observed in these figures, even when the resources assigned to police and military help are fewer than those assigned to economical and social help, almost the totality of the first is aimed at four countries. Meanwhile, the second is spread across a slightly larger number of countries, which proves the assessment of the risks (particularly violence and crime) is located in four countries: Colombia, Mexico, Peru, and Bolivia—the biggest drug producers or distributors in the region.[19]

However, it is not only a matter of resources. The United States needs to put into practice a hemispheric spirit of cooperation. This new context of security would have cross-cutting problems that require multifaceted responses by different national organizations and in some cases, partnerships between governments, the private sector, and civil society. In this way, Plan Colombia can be analyzed.

Considering that since 1971 the United States and Colombia have promoted an institutional collaboration to undertake a "war against drugs," this plan is also directed to slow down activities against armed groups such as the Revolutionary Armed Forces of Colombia and the National Liberation Army (FARC and ELN, in Spanish). In this sense, the founding in 1998 of Plan Colombia is an acknowledgement that "added counterinsurgency tactics [are needed] to counternarcotics goals" (Guaqueta 2005), declaring the FARC and the ELN as Foreign Terrorist Organizations, trying to position the problem of Colombian national security to a hemispheric level. The effects of this displacement have, however, affected the everyday life of the inhabitants of Colombia, since the plan considers the implementation of security and surveillance services in distinct spheres of social life. For instance, the support for institutions of the penitentiary system is established, giving assistance for the treatment, surveillance, and security of prisons, support to the Colombian Prison Service, and the use of software for managing information in the prisons and the follow up of parolees (Rivera and Wilkey 2002). In the same way, it considers the creation of favorable conditions for the privatization of public resources related to water, energy, and biological routes and to increase the number of paramilitaries required to guard future investments and to create programs of social cleaning to eliminate the possibility of protests in the region (Salazar 2001).

In general, Plan Colombia suggests that the inhabitants of the Colombian regions and of neighboring countries, especially indigenous groups, are potential threats to security, which in the future could destabilize the nation-states of Latin America (Radcliffe 2007). In this sense, Plan Colombia has increased the scale of violence in the region and the number of refugees that escape from the conflict zones.

The objective announced when Plan Colombia (1999) was put in practice was to reduce to 50% the cultivation, processing, and distribution of drugs—especially cocaine—in the following 6 years. However, its production was only reduced, according to figures from the Integral System Project for the Monitoring of Illicit Crops (made up of the Department of State, the United Nations, and the Direction of Narcotics), 11.6% toward the end of the term, with a tendency to increase such percentages. The Washington Office for Latin American Matters made public in 2006 the extent to which cocaine was being cultivated by in new areas of Colombia, Peru, and Bolivia. In fact, this has resulted in the re-structuring of the mafias, generating 22 new more drug cartels.[20]

The central axis of Plan Colombia is the re-structuring and modernizing of the armed forces of the Colombian government, as well as the strengthening of the military. To this end, the United States invested $4 million between 2000 and 2006 for military assistance. Thus, Colombia has become the second largest recipient of foreign training after Iraq. The figures are remarkable: in 1999 there were 2,476 foreign trainees, almost tripling their presence by 2006, reaching a total of 7,729. Similarly, with these resources, the Colombian government has acquired different security and surveillance technologies including terrestrial and satellite tracking, cryptographic devices and night vision equipment, radar systems, thermal image generators, infrared detectors, CCTV, and biometric devices, as well as electronic equipment for the combat and control of disturbances. In addition, security companies such as DynCorp, MPRI, Northgroup Grumman (for the installation of radars), AirScan (for air surveillance services), and Lockheed Martin act freely in Colombia without any type of control and evading international norms for armed conflicts. In general, the result of this process of security has been reflected in the fact that between August 2002 and December 2004, a total of 6,332 arbitrary arrests, 3,127 extrajudicial executions, and 337 forced disappearances of some paramilitary groups (such as the so-called "Águilas Negras" [Black Eagles]) were registered.[21] These results are distressing in the sense that the civil population has been involved in networks of informants or collaborators with the public force. According to the Colombian Ministry of Defense, Plan Colombia allowed the government to have full or partial control of approximately 90% of the country in 2007, compared with the almost 70% it had in 2003.[22]

In this sense, the Merida Initiative is included, which has as its objective the reduction of asymmetry between agencies (police, intelligence, and army) in Mexico and Central America with respect to drug trafficking, whose chief perpetrators possess arms and advanced information equipment, in the same way it pretends to strengthen communication, inspection, and analysis of data equipment, through the incorporation of advanced computer and software systems. Conversely, the initiative is intended to professionalize the police and the prosecutors in the use of such databases and telecommunication systems. The training would be provided by U.S. judicial agents or private contractors (Freeman 2008). In the words of the White House press secretary, the Merida Initiative implies the activation of:

- Non-intrusive inspection equipment; ion scanners; canine units for Mexican customs, for the new federal police and the army, for intercepting drug, arms, money and human trafficking.
- Technologies to improve and ensure communication systems in order to favor the collection of information, as well as guarantee that vital information may be accessible to the authorities.
- Technical and training devices for strengthening judicial institutions: for the investigation by the new police force, software for the handling of packages to consign investigations destined for trial, new offices for citizens demands and professional responsibility, as well as the establishment of witness protection programs.
- Helicopters and surveillance airplanes to support activities of interception and rapid operative answers on behalf of the security agencies in Mexico.[23]

Funding for the Merida Initiative projects for Mexico and Central America is intended to strengthen cooperation in matters of security by reducing the risks inherent in controlling gangs involved in the trafficking of drugs, goods, and human beings. In general, as stated by Fyke and Meyer (2008), after several years this is the first proposal that establishes economic support to Central America in the matter of security. As these same authors state, in this region the responsibility for acts of insecurity is localized in the gangs, organized crime, and drug trafficking. In this sense, the Merida Initiative advocates the installation of surveillance technologies, classification, and social control such as fingerprint reading systems, new equipment for the inspection of air and maritime ports, and equipment and software (eTrace) for the tracking of arms, as well as the creation of a center for crime information related to drugs in the whole Central America region.

In this way, the Merida Initiative intends to balance an "asymmetry" in the administration and managing of security that Mexico and the countries of Central America guard with respect to the United States. However, the Merida Initiative goes beyond the sense of a mere strategy for surveillance, since it also intends to generate a connection between the different security devices, which would allow the broadening of the regional closeness between the United States, Mexico, and Central America in combating crime.[24] The idea is to articulate the different security spaces that each member of the initiative constructs, so that it might guarantee in the region the control of delinquency and organized crime. Such a connection derives from the same architecture of security that the United States has put in practice, on which interweaves political, bureaucratic, military, judicial, and police systems in an effort to control crime. The Merida Initiative would try to fight crime and the risks associated with combating drug and money trafficking, and the threat of terrorism, linking more advanced surveillance technologies with better-trained human resources in each country's jurisdiction and a better governmental administration. This type of strategy strengthens others of a more particular character, such as that established between Mexico and the United States, for instance, to apply a system of wiretapping between both countries, to follow cell phone users while they travel, a process which requires a large storage capacity but one that makes it possible to identify users through their voice signature. This technology has been implemented, according to spokespeople, to combat criminal gangs linked to drug, arms, and human trafficking.[25]

Both Plan Colombia and the Merida Initiative are defined as strategies of hemispheric security. However, their devices are articulated to the underlying logic of archipelagos of security, which have been constructed since the decade of the 1990s in the majority of Latin American countries. In both cases, it is possible to observe the construction of a mechanism of surveillance and security that goes beyond the "war" against terrorism, the trafficking of drugs or transnational organized crime, and that is anchored within the distinct spheres of the everyday life of the societies in the region. These mechanisms have been involved since the intervention of the telephone, satellite control of the populations' movements, the control of prisons and in the whole penitentiary system, to the formation of databases of the population with information of different types. In this sense, the activation of surveillance technologies in Latin America strengthens and accelerates a tendency to create strategies designed to slow down the increase of criminal violence. However, it introduces a distinct purpose to the security logic of the region, in the way in which the manipulation of different databases and information—that involve different governments on different scales—allow for the provision of a larger capacity to plan and program security strategies.

The implications foreseen by the North American government for both Plan Colombia and the Merida Initiative accentuate the importance given to the security of the State and the upkeep of social order over civil liberties of the population in the region of Latin America. This outcome should not be surprising since the concept of human security itself, as established by the OAS, subordinates social insecurity (in terms of poverty, exclusion, and health) to the existence of state security. In fact, the language of the OAS deals with the problems of social insecurity in relation to state security. Accordingly, the most important thing is to guarantee control of the population rather than increasing their levels of life expectancy. Even more, the definition of security as implemented by international organizations through Plan Colombia and the Merida Initiative is applied regardless of the characteristics of each country in the region. For example, Nicaragua and Bolivia are countries with relatively low levels of violence, even though they are certainly politically unstable, that have not reached the criminal statistics of countries such as Brazil, Colombia, or Mexico, as well as those in the northern part of Central America.

In this sense, it can be stated that the proposals of hemispheric security previously mentioned, when linked with the archipelagos of security in each country, potentially paint security as a social principle of organization above politics, tending to decrease inequality, and social exclusion—in fact, encouraging them to worsen. This outcome is to be expected since security is being tranformed into a form of government, and the surveillance devices connected to it try to maintain control over those events that affect the stability of the state. Then, those hemispheric surveillance devices are susceptible to fit together, providing better supervision of everyday life, with the aim of reducing the "abnormal development of things."

Here the work carried out by Waever (1995, 2005) generates relevant results considering that for this author, security could actually mean more militarization, and thus, the state—conceptually referred to—remains the principle security provider, as well as to the security which is defined from national sovereignty. Wider security therefore means more issues are approached according to the logic of securitization; that is, framed in the way traditionally reserved for military issues (e.g., supposing that threats faced by a state are of such dimension [such as drug and arm trafficking or terrorism] that only a force like the army and their logic could face them). Securitization, in this sense, justifies extreme measures—whether or not states limit democracy "for democratic reasons." Thus, "security" becomes a means to justify the logic by which the state has the right to transcend normal rules when facing particular threatening possibilities (Wæver 2005). From this perspective, the concept of "security" refers to national security, although it involves local or international dynamics: concerns about military issues ends when applying the same logic to other sectors (such as public or private security), of linking "the discussion from state by apply-ing the similar moves to society" (Weaver 1995). In this sense, the concept of "security" refers to the presence of a security problem, to the threat to society, and some strategy, which responds to it if is articulated by a pre-determined institution in a specific place (Wæver 1995). Consequently, the metamorphosis of the security matter in Latin America responds to the use of a logic of securitization of the state in all forms of everyday life, allow-ing the use of strategies of government-based surveillance technology of the population, harmonizing national public policies in the context of the hemisphere, insinuating itself into the everyday lives of Latin Americans.

## SECURITY IN THE SCENARIOS OF
## DEMOCRATIC TRANSITION

It has been observed how the constant formation of borders fragments—yet interconnects in different ways—the spaces in Latin American urban forming security archipelagos that intend to hold back so-called "crime waves," thus limiting the closeness of those responsible for the prolifera-tion of crime. The perpetrating of a culture of fear is articulated with the discussions of security, which leads to suspicion of all those considered potentially delinquent. It is indeed certain that those excluded from the policies of economic development in the region turn out to be the main social group that is feared; it is also a fact that in the policy of fear manage-ment, practically any person or group could be considered a potential risk to the "normal development of things."

In the spaces of management of fear referred to here—such as closed neighborhoods, commercial centers, private and governmental buildings, parks, business districts, streets, and avenues—policies are implemented that, at the insistence of reducing risk, involve surveillance of large num-bers of people who cross their borders. In this sense, it could be understood as a process of differentiating social-space specifically as a governmental response to slow down the increase of criminal violence of which, on a grand scale impedes the recognition of the problem as a result of social transformations in the marked regions, and above all, through the pro-cesses of exclusion and social inequality. In Latin America, the topic of criminal violence is intended to be solved through the application of dif-ferent and differentiated logics of security, favoring the configuration of a blurred character always seen as an "internal enemy," an "other" that inhabits cities and which animates certain spaces of fear, who it is neces-sary to manage not only from islands of security but from a complete secu-rity archipelago.

In regards to this archipelago, wider machines of security tend to group together, as in the Merida Initiative and Plan Colombia, whose devices are directed toward the elimination of terrorism risks, drug dealing, and transnational organized crime and which serve, in the same way, to watch over and manage those sectors of the population that can be considered a danger to "public peace." These supranational machines come, without a doubt, to reinforce in different spheres the logic of securitization in everyday life in Latin America, established at the end of the last century. This scenario has developed in a constantly growing atmosphere of inequality and social exclusion and, no less importantly, in a scenario of democratic transition where it is possible to observe that authoritarian practices still prevail. In this sense, the consolidation and depth of the securitization logic may seem to allow that these government practices are consolidated. Their most clear expression can be noticed in the recent and recurrent mobilizations of the police and the army, through checkpoints in highways, streets, and avenues. The formation of "states of exception" in different social spaces apparently will be based upon a strategy more or less common in the following years, as a form of government that will seek to end with the proliferation of the forms of violence generated by groups of criminals and mercenaries. The objective of this strategy consists in creating voluntarily, a state of permanent urgency—even if not declared in a technical sense—through a more political than judicial action (Agamben 2003; Diken and Bagge Laustsen 2005).

Also, following with Wæver's line of thought, the politics of hemispheric security put in practice in Latin America, such as the Merida Initiative and Plan Colombia (which follow the logic of human security as defined by the Declaration on Security in the Americas of the OAS) would face the appearance of threats that follow more complex and multidimensional patterns: from social dangers and economic and urban problems to the threats toward the population in general and the development of everyday life (such as criminal violence, the use of drugs, or other discomfort derived from poverty or inequity). This argument appears to be sustained by some academics and members of the North American army (Manwaring et al. 2003), to highlight that insecurity is sustained by drug-trafficking, terrorism, organized crime, or illegal trafficking as a hemispheric matter, a problem that requires transnational solutions, and which must harmonize the public policies of each country in the American region. In the case of the Merida Initiative or Plan Colombia, a constant adjustment to concepts of security can be observed, through the use of extreme measures such as the militarization of the streets or national borders, the construction of urban forts surrounded by electronic surveillance devices, or putting into practice legislation that sanctions the creation of databases to collect the biometric features of the population, measures that finally reflect a scenario of permanent emergency toward any perceived danger. Without a doubt, these extreme measures are not only declared and financed by the Latin American states, they are also sustained by private institutions (such as some private security agencies), giving continuity to a regional logic of security in which the majority of social actors participate in some way or another.

This hemispheric insecurity, in terms of what it has cost over the last few years, implies the articulation of a complex architecture, in which criminal violence is an important manifestation of part representing several causes (immigration, arms smuggling, drug trafficking, money laundering, poverty, and urban population growth). As an answer to these patterns of insecurity, the securitizing actors (the state, civil organizations, and private security companies) look for multidimensional policies that act on the same levels and with the same magnitude as the growth of threats (road and border surveillance, politics for the tracking of merchandise, politics for the "combating" of poverty, efficient city planning, and birth rate control). According to this logic of hemispheric securitization, there would be a close relationship between political and social problems with those that may generate threats, such as criminal violence.

## CONCLUSION

Within this context, the main threat against weak democratic institutions in Latin America may seem to be, paradoxically, the obsessive compulsion to guarantee at all costs the security of the population, even against the individual guarantees themselves. There is, in Latin American countries, the application of security polices, whose primary mechanism is one of exception. With a more political than legal sense, these security policies are seen as a way of classification, administration, and control of threats and every class of risk that affects the everyday of citizens. In Latin American countries, the political mechanism of exception requires any dangerous social action, increasing alarm and reaction against insecurity, crime and violence, not only of those in charge of providing civil security, but of the population in general. In the countries of the region, the cities have been reconfigured by fear: there are zones that are considered wealthy and highly secure, and there are poorer zones, which are seen as highly crime ridden. This reconfiguration locates each entity as a principal piece of political and social functioning. In this sense, local policies against crime and violence are communicated with regional and hemispheric parallels, searching to increase the space of security. The application of this class of mechanisms—on their different levels—increases correspondingly the levels of mistrust, fear, and social conflict. The history of Latin America has been one of social relationships based on authoritarianism and suspicion; a political space with continuous scandals of corruption and nepotism, as well as inefficient legal systems which are fixed through relationships of patronage. Therefore, the employ of surveillance systems and security measures provoke terror and not well-being and stability day to day. In the Latin American region, the creation of suspects has been a recurring practice, and the tactics of poorly skilled security bodies are well known. With the installation of platforms such as the Merida Initiative or Plan Colombia, in countries with an already fragile social and political development, with democratic institutions still weak, and even more, with unequal standards of living, the public space seems to remain even narrower and more isolated.

## NOTES

1. Source: Ministerio de Justicia, Seguridad y Derechos Humanos-República Argentina [Ministry of Justice, Security and Human Rights- Republic of Argentina].

2. UN Office on Drugs and Crime, Division for Policy Analysis and Public Affairs, "Seventh United Nations Survey of Crime Trends and Operations of Criminal Justice Systems, covering the period 1998–2000." Available at http://www.unodc.org/pdf/crime/seventh_survey/7sc.pdf (December 10, 2008).

3. Source: UN Office on Drugs and Crime, Division for Policy Analysis and Public Affairs.

4. This indicator measures citizen's fears of crime and insecurity, as well as the modification of their personal habits and expenses on forms of protection.

5. Inter-American Development Bank. Data Bank http://www.iadb.org/research/statistics.cfm?lang=en (December 10, 2008).

6. Geneva Declaration Secretariat (2008), "Global Burden of Armed Violence", Geneva, Swaziland. Available at http://www.genevadeclaration.org/pdfs/Global-Burden-of-Armed-Violence.pdf (December 10, 2008).

7. It turns out to be meaningful that during 2006, the main cause of death in El Salvador was "aggression with the firing of another weapon," causing a total of 2,793 deaths. *Dirección General de Estadísticas y Censos*. El Salvador. http://www.digestyc.gob.sv/. (December 10, 2008).

8. Geneva Declaration Secretariat (2008), "Global Burden of Armed Violence", Geneva, Swaziland. Available at http://www.genevadeclaration.org/pdfs/Global-Burden-of-Armed-Violence.pdf (December 10, 2008).

9. Geneva Declaration Secretariat (2008), "Global Burden of Armed Violence", Geneva, Swaziland. Available at http://www.genevadeclaration.org/pdfs/Global-Burden-of-Armed-Violence.pdf (December 10, 2008).

10. Informe Latinobarómetro. http://www.latinobarometro.org/ (December 15, 2008).

11. Comisión Económica para América Latina y el Caribe-Estadísticas (CEPAL) (Economic Commission for Latin America and the Caribbean-Stadistics) http://www.eclac.cl/estadisticas/ (December 15, 2008).

12. Geneva Declaration Secretariat (2008), "Global Burden of Armed Violence", Geneva, Swaziland. Available at http://www.genevadeclaration.org/pdfs/Global-Burden-of-Armed-Violence.pdf (December 10, 2008).

13. "Según el Gobierno, la cumbia villera incide en la inseguridad" ("According to the Government, cumbia villera insights insecurity"), *La Nación*, 4/08/04.

14. The following information that is presented was obtained from the analysis of 18 documents of an equal number of private security companies from companies that offer their protection and personnel, and electronic surveillance services in distinct Latin American countries.

15. The information with respect to these themes linked to reform, training and technological modernization can be checked in the Report on the Security Sector in Latin America and the Caribbean (FLACSO 2007).

16. Organization of American States (2003), "Declaration on Security in the Americas." http://www.oas.org/documents/eng/DeclaracionSecurity_102803.asp (December 15, 2008).

17. The assistance is directed to the following countries: Colombia, Mexico, Perú, Bolivia, Ecuador, Haiti, El Salvador, Honduras, Guatemala, Panama, Brasil, Bahamas, Nicaragua, Dominican Republic, Jamaica, Paraguay, Belize,

Chile, Argentina, Suriname, Costa Rica, Venezuela, Guyana, Trinidad and Tobago, Uruguay, Antillas Holandesas, Barbados, St. Lucia, Antigua and Barbuda, St. Kitts and Nevis, Dominica, Granada, Martinica, Aruba, St. Vincent, and the Grenadinas and Bermuda. Just in Facts. A civilian guide to U. S Defense and Security assistance to Latin America and the Caribbean www.justf.org (December 15, 2008).

18. Also added to the list of previously mentioned countries, Cuba was also included. Just in Facts. A civilian guide to U. S Defense and Security assistance to Latin America and the Caribbean www.justf.org (December 15, 2008).
19. These resources are estimated in accordance to the budgets assigned to programs in which both Plan Colombia as well as the Merida Initiative are part of. Just in Facts. A civilian guide to U.S. Defense and Security assistance to Latin America and the Caribbean. www.justf.org (December 15, 2008).
20. *La Jornada*, November 19,2008.
21. *La Jornada*, November 19, 2008.
22. U.S. Government Accountability Office, "PLAN COLOMBIA Drug Reduction Goals Were Not Fully Met, But Security Has Improved; U.S. Agencies Need More, A Report To The Detailed Plans For Reducing Assistance." www.gao.gov (December 15, 2008).
23. Office of the Spokesman, October 22, 2007.
24. Office of the Spokesman, U.S. Department of State, October 23, 2007.
25. *La Jornada*, May 27, 2007.

# Conclusion
## Security and Everyday Life

*Willem de Lint*

In the summer of 2010, more than $1 billion was spent on the biggest security operation in Canadian history for the G20 and G8 summit meetings in Toronto and Huntsville, Ontario. Coverage of the event by Canadian and international news outlets toggled between the high-level intergovernmental discussion on deficit reduction targets and images of the clashes with protesters around the "red zone" of internationally protected persons. On one side, host Canadian Prime Minister Stephen Harper's belt-tightening agenda and the question of national economic independence versus global governance; on the other, protesters squeezed by public order police phalanxes (at a police to protester and bystander ratio of 5:1 and 10:1, respectively) into and out of the "free speech zone" seemingly for the explicit and singular purpose of facilitating snatch and grab arrests of individual "troublemakers." The dark hypothesis proffered by this tightly choreographed flirtation with a classic police riot? Spectacle *is* message.

However, unlike the doubly fictional clashes between *1984*'s Oceania and Eurasia and beyond ideological fodder, disasters and catastrophes do have a basis in empirical fact, as things do crash and burn. Harper, in summing up the accomplishment of talks at the summit, said to reporters that representatives of the world's leading economies understood what is at stake, that the world cannot afford a failure like that of Lehmann Brothers (and the subsequent October 2008 financial crisis); the scalar is global. The security operation was presented in postulations equally hyperbolic; its failure would be paradigmatically catastrophic, another September 11, 2001 (9/11). In fact, opinion polls regularly show up the gap between the interests of the mobile global elites and the fixed masses. At the same time, it has been powerful transnational capital and geopolitical interests that have sought to avoid a transnational rule of law. Thus, the dissonance behind the attempt to connect security operations with financial regulation as too big to fail and why some protesters are saying that, on the contrary, both the remedy of the summit and the fact on the ground of the police and security operations of the Integrated Security Unit (overseeing operations)—packaged in the differential arbitrariness and secrecy that recalls the dark ages—ought to be too big to succeed.

Although not an explicit objective of this volume (it is the subject of many others), dissonance between the concept and reality of security is seen perhaps most unequivocally in the rupture between the everyday experience of our biological life on the planet and its representation in, most importantly, our social and political institutions. We are perhaps at the apotheosis of finance or casino capitalism (pushed forward by "bubbles," "shock," or "disaster" capitalism as Klein [2007] puts it), where the drive for profits outruns risk-averse resource extraction and pushes aside cautious stewardship policy. Ironically, the check on appetite that is performed by the limitations of the sustainability of our quotidian or existential humanness is superseded by the methodology and constitution of the market and its forces. According to the U.S. Supreme Court, large corporations have almost unlimited rights to combine as consortia and speak as citizen-subjects. If such entities have a "guiding mind and will" they can also easily transmogrify, splitting and re-splitting agency and corporate body. In the meantime, the word "sustainability" is anathema, understood as stasis or corporate death. So we experience regular irruptions as natural resources are recast as financial abstraction and converted into risk and collateralized debt in commodity index funds. Presented a daily diet of the dividends (bankruptcy, pollution, starvation, environmental, and species degradation), the (human) citizen or news consumer is alarmed not only by the impact but the prognosis for recovery or correction. Where ecology is a concept that may be written off with the term "externality," capitalized as a dump-site, or acquired in a lottery of resource discovery, the rupture between the lived experience and the lived politics is such as to exacerbate the condition of insecurity. As property, commodity, and backstop to politics and economy security is packaged for resale, pitched by candidates for elective office, and referenced matter-of-factly to block passage, arrest mobility, or force information into or out of private places. This leads to a question, only suggested in rough outline after a brief review of some underlying themes, is what makes "security" (as in "security operations" that run the gamut between war-making and peacekeeping, policing, and security) the object of spectacle the weak and faulty unity of its particular suturing of economy and society?

Scholarship in security in the past 20 years or so may be reviewed on this question of the proper intermediary and referent. The normative question has been posed through word associations intended to harness security, each sufficient to privilege a version of the quotidian or every day. Security is given preferential placement in attachments, hyphenations, and objectifications or the word-couplings chosen to restrict the play of freedoms, autonomy, chance, or choice—couplings repeated to assure some preferred organizational and institutional predictabilities and avoid unwanted harm and losses, particularly from a perceived lack of governance. Perhaps most familiar among these is national security, a concept that, as explored by Neocleous (2008), has its origins in social security. Others include human, green, trade, water, and food security. Is the most pressing problem in the future life-world the availability of and ready access to fresh water, breathable air, and healthy food and that competition over these essentials does not overcome the bulk of our political, social, and cultural energies?

In these hyphenations, how we think about everyday security is based on overlapping popular and scholarly ideas. Some of the scholarly threads include: critical security studies and its various constellations and counterpoints (C.A.S.E. Collective 2006; Mutimer 2009); post-Foucauldian work that advances the idea of the tripartite distinction between sovereignty, discipline, and security; postmodernist scholarship that distinguishes binary, objective relations of the individual or sovereign and a state-based territorialized subject from the denizen and the fluid networks of societies of control (Jones 2000; O'Connor and de Lint 2009); the corpus of thought following Beck (1992) and Giddens (1991) maintaining that catastrophic risk and reflexive modernity combine to produce a regulatory regime based on precaution and avoidance of bads rather than rights protection (Mythen 2006); postwar or post-grand ideology arguments (e.g. Fukuyama 1989; Hobsbawm 1990) that understand the transition in everyday security as a consequence of the re-division of threat: thus asymmetrical warfare, unease, pre-crime (Pickering and McCulluch 2009; Suskind 2003).

Another object of investigation is more traditionally sociological: the relationship between trust, monitoring and rule, and governmental power relations. Undertaking daily routines may involve the protection or maintenance of our self-perceptions as securitized identities (Rose 1999: 240), how security optics perform more or less as simulacrum (de Lint 2008b), and how governing relations are structured or practiced. These relations are also sufficiently thick and reflexive to dramatically alter the 'we' that undertakes such routines.[1] A common thread is that the sovereign-subject relation is being displaced, even within liberal democracies. What is replacing it is a question of debate (see Bigo 2001; Brodeur 2005; Brodeur and Shearing 2005, Ericson 2007, O'Malley 2008; Ashworth and Zedner 2008; Aradau and van Munster 2007).[2] Although there is reasonable clarity regarding the role of the individual and state authority within liberal democracies as a contest, the legitimacy of which depends upon a reasonable chance of victory for the lesser contestant, an equivalent claim on the emerging paradigm of security or security governance is yet to find expression. However, a few provisional claims may be made.

One is that at the very least there is a devaluing of the citizen-subject. The 'free and rights-bearing' individual, the subject-individual as a basis for security governance, is challenged from a number of fronts. It is challenged in the courts where corporations or associations are presumed to have constitutional rights (that may then trump the rights of human individuals). It is also challenged by precautionary or pre-emptive public policy, which acts not against the individual as a decision maker but against the chance of decisions that are deemed unsafe, dangerous, or disordering.

This devaluation is occurring in the realm of criminal justice in which the values and principles of the criminal law have informed the structures and procedures that have in turn, in liberal democracies, made individuals as citizens a counterweight against corporatist, authoritarian, and even fascist inclinations of governments. Criminologists have noted a shift in the orienting locus of criminal justice that, of course, has followed or matched the changing nomenclature elsewhere as modernity, liberalism, and capitalism unfolds. Accordingly, we see significant slippage from the orienting presumption of the citizen-subject as terms (including prevention, precaution, and risk) form the basis of a "security society." Under a logic of security the adage that it is better that 99 guilty persons should go free than that one innocent person should be wrongly punished is changed to follow former Vice President Dick Cheney's 1% doctrine that it is better that 99 innocent people are falsely interdicted than that one terrorist fails to be stopped. In the security society, the individual is not protected by the operation of criminal justice as a backward-looking enterprise that responds post-hoc to proven acts already committed. On the contrary, criminal justice in the frame of security selectively utilizes (Harcourt 2003) the preventative and precautionary discourse to proactively control criminal justice outcome, output, or product. Evaluation of effectiveness is not through evidence of how a moral order was restored through clearances of crime, but through how a cybernetic order is being achieved by matching previous to future forecasts and predictions in the "taming of chance."

Devaluation of the citizen-subject is being accomplished as the mobility claims of transnational enterprises put pressure on economic and sovereign demarcations. The border is exemplary in the installation of the new security paradigm because it offers the discursive means to dissolve the distinction between internal and external threats where, as Feeley and Simon (1994: 181) put it, "the border is everywhere." Security measures 'connect dots' using 'fusions' or the introduction and expansion of linkages and interoperability between law enforcement and military, public and private, or broadly, security and justice affiliates. The consequence is not simply the diminution of the rights-protected citizen-subject, but the production of a contingent individual and persons made up (Hacking 1985) from these fusions and the extension of the presumptive domain in which the interpolation holds up. The battle line between what may be called, according to Foucault, "systems of exclusion" (de Lint and Bahdi in press)–that is, between the truths and knowledge of modern law on one hand and the security paradigm on the other—is of no small interest. Also key is the mechanism by which the displacement of one paradigm by another is achieved (O'Connor and de Lint 2009). Borderlands are rebordered (Andreas and Bierstekker 2003), expanded outward, bringing ubiquitous surveillance and pre-emptory instruments into the data-streams of everyday life. As the variety and scope of fusions and the interoperabilities between national security and policing, and foreign and domestic intelligence-based operations proliferate and circulate, the practical distinction between the national and international security ambit falls away. Consequently, political and civil rights and the idea of political governance as predicated on the adversarial character of the individual-state relationship are recast as a traditional modernist political ideal (classic liberalism) that has been superseded by postmodern political 'realities.' These realities take from popular and scholarly discourses to reframe 'necessities.' For instance, as Mythen summarizes in this volume, 9/11 is popularly understood as "both a historical watershed and a catalyst for a new phase of political struggle, legal transformation, and military expansion."

Which brings us to a key point in our thinking about security and everyday life: the importance of ideology, or more prosaically, the hopeful projection of thinking about ways of living. How we think about security is a matter of politics or power relations, and most of us are increasingly aware that "security talk" is monopolized by experts for a particular agenda, be it for commercial, military, or policing applications or in the exploitation of private or public goods. Those who believe security is a public good will have been informed by and in turn reiterate the terms of classic liberal thought and more recent variants of liberal democratic thinking, with its emphasis on rights, equality, access to justice, transparency, and checks and balances (eg. Loader and Walker 2007; Zedner 2008). Although we have been told that ours is a time when the great ideological clash between communism and capitalism—and more narrowly between welfare liberalism and neoliberalism—is behind us, it would seem on the contrary that there is a continuous if somewhat submarine or subterranean skirmish concerning the successor ideology, or which way of thinking will see us through these troublesome times. Here we are looking for something beyond the merely descriptive. That is to say, it is necessary to acknowledge first and foremost that there is a widening gulf between what our institutions are ready and capable of delivering in terms even of risk or security assessments and what we need from them in the form of answers and solutions.

Those who prefer to believe, on the contrary, that security is a market or best addressed by privatization or marketization will listen keenly to Milton Friedman economists on how to think our way forward and blame security's relative absence (i.e., the absence of framing social problems as security problems) on clumsy bureaucracies, regulatory restrictions of big government, or socialized service delivery systems. Will scarcity be maintained or even orchestrated following the economic idea that conflict over access to basic and valued goods is the necessary preamble to further distributions, including allocations of security? This depends upon the idea, the a priori necessity of an interminable contest over scarce goods, material or otherwise, that acts to frame a problem that then is busily instantiated through policy and practice in a self-fulfilling prophecy. It is here that security is most vexing as a commodity or product of so-called expert or specialist enterprise or intervention. What are we to make of the proliferation of technologies that claim to enhance personal, public, and even social security in an age of market consolidation and venture finance capitalism, and where there is such a rampant proliferation of dangerous weapons and goods often by the very same corporate agents who have been staking their claim on the need for greater and better prophylactic measures in what comes to represent nothing so much as a protection racket?

In his lectures on security, territory, and population (Foucault 2007), Foucault distinguished a shift in the model of government and technologies of power with a transition from territorial safety to population security. The new model of government, governmentality, has "population as its target and political economy as major form of knowledge" and involves "apparatuses of security as its essential technical instrument." For Foucault, the discovery of the population variable is important not simply in taking the measure of the sovereign's wealth in an imposition of rule or administration by police, but in the allocation of optimal measures and in its configuring political problems (now associated with liberalism) as a question of a balance between too much and too little. Foucault argues that for neoliberal governments, intervention is restricted to producing the conditions of competition, an ongoing concern given the tendency toward monopoly.

According to Donzelot (2008), liberalism and neoliberalism's emphasis on the limit of rule and the maintenance of productive capacities distinguishes it from the (failed) policy of welfarism and its "logic of automatic compensation for all adversities, real or otherwise" (132). The state is restricted to stimulating the conditions in which the entrepreneurial self may play the game while sufficiently maintaining system credibility. To avoid welfarism's failure as a game of inclusions without limits, (neo)liberalism's rules simultaneously define the terms of participation, regulate some to the margins, and put out the promise that a return to full participation is possible. Donzelot (2008: 130) argues that the limit on "the game of inequalities" that characterizes a neoliberal political economy is "that of exclusion. Everything must be done to avoid some players being definitively excluded from the game; otherwise it loses its sense and credibility." Social policy is "not aimed to reduce inequalities," it is a "struggle against exclusion" that "neglects the social and even condemns it" (Donzelot 2008: 131).

Government is conceived through management of limits, or in the restriction on its impositions for society, with emphasis on economic progress rather than state advancement. In other words, the apparatus of security modulates and is modulated by political economy. Just as freedom is produced or constructed through government or state interventions and can lead through strong interpolations or elicitations to its opposing number (see Holquist 1997)—that is, unfreedom—so to security is produced and constructed sometimes without due regard for limits or restrictions to produce its opposite. Where governmentality is exercised as the model of government, we should expect that security will be constructed through the restraints of political economy. This produces the observation that the best curtailment on runaway security is already the most powerful form of knowledge: political economy.

Missing from Foucault's analysis is the role of various intermediations and the structured and institutional manipulation of what passes as knowledge within the apparatus of security itself. No doubt as a consequence of Foucault's view of power (cf. Digeser 1992), the positive exercise of information control becomes a wash in the availability of reversals. Nonetheless, the power of the mode of governmentality resides in how information is rendered a commodity of politics. The security apparatus adds and subtracts information and does so most vigorously to supplement the vitality of the sovereign or to produce the appearance of a secure economic order. So rampant is information control (through secrecy, persuasion, espionage, and evaluation [Wilsnack 1980]) that the effects we are encouraged to work with *qua* "political economy" or "security apparatus" are themselves thrown off by institutional shadow boxers or avatars to distract and confound.

It is now well established that security and surveillance dispositifs are inserted wherever everyday life may be threatened by a risk of certain kind of uncertainty, events (singular, exceptional, or as effect) may be swept up and into the vortex of security and surveillance to produce a rebranding of the very elements of 'the social.' Having reframed social problems as security risks, securitization (Waever 1995) produces its own nomenclature, so that now to speak of social problems it is necessary to do so in the constituent terms of the "security society." Moreover, it is not only that everything in everyday life is a security issue, but to say that it is a security issue is already to call upon a certain political economy of remedy or address. Much of the power of the security utterance today is attributable to the form or modality of closure that attends the utterance. Deep in the security apparatus is the privileged place of a different order of politics: the politics of knowledge exclusions or decision making about the representations of populations in information that is powerful *because* it excludes as it offers a difference: to policy, the fate of political and economic authorities, or the life-chances of the truth regimes including the version of political economy holding sway. It is by oblique or direct reference to this dark art and archive of actionable information that security gains its greatest power in the hyphenation security intelligence (de Lint 2008b). At the same time, however, the act of rendering information an arcane, privileged commodity and of creating indispensible "centers of calculation" or unassailable bastions of technological supremacy drives security agents and agencies in the direction of monopoly. Note that security and weapons and intelligence represent an extremely large market that is dominated by corporate behemoths whose comprehensive failure would likely produce dangers not too dissimilar to the dangers that may well be stoked by their growth and combination.

Consequently, as an essential technical instrument of governmentality, the security apparatus is somewhat confounding. On one hand, it is an instrument for effecting exclusions 'from the game.' On the other, it will need to be framed to maintain the sense and credibility of the political economy in the avoidance of monopolistic tendencies and the furtherance of conditions of competition. Across internal and external policing and security sectors, the security apparatus is periodically subject to waves of privatization to compel the proper disciplining of market and state forces. Maintaining sense and credibility through reproduction of the conditions of competition requires that there is an equal antipathy toward overweening state and market monopolies. But what are the instruments available to assure that security conglomerates or assemblages do not become, in the current parlance, too big to fail (i.e., monopolistic or dysfunctional)? Where are the measures? Who can produce the evidence when penalties or game exclusions are also the product of these instruments of governmentality?

Of course, "we" would like to say that more research is needed to pursue this question of how to prepare an effective antidote to the security apparatus in the absence of a strong counter-hegemony and knowledge base. Unfortunately, "we" await increasingly catastrophic security irruptions, served up by expert monopolies, with decreasing access to security-free zones.

In Botello's analysis of the Meridia Initiative and Plan Columbia, these hugely expensive foreign interventions were threaded into the social fabric of Mexico and Columbia and, indeed, Latin America more generally, as "archipelagos of security" that "functioned as dikes that allow the maintaining and control of social groups considered dangerous–social groups, evidently, identified with certain sectors of the excluded and marginalized." It may be added that in their redrawing or displacement of formal and informal domestic internal security structures, they foster a brand of harsh neoliberalism that only exacerbates the conditions feeding organized crime. In Latin America, this imposition produces, as Botello writes, a commonplace:

> to hear talk about the safest routes to use to cross the city, at different hours and days, since one route may be safe one day at a specific time, but it may not be a few minutes later.

A more prosaic instance of securitization is found in Salter's essay on airport security. As Salter argues, impositions against longstanding freedoms cannot be accomplished in liberal democracies without a fair quotient of consent, and this is reflected in the cultural sensibilities of everyday discourse. We agree not to make jokes about bombs or terrorists at airports because we prefer to align ourselves against the 'other' or the 'monster' in conditions of existential danger; to do otherwise is akin to yelling out 'fire' in a crowded theater as a 'joke'. As Salter argues, the capacity to "play language in ways that fundamentally unsettle the claims to knowledge, security, and authority" may still be a powerful antidote to such claims. If not—and what comes to mind is the grim penalty against humorous expression that sets the background for *1984*—security apparatuses have not left much of a 'humanity' remainder.

Israel is sometimes understood as the apotheosis of the security state. It is built on exception and governed through security. What constitutes the population and societal basis of Israel is registered through the prism of a highly fraught exercise that calculates the dominant or privileged binary through the rhetorical combination of existential and exceptional necessity. But, to follow Donzelot's analysis, is there here a tension between the maintenance of economic vitality or *homo economicus* and that of the sovereign? Many commentators have argued that the Israeli state cannot long continue to comprise and re-comprise populations through the prism of the exceptional state without producing too much unexpected and counterproductive market uncertainties. To the extent that such market uncertainties include the regular predictabilities of civil society buttressed by the rule of law, the agent for collapse may well be internal. In recounting the story of Tali Fahima, a Jewish Mizrachi woman of a working class origin who was tried and convicted for befriending and offering existential assistance to the chief of the al-Aqsa Martyrs Brigades in the Palestinian town of Jenin, Sion exposes this fault-line between occupier and occupied, friend and foe, exception and quotidian.

Mythen, Bahdi, Virta, and Staudt speak to the reconfiguration of internal security within liberal democracies that, although it is not without the baggage of colonization, is perhaps several iterations of accommodation beyond the Israeli benchmark. Mythen notes that like other institutions and areas of policy of the new security agenda, counterterrorism legislation in the United Kingdom may be analyzed "as a means of establishing the links between political desires, pre-imaginings of harm and the use of pre-emptive regulation." As many commentators have noted, the alignment between neoliberal and neoconservative political views and the mediated framings and imaginings of harm, risk, and dangers has pushed policy makers toward pre-emptive or pre-cautionary models of policy intervention, and this is exemplified in counterterrorism legislation throughout the world. As Mythen concludes, the proliferation of policy on hypothetical scenarios stemming from an extremely low tolerance for risk has real and deleterious impacts. To take us again to the point we are making borrowing from Donzelot, that impact is also at loggerheads with the ideological foundation of the political economy (in economic vitality) that otherwise should modify the security apparatus.

In adaptations putatively to accord to the 'war on terrorism' the reconfiguration of domestic security and indeed of the rights and protections that are normally granted is such as to twist the result, even in liberal democracies such as Canada, to a grotesque parady. Bahdi reviews how Maher Arar, Abdullah Almalki, Ahmad El Maati, and Muayyed Nurredin were all subjected to torture in foreign prisons or holding cells while Canadian government officials looked away. Canada's deliberate failure to protect these men (or proactive effort to out-source torture) in the service of a claim to information of domestic and foreign law enforcement and security intelligence interests that was predicated not on the rule of law but on the rule of particular sovereign excess, comprises, as Bahdi argues, a "legal regime which has pulled lawlessness into itself." In bringing the concept of meta-framing to public events in the instance of the Pope's visit to Israel, Bacj explores the idea that order in social life is provided through the communications of the security apparatus, and that how these ritual events guide public order is a matter that acts with great subtleness. In my own chapter, I postulate that there may be more behind some events than meets the eye, that being seen to be doing security is a matter of necessity and exceptionalism such that the exploitation of optics and knowledges produces a kind of governance that may be so hooked on the spectacular security fix that it requires regular episodic events.

It would be perhaps a hopeful gesture to summarize Staudt and Virta's chapters by way of indicating how they point to the places of even more serious fracture (suggesting perhaps even collapse) in the security apparatus as an instrument of governmentality. After all, an edifice constructed without adequate recourse to humor, the rule of law, or an apt regard of the need for risk taking is already likely to be brittle and crotchety. In her examination of the border security apparatus between Mexico and United States, Staudt finds somewhat hopefully that "border people challenge and resist the ways [border security] policies aim to shape their lives" and notes that the resistances are enjoined by some local municipalities in Texas. In particular, there are constitutional challenges against the imposition of the Border Wall, an Israelification that undermines federalism and the separation of powers while it tears families and communities apart. Staudt points out that there are many available antidotes to the realist security discourse that has spread its prolific seed, with human security already more than 15 years old. Alas, even with the election of Barak Obama, the wall continues, supported by the loaded dice of American presidential political poker.

Nor is the outlook any rosier in Europe, where, according to Virta, "internal policy is giving way to the expansive logic of security." This has developed out of the third Pillar of the European Union concerning "justice and home affairs." As elsewhere, prevention, precaution, and pre-emption are the catch-words that have stimulated the 'ban-optic' security apparatus. As Virta documents, "fortress Europe" is becoming a governable singularity through the interoperability of police and security agencies that have built up the bandwidth between local, regional, national, and transnational conductivities. This is being accomplished in no small part through localized developments, including community policing initiatives, which are "governing through counter-terrorism." Because community policing is a feel-good term connoting a solidaristic altruism, the combination of community, policing, and counterterrorism may appear at first to be a modifying force. Virta concludes that the direction of impact is not that power relations will be softened but that they will be hardened, as openness, transparency, mutuality, and consent are displaced by secrecy and distrust.

This brings us back to our objective in bringing together a cross-section of essays following the hypothesis that security is displacing or modifying everyday social practices, sometimes profoundly. In particular in the examination of borders and airports by Staudt and Salter, we see how commonplace activities are disaggregated and recombined through the security sieve. Although it is obvious that this screening is indeed explicitly political, discourses of risk, precaution, and prevention provide a familiar palliative. Just as 'community policing' asks "who can be against community and policing?" these terms ask: "who can be against and what can be bad about taking precautions against mishaps?"

It is useful to place these terms in the further context of the relative vacuum of successor counter-ideologies to neoliberalism and global finance capitalism. The effort made to aggrandize or trump up al-Qaeda as a worthy and powerful 'other' is itself a sensible prophylactic if the more significant fear is that the substance and direction of public anxieties is not completely servile and may yet outflank governmental and economic vitalities, particularly their combination in enterprises such as the G8 and G20 summits. The everyday and periodically spectacular security episodes that comprise our daily relation with social, political, and even cultural institutions do comprise a coherent template. Outflanking, were that to occur, would no doubt require the unleashing of positive proactive policy instruments and renewed refreshments of domestic political institutions. Indeed, it is likely where elites suddenly find themselves standing shoulder-to-shoulder outside the gates that a reinvigorated common security program will be launched. The spectacle of the G8 and G20, its "red zone" participants enjoying a $1 billion security detail, is a case in point. As business owners, bankers, and media cannot readily distinguish their outsider status from the ranks of the masses, they are on the brink of an emergent solidarity experience. The security apparatus has a distracting if not mesmerizing and perhaps even mystifying influence, but its apotheosis may have passed.

## NOTES

1. Althusser (1971) referred to this as "hailing." In much critical security studies, scholarship 'securitization' may be contrasted to 'alienation' inasmuch as it involves both the hard relations of material forces and the interjection

of meanings and discourses between actors and institutions, subjects and states, individuals and populations.

2. For instance, Bigo (2005) has framed the concept of the 'banopticon', consisting of criminal profiling, management of movement, and exceptionalism. Bigo, D. (2005) Global (in)security: the field of the professionals of unease management and the Ban-opticon. *Traces: a multilingual series of cultural theory*.

# Bibliography

Aaltola, M. (2005) The international airport: the hub-and-spoke pedagogy of the American Empire. *Global Networks,* 5(3): 261–278.

Abelson, A. (2006) "Seguridad privada en Chile: tema pendiente para el ministerio de Seguridad Pública," *Boletín del Programa Seguridad y Ciudadanía,* 6 (Aug.), FLACSO, Chile.

Adam, B., Beck, U., and Van Loon, J. (eds.) (2000) *The Risk Society and Beyond: Critical Issues for Social Theory.* London: Sage.

Adey, P. (2004) Secured and sorted mobilities: examples from the airport. *Surveillance and Society,* 1(4): 500–519.

Adey, P. (2008) Airports, mobility and the calculative architecture of affective control. *Geoforum,* 39(1): 438–451.

Agamben, G. (1998) In D. Heller-Roazen (trans.), *Homo Sacer: Sovereignty and Bare Life.* Stanford: Stanford University Press.

Agamben, G. (2003) *État d'exception. Homo Sacer II, 1.* Éditions du Seuil, Paris.

Agamben, G. (2005) In K. Attell (trans.), *State of Exception.* University of Chicago Press.

Agathangelou, A. M., and Ling, L. H. M. (2004) Power, borders, security, wealth: lessons of violence and desire from September 11. *International Studies Quarterly,* 48: 517–538.

Aiken, S. J. (2007) Risking rights: An assessment of Canadian border security policies. In Y. S. R. Grinspun (ed.) *Whose Canada?*, Montreal: McGill-Queen's University Press.

Alden, E. (2008) *The Closing of the American Border: Terrorism, Immigration and Security Since 9 11.* New York: Harper Collins.

Al-Haj, M. (2005) National ethos, multicultural education, and the new history textbooks in Israel. *Curriculum Inquiry,* 35(1): 47–71.

Althusser, L. (1971) Ideology and ideological state apparatuses. In *Lenin and Philosophy and other Essays 122–89.* London: New Left Books.

Alvarado, A., and Arzt, S. (2001) *El Desafío de México: Seguridad y Estado de Derecho.* México: El Colegio de México.

Amoore, L. (2007) Vigilant visualities: the watchful politics of the war on terror. *Security Dialogue,* 38(2): 139–156.

Amoore, L., and de Goede, M. (2008) Governing by risk in the war on terror. In L. Amoore and M. de Goede (eds.), *Risk and the War on Terror.* London: Routledge. 5–19.

Anderson O'Gorman, B. R. (1983) *Imagined Communities: Reflections on the Origin and Spread of Nationalism.* London: Verso.

Andreas, P., and Bierstekker, T. (2003) *The Rebordering of North America: Integration and Exclusion in a New Security Context.* London: Taylor and Francis.

Aparecida, M. L. (1996) Violencia, cultura popular e organizacoes comunitarias. In G. Velho and M. Alvito (organizadores). *Ciudadanía e violencia.* Río de Janeiro: UFRJ-FGV.

Aradau, C., and van Munster, R. (2007) Governing terrorism through risk: taking precautions, (un)knowing the future. *European Journal of International Relations*, 13(1): 89–115.

Aradau, C., Lobo-Guerrero, L., and van Munster, R. (2008) Security, technologies and the political. *Security Dialogue*, 39(2): 147–154.

Aradau, C., and van Munster, R. (2009) Exceptionalism and the 'war on terror': criminology meets international relations. *British Journal of Criminology*, 49/5: 686–701.

Aretxaga, B. (2003) Maddening states. *Annual Review of Anthropology*, 32: 393–410.

Arizaga, M. C. (2000) Las murallas y barrios cerrados. La morfología espacial del ajuste en Buenos Aires. *Nueva Sociedad*, Caracas;166: 26–37.

Arriagada, I., and Godoy, L. (1999) *Seguridad ciudadana y violencia en América Latina: diagnostico y políticas en los años noventa.* Chile, CEPAL-ECLAC.

Arteaga Botello, N. (1998) *En Busca de la Legitimidad: Violencia y Populismo Punitivo en México 1990–2000.* México: Universidad Autónoma de la Ciudad de México.

Arteaga Botello, N. (2006) *Pobres y Delincuentes. Estudio de Sociología y Genealogía.* México: Universidad Autónoma del Estado de México, Miguel Ángel Porrúa Editores.

Ashworth, A., and Zedner, L. (2008) Defending the criminal law: reflections on the changing character of crime, procedure, and sanction. *Criminal Law and Philosophy*, 2: 21–51.

Augé, M. (1995) In J. Howe (trans.), *Non-places: Introduction to an Anthropology of Supermodernity.* New York: Verso.

Bacevich, A. J. (2007) Introduction. In Bacevich (ed.), *The Long War: A New History of U.S. National Security Policy Since World War II.* New York: Columbia University Press.

Bahdi, R. (2003) No exit: racial profiling and the war against terrorism. *Osgoode Hall Law Journal*, 41(2,3): 293–316.

Bahdi, R. (2009) Torture, tort and terror: the non-delegable duty to protect nationals in the context of anti-terrorism. *Supreme Court Law Review,* 44: 231–262.

Bajc, V. (2007a) Introduction: debating surveillance in the age of security. *American Behavioral Scientist,* 50(12): 1567–1591.

Bajc, V. (2007b) Surveillance in public rituals: security meta-ritual and the 2005 U.S. Presidential Inauguration. In Bajc and Torpey (eds.). Special Issue: Watching Out: Surveillance, Mobility, and Security, *American Behavioral Scientist*, 50 (12 August). INITIALS FOR EDITORS/PAGE NUMBERS

Bajc, V. (2010) On surveillance as solution to security issues. In G. Cassano and R. Dello Buono (eds.), *Crisis, Politics, and Critical Sociology.* Leiden: Brill; 183–196.

Bajc, V. (forthcoming) *Christian Pilgrimage in Jerusalem: Performing Social Realities.* University of Chicago Press.

Bajc, V., and Torpey, J. (eds) (2007) Watching Out: Surveillance, Mobility, and Security. Special Issue. *American Behavioral Scientist*, 50(12 August).

Balzacq, T. (2005) The three faces of securitization: political agency, audience, and context. *European Journal of International Studies*, 11(2): 171–201.

Balzacq, T. (2008) The policy tools of securitization: information exchange, EU foreign and interior policies. *Journal of Common Market Studies*, 46(1): 75–100.

Barnett, M. N., and Adler, E. (1998) Studying security communities in theory, comparison, and history. In E. Adler and M. N. Barnett (eds.), *Security Communities.* New York: Cambridge University Press; 413–441.

Bar-Tal, D. (1996) Development of social categories and stereotypes in early childhood: the case of 'The Arab' concept formation, stereotype and attitudes by Jewish children in Israel. International Journal of Intercultural Relations, 20(3–4): 341–370.

Bateson, Gregory. (1953) The position of humor in human communication. In H. von Foerster (Ed.), *Cybernetics: Circular Causal and Feedback Mechanisms in Biological and Social Systems*. Ninth Macy Conference. New York, 1-47.

Bateson, G. (1956) The message 'this is play.' In B. Schaffner (ed.), *Group Processes; Transactions of the Second Conference, October 9–12, 1955, Princeton, N.J.* New York: The Josiah Macy, Jr. Foundation; 145–242.

Bateson, G. (1958 [1936]) Epilogue 1958. In *Naven. A Survey of the Problems Suggested by a Composite Picture of the Culture of a New Guinea Tribe Drawn from Three Points of View.* 2nd ed. Stanford, CA: Stanford University Press; 280–303.

Bateson, G. (2000a [1972]) A theory of play and fantasy. In *Steps to an Ecology of Mind*. University of Chicago Press; 177–193.

Bateson, G. (2000b [1972]) Toward a theory of schizophrenia. In *Steps to an Ecology of Mind*. University of Chicago Press; 201–227.

Bateson, G. 2002 [1979] *Mind and Nature: A Necessary Unity*. Cresskill, NJ: Hampton Press, Inc.

Baudrillard, J. (1981) *For a Critique of the Political Economy of the Sign*. St. Louis, MO: Telos Press.

Beck, U. (1992) *Risk Society: Towards a New Modernity*. London: Sage.

Beck, U. (1995) *Ecological Politics in an Age of Risk*. London: Sage.

Beck, U. (1999) *World Risk Society*. Cambridge, Cambridgeshire: Polity Press.

Beck, U. (2002) The terrorist threat: world risk society revisited. *Theory, Culture and Society*, 19(4): 39–55.

Beck, U. (2009) *World at Risk*. Cambridge, Cambridgeshire: Polity.

Bell, C. (1997) *Ritual. Perspectives and Dimensions*. New York: Oxford University Press.

Benatta v. Attorney General of Canada (2008) 07-CV-336613PD3 (Statement of Defence).

Benford, R., and Snow, D. (2000) Framing processes and social movements: an overview and assessment. *Annual Review of Sociology*, 26: 611–639.

Ben-Eliezer, U. (1995) A nation-in-arms: state, nation, and militarism in Israel's first years. Comparative Studies in Society and History, 37: 22, 264–285.

Berkovitch, N. (1997) Motherhood as a national mission: the construction of womanhood in the legal discourse in Israel. *Women's Studies International Forum*, 20(5/6): 605–519.

Bigo, D. (2001) The Möbius ribbon of internal and external security(ies). In M. Albert, D. Jacobson, and J. Lapid (eds.), *Identities, Borders, Orders. Rethinking International Relations Theory*. Minneapolis: University of Minnesota Press.

Bigo, D. (2002) Security and immigration: toward a critique of the governmentality of unease. *Alternatives: Global, Local, Political*, 27(special issue): 63–92.

Bigo, D. (2007) Detention of foreigners, states of exception, and the social practices of control of the Banopticon. In P. Kumar Rajaram and C. Grundy-Warr (eds.), *Borderscapes: Hidden Geographies and Politics at Territory's Edge*. Minneapolis: University of Minnesota Press; 3–33.

Binford, L. (1999) A failure of normalization: transnational migration, crime, and popular justice in the contemporary neoliberal Mexican social formation. *Social Justice*, 26(3): 123–144.

Birnbaum, J. (2004) Jacques Derrida: "I am at war with myself." *Le Monde*, August 19.

Black, D., and Baumgartner, M. P. (1980) On self-help in modern society. In D. Black (ed.), *The Manners and Customs of the Police*. New York: Academic Press.

Black, D. and M.P. Baumgartner. 1987. "On Self-Help in Modern Society." *Dialectal Anthropology*. 12: 33-44.

Bodemer, K., Kurtenbach, S., and Meschkat, K. (2001) *Violencia y regulación de conflictos en América Latina*. Venezuela: Editorial Nueva Sociedad.

Bogard, W. (1996) *The Simulation of Surveillance. Hypercontrol in Telematic Societies*. Cambridge University Press.

Boutellier, H. (2005) *The Safety Utopia*. Dordrecht: Kluwer Academic Publishers.

Boyle, P., and Haggerty, K.D. (forthcoming) Spectacular security: mega-events and the security complex. *British Journal of Sociology*.

Briceño-Leon, R. (2007) Caracas. In K. Koonings and D. Kruijt (eds.), *Fractured Cities: Social Exclusion, Urban Violence & Contested Spaces in Latin America*. London: Zed Books; 86–100.

Brigham, J. (2005) Anti-anti terror: color coding and the joke of homeland security. *New Political Science,* 27(4): 481–496.

Brighenti, A. (2006) Dogville, or, the dirty birth of law. *Thesis Eleven,* 87(1): 96–111.

Brodeur, J.-P. (2005) Trotsky in blue: permanent policing reform. *Australian and New Zealand Journal of Criminology,* 38(2): 254–267.

Brodeur, J.-P., and Shearing, C. (2005) Configuring security and justice. *European Journal of Criminology,* 2(4): 379–406.

Brogden, M., and Nijhaar, P. (2005) *Community Policing. National and International Models and Approaches*. Collompton: Willan Publishing.

Bronner, M. (2006) 9/11 live: the NORAD tapes. *Vanity Fair,* 8/1.

Brosh, H. (1993) The influence of language status on language acquisition: Arabic in the Israeli setting. *Foreign Language Annals*, 26(3): 347–358.

Brugués, A., Cortéz, W. W., and Aarón Fuentes, N. (1998) Inseguridad pública en la frontera norte. en *Ciudades*, Puebla, 40: 18–24.

Buck-Morss, S. (2003) *Thinking past terror: Islamism and critical theory on the left*, Verso, Londres, Reino Unido.

Burkitt, I. (2005) Powerful emotions: power, government and opposition in the "War on Terror." *Sociology*, 39(4): 679–695.

Burnett, J., and Whyte, D. (2005) Embedded expertise and the new terrorism. *Journal for Crime, Conflict and the Media*, 1(4): 1–18.

Butler, J. (2004) *Precious Life: The Power of Mourning and Violence*. London: Verso.

Buzan, B. and Hansen, L. (2009) *The Evolution of International Security Studies*. Cambridge University Press, Cambridge, UK.

Buzan, B. and Waever, O. (2007) After the Return to Theory: The Past, Present and Future of Security Studies. In: Collins, Alan, (ed.) *Contemporary Security Studies*. Oxford University Press, Oxford, UK, 383–402.

Buzan, B., and Waever, O. (2009) Macrosecuritization and security constellations: reconsidering scale in securitization theory. Review of International Studies, 35(2): 253–276.

Buzan, B., Waever, O., and de Wilde, J. (1998) *Security: A New Framework for Analysis*. Boulder, CO: Lynne Rienner Publishers.

C.A.S.E. Collective. (2006) Critical approaches to security in Europe: a networked manifesto. *Security Dialogue*, 37(4): 443–487.

CAIR-Can, Annual Review 2003–2004, HTTP: http://www.caircan.ca/downloads/CAIR-CAN_2004.pdf). October 30, 2010.

CNN (2006) Thousands march for immigrant rights. CNN. Available at http://articles.cnn.com/2006-05-01/us/immigrant.day_1_thousands-march-largest-protests-immigration-laws?_s=PM:US. Accessed October 19, 2010.

Calarco, M., and DeCaroli, S. (eds.) (2007) *Giorgio Agamben: Sovereignty and Life*, Stanford: Stanford University Press.

Caldeira, T. P. R. (1996) Fortified enclaves: the new urban segregation. *Public Culture*, 8(2): 303–328.

Caldeira, T. P. R. (2000) *City of Walls: Crime, Segregation, and Citizenship in São Paulo*. Berkeley: University of California Press.

Caldeira, C. (2000) El crimen organizado en Brasil. *Nueva Sociedad* (Caracas), 167: 99–113.

Campbell, D. (2007) The biopolitics of security: oil, empire, and the sports utility vehicle. In E. Dauphinee and C. Masters (eds.), *The Logics of Biopower and the War on Terror: Living, Dying, Surviving*. New York: Palgrave Macmillan; 129–156.

Canada (Prime Minister) *v.* Khadr, (2010 SCC 3) Pue, W. (2003) "The War on Terror: Constitutional Governance in a State of Permanent Warfare?", *Osgoode Hall Law Journal*, 41(2 &3): 267–292.

Capano, M., and Feleci, S. (1999) La comunidad y el municipio en la prevención de la violencia urbana. Casos en la Argentina. *Nuevas visiones para los municipios*. Cuadernos del IFAM, No. 6. Argentina, Ministerio del Interior.

Carranza, E. (2004) "Políticas públicas en materia de seguridad de los habitantes ante el delito en América Latina," *Seguridad ciudadana y orden público en América Latina*, México, Editorial Nueva Sociedad.

Castells, M. (1998) *La Era de la Información:El fin de Milenio*. España, Alianza Editorial.

Chappell, B. (2006) Rehearsals of the sovereign: states of exception and threat governmentality. *Cultural Dynamics*, 18(3): 313–334.

Charlton, N. G. (2008) *Understanding Gregory Bateson: Mind, Beauty, and the Sacred Earth*. Albany: State University of New York Press.

Chesney, R. (2007) State secrets and the limits of national security litigation. *The George Washington Law Review*, 75: 1249–1332.

Chinchilla, L. (2005) Experiencias de participación ciudadana en la prevención del crimen en Centroamérica. *Crimen y Violencia en América Latina*. Colombia: Fondo de Cultura Económica.

Clarke, R. (2004) *Against All Enemies: Inside America's War on Terror*. New York: Free Press.

Clark, P. (2007) *Learning From Experience—Counter Terrorism in the UK since 9/11*. London: Policy Exchange.

Cockfield, A. (2007) Protecting the social value of privacy in the context of state investigations using new technologies. *University of British Columbia Law Review*, 40(May 1): 41–66.

Cohen, S. (2001) *States of Denial: Knowing about Atrocities and Suffering*. Cambridge: Polity Press.

Cohen, Y., Haberfeld, Y., and Kristal, T. (2007) Ethnicity and mixed ethnicity: educational gaps among Israeli-born Jews. *Ethnic and Racial Studies*, 30(5): 896–917.

Cohn, Carol and Cynthia Enloe. 2003. "A Conversation with Cynthia Enloe: Feminists Look at Masculinity and the Men Who Wage War." *Signs: Journal of Women in Culture and Society*, 28(4): 1187–1207.

Concha-Eastman, A. (2000) Violencia urbana en América Latina y el Caribe: dimensiones, explicaciones, acciones. In S. Rotker (ed), *Ciudadanía del miedo*. Caracas, Venezuela: Nueva Sociedad–The State University of New Jersey.

Connelly, J. (2001) Politicisation and political participation: beyond apathy. *Finnish Yearbook of Political Thought*, 5: 154–186.

Cornelius, Wayne. 2001. "Death at the Border: Efficacy and Unintended Consequences of U.S. Immigration Control Policy." *Population and Development Review* 27(4): 661–685.

Crelinsten, R. (2007) Counter terrorism as global governance: a research inventory. In M. Ranstorp (ed.), *Mapping Terrorism Research*. New York: Routledge.

Crelinsten, R. (2009) *Counterterrorism*. Cambridge: Polity Press.

Curry, M. R. (2004) The profiler's question and the treacherous traveler: narratives of belonging in commercial aviation. *Surveillance and Society*, 1(4): 475–499.

Davies, C. (2007) Humor and protest: jokes under Communism. *International Review of Social History,* 52(15): 291–305.

Davis, M. (1992) Fortress Los Angeles: the militarization of urban space. In M. Sorkin (ed.), *Variations a Theme Park: The New American City and the End of Public Space.* New York: Hill and Wang.

Davis, M. (2006) *Le Pire des Mondes Possibles.* Paris: La Découverte.

Dayan, D., and Katz, E. (1992) *Media Events. The Live Broadcasting of History.* Cambridge, MA: Harvard University Press.

De Andrade de Melo, R. (2002) A pobreza como locus preferencial da violencia. In Helenilda Cavalcanti y Joanildo Burity (organizadores*),* *Polifonia da Miseria, Uma Construcao de Novos Olhares.* Recife, Fundacao Joaquim Nabuco.

De Certeau, M. (1986) The laugh of Michel Foucault. In B. Massumi (trans.), *Heterologies: Discourse on the Other.* Minneapolis: University of Minnesota; 193–198.

de Goede, M. (2008) Beyond risk: premediation and post 9/11 security imagination. *Security Dialogue,* 39(2): 155–176.

de Kool, W. (2008) The signalling of Islamist radicalism and terrorism by Dutch local policeofficers. In S. Virta (ed.), *Policing Meets New Challenges:Preventing Radicalisation and Recruitment.* Tampere: Tampere University Press.

de Larrinaga, M., and Salter, M. (2010) Cold CASE: A Manifesto for Canadian Critical Security Studies. Paper presented at the 82nd Annual Conference of the Canadian Political Science Associatio, Montreal, Concordia University.

De León E., Rosa, C., Ogaldes, C., and Lopez, C. (1999) Guatemala: diagnostico de la problemática posconflicto. In *Violencia Social en Centroamérica: Ensayos Sobre Gobernabilidad y Seguridad Ciudadana.* Managua, Nicaragua, CRIES.

de Lint, W. (2006) Intelligence in policing and security: reflections on scholarship. *Policing & Society: An International Journal of Research and Policy,* 16/1: 1–6.

de Lint, W. (2008a) Intelligent governmentality. *The Windsor Yearbook of Access to Justice,* 27/1: 195–240.

de Lint, W. (2008b) The security double take: the political, simulation and the border. *Surveillance and Society, Special Issue: Smart Borders and Mobilities: Spaces, Zones and Exclusions,* 5/2: 166–187.

de Lint, W., and Bahdi, R. (in press). Brokering access to national security. In M. Larsen and K. Walby (eds.) *Brokering Access in Information.* University of British Columbia Press.

de Lint, W., and Virta, S. (2004) Security in ambiguity. Towards a radical security politics. *Theoretical Criminology,* 8(4): 465–489.

de Lint, W., Virta, S., and Deukmedjian, J. (2007) Simulating control: a shift in policing. *American Behavioural Scientist,* 50/12: 1631–1647.

de Lint, W. and Hall, A. 2009. Intelligent Control: Developments in Public Order Policing in Canada. Toronto: University of Toronto Press.

den Boer, M., Hillebrand, C., and Nölke, A. (2008) Tightening the net around radicalisation and recruitment: notes on the legitimacy of European counter-terrorism initiatives. In S. Virta (ed.), *Policing Meets New Challenges: Preventing Radicalisation and Recruitment.* Tampere: Tampere University Press.

Dean, M. (1999) *Governmentality: Power and Rule in Modern Society.* London: Sage.

Deukmedjian, J. E. (2006) From community to intelligence: executive realignment of RCMP mission. *Canadian Journal of Criminology and Criminal Justice,* 48(4): 523–542.

Deleuze, G., and Guattari, F. (1989) *Mil Mesetas: Capitalismo y Esquizofrenia.* Valencia, España: Pre-textos.

Del Olmo, R. (2000) Ciudades duras y violencia urbana. *Nueva Sociedad,* núm. 167, Caracas.

Desrosières, A. (1998) *The Politics of Large Numbers: A History of Statistical Reasoning.* Cambridge, MA: Harvard University Press.

Diab, R. (2008) *Guantanamo North: Terrorism and the Administration of Justice in Canada.* Halifax, Nova Scotia: Fernwood Publishers.

Digeser, P. 1992. "The Fourth Face of Power." *The Journal of Politics,* 54/4: 977–1007.

Diken, B., and Bagge Laustsen, C. (2005) *The Culture of Exception. Sociology Facing the Camp.* New York: Routledge.

Diprose, R., Stephenson, N., Mills, C., Race, K., and Hawkins, G. (2008) Governing the future: the paradigm of prudence in political technologies of risk management. *Security Dialogue,* 39(2): 267–288.

Donzelot, J. (2008) Michel Foucault and liberal intelligence. *Economy and Society,* 37/1: 115–134.

Dor, D. (2001) *Newspapers Under the Influence.* Tel-Aviv: Babel. [In Hebrew.]

Doty, R. (2009). *The Law into Their own Hands: Immigration and the Politics of Exceptionalism.* Tucson: University of Arizona Press.

Douglas, M. (1991) Jokes. In C. Mukerji and M. Schudson (eds.), *Rethinking Popular Culture: Contemporary Perspectives in Cultural Studies.* Berkeley: University of California Press; 291–310.

Duce, M., and Pérez Perdomo, R. (2005) La seguridad ciudadana y la reforma del sistema de justicia penal en América Latina. *Crimen y Violencia en América Latina.* Colombia: Fondo de Cultura Económica.

Duclos, D. (1995) Topologie de la peur. *Espaces et Sociétés,* 77: 21–44.

Dundes, A., and Hauschild, T. (1983) Auschwitz jokes. *Western Folklore,* 42(4): 249–260.

Dunn, T. (1996) *The Militarization of the U.S.-Mexico Border 1978–1992.* Austin: University of Texas, Center for Mexican American Studies.

Dunn, T. (2009) *Blockading the Border and Human Rights.The El Paso Texas Operation that Remade U.S. Border Enforcement.* Austin: University of Texas Press.

Durkheim, É., and Mauss, M. (1963) *Primitive Classification.* London: Cohen and West.

Drennan, L., and McConnell, A. (2007) *Risk and Crisis Management in the Public Sector.* London: Routledge.

Dyzenhaus, D. (2006) *The Constitution of the Law: Legality in a Time of Emergency.* Cambridge: Cambridge University Press.

Ellin, N. (1977) Shelter from the storm, or form follows fear and vice versa. In N. Ellin and E. J. Blakely (eds), *Architecture of Fear.* NY: Princeton Architectural Press.

Ellis, B. (2001) A Model of Collecting and Interpreting World Trade Centre Disaster Jokes *New Directions in Folklore 5.* On-line journal available at http://www.temple.edu/isllc/newfolk/wtchumor.html

Ellis, B. (2002) Making a Big Apple Crumble: The Role of Humor in Constructing a Global Response to Disaster *New Directions in Folklore 6.* On-line journal available at http://www.temple.edu/isllc/newfolk/bigapple/bigapple1.html

Enloe, C. (2007) *Globalization & Militarism: Feminists Make the Link.* New York: Rowman & Littlefield.

Ericson, R. V. (2007) *Crime in an Insecure World.* Cambridge: Polity Press.

Eschbach, K., Hagan, J., Rodríguez, N., Hernández-León, R., and Bailey, S. (1999) Death at the Border. *International Migration Review,* 33(2): 430–454.

Evans-Pritchard, E. E. (1965) *Witchcraft, Oracles and Magic among the Azande.* Oxford: Clarendon Press.

Ewald, F. (1991) Insurance and risk. In G. Burchill, C. Gordon, and P. Miller (eds.), *The Foucault Effect: Studies in Governmentality.* University of Chicago Press; 197–210.

Facultad Latinoamericana de Ciencias Sociales (FLACSO). (2007) In L. Dammert (coord.), "Report on the Security Sector in Latin America and Caribbean," Santiago, Chile.

Falk, R. A. (2004) *The Declining World Order: America's Imperial Geopolitics.* New York; Routledge.

Feldman, L. C. (2007) Terminal exceptions: law and sovereignty at the airport threshold. *Law, Culture and the Humanities,* 3(2): 320–344.

Ferguson, S. (1976). Satellite television: Promise or threat to the third world? *The International and Intercultural Communication Annual,* 3: 121–129.

Feeley, M., and Simon, J. (1994) Actuarial justice: The emerging new criminal law. In D. Nelken (ed.), *The Futures of Criminology.* London: Sage Publications; 171–184.

Fierke, K. M. (2007). *Critical Approaches to International Security.* Cambridge: Polity.

Fine, G. A. (2004) Review of *Engaging Humor* by Elliot Oring. *Journal of American Folklore,* 117(464): 224–255.

Fine, G. A., and de Soucey, M. (2005) Joking cultures: humor themes as regulation in group life. *Humor,* 18(1): 1–22.

Floyd, R. (2007) Human security and the Copenhagen School's securitization approach: conceptualizing human security as a securitizing move. *Human Security Journal,* 5(winter): 38–49.

Flynn, S. E. (2007) *The Edge of Disaster: Rebuilding a Resilient Nation.* New York: Random House.

Foucault, M. (1970) *The Order of Things: An Archaeology of the Human Sciences.* New York: Vintage.

Foucault, M. (1977) In A. Sheridan (trans.), *Discipline and Punish: The Birth of the Prison.* New York: Vintage.

Foucault, M. (1979) *Discipline and Punish: The Birth of a Prison.* New York: Random House.

Foucault, M. (1994) On the government of the living. In R. Hurley et al. (trans.) and P. Rabinow (ed.), *Essential Works of Michel Foucault 1954–1984. Ethics.* New York: New Press; 81–85.

Foucault, M. (2000a) Truth and power. In R. Hurley et al. (trans.) J. D. Faubion (ed.), *Essential Works of Michel Foucault 1954–1984. Power.* New York: New Press; 1–89.

Foucault, M. (2000b) Truth and juridical forms. In R. Hurley et al. (trans.) and J. D. Faubion (ed.), *Essential Works of Michel Foucault 1954–1984. Power.* New York: New Press; 1–89.

Foucault, M. (2001) In G. Burchill (trans.) and F. Gros (eds.). *The Hermeneutics of the Subject: Lectures at the Collège de France 1981–1982.* New York: Picador. PAGE NUMBERS

Foucault, M. (2003) *Abnormal: Lectures at the College de France, 1974–1975.* New York: Picador.

Foucault, M. (2004) *Sécurité, Territoire, Population. Cours au Collège de France 1977–1978.* Seuil, Gallimard, Paris, France.

Foucault, M. (2007[2004]) In G. Burchell (trans.), *Security, Territory, Population. Lectures at the Collège de France 1977–1978.* New York: Palgrave-Macmillan.

Foucault, M. (2008) In G. Burchill (trans.) and M. Senellart (ed.), *The Birth of Biopolitics: Lectures at the Collège de France 1978–1979.* New York: Palgrave. PAGEs

Frank, R. (2004) When the going gets tough, the tough go photoshopping: September 11 and the newslore of vengeance and victimization. *New Media & Society,* 6(5): 633–658.

Frankfort, H. 1978 [1948] *Kingship and the Gods: A Study of Ancient Near Eastern Religion as the Integration of Society and Nature.* Chicago, IL: University of Chicago Press.

Freiberg, K., and Freiberg, J. (1996) *NUTS! Southwest Airlines' Crazy Recipe for Business and Personal Success*. Austin, TX: Bard Press.

Freedman, L. (2000) "Human Rights and Women's Health" *Women and Health* Marlene Goldman and Maureen Hatch (eds.) New York: Academic Press, 428–438.

Freeman, L. (2008) Déjà vu: La política antidrogas en la relación México-Estados Unidos. *Foreign Affaire en Español*, ITAM, México D. F., México, 8(3): 15–23.

Freud, S. (1960) In J. Strachey (trans.) and A. Richards (ed.), *Jokes and Their Relation to the Unconscious*. London: Penguin.

Freud, S. (1961) Humour. In J. Strachey (trans.) and A. Dickson (ed.), *Art and Literature*. London: Penguin; 425–434.

Friedman, J. (1999). Cultural insecurities and global class formation. In M. Tehranian (ed.), *Worlds Apart: Human Security and Global Governence*. London: I. B. Tauris: 125–152.

Frühling, H. (2005) La reforma de la policía y el proceso de democratización. *Crimen y Violencia en América Latina*. Colombia: Fondo de Cultura Económica. COMPLETE

Fuller, G. (2002) The arrow-directional semiotics: wayfinding in transit. *Social Semiotics* 12(3): 131–144.

Fuller, G., and Harley, R. (2005) *Aviopolis: A Book About Airports*. London: Black Dog Publishing.

Fuller, G. (2008) Welcome to Windows 2.1: Motions aesthetics at the airport. In M. B. Salter (ed.), *Politics at the Airport*. Minneapolis: University of Minnesota Press; 161–173.

Fukuyama, F. (1989) The end of history? *National Interest*, 16: 3–18.

Furedi, F. (2002) *Culture of Fear: Risk Taking and the Morality of Low Expectation*. London: Continuum.

Furedi, F. (2005) Terrorism and the politics of fear. In C. Hale, K. Hayward, A. Wahidin, and E. Wincup (eds.), *Criminology*. Oxford: Oxford University Press.

Furedi, F. (2005) *Politics of Fear. Beyond Left and Right*. London: Continuum.

Furedi, F., (2007) *Invitation to Terror: The Expanding Empire of the Unknown*. London: Continuum Press.

Fyke, J., and Meyer, M. (2008) No todo lo que es oro brilla y no todo lo que brilla es oro ¿Amenazas para México? *Foreign Affaire en Español*. ITAM, México D. F., México; 8(3): 25–31.

Ganser, D. 2005. "Terrorism in Western Europe: An Approach to NATO's Secret Stay-Behind Armies," *Whitehead Journal of Diplomacy and International Relations*. 6/1: 69-94

García, P. J. , and Villá, M. (2001) De la sociedad vigilante a la urbanidad preventive. *Perfiles Latinoamericanos*, núm. 19.

Garfinkel, H. (1956) Conditions of successful degradation ceremonies. *The American Journal of Sociology*, 61/5: 420–424.

Garland, D. (1990) *Punishment and Modern Society: A Study in Social Theory*. University of Chicago Press.

Garland, D. (2000) The culture of control in high crime societies: some preconditions of recent 'law and order' policies. *British Journal of Criminology*, 40: 347–375.

Gellman, B., and Schmidt, S. (2002) Shadow government is at work in secret. *Washington Post*, March, 1, A01.

Giddens, A. (1987) *The Nation State and Violence*. Berkeley: University of California Press.

Giddens, A. (1991) *Modernity and Self-Identity: Self and Society in the Late Modern Age*. Stanford, CA: Stanford University Press.

Giglia, A. (2001) Los espacios residenciales cerrados: el caso de Villa Olímpica. In M. A. Portal (coord.). *Vivir la diversidad. Identidades y culturas en dos contextos urbanos*, México, CONACYT.

Gilmore, R. W., and Gilmore, C. (2008) Restating the obvious. In M. Sorkin (ed.), *Indefensible Space: The Architecture of the National Insecurity State*. New York: Routledge; 141–162.

Giraldi, P. (2008) FBI whistleblower Sibel Edmonds spills her secrets. *American Conservative*, January 28.

Gittell, J. (2002) *The Southwest Airlines Way: Using the Power of Relationships to Achieve High Performance*. New York: McGraw-Hill.

Glassner, B. (1999) *The Culture of Fear: Why Americans are Afraid of the Wrong Things*. New York: Basic Books.

Goffman, E. (1986 [1974]). *Frame Analysis. An Essay on the Organization of Experience*. Chicago: Northwestern University Press.

Goldsmith, A. (2008) The governance of terror: precautionary logic and counterterrorist law reform after September 11. *Law & Policy*, 30(2). Holloway, J. (2002) *Change the World Without taking Power: the Meaning of Revolution Today*. London: Pluto Press.

Gordon, A. (2004) *Naked Airport: A Cultural History of the World's Most Revolutionary Structure*. New York: Metropolitan Books.

Gross, M. L. (2003) Fighting by other means in the Mideast: a critical analysis of Israel's assassination policy. *Political Studies,* 51: 350–368.

Grusin, R. (2004) Premediation. *Criticism*, 46(1): 17–39.

Guaqueta, A. (2005) Change and continuity in U.S–Colombian relations and the war against drugs. *Journal of Drug Issues,* 35(1): 27–56.

Habermas, J. (2001) *The Postnational Constellation: Political Essays*. Cambridge: MIT Press.

Hacking, I. (1985) Making up people. In T. L. Heller, M. Sosna, and D. E. Wellbery (eds.), *Reconstructing Individualism*. Stanford, CA: Stanford University.

*The Hague Programme: Strenghtening Freedom, Security and Justice in the European Union*. Council of the European Union. Brussels, November 2004.

Handelman, D. (1998) *Models and Mirrors: Towards an Anthropology of Public Events*. 2nd Edition. New York, NY and Oxford, UK: Berghahn Books.

Handelman, D. (1992) Passages to play: paradox and process. *Play and Culture,* 5: 1–19.

Handelman, D. (2004) *Nationalism and the Israeli State: Bureaucratic Logic in Public Events*. Oxford: Berg.

Handelman, D. (2006a) Framing. In J. Kreinath, J. Snoek, and M. Stausberg (eds.), *Theorizing Ritual*. Leiden: Brill; 571–582.

Handelman, D. (2006b) Postlude: Towards a braiding of frame. In D. Shulman and D. Thiagarajan (eds.), *Behind the Mask: Dance, Healing, and Possession in South India*. Ann Arbor: University of Michigan; 248–264.

Handelman, D., and Lindquist, G. (eds.) (2005) *Ritual in Its Own Right*. New York, Oxford: Berghahn Books.

Handy, J. (2004) Chicken thieves, witches and judges: vigilante justice and customary law in Guatemala. *Journal of Latin American Studies*, 36(3): 533–561.

Haggerty K. D., and Ericson, R. V. (2000).The surveillant assemblage. *British Journal of Sociology,* 51(4): 605–22.

Hajjar, L. (2005) *Courting Conflict: The Israeli Military Court System in the West Bank, and Gaza*. Berkeley: University of California Press.

Harcourt, B. (2003) The shaping of chance: actuarial models and criminal profiling at the turn of twenty-first century. *University of Chicago Law Review*, 70/1: 105–128.

Hass, E. (2009) International Women's Media Foundation honors Israeli journalist Amira Hass with 2009 Lifetime Achievement Award. *Democracy Now*, October 21.

Helman, S. (1999) From soldiering and motherhood to citizenship: a study of four Israeli peace protest movements. *Social Politics: International Studies in Gender, State & Society,* 6(3): 292–313.

Hinton, M. S. (2006) *The State on the Streets: Police and Politics in Argentina and Brazil, United States of America.* Boulder, CO: Lynner Rienner Publishers.

Hobsbawm, E. J. (1990) *Nations and Nationalism Since 1780: Programme, Myth, Reality.* Cambridge: Cambridge University Press.

Hoffman, B. (1999). Introduction. In I. Lesser, B. Hoffman, J. Arquilla, D. Ronfeldt, M. Zanini, and B. Jenkins (eds.), *Countering the New Terrorism.* Santa Monica: RAND.

Holquist, P. (1997). "Information is the alpha and omega of our work": Bolshevik surveillance in its pan-European context. *Journal of Modern History,* 69(3), 415–450 .

Hornquist, M. (2004) The birth of public order policy. *Race and Class,* 46(1): 30–52.

Hörnqvist, M. (2007) The organised nature of power. On productive and repressive interventions based on considerations of risk. *Dissertations in Criminology,* no 21, Stockholm University.

Huang, J. (1995) Structural disarticulation and third world human development. *International Journal of Comparative Sociology,* Dharwar, 36(3–4): 164–183.

Hughes, G., and Rowe, M. (2007) Neighbourhood policing and community safety: researching the instabilities of the local governance of crime, disorder and security in contemporary UK. *Criminology and Criminal Justice,* 7(4).

Humphreys, S. (2006) Legalizing Lawlessness: On Giorgio Agamben's state of exception. *The European Journal of International Law ,* 17(3): 677–687.

Huysmans, J. (1998) Security! What do you mean? From concept to thick signifier. *European Journal of International Relations,* 4(2): 226–255.

Huysmans, J. (2004) Minding exceptions: the politics of insecurity and liberal democracy. *Contemporary Political Theory,* 3: 321–341.

Isin, E. (2004) The neurotic citizen. *Citizenship Studies,* 8(3): 217–235.

Iyer, P. (2001) *The Global Soul: Jet Lag, Shopping Malls and the Search for Home.* New York.

Jaffer, J. (2007) *Administration of Torture: A Documentary Record From Washington to Abu Ghraib and Beyond.* New York: Columbia University Press.

Jarrín R., Osvaldo (2004) La junta de seguridad ciudadana: el Caso Sucumbios. *Seguridad ciudadana y orden público en América Latina,* México, Editorial Nueva Sociedad.

Jenkins, D. (2002) A primer on airport security. In A. Roberts (ed.)., *Governance and Public Security.* New York: Campbell Public Affairs Institute, Maxwell School, Syracuse University; 69–94.

Jenkins, D. (2003) In support of Canada's Anti-Terrorism Act: a comparison of Canadian, British, and American anti-terrorism law. *Saskatchewan Law Review,* 66: 419–54.

Jiang, F. (ed.). (2005) *Media Abroad in China.* Beijing: CFLACPC (China Federation of Literary and Art Circles Publishing Corporation). [In Chinese.]

Jones, T. (2000) Digital rule. Punishment, control and technology. *Punishment and Society,* 2: 5–22

Kaldor, M. (2006) *New & Old Wars. Organized Violence in a Global Era.* Cambridge: Polity Press.

Kalajdzic, J. (2009) Access to Justice for the Wrongfully Accused in National Security Investigations, (2009) 2 Windsor Yearbook of Access to Justice, XXX (forthcoming).

Kearon, T., Mythen, G., and Walklate, S. (2007) Making sense of the terrorist risk: public perceptions of emergency advice. *Security Journal,* 20(2): 77–95.

Kellner, D. (2002) September 11 and terror war: The Bush legacy and the risks of unilateralism. *Logos,* 1(4): 19–41.

Kelman, H. C. (1999) The interdependence of Israeli and Palestinian national identities: the role of the other in existential conflicts. *Journal of Social Issues,* 55(3): 581–600.

Ketcham, C. (2007) High-fivers and art student spies: what did Israel know in advance of the 9/11 attacks? *Counterpunch,* March 3.

Khazzoom, A. (2003) The great chain of Orientalism: Jewish identity, stigma management and ethnic exclusion in Israel. *American Sociological Review,* 68(4): 481–510.

Kimmerling, B. (1985) The Interrupted System: Israeli Civilians in War and Routine *Times.* Transaction Books.

Kimmerling, B. (2001) *The Invention and Decline of Israeliness: State, Society, and the Military.* Berkley: The University of California Press.

King, M. (1993) The 'truth' about autopoiesis. *Journal of Law and Society,* 20(2), summer: 218–236.

Kleemans, E. R. (2008) Introduction to special issue: Organised crime, terrorism and European Criminology. *European Journal of Criminology,* 5(1).

Klein, N. (2008) *The Shock Doctrine: The Rise of Disaster Capitalism.* Vintage.

Koonings, K., and Kruijt, D. (2007) Fractured cities, second-class citizenship and urban violence. In K. Koonings and D. Kruijt (eds.), *Fractured Cities: Social-Exclusion, Urban Violence & Contested Spaces in Latin America.* London: Zed Books; 7–22.

Korn, A. (2004) Israeli press and the war against terrorism: the construction of the 'liquidation policy.' *Crime, Law & Social Change,* 41: 209–234.

Kretsedemas, P., and Brotherton, D. (eds.) (2008) *Keeping Out the Other: Immigration Enforcement Today.* New York: Columbia University Press.

Kuipers, G. (2005) Where was King Kong when we needed him? Public discourse, digital disaster jokes, and the functions of laughter after 9/11. *The Journal of American Culture,* 28(1):70–83.

Lacarrieu, M., and Thullier, G. (2001) Las urbanizaciones privadas en Buenos Aires y su significación. *Perfiles Latinoamericanos,* núm. 19.

Lacquer, W. (2000) *The New Terrorism: Fanaticism and the Arms of Mass Destruction.* London: Oxford University Press.

Lambert, R. (2008) Ignoring the lessons of the past. *Criminal Justice Matters,* 73(1): 22–23.

Lazar, N. C. (2006) Must exceptionalism prove the rule? An angle on emergency government in the history of political thought. *Politics and Society,* 34(2): 245–275.

Lappalainen, P. (2002) *Poliittisen Tyylin Taito.* Tampere: Vastapaino.

Leeds, E. (2007) Rio de Janeiro. In K. Koonings and D. Kruijt (eds.), *Fractured Cities: Social Exclusion, Urban Violence & Contested Spaces in Latin America.* London: Zed Books; 23–35.

Lesser, I., Hoffman, B., Arquilla, J., Ronfeldt, D., Zanini, M., and Jenkins, B. (eds.) (1999), *Countering the New Terrorism.* Santa Monica: RAND.

Levy, D., and Sznaider, N. (2006) Sovereignty transformed: a sociology of human rights. *The British Journal of Sociology,* 57(4).

Levi, M. (2009) Making counter-law: on having no apparent purpose in Chicago. *British Journal of Criminology,* 49: 131–149.

Lin, H.-Y. (1999). Cultural security: The deep structure and subject of national security. *Journal of National Security,* 8: 31–33. [In Chinese.]

Lloyd, J. (2003) Airport technology, travel, and consumption. *Space and Culture,* 6: 93–109.

Lippmann, W. (1922 [1997]) *Public Opinion.* New York: Free Press Paperbacks.

Lipset, D. (1980) *Gregory Bateson: The Legacy of a Scientist.* Boston, MA: Beacon Press.

Liu, Y.-J. (2001). On the basic meaning of national security and its history. *Journal of North China Electric Power University (Social Sciences),* 4: 62–65. [In Chinese.]

Loader, I. (2002) Policing, securitization and democratization in Europe. *Criminal Justice*, 2(2): 125–153.

Loader, I., and Walker, N. (2007) *Civilizing Security*. Cambridge: Cambridge University Press.

Londoño, J. L., and Guerrero, R. (1999) *Violencia en América Latina. Epidemiología y costos*. Banco Interamericano de Desarrollo, Documento de trabajo R-375.

Lustgarten, L., and Leigh, I. (1994*) In From the Cold: National Security and Parliamentary Democracy*. Oxford: Clarendon Press.

Lustick, I. (1993) *Unsettled States, Disputed Lands: Britain and Ireland, France and Algeria, Israel and the West Bank-Gaza*. Ithaca: Cornell University Press.

Lyng, S. (1990) Edgework: a social psychological analysis of voluntary risk taking. *American Journal of Sociology*, 95(4): 851–886

Lyon, D. (2003) Airports as data filters: converging surveillance systems after September 11th. *Information, Communication and Ethics in Society,* 1(1):13–20.

Lyon, D. (2006) Airport screening, surveillance, and social sorting: Canadian responses to the 9/11 in context. *Canadian Journal of Criminology and Criminal Justice*, 48(3): 397–411.

Lyotard, J.-F. (1986) *L'Enthousiasme*. Paris: Galilée.

Macioti, M. I. (2002) Pilgrimages of yesterday, jubilees of today. In W. Swatos and L. Tomasi (eds.), *From Medieval Pilgrimage to Religious Tourism. The Social and Cultural Economics of Piety*. Praeger.

Mann, J. 2004a. "The Armegeddon Plan." The Atlantic Monthly. March.

Mann, J. (2004a) *Rise of the Vulcans: The History of Bush's War Cabinet*. New York: Penguin.

Manwaring, Max et.al. (2003) *Building Regional Security Cooperation in the Western Hemisphere: Issues and Recommendations*. Shaping the regional environment of security in Latin America, Special Series. US Army War College and North South Centre, University of Miami.

Martin, H.-P., and Shuman, H. (1998) *Las Trampas de la Globalización: El Ataque Contra a la Democracia y el Bienestar*. España, Taurus.

Martínez, Oscar. 1996. *Border People*. Tucson: University of Arizona Press.

Masco, J. (2008) Survival is your business: engineering ruins and affect in nuclear America. *Cultural Anthropology*, 23(2): 361–398.

Masco, J. (2006) *The Nuclear Borderlands: The Manhattan Project in Post Cold-War New Mexico*. Princeton: Princeton University Press.

McCulloch, J., and Pickering, S. (2009) Pre-crime and counter-terrorism: imagining future crime in the 'War on Terror.' *British Journal of Criminology*, advance access archive, doi:10.1093/bjc/azp023.

McGhee, D. (2008) *The End of Multiculturalism: Terrorism, Integration and Human Rights*, London: McGraw Hill.

Mesquita P. N., and Loche, A. (2005) Las asociaciones entre la policía y la comunidad en el Brasil. *Crimen y Violencia en América Latina*. Colombia: Fondo de Cultura Económica. EDITORS

Miles, S. J., and Mangold, W. G. (2005) Positioning Southwest Airlines through employee branding. *Business Horizons,* 48(6): 535–545.

Milnes, P. D. (2008). *Cultural Interaction Analysis*. 2nd ed. Guildford, WA: Belco Consulting.

Morgan, M. (2004) The origins of terrorism. *Parameters*, spring edition: 29–43.

Morrison, A., Buvivnic, M., and Shifter, M. (2005) América violenta: factores de riesgo, consecuencias e implicaciones para las políticas sobre la violencia social y domestica. *Crimen y Violencia en América Latina*. Colombia: Fondo de Cultura Económica.

Mutimer, D. (2009) My critique is bigger than yours: constituting exclusions in critical security studies. *Studies in Social Justice*, 3/1: 9–22

Mythen, G. (2004) *Ulrich Beck: A Critical Introduction to the Risk Society*. London: Pluto Press.

Mythen, G. (2005) From goods to bads? Revisiting the political economy of risk. *Sociological Research Online*, 10(3): http://www.socresonline.org.uk/10/3/mythen.html. (accessed 4 July 2009).

Mythen, G. (2008) Sociology and the art of risk. *Sociology Compass*, 2/1: 299–316.

Mythen, G., and Walklate, S. (2006a) Criminology and terrorism: which thesis? Risk society or governmentality?' *The British Journal of Criminology*, 46(3): 379–398.

Mythen, G., and Walklate, S. (2006b) Communicating the terrorist risk: harnessing a culture of fear? *Crime, Media, Culture: An International Journal*, 2(2): 123–142.

Mythen, G., and Walklate, S. (2008) Terrorism, risk and international security: the perils of asking what if? *Security Dialogue*, 39(2–3): 221–242.

Mythen, G., Walklate, S., and Khan, F. (2009) 'I'm a Muslim, but I'm not a Terrorist': Risk, victimization and the negotiation of risky identities. *British Journal of Criminology*, doi:10.1093/bjc/azp032, viewable on advance access archive at: http://bjc.oxfordjournals.org/cgi/content/abstract/azp032v1.

Naím, M. (2005) *Illicit*. New York: Random House.

Nathan, D. (1986) *Women and Other Aliens: Essays from the U.S.-Mexico Border*. El Paso, TX: Cinco Puntos Press.

Neira, A. (1995) *La Sustentabilidad de la Metropolis Latinoamericanas, México*. Foro del Ajusco II. El Colegio de México-PNUMA.

Nelson, A. K. (2007) The evolution of the national security state. In A. Bacevich (ed.), *Ubiquitous and Endless*. 265–301.

Neocleous, M. (2006) From social to national security: on the fabrication of economic order. *Security Dialogue*, 37(3): 363–384.

Neocleous , M. (2008) *Critique of Security*. Edinburgh: Edinburgh University Press.

Newburn, T. (2001) The modification of policing: security networks in the late modern city. In *Urban Studies*. London: vol. 38, no. 5–6, pp. 829–848.

Nordstrum, C. (2006) *Global Outlaws*. Berkeley: University of California Press.

Novaes, J. R. (2002) Trábalo infantil: exclusao social. In H. Cavalcanti and J. Burity (organizadores*)*, *Polifonia da Miseria, Uma Construcao de Novos Alhares*. Recife, Fundacao Joaquim Nabuco.

Nye, J. S. (2004) *Soft Power. The Means to Success in World Politics*. New York: Public Affairs.

Offner, A. (2007) Liberation or dominance? The ideology of U.S. national security policy. In A. Bacevich (ed), *The Long War. A History of US National Security Policy Since World War II*. Columbia: Columbia University Press.

O'Connor, D., and de Lint, W. (2009) Frontier governance: the folding of the Canada-US border. *Studies in Social Justice*, 3(1): 39–66.

O'Donnell, (1999) *Counterpoints: Selected Essays on Authoritarianism and Democratization*. Notre Dame, IN: University of Notre Dame Press.

O'Malley, P. (2008) Experiments in risk and justice. *Theoretical Criminology*, 12: 451–469.

O' Malley, P. (2009) Experiments in risk and criminal justice. *Theoretical Criminology*, 12(4): 451–469.

O'Neill, W. (2007) The 'Good' War. National Security and American Culture. In A. Bacevich (ed.) 517–549.

Ould Mohamedou, M. (2007) *Understanding Al Qaeda: The Transformation of War*. London: Pluto Press.

Oring, E. (1987) Jokes and the discourse on disaster. *The Journal of American Folklore*, 100(397): 276–286.

Oring, E. (2003) *Engaging Humor*. Urbana: University of Illinois Press.

Packer, J. (2003) Disciplining mobility: governing and safety. In J. Z. Bratich, J. Packer, and C. McCarthy (eds.), *Foucault, Cultural Studies and Governmentality*. Albany: State University of New York Press; 135–161.

Paolucci, P., and Richardson, M. (2006) Sociology of humor and a critical dramaturgy. *Symbolic Interaction,* 29(3): 331–348.

Palonen, K. (1993) From Policy and Polity to Politicking and Politicization. In Palonen and Parvikko (eds.), Reading the Political, Exploring the Margins of Politics. *The Finnish Political Science Association.* Helsinki.

Pape, R. (2003) The strategic logic of suicide terrorism. *American Political Science Review,* 97(3): 1–19.

Parks, L. (2007) Points of departure: The culture of US airport screening. *Journal of Visual Culture,* 6(2): 183–200.

Pascual, M. (2007) Violencia y miedo urbano: reflejos de la ciudad de México. In R. Sosa (coord.), *Sujetos, Víctimas y Territorios de la Violencia en América Latina.* México: Universidad de la Ciudad de México.

Pastor, M., and Wise, C. (1999) Stabilization and its discontents: Argentina's economic restructuring Brazil. In P. R. Kingstone and T. J. Power (eds.), *Democratic Brazil: Actors, Institutions, and Processes.* Pittsburgh: University of Pittsburgh Press.

Patane, V. (2006) Recent Italian efforts to respond to terrorism at the legislative level. *Journal of International Criminal Justice,* 4: 1166–1180.

Patton, C. V., and Sawicki, D. S. (1993) *Basic Methods of Policy Analysis and Planning.* New Jersey: Prentice Hall.

Pegoraro, J. (2000) Violencia delictiva, inseguridad urbana. La construcción social de la inseguridad ciudadana. *Nueva Sociedad,* núm. 167.

Peled, Y. (1993) Strangers in utopia: the civic status of the Palestinians in Israel. *Teoria Ve'Bikoret* (Theory and Criticism) 3: 21–35. [In Hebrew.]

Peled, Y., and Shafir, G. (1996) The roots of peacemaking: the dynamics of citizenship in Israel, 1948–93. *International Journal of Middle East Studies,* 28(3): 391–413.

Peralva, A. (2001) *Violence et Démocratie. Le Paradoxe Brésilien.* Paris, Francia, Balland.

Pither, K. (2008) *Dark Days: The Story of Four Canadians Tortured in the Name of Fighting Terror.* Toronto: Viking Canada.

Prados, J. (2006) *Safe for Democracy: The Secret Wars of the CIA.* Ivan R Dee: Chicago.

Prévôt, S., and Marie-France (2001) "Fragmentación espacial y social : conceptos y realidades, *Perfiles Latinoamericanos,* núm. 19, México, FLACSO, pp. 33–56.

Priest, D., and Gellman, B. (2002) U.S decries abuse but defends interrogation. *Washington Post,* Thursday, December 26.

Pue, Wesley, The War on Terror: Constitutional Governance in a State of Permanent Warfare? (2003) Osgoode Hall Law Journal pp. 267–292, 2003.

Radcliffe, S. A. (2007) Latin American indigenous geographies of fear: living in the shadow of racism, lack of development, and anti-terror measures. *Annals of the Association of American Geographers,* 97(2): 385–397.

Ranstorp, M. (2007) Introduction: mapping terrorism research—challenges and priorities. In M. Ranstorp (ed.), *Mapping Terrorism Research.* New York: Routledge.

Ratcliffe, J. (ed.) (2004). *Strategic Thinking in Criminal Intelligence.* Marrickville, Australia: Federation Press.

Ratcliffe, J. (2008) *Intelligence-Led Policing.* Cullompton: Willan Publishing.

Ratner, S. R. (2001) *Accountability for Human Rights Atrocities in International Law.* Cambridge: Cambridge University Press.

Razack, S. (2008) *Casting Out: The Eviction of Muslims from Western Law and Politics.* Toronto: University of Toronto Press.

Reus-Smit, C. (1992) Realist and resistance utopias: Community, security and political action in the new Europe. *Millennium—Journal of International Studies,* 21(1): 1–28.

Rico, J. M., and Chinchilla, L. (2002) *Seguridad Ciudadana en América Latina.* México: Siglo Veintiuno Editores.

Rivera, G., and Wilkey, W. (2002) Plan Colombia: a successful long-term effort. *Corrections Today*, 64(7): 142.

Roach, K. (2001) The dangers of a charter-proof and crime-based response to terrorism. In R. D. and Patrick Maclem (eds.), *The Security of Freedom: Essays on Canada`s Anti-Terrorism Bill*.Toronto: University of Toronto Press; 131–150.

Roach, K. (2003) *September 11: Consequences for Canada*. Montreal: McGill-Queen's University Press.

Roberts, B. (2008) 'Minister warns of peril as he pushes for 42-day lock-up', *Daily Mirror*, 23 January.

Rosanvallon, P. (2006) *La Contre-Democratie*. Vastademokratia. Vastapaino. Tampere. [In Finnish.]

Ruddock, P. (2004) A new framework: counter-terrorism and the rule of law. *The Sydney Papers* ,16(2): 112–121.

Romero Vázquez, B. (2000) Notas para un modelo alternativo de seguridad ciudadana. *Diálogo y Debate de Cultura Política*, 12: 101–119.

Romo, D. (2005) Ringside Seat to a Revolution: an Underground Cultural History of El Paso and Juárez: 1893–1923. El Paso: Cinco Puntos Press.

Ron, J. (2000) Savage restraint: Israel, Palestine and the dialectics of legal repression. *Social Problems*, 47(4): 445–472.

Rose, N. 1999. Powers of Freedom: Reframing Political Thought. New York: Cambridge University Press.

Rotker, S. (2000) Ciudades escritas por la violencia (a modo de introducción). In S. Rotker (ed.), *Ciudadanías del Miedo*. Caracas, Venezuela, Nueva Sociedad–The State University of New Jersey.

Ruiz Harrell, R. (1998) *Inseguridad y Mal Gobierno*. México: Sansores&Aljure.

Ruppert, M. 2004. Crossing the Rubicon: The Decline of the American Empire in the Age of Peak Oil. Gabriola Island: New Society Publishers.

Ruesch, J., and Bateson, G. (1951) *Communication: The Social Matrix of Psychiatry*. New York: Norton.

Saban, I., Jury, V., Hatib, J., Hanin N., Solomon, E., and Shchade, N. (2008) *Confidential Evidence and Legal Critic of Administrative Arrest*. Haifa: The Clinique for the Rights of the Arab Minority, Law School, Haifa University. [In Hebrew.]

Sáenz, B. A. (1992) Exile. In *Flowers for the Broken*. Seattle: Broken Moon Press.

Safferling, C. (2006) Terror and law: German responses to 9/11. *Journal of International Criminal Justice*, 4: 1152–1165.

Salamon, L. (2002) *The Tools of Government: A Guide to the New Governance*. Oxford University Press.

Salazar, G. (2001) "Origen y motivos de la violencia urbana en Santiago y Rancagua (Chile, 1980–1999). In K. Bodemer et al. (eds.), *Violencia y Regulación de Conflictos en América Latina*. Caracas, Nueva Sociedad, Asociación Alemana de Investigación sobre América Latina-Heinrich Boll Stiftung.

Saldomando, Á. (1999) Nicaragua: los rostros de la violencia. In *Violencia Social en Centroamérica: Ensayos Sobre Gobernabilidad y Seguridad Ciudadana*. Managua, Nicaragua, CRIES.

Salter, M. (2003) *Rights of Passage: The Passport in International Relations*. Boulder, CO: Lynn Rienner Publishers.

Salter, M. B. (2006) The global visa regime and the political technologies of the international self: borders, bodies, biopolitics. *Alternatives: Global, Local, Political*, 31(2): 167–189.

Salter, M. B. (2007) Governmentalities of an airport: Heterotopia and confession. *International Political Sociology*, 1(1): 49–66.

Salter, M. B. (2008) Airport assemblage. In M. B. Salter (ed.), *Politics at the Airport*. Minneapolis: University of Minnesota Press; ix–xix.

Salter, M. (2008) Risk quantification and aviation security. *Security Dialogue*, 39(2): 243–266.

Salter, M. B. (2008a) Imagining numbers: risk, quantification and aviation security. *Security Dialogue,* 39(2–3): 243–266.

Sands, P. (2009) *Torture Team: Rumsfeld's Memo and the Betrayal of American Values.* New York: Palgrave Macmillan.

Santana, A. (2002) America Latina: pobreza, drogas y economía subterranean. In H. Cavalcanti and J. Burity (organizadores), *Polifonia da Miseria, Uma Construcao de Novos Olhares.* Recife, Fundacao Joaquim Nabuco.

Sassen, S. (2008) *Territory, Authority, Rights. From Medieval to Global Assemblages.* Princeton, NJ: Princeton University Press.

Sasson-Levy, O., and Rappoport, T. (2003) Body, gender, and knowledge in protest movements: The Israeli case. *Gender and Society,* 17(3): 379–403.

Scarry, E. (1985) *The Body in Pain: The Making and Unmaking of the World.* Toronto: Oxford Univerity Press.

Scheppele, K. L. (2004) Law in a time of emergency: states of exception and the temptation of 9/11. *University of Pennsylvania Journal of Constitutional Law,* 6:1001–1180.

Schlesinger, P. (1991) *Media, State and Nation: Political Violence and Collective Identities.* London: Sage.

Schmitt, C. (1985) In G. Schwab (trans.), *Political Theology: Four Chapters on the Concept of Sovereignty.* Cambridge, MA: MIT Press.

Schteingart, M. (2001) La división social del espacio en las ciudades. *Perfiles Latinoamericanos,* num. 19.

Silke, A. (2008) Holy warriors: exploring the psychological processes of jihadi radicalisation. *European Journal of Criminology,* 5(1): 99–123.

Silvestri, S. (2008) Revising the European Security Strategy. Paper presented in the international conference "European Interests and Strategic Options" in Paris. May 2008.

Sinai, J. (2007) New trends in terrorism studies. In M. Ranstorp (ed.), *Mapping Terrorism Research.* New York: Routledge.

Simmel, G. (1994) The picture frame: an aesthetic study. Theory, Culture and Society, 11(1): 11–17.

Simonett, H. (2001) Narcorridos: an emerging micromusic of Nuevo L. A. *Ethnomusicology,* 45(2).

Skocpol, T. (1985) Strategies of analysis. In: P. Evans, D. Rueschemeyer, and T. Skocpol (eds.), *Bringing The State Back In.* Cambridge: University Press.

Slevin, P. (2010) Deportation of illegal immigrants increases under Obama administration. *Washington Post.* Available online at http://www.washingtonpost.com/wp-dyn/content/article/2010/07/25/AR2010072501790.html?hpid=topnews. Accessed October 19, 2010.

Sloggett, D. (2008a) *Perspectives on Terrorism Recruitment and Community Impact Assessment.* Paper presented in Police National CBRN Centre, London, June 2008.

Sloggett, D. (2008b) *Perspectives on the CBRN threat to the UK.* Paper presented in Police National CBRN Centre, London, June 2008.

Smulovitz, C. (2005) La inseguridad y el miedo de la ciudadanía: Respuestas públicas y privadas en la Argentina. *Crimen y Violencia en América Latina.* Colombia: Fondo de Cultura Económica.

Snow, D., and Corrigall-Brown, C. (2005) Falling on deaf ears: confronting the prospect of non-resonant frames. In Croteau, Ryan, and Hoynes (eds.), *Rhyming Hope and History: Activism and Social Movement Scholarship.* Minneapolis: University of Minnesota Press; 222–238.

Solove, D. (2007) I've got nothing to hide and other misunderstandings of privacy. *San Diego Law Review,* 44:745–772.

Solove, D. (2008) *Understanding Privacy.* Cambridge, MA: Harvard University Press.

Sorkin, M. (2008) Introduction: the fear factor. In Sorkin (ed.), *Indefensible Space: The Architecture of the National Insecurity State.* New York: Routledge; vii–xvii.

Sosa, R. (2004) Pobreza, violencia y seguridad pública en los años neoliberals. In R. Sosa (coord.), *Sujetos, Victimas y Territorios de la Violencia en América Latina.* México: Universidad de la Ciudad de México.

Spalek, B. (2008) Terrorism: emerging critiques. *Criminal Justice Matters,* 73(1): 10–11.

Spalek, B; El Awa, S. and Zahra-McDonald, L. (2008): Police-Muslim engagement and partnerships for the purposes of counter-terrorism. Project report. University of Birmingham.

Spencer, L. (2008) *Touching History: the Untold Story of the Drama that Unfolded in the Skies over America on 9/11.* New York: Free Press.

Spivak, G. C. (1990) In S. Harasym (ed.), *The Postcolonial Critic.* London: Routledge.

Staudt, K. (1998) *Free Trade? Informal Economies at the U.S.-Mexico Border.* Philadelphia: Temple University Press.

Staudt, K. (2008a) Bordering the Other in the U.S. Southwest: El Pasoans Confront the Local Sheriff on Immigration Enforcement." In Kretsedemas and Brotherton, pp.291–313.

Staudt, K. (2008b) Gendering development. In G. Goertz and A. G. Mazur (eds.) *Politics, Gender, and Concepts: Theory and Methodology.* New York: Cambridge University Press; 136–56.

Staudt, K. (2008c) *Violence and Activism at the Border: Gender, Fear and Everyday Life in Ciudad Juárez.* Austin: University of Texas Press.

Staudt, K. (2009) Violence at the Border: Broadening the Discourse to Include Feminism, Human Security, and Deeper Democracy." In K. Staudt, T. Payan, and Z. Anthony Kruszewski (eds.), *Violence, Security and Human Rights at the U.S.-Mexico Border.* Tucson: University of Arizona Press.

Staudt, K., and Coronado, I. (2002) *Fronteras no Más: Toward Social Justiceat the U.S.-Mexico Border.* New York: Palgrave.

Staudt, K. and Stone, C. (2008) Division and fragmentation: the El Paso experience, with Clarence Stone. In M. Orr (ed.), *Community Organizing and Political Change in the City.* University Press of Kansas, (2007), pp. 84–108.

Stone, D. (1988 [1997]) *Policy Paradox: The Art of Political Decision-Making.* New York: W. W. Norton.

Strauss, L., 1996 [1933]. 'Notes on Carl Schmitt's Concept of the Political', in Carl Schmitt, *The Concept of the Political* (Chicago: University of Chicago Press.

Stritzel, H. (2007) Towards a theory of securitization: Copenhagen and beyond. *European Journal of International Relations,* 13(3): 357–383.

Stuart, D. (2005) Avoiding myths and challenging Minister of Justice Cotler to undo the injustices of our anti-terrorism laws. *Criminal Law Quarterly,* 11–26.

Sunstein, C., and Vermeule, A. (1998) *Conspiracy Theories. Social Science Research Network.* http://ssrn.com/abstract=1084585

Suskind. R. (2004) *The One Percent Doctrine: Deep Inside America's Pursuit of its Enemies Since 9/11.* New York: Simon and Schuester.

Székely Pardo, M. (1994) *Cambios en la pobreza y la desigualdad en México durante el proceso de ajuste y estabilización,* México: El Colegio de México, Centro de Estudios Económicos, Documento de Trabajo, núm. 12.

Tapia-Valdes, J. A. (1982) A typology of national security policies. *Yale Journal of World Public Order,* 9(10): 15–30.

Taylor, C. (1984) Foucault on freedom and truth. *Political Theory,* 12/2: 152–183.

Teutli, H. (2000) Seguridad pública y violencia social en México: en los limites de la gobernabilidad. *Diálogo y Debate de Cultura Política,* Num. 12.

Thompson, E. P. (1982). *Beyond the Cold War: A New Approach to the Arms Race and Nuclear Annihilation* (1st U.S. ed.). New York: Pantheon Books.

Thurlow, C., and Jaworski, A. (2006) The alchemy of the upwardly mobile: symbolic capital and the stylization of elites in frequent-flyer programmes. *Discourse and Society,* 17(1): 99–135.

Tickner, A. (2002) *Gendering International Relations*. New York: Columbia University Press.

Tilly, C. (1990) *Coersion, Capital, and European States, AD 990–1992*. Oxford: Basil Blackwell.

Tilly, C. (1985) War making and state making as organized crime. In P. Evans, D. Rueschemeyer, and T. Skocpol (eds.), *Bringing the State Back In*. Cambridge: Cambridge University Press; 169–187.

Tilley, N. (2003) Community policing, problem-oriented policing and intelligence-led policing. In T. Newburn (ed.), *Handbook of Policing*. Cullompton: Willan Publishing.

Tirman, J. (2004) Introduction: The movement of people and the security of states. In Tirman (ed.), *The Maze of Fear: Security and Migration after 9/11*. New York: New Press; 1–16.

Torpey, J. (1998) Coming and Going: On the State Monopolization of the Legitimate 'Means of Movement'. *Sociological Theory*, 16(3): 239–259. New York: Cambridge University Press.

Tulloch, J. (2006) *One Day in July: Experiencing 7/7*. London: Little Brown.

Vedby Rasmussen, M. (2004) It sounds like a riddle: security studies, the war on terror and risk. *Millennium: Journal of International Studies*, 30(2): 381–395.

Vedby Rasmussen, M. (2006) *The Risk Society at War: Terror, Technology and Strategy in the Twenty-First Century*. Cambridge, Cambridgeshire: Cambridge University Press.

Velho, G. (1996) Violencia, reciprocidade e desigualdade: uma perspectiva antropológica. In G. Velho and M. Alvito (organizadores), *Ciudadania e Violencia*. Río de Janeiro: UFRJ-FGV.

Vianna, H. (1996) O funk como símbolo da violencia carioca. In G. Velho and M. Alvito (organizadores), *Ciudadanía e Violencia*. Río de Janeiro: UFRJ-FGV.

Vilas, M. C. (2001) (In) justicia por mano propia: linchamientos en el México contemporáneo. In *Revista Mexicana de Sociología*. México, Vol. 63, núm. 1, pp. 131–160. FIX

Virta, S. (2008) Community policing meets new challenges. In S. Virta (ed.), *Policing Meets New Challenges: Preventing Radicalisation and Recruitment*. Tampere: Tampere University Press.

Virta, S., and Hukkanen, V. (2008) Community policing reform in Finland. In S. Virta (ed.), *Policing Meets New Challenges: Preventing Radicalisation and Recruitment*. Tampere: Tampere University Press.

Volkov, V. (1999) Violent entrepreneurship in post-communist Russia. en *Europa-Asia Studies*, Abingdon, vol. 51, núm. 5, pp. 741–754.

V. Spike Peterson and Runyan, A. (1998) *Global Gender Issues*. 2nd ed. Boulder, CO: Westview.

van Loon, J. (2003) *Risk and Technological Culture: Towards a Sociology of Virulence*. London: Routledge.

Van Munster, R. (2007) The war on terrorism: when the exception becomes the rule. *International Journal for the Semiotics of Law*, 141–153.

Von Hippel, K. (2007) Responding to the roots of terror. In M. Ranstorp (ed.), *Mapping Terrorism Research*. New York: Routledge.

Vygotksy, L. (1962 [1934]) In Haufmann and Vakar (eds.), *Thought and Language*. Cambridge: MIT Press.

Wacquant, L. (1999) *Les prisons de la Misère*. Francia: Raisons d'Agir.

Wacquant, L. (2004) Punir les pauvres. In *Le nouveau gouvernement de l'insegurité sociale*. Francia: Agone.

Wacquant, L. (2008) The militarization of urban marginality: Lessons from the Brazilian metropolis. *International Political Sociology*, (2), Blackwell Publishing, Oxford, UK, 56–74.

Wantanabe, T. and H. Becerra (2006) "500,000 Pack Streets to Protest Immigration Bills." *Los Angeles Times*. Available online at http://articles.latimes.com/2006/mar/26/local/me-immig26. Accessed October 19, 2010.

Ward, P. (1993) Social welfare policy and political opening in Mexico. *Journal of Latin America Studies*, 25(3): 613–628.

Waever, O. (1995) Securitization–desecuritization. In R. Lipchutz (ed.), *On Security*. New York: Columbia University Press; 46–86.

Waever, O. (2005) Constellations of securities in Europe. In E. Aydinli and J. N. Rosenau (eds.), *Globalization, Security, and the Nation-State. Paradigms in Transition*. SUNY Press.

Walker , R. (2006) Lines of insecurity: international, imperial, exceptional. *Security Dialogue*, 37: 65–82 .

Walklate, S., and Mythen, G. (2008) How scared are we? *British Journal of Criminology*, 48(1): 209–225.

Weaver, O. (1995) Securitization and desecuritization. In R. D. Lipschutz (ed.), *On Security*. New York: Columbia University Press; 46–86.

Welch, M. (2006) Seeking a safer society: America's anxiety in the war on terror. *Security Journal*, 19: 93–109.

Wendt, A., and R. Duvall. (2008) Sovereignty and the UFO. *Political Theory*, 36(4): 607–633.

Whitehead, A. N., and Russell, B. (1910, 1912, 1913) Principia Mathematica. 3 vols. Cambridge: Cambridge University Press.

Wilder, C., and Collins, S. 1994. Patterns of interactional paradoxes. In: Cupach and Spitzberg (eds.), *The Dark Side of Interpersonal Communication*. Los Angeles: L. Erlbaum.

Wilford, H. (2009) *The Mighty Wurlitzer: How the CIA Played America*. Cambridge, MA: Harvard University Press.

Williams, M. C. (2003) Words, images, enemies: securitization and international politics. *International Studies Quarterly*, 47(4): 511–531.

Williams, P. (1991) *The Alchemy of Race and Rights: Diary of a Law Professor*. Cambridge, MA: Harvard University Press.

Wilkinson, P. (2007) Research into terrorism studies: achievements and failures. In M. Ranstorp (ed.), *Mapping Terrorism Research*. New York: Routledge.

Wilsnack, R. (1980). Information control: a conceptual framework for sociological analysis. *Journal of Contemporary Ethnography*, 8/4: 467.

Wittgenstein, L. (1953) In G.E.M. Anscombe (trans). *Philosophical Investigations*. New York: The MacMillan Company.

Wonders, N. A. (2006) Global flows, semi-permeable borders and new channels of inequality: border crossers and border performativity. In S. Pickering and L. Weber (eds.), *Borders, Mobility and Technologies of Control*. The Netherlands: Springer; 45–62.

Wyn Jones, R. (1999). *Security, Strategy, and Critical Theory*. Boulder, CO: Lynne Rienner Publishers.

Zedner, L. (2007) Pre-crime and post-criminology? *Theoretical Criminology*, 11(2): 261–281.

Zedner, L. (2008) Terrorism, the ticking bomb and criminal justice values. *Criminal Justice Matters*, 73(1): 18–19

Zhang, C.-R. (2003) Build up new world order through promotion of Chinese history, education and culture. *Journal of Chengdu University,*1: 8–10. [In Chinese.]

Zhang, J., and Qi, C.-A. (2003) Cultural reasons for the collapse of the Soviet Union. *Socialism Studies*, 6: 32–35. [In Chinese.]

Zhu, C.-R. (1999) On China's cultural security strategy in the twenty first century. *Journal of Jiangnan Social University*, 1: 9–13. [In Chinese.]

Zukin, S. (1995) *The Cultures of Cities*. Cambridge, MA: Blackwell.

# Contributors

**Reem Bahdi** is Associate Professor, Faculty of Law, University of Windsor. She is Co-Director of KARAMAH, the Project on Judicial Independence and Human Dignity, an initiative that supports access to justice in Palestine through research, continuing judicial education, and directed civil society engagement. She is the Editor-in-Chief (with Dr. Chris Waters) of the *Windsor Yearbook of Access to Justice* and board member of the International Association of Law Schools and the BC Civil Liberties Association. Her current research focuses on the human rights dimensions of national security laws and policies in Canada and access to justice in the Palestinian context.

**Vida Bajc** is Assistant Professor at Methodist University. She completed her Ph.D. in Sociology at the University of Pennsylvania (May 2008) and subsequently a Postdoctoral Fellowship at The Surveillance Studies Centre at Queen's University, Canada (2008-2009). Her research connects framing theory, ritual, surveillance and security, globalization, culture, and Christianity. Her book manuscript, *Christian Pilgrimage in Jerusalem: Performing Social Realities,* under contract with the University of Chicago Press, is based on years of on-going ethnographic fieldwork in Jerusalem. She is currently completing an edited book on surveillance and security in the Olympic Games, forthcoming with Palgrave. She is guest editor of three journal special issues: "Watching Out: Surveillance, Security, and Mobility" (with John Torpey) for the *American Behavioral Scientist* (2007); "(Dis)Placing the Center: Pilgrimage in a Mobile World" (with Simon Coleman and John Eade) for *Mobilities* (2007); and "Collective Memory and Tourism" for *Journeys: The International Journal of Travel and Travel Writing* (2006).

**Nelson Arteaga Botello** is Professor and researcher of sociology in the Faculty of Political and Social Science at the Universidad Autónoma del Estado de México. He received his doctorate at the University of Alicante, Spain. His main research interests are problematization fields and dispositifs through violence, inequality, public security, and surveillance. His publications include *Sociedad de la vigilancia en el Sur-Global. Mirando América Latina* (2009); "The Merida Initiative: Security-Surveillance Harmonization in Latin America," *European Review of Latin American and Caribbean Studies*, Ámsterdam, No. 87, October 2009; "An Orchestration of Electronic Surveillance: A CCTV Experience in Mexico," *International Criminal Justice Review*, Georgia State University/SAGE Publications, EE.UU. (2007); and "Privacy and Surveillance in Mexico and Brazil," in Elia Zureik, L. Lynda Harling Stalker, Emily Smith, David Lyon, and Yolan de E. Chan (eds.), *Privacy, Surveillance and the Globalization of Personal Information: International Comparisons*, Montreal, Kingston: McGill-Queen's University Press, (2010).

**Kuo Huang** is Associate Professor at Heilongjiang University, the People's Republic of China. She obtained her M.A. degree in Communication at the University of Westminster, the United Kingdom. She is currently completing her PhD. thesis at the Centre for International Communication at Macquarie University, Australia, on the topic of *Chinese Boxes: Participation among Reality TV Audiences—Two Chinese Case Studies*. She is the winner of 2009 Higher Degree Research Award for Contributions to Improving Faculty Research Climate in the Faculty of Arts, Macquarie University. Her research interests focus on cultural studies, audience studies, media economics, and the new media. She is the author of *Multimedia Technology: How It Changes Classroom and Communication* (2009, published by VDM Verlag, Dr. Müller). She has conducted several research projects and published numerous journal articles in English and Chinese, including "Selling participation to audiences in China" and "Understanding diaspora cultures in the context of globalization." She is a regular participant at the annual meetings of the International Communication Association, the International Association of Media and Communication Research, and the World Media Economics.

**Fei Jiang** is Associate Professor at the Institute of Journalism and Communication, the Chinese Academy of Social Sciences. His PhD degree is from Sichun University, People's Republic of China. He is engaged in communication theory, intercultural communication theory, media discourse, transnational media corporations, and postcolonial theory studies. He has held a number of visiting scholar awards: in 2004 at the Journalism, Media and Communication Department, the Stockholm University; in 2005 as the winner of "Special Awards for Canadian Studies" at the University of Toronto, the University of British Columbia, and the University of Concordia; in 2007–2008 at the Annenberg

School for Communication, the University of Pennsylvania; in 2009 at the Institute of Communication, the National Chengchi University, Taiwan; and in 2009 at the Department of Media and Communication, the City University of Hong Kong. He is the author of *The Postcolonial Context of Intercultural Communication,* which won the WU-Yuzhang Award in 2007 and the HU-Sheng Award in 2009. He has conducted several research projects, including "Media discourse: How global media and experts determine people's view on China," funded by the Chinese National Social Science Foundation (2005–2008); "Approaches to intercultural communication theory," funded by the Chinese Academy of Social Sciences (2005–2008); "The Chinese perspective: The development of communication studies in China for thirty years——from 1978 to 2008", funded by the Chinese Academy of Social Sciences (2007–2011); and "Research on strategies of transnational media coporations from the intercultural perspective," funded by the Chinese Academy of Social Sciences (2008–2012). He published numerous journal articles and has presented at the International Communications Association and the International Association of Media and Communication Research. Contact: taiheshusheng@gmail.com.

**Willem de Lint** is Professor of Criminal Justice at Flinders Law School, Flinders University of South Australia. He has published more than three dozen research papers, books, or book chapters in venues including the *British Journal of Criminology, Theoretical Criminology,* and the *American Behavioral Scientist.* He is on the editorial board of the *Canadian Journal Criminology and Criminal Justice, Policing and Society,* and the *Open Law Journal.* His last book, *Intelligent Control-Developments in Public Order Policing in Canada* (co-authored with Alan Hall), was reviewed in the *Canadian Review of Sociology* as 'a must read for anyone in criminology and socio-legal studies in North America.' His current work concerns the interrelationships between security and justice.

**Gabe Mythen** is Senior Lecturer in Sociology in the School of Sociology and Social Policy at the University of Liverpool. He has published work in the areas of risk perception, human security, and the management and regulation of terrorism in journals such as the *Sociological Review, Current Sociology, British Journal of Criminology, Security Journal,* and *Environmental Politics.* He is author of *Ulrich Beck: A Critical Introduction to the Risk Society* (Pluto Press, 2004) and co-editor of *Beyond the Risk Society: Critical Reflections on Risk and Human Security* (Open University Press, 2006). He is presently writing a third book to be published by Palgrave Macmillan entitled *Understanding the Risk Society: Crime, Security and Welfare.*

**Mark B. Salter** is associate professor in the School of Political Studies at the University of Ottawa. He is editor of *Mapping Transatlantic Security Relations* (2010) and *Politics at the Airport* (2008). Recent research appears in *Geopolitics, Security Dialogue, International Political Sociology, Citizenship Studies,* and *Alternatives.*

**Liora Sion** is Lecturer in Sociology at the School of Sociology and Social Policy at Nottingham University, the United Kingdom. She teaches courses on gender, militarization, and postconflict operations, with the focus on Israel and the Balkans. She is completing a book manuscript about peacekeeping in the Balkans and has published journal articles on the female peacekeepers in Bosnia and Kosovo, body and sexuality among the reserve soldiers in Israel, and peacekeepers' perceptions of their missions. Her current research agenda involves the question of the boundaries of the Israeli society, particularly how and in what terms can a citizen be expunged from the collective.

**Kathleen Staudt,** PhD (University of Wisconsin 1976) is Professor of Political Science at the University of Texas at El Paso. She has published 15 books, six of which focus on the U.S.-Mexico border. The latest of these are coedited collections entitled *Human Rights Along the U.S.-Mexico Border: Gendered Violence and Insecurity* (Tucson: University of Arizona Press, 2009) and *Cities and Citizenship at the U.S.-Mexico Border: The Paso del Norte Metropolitan Region* with colleagues at El Colegio de la Frontera Norte, César Fuentes and Julia Monárrez (NY: Palgrave USA 2010). She teaches courses on democracy, the border, leadership and civic engagement, public policy, and women and politics. She is active in various community-based organizations focused on social justice and civil and human rights.

**Sirpa Virta** is Professor of Public Administration and Police Management at the University of Tampere, Finland. She has been researching, writing, and consulting in higher police education in Finland since the late 1990s. She is the author of many articles, books, and reports in Finnish and in English about community policing, safety partnerships and networks, police management, and security strategies.

# Index